D. WAYNE

THE HIGH-ROLLING AND FAST TIMES OF AMERICA'S PREMIER HORSE TRAINER

CARLO DEVITO

Contemporary Books

Chicago New York San Francisco Lisbon London Madrid Mexico City
Milan New Delhi San Juan Seoul Singapore Sydney Toronto

Library of Congress Cataloging-in-Publication Data

DeVito, Carlo.
    D. Wayne : the high-rolling and fast times of America's premier horse trainer /
Carlo DeVito.
        p.   cm.
      ISBN 0-07-138737-4
      1. Lukas, D. Wayne.   2. Horse trainers—United States—Biography.
3. Horse racing—United States.   I. Title.

   SF284.52.L85 D48   2002
   798.4'0092—dc21   2001054818
   [B]

Contemporary Books

A Division of The McGraw·Hill Companies

1 2 3 4 5 6 7 8 9 0   AGM/AGM   1 0 9 8 7 6 5 4 3 2

ISBN 0-07-138737-4

This book was set in Sabon
Printed and bound by Quebecor Martinsburg

Interior design by Nick Panos
Interior photographs courtesy of D. Moths unless otherwise noted.

McGraw-Hill books are available at special quantity discounts to use as premiums and
sales promotions, or for use in corporate training programs. For more information, please
write to the Director of Special Sales, Professional Publishing, McGraw-Hill, Two Penn
Plaza, New York, NY 10121-2298. Or contact your local bookstore.

This book is printed on acid-free paper.

For my wife, Dominique, the real horse lover in our family,
for my brother Eugene,
and for my parents,
who instilled in me a love of sports and competition

CONTENTS

v

ACKNOWLEDGMENTS

First, I'd like to thank and commend D. Wayne Lukas for his cooperation in the preparation of this book. He made himself available for a lengthy interview, and never flinched or refused to answer any questions I put to him. He did this without the manuscript being made available to him.

It has been my hope to present the best possible biography of D. Wayne Lukas's controversial and accomplished career and life. In doing so, I don't believe I violated any trust in the conveyance of his opinions and quotes, nor have I withheld any information or opinions, good or bad, that I thought would result in a well-rounded, objective picture of his life. I've attempted to present both praise and criticism from the various corners of the professional racing world, as I independently saw fit.

Second, I would like to thank Dauna Moths, Mr. Lukas's sister, for her willingness to share the contents of the family scrapbook with me. She too did not see or approve the manuscript or pages. Mrs. Moths also contributed many cherished family photos in an effort to help the author achieve a fuller picture of her brother's life, especially the early years. As I stated to her, I only hope my sisters speak as highly of me as she does of Wayne.

Of course, there are others. Leonard Lusky of Moonlight Press was an invaluable adviser and sounding board. I would also like to thank Richard Chamberlain, editor of *The Quarter Racing Journal*, for his time and assistance in helping me to re-create the quarter horse years; and William Nack, for his advice, guidance, and opinions.

Any author of such an effort also owes a huge debt of gratitude to those who went before him. Several writers' works have proved invaluable to me. Carol Flake's major profile of Mr. Lukas from *The New Yorker* set an incredible standard, while Nack's major profiles of Lukas from *Sports Illustrated* were invaluable in providing insight and information. And finally, Ross Staaden's book, *Winning Trainers*, was as essential a piece of reportage as one could hope to find. I have leaned heavily on these works, and have cited them consistently throughout the book. Also invaluable was *New York Times* racing correspondent Joe Drape and his book *The Race for the Triple Crown*, which was chock-full of anecdotes and stories.

Obviously, the *Daily Racing Form* was an invaluable source of information, as were the countless newspapers, magazines, and racetrack publicity notes that went into the making of this book. As I amassed almost five hundred articles from these publications, I was grateful to the many journalists who cover the track on a daily basis. I thank them for bringing the backstretch to life for those of us who cannot be there every day.

My deepest appreciation to Stuart Teacher, publisher of Running Press Books, for allowing me to pursue this project despite my obligations and responsibilities to him and our staff in Philadelphia. Without his cheerful assent this opportunity would have passed beyond my reach. Also thanks to Shari and Lowell Lukas.

I owe a debt of special thanks to Greg Jones and Gilbert King for their ear and opinions, and to Rick Wolff of Time Warner Books for his advice and help. I would also like to thank equine writer Audrey Pavia, who withstood my questioning of horse breeds and confirmation.

Thanks, too, to my editor, Michele Pezzuti. This book was her idea. Were it not for her excitement and enthusiasm, I might have given up under the massive weight of the undertaking. She was cheerleader, coach, and friend, and I thank her and her colleagues at Contemporary Books and McGraw-Hill Publishing for this opportunity.

Thanks also to Craig Bolt and Peter Weissman, who caught many of my mistakes and improved my work tremendously.

A special thanks to my agents, Bert Holtje and Gene Brissie of James Peter Associates, for their encouragement and assistance, and for their belief in me.

To my brother Eugene T. Venanzi II, I am grateful for the use of his excellent sports library and for his knowledge of horse racing. I would also like to thank my parents, siblings, and other close family members for their enthusiasm, understanding, and forbearance during the course of the writing of this book.

And finally I want to thank my wife, Dominique. She is the real horse lover in our household, and a premiere animal book publisher. She was friend, counselor, confessor, secretary, expert, confidante, and pillar during the writing of this book. She helped transcribe interviews, exchange E-mail, and follow up with various and sundry items. My successes in my job and work are a result of her effort, love, and understanding. She makes my failures and disappointments seem inconsequential.

PROLOGUE

"Every horseman and horsewoman alive, from a superstar trainer like D. Wayne Lukas to the most obvious dreamer in the backwaters of racing, wants to believe that among the babies in the barn that are just beginning their racing careers there is *the* one. The big horse. That magical equine athlete who in the springtime of his third year on this earth can grow fast enough to win one—or better, all three— of the races that make up the Triple Crown," wrote Joe Drape in his exciting book *The Race for the Triple Crown*, which highlighted the 2000 Triple Crown season. In 1999, D. Wayne Lukas was about to realize that dream. His "big horse" had won the first two legs of the Triple Crown—the Kentucky Derby and the Preakness—and with just the Belmont Stakes remaining, the trainer was attempting a feat that hadn't been achieved since jockey Steve Cauthen rode Laz Barrera's lightning fast colt, Affirmed, in 1978.

"I've probably in my career never misjudged a horse early on as I did with this one," Lukas said about Charismatic. "But he got better and better every day. There's a well-known song that says: 'It's a lifetime of chance and a chance of a lifetime.' We took some chances with this one."

The chestnut colt, foaled in March 1996, was the son of Summer Squall (Storm Bird) out of Bali Babe (Drone), and was the great-grandson of Secretariat. For Lukas, Charismatic had been a problem horse. The horse had not performed up to the expectations he and Bob and Beverly Lewis had when they bought him as a yearling.

Charismatic had sunk so low in his career that Lukas and the Lewises agreed they would run him in two claiming races, hoping it might help him regain a sense of confidence that they thought the horse had lost. Charismatic won the second race and found the will to win, but could have been bought at that time for a mere $62,500. As the horse grew stronger, Lukas pressed, asking him to race on April 18, just weeks before the Derby. He won the Lexington Stakes at Keeneland. Still, despite his improvements, Charismatic wasn't proving he could win the Derby. They took some chances in those rides.

A sidebar to the racing season of 1999 was the attempted comeback of a troubled yet brilliant rider named Chris Antley. The young Antley had been a fearless, smart rider—and a winner. However, Antley had found the excesses of success difficult to turn down. When his drinking and drug abuse spiraled out of control, so had his career. He had proven to be unreliable, to the point of not even showing up. Soon, Antley couldn't get a mount, and he quickly found himself out of racing.

Relegated to the sidelines, Antley faced a difficult decision: get some help and come back, or give up and face oblivion. Ever the fighter, Antley gamely attempted his comeback. He successfully honed down his ballooning weight, sobered up, and started working the backstretch, looking for mounts.

D. Wayne Lukas and Bob and Beverly Lewis had all entered better combinations in a Triple Crown event than the team they assembled with Antley and Charismatic. But it worked. Charismatic, the majestic-looking underachiever, and Antley, the struggling jockey attempting a comeback, combined to give Lukas and the Lewises the ride of their lives. Winning the Kentucky Derby and the Preakness, they now found themselves the most unlikely pair to achieve what had not been accomplished by better-paired teams in the previous twenty-one years. The press loved it. This duo was tailor-made for the media. And the media ate it up.

And so the Lewises and Lukas were now watching as their horse and his comeback kid jockey raced toward the finish line and history. Millions were viewing on television. At about the eighth pole, sixty yards from paydirt, the horse started to slow down. "It was almost like letting out air," said Antley, who could not tell exactly when it happened. "He eased off the run he started on." And like that, Lemon Drop Kid shot past, followed by Vision And Verse. Charismatic gamely held on for third. But something was terribly wrong.

Just after passing the finish line, Antley leaped off the horse, landing in the dirt but still holding onto the reins. He quickly jumped up and grabbed one of the horse's legs. A hush fell over the second largest crowd in Belmont Stakes history. The nation watched.

Tears streamed down the mud-caked face of the crying jockey as he tended his wounded horse. Flashbacks of Ruffian (buried at the Belmont's infield) and Go for Wand, long since put down, filled terror-stricken faces, yet no one dared to say it aloud. Lukas, taking his jacket off, rushed onto the track. So did about a dozen other track officials and veterinarians.

"We're devastated at the thought that anything could be wrong with Charismatic," Bob Lewis said as the confusion continued, with no word on the horse's status.

William Nack, famed turf writer for *Sports Illustrated*, wrote that events were moving with "a kind of funereal sadness." The fans were filled with sympathy, "pleading, 'Please be careful with him!'" and Nack described D. Wayne Lukas approaching the scene with "face ashen, taking the longest walk of his life."

As the horse was loaded onto the truck, Antley was being interviewed on television. Still crying, the heartbroken jockey said, "He gave us a lot. He gave America a lot."

"There's a certain element of the public, even my wife [Laura], who is a [quarter horse] trainer, that can't handle this part of the game," Lukas told CNNSI.com. "We can't always play out these Hollywood scripts the way we want to."

From the peaks to the valleys and back again, such are the life and times of a successful horse trainer. Especially D. Wayne Lukas.

INTRODUCTION

"If thoroughbred horse racing is 'The Sport of Kings,' then its absolute ruler is D. Wayne Lukas," wrote newspaper writer Dan Peterson.

D. Wayne Lukas is America's most successful trainer. And when he burst onto the thoroughbred scene in the 1970s he was also the most unorthodox. Thoroughbred horse racing had long been the bastion of wealthy families, who refused to share or breed their horses with others, and kept their foals as their own. The great trainers up to that time had either worked for one of these families or for one of the few famous breed farms. A handful had gotten lucky with a lesser horse bought at auction or gotten lucky with a horse that a more successful firm didn't have the time or inclination to develop. To establish winning stables, many trainers and farms found winning broodmares and bred them with winning stallions, hoping that these combinations would breed winning thoroughbreds.

Laura Hillenbrand's bestselling book, *Seabiscuit*, details a world in which a few elite families and a few elite farms virtually ran racing from the 1920s and 1930s up to the late 1960s. In the early 1970s, both death and the economic realities of the business were forcing changes. Horses were too expensive for individuals to control. Syndicates were created. In order to meet expenses, prize yearlings were being put up for sale. In previous years, yearlings bought at auction were considered a sucker's game. Only a few had ever won major races in modern racing.

D. Wayne Lukas burst on the scene just as this old, clannish mentality was breaking down. The expenses were so great in keeping great horses that syndicates were being formed to buy, sell, and breed champion racehorses. Lukas, as part of this progression, took the next step and completely changed the rules by which trainers governed racing. He then turned the racing world upside down.

Unlike any other syndicate or group, Team Lukas bought yearlings through all manner of sales, and raised racehorses. Once their racing careers were ended, he sold the mares and stallions to the highest bidder and plowed the money back into buying more thoroughbreds to race.

D. Wayne has made Team Lukas the winningest formula in horse racing history. He has saddled more than nine hundred stakes-winning mounts in his career, far exceeding anyone else in the business, and has spent more time in the winner's circle than a good number of the other best trainers put together. Lukas holds many of the records in quarter horse racing and in thoroughbred racing in the United States. He's won all the biggest races, has been America's Eclipse champion trainer four times, holds the record for most Eclipse champion horses (twenty) and most Breeders' Cup wins (fifteen), led all trainers in earnings fourteen of the past seventeen years, and has won thirteen Triple Crown races—four Kentucky Derbys, five Preaknesses, and four Belmonts—including an unprecedented six in a row, beginning with the '94 Preakness. He's been elected to the Horse Racing Hall of Fame, and his horses have earned more than $200 million. The only other trainer to exceed $100 million in earnings is Hall of Famer Charlie Whittingham, who died a few years ago, thirty years older than Lukas.

As the Triple Crown and other high profile races come up each year, Lukas is invariably in the news. He is the most sought out trainer on the backstretch. Always good for a quote, he has never shied from the spotlight, whether in its dazzling brilliance or its harshest glare. You always know where to find him. Lukas is up every morning at three o'clock, runs five different barns (in five different parts of the country) and phone conferences with each every day. In operating one of the largest horse concerns in America, he attends auctions around the country, and competes with the largest and wealthiest horse racing owners in the world, including the European contingents and the Arab sheiks, both of which offer huge sums for promising horses.

Simply put, he is the Vince Lombardi of American horse training, with the highest profile of any horse racing professional in the business. Married four times, lastly to a rival trainer's assistant, Lukas has been the focus of controversy his entire career. He has also been a success at almost every level of competition. From his days as a basketball coach to his meteoric rise in the world of quarter horses and thoroughbreds, Lukas has always been in the middle of the whirlwind. His story is breathtaking, exhilarating, and heartbreaking.

Lukas is known for clean talking (he rarely swears, and doesn't allow it in his barns), clean walking (he is always impeccably dressed, even when in jeans), and loving clean barns (they are known in horse racing circles to be the cleanest and prettiest on the backstretch at any racetrack). Lukas is a walking ad for himself and horse racing. He is known to be temperamental, a workaholic, demanding and sarcastic, and also generous and understanding.

But getting back to D. Wayne Lukas's place in the changing history of horse racing: among the changes he's wrought, Lukas was the first to run multiple stables in the same way McDonald's (his favorite analogy, which he's used many times) runs its franchises. Each barn, as mentioned above, is impeccably kept. And each barn has the same rules and credo, which is "run 'em while they're hot." And each barn has a head trainer who has a phone call scheduled with D. Wayne no matter where he is, long before six in the morning.

Another aspect of Lukas's mode of operation that has changed the face of horse racing is his unique idea about finding horses, running them to win, then selling them off after they have outlived their racing years.

And then there's Lukas's innovative training methods. For years his horses have been among the most pampered athletes on the backstretch. They sleep in deep straw beds in manicured barns. But he's also been known to try almost anything to goad a horse into winning. He has whipped some horses up into champions and ground others down into, quite literally, dust. Having had more than his share of horses break down, opponents and critics have said that Lukas has been too hard on his animals. But he makes no apologies. He's in the horse racing business. And his job is to win.

In the history of horse racing there has been no meaner group of fishwives than rival trainers. They take shots at each other both on the record and off. Whoever is on a winning streak is the best candidate for target practice. And no one has ever been on a bigger winning streak than D. Wayne Lukas. All the great trainers of history, including Charlie Whittingham and John Nerud, have at one time or another been attacked and have had to defend themselves and their methods. In fact, in a sport where men and women will attempt almost anything to gain the slight edge that makes the difference between winning and losing, winners take a chance at being a little too far out front.

But perhaps Lukas's most important legacy is the people he will have left behind. Like all the great coaches in other sports, he has been running a successful school while running a successful stable. A legion of new, young, hot trainers have come forward from his many barns to take a place in the starting gate next to their teacher. Though Lukas's methods have been questioned and criticized and his business sense ridiculed, the old guard that constitutes his greatest detractors has been giving way to the likes of Lukas protégés like Todd Pletcher, Mark Henning, Bobby Barnett, Dallas Stewart, Randy Bradshaw, and Kiaran McLaughlin. Like him, they believe in clean language, clean barns, clean dress, and intensity. Few, if any, can match that legendary intensity, but they emulate everything else they can. His stamp on each of them is unmistakable.

The great influence Lukas has had on thoroughbred horse racing, and his way of doing it, has made him a lightning rod. Lukas is always where the electricity is. He is arrogant, charming, demanding, gregarious, driven, and a born salesman. He is either the man you love or the man you love to hate. But both supporters and critics alike have given Lukas his due. Whatever problems you may have with him—

and there are many who would get in line—they cannot take away the success he's had. And the cost has not been cheap.

He gets up every morning between three-thirty and four o'clock. He was 24/7 before anyone knew what that meant. He sleeps little, taking catnaps from time to time to get the rest and REM cycles he requires. He has sacrificed three marriages on the altar of success. And he almost lost his son, Jeff, to a major racing accident. Lukas has had more rivalries and made more enemies through his competitive nature than some small countries or large states.

Wayne grew up a farm boy in Antigo, Wisconsin, and learned early, he says, that the guy with the smile, the good tan, and the nice car gets the girl. He has never seen a horse or an expensive suit he didn't want to buy. Indeed, it's been some high-rolling and fast times for D. Wayne Lukas.

ONE

THE LAST BIG RACE

Saratoga, August 2000

Despite the tony surroundings and visits by First Lady—and then Democratic senatorial hopeful—Hillary Rodham Clinton, August and Saratoga had not been good to D. Wayne Lukas. First, the press was having a field day with his horse LaSalle Street. The young horse had been bought by Lukas and owner Michael Tabor in 1999. "Notable for his absence throughout his two-year-old year, LaSalle Street finally debuted yesterday at Saratoga," Bill Finley opined on August 2, 2000. "Mr. Tabor probably wants his money back," Finley chided as LaSalle Street, with veteran jockey Pat Day up, finished a miserable ninth, losing by 20½ lengths.

Lukas, trying to put a positive spin on his problem, said, "I think he needed that one. He wasn't as tight as I wanted him to be. He's got some talent. I can't be that far off. . . ."

Lukas's other horse, a $1.95 million purchase, Yonaguska, also lost. Yonaguska had previously won the Flash Stakes, but was beaten by one of the losers in that race, Zip City, in the Stanford Stakes.

"Between LaSalle Street and Yonaguska," Finley wrote, "Lukas ran $3.95 million worth of horseflesh only to get $21,740 back in purse monies."

Eighteen days later Lukas had a record of 1–34, with a twenty-two-race losing streak. His low point was when LaSalle Street finished dead last in an important stakes race, and then Cash Run, his 1999 Breeders' Cup Juvenile Fillies winner, failed to dominate a field she should have outclassed in the Grade 1 Ballerina Stakes. Worse, Cash Run let Dream Supreme, owned by George Steinbrenner, intimidate her on the backstretch run. Traffic had clogged the field and caused some bumping.

Frustrated, Lukas exploded: "If we're going to let them bang off each other in the stretch 150 yards from the wire, we need to know that so we can turn them loose and tell them to get a little tougher and run the other over." He filed a protest.

Dream Supreme jockey Pat Day, a sometime and favorite employee of Team Lukas, offered a dissenting opinion: "Cash Run was the filly that caused the traffic trouble, not us. My filly ran a superb race today."

The stewards let the results stand.

While Saratoga is probably one of the poshest resorts in America, where the moneyed families come to meet, greet, and do business, horse trainers come there to race. They race three-year-olds and they race two-year-olds. And Saratoga is where some horseplayers and horse experts begin to identify the Derby hopefuls for the next season.

Like any coach or athlete, you are only as good as your last event. Whether it's a basketball game or a tennis match, that's how you're remembered until tomorrow. In horse racing it is only more so. And there is no greater stage for throughbred racing professionals than the Triple Crown races. The Kentucky Derby, the Preakness, and the Belmont Stakes are the sport's three premiere races. While the Breeders' Cup is also highly prized, it does not come close in media hype and coverage to these big three.

More than any other trainer, Wayne Lukas has made the Triple Crown events his own personal forum. But the campaigning for these events starts long before most of the betting public really knows what's going on. The Triple Crown features three-year-old horses— colts, actually, and now and then a filly—which for the most part begin to make an impression, or not, the year before, as two-year-olds. For Team Lukas, Saratoga in the year 2000 was the first sign of trouble. Something ominous was on the horizon.

The Preps

January, February, March, and April are the months that make up the prep season. If the horse you're campaigning shows well in some of the four dozen big prep races, then you're going to the show.

No one in thoroughbred racing has been as loaded for bear as D. Wayne Lukas at the start of each prep season. Without exception, each year in his various barns Lukas can find a wide array of young three-year-olds like bullets in a gun. And make no mistake about it, when it comes to Triple Crown races, Wayne comes with a loaded gun. While the 2001 racing season did not see Lukas enter with the best horses, they certainly were horses that most experts thought would perform better than they did.

Trainers use the preps, as they are known, to raise the profiles of their horses through victories and finishes. The higher the rating, the higher profile the win is. The first prep is the Tropical Park Derby, which is usually run on January 1. The last prep for the Kentucky Derby is generally the Coolmore Lexington Stakes, in the third week of April. Because it is run so close to the Derby, this race is usually for late developing horses, or is witness to the last-ditch efforts of desperate trainers trying to get a last-minute invite to the big dance. In fact, Lukas had used the race as a tune-up for two Kentucky Derby winners.

Trainers like Lukas, Nick Zito, Bob Baffert, Elliott Walden, Todd Pletcher, and others will crisscross the United States, racing different horses in different races, mixing and matching jockeys with horses, hoping to find the one dynamic duo that will propel them to the Kentucky Derby and then to the Triple Crown. In the meantime, they are still racing a dozen horses on any given day. It is not uncommon for D. Wayne Lukas to have an afternoon race, for example, at Gulfstream in South Florida and then fly to California to saddle two horses in a big purse race that evening. This takes its toll on all the trainers, both mentally and physically. It is a long, grueling, worrying season.

In the prep season the big name trainers may have as many as a score of horses with big stakes potential. In 2000, Lukas had twenty-one horses nominated to the Triple Crown. Among them, names like Duality, Drumcliff, Unbridled Time, and Yonaguska fell off one by one, as horses do every spring. The big horses that showed promise to the last were Gold Trader, High Cascade, Turnberry Isle, and Scorpion.

At the end of a Triple Crown campaign, as always, Lukas would tell the crowd to watch out for his horses for next year. When he said this in 2000, he was standing in the Belmont Stakes winner's circle, holding the reins to Commendable. Speaking of his growing cadre of 2001 Triple Crown candidates, Lukas told Associated Press reporter Richard Rosenblatt: "Every time I look up, I've got another. I have seven of them now, and the first string is getting crowded. This is our best year so far. This is our best jump start." Was it optimism? Salesmanship? Wishful thinking? Whatever it was, Lukas would find the promise hard to deliver on.

High Cascade

The first horse Lukas began to campaign was High Cascade, a large chestnut, bred by Woodman out of Ruby Slippers. The owner was Padua Stables, which is to say, it was owned by Satish Sanan, another in a long line of deep-pocketed owners whom Lukas seemed to find in an inexhaustible supply.

Sanan had made his money in the computer business, and was known for loving work, food, and horses, not always in that order. Born in India, he had been educated in England and come to America halfway through his career, where, along with the burgeoning information age, he prospered and profited to gigantic proportions. One of the things Sanan wanted most was to build a successful racing stable.

To that end he spent well in excess of $100 million to build a state-of-the-art facility. In charge, along with himself, was none other than D. Wayne Lukas. While Lukas had set up similar arrangements before, most notably with former San Diego Chargers owner Gene Klein, this new venture, though heavily invested with land, building equipment, and horses, was not as successful as several other similar ventures.

High Cascade was a good example of the mediocre luck that had bitten Lukas and Padua Stables. The horse's first two starts, at Hollywood Park, were a bust. Then, on August 12, 1999, High Cascade raced at Del Mar Racetrack and won by 5½ lengths, leading from gate to wire. But he followed it by taking a tremendous drubbing in the Del Mar Futurity, finishing dead last.

"But the maiden win must be reviewed in a different, more encouraging light now, considering that High Cascade defeated Point Given, who came up a nose short in the Breeders' Cup Classic before winning the Hollywood Futurity," Horseplayerdaily.com wrote. High Cascade had beaten Point Given by a nose, and during the prep season Point Given would be considered the favorite to take the Kentucky Derby. As Point Given's stock rose, more people wondered if High Cascade had another such win somewhere inside him.

In mid-January he entered High Cascade in the Golden Gate Derby; Russell Baze was on top. Baze is one of racing's top jockeys; Lukas had insisted on Baze for the colt, hoping he could come up with a team early to top the Kentucky Derby contender list. In muddy going, High Cascade fought valiantly on the inside track, struggled for the lead, but came in second. It was a disappointment.

Lukas then shipped High Cascade from California to Florida, to race in the Fountain of Youth Stakes at Gulfstream Park. Given his finishes, Team Lukas still had hope for the young, struggling colt. Again Lukas insisted on Russell Baze, who consented, and raced for the first time in his illustrious career at Gulfstream.

"Last year he was a little high strung, and hard to get to relax," assistant trainer Randy Bradshaw told the *San Francisco Chronicle*. "Russell did a great job of getting him to relax." Lukas was so sure that things would break right for him and his horse that Ray Harris, Baze's agent, told the *Thoroughbred Times* that "Lukas told me he wants Russell to ride in the Kentucky Derby for him. He thinks he'll run several horses in it."

But despite all the grandiose plans, on February 17, 2001, the ride went bust, and High Cascade finished a disappointing eleventh and last. "Russell Baze was fighting High Cascade going into that first turn and he doesn't like that and was rank," Lukas told the press after the race. "He probably should have gone with him."

Gold Trader

"Trainer D. Wayne Lukas has enjoyed success in the past preparing Triple Crown prospects in Northern California. And he may continue the trend this year, as Gold Trader, an Overbrook Farm homebred, won the first stakes of his career on February 10 with a victory in the $100,000 Golden State Mile," the *Thoroughbred Times* reported.

"He's one of our top two or three prospects," assistant trainer Bradshaw said. "He's bred as well as any colt we've got. If you look at his pedigree, it takes about twelve pages."

Team Lukas was feeling good about Gold Trader, and so were the beat writers. However, Lukas rested the colt. He trained and worked him for five weeks, then entered him in the San Felipe Stakes at Santa Anita on March 17.

"He's coming back off a five-week layoff, so you always have to be concerned about that," Lukas said. "I'm not a great trainer off lay-offs." Point Given, the pre-Derby favorite, would also be tuning up in this same race.

"It's time to get into the fray, " Lukas said. "I think there are some questions to be answered by every horse in the race, not just ours, and including Point Given." Still, Lukas couldn't help but brag about his horse: "Mentally, he's so solid. You can do almost anything with him in a race. . . . He will stalk a horse and just pounce on 'em, but I want to see him carry it a little further. He didn't get that up at Golden Gate because he made the lead and just cruised."

The race started with great promise. Gold Trader fought for the early lead and pressed the pace for the first half. But something was wrong. Point Given cruised to the easy win, and Gold Trader was pulled up before the finish line. In midstretch he had fractured his cannon bone on his right hind leg. The horse had to be euthanized, and was given a lethal injection.

"He was running fine; it was just one bad step," said jockey David Flores.

"These horses are very fragile, so you can't get excited yet," Bob Baffert, the trainer of Point Given, said. "I feel bad about Gold Trader. That's the tough part of the game. That's what I mean. You never know when one of those things are going to happen. You have to hold your breath and can't take anything for granted. To me, it took away from the win."

Lukas took it hard. Gold Trader was an excellent colt with great promise. The horse's death "was a great blow to us," he said.

Scorpion

In Scorpion's second year, his first year of racing, he never finished out of the money. Early on it looked like Lukas might have another prodigy on his hands, like his earlier successes, Landaluce and Capote. But as the season wore on, Scorpion finished ninth in both the Champagne Stakes at Belmont and the Breeders' Cup Juvenile at Churchill Downs. Before the Breeders' Cup, Lukas explained that Scorpion had suffered from a breathing problem and had "displaced his soft palate that day." He believed that it led to Scorpion's poor showing.

"We think we've got that behind us, but we don't know," he said. "He's a talented horse and I thought he'd really run big in the Champagne." Lukas was looking at one other possible explanation for the Seattle Slew colt's breathing problem: "As crazy as it sounds, they say that he's holding his breath. Both riders and two highly respected vets say that. So, I'm going to have to go along with it. . . . They claim it's a relaxation thing, so we're going to address it that way." Part of the adjustment was to race the horse without blinkers, as he had in the Champagne.

Despite all this, as late as March 3, Gold Trader—a true contender—and Scorpion were still ranked among the *Daily Racing Form*'s top twenty-five Derby prospects. Scorpion ran in the Gotham Stakes at Aqueduct in New York. Favored to win, he finished thirteen lengths behind the leader, placing fifth. Sounding as if he were looking for an excuse, Lukas said Scorpion didn't handle what the trainer called a deep and cuppy track, and now this colt would get one more chance to prove himself when he met Point Given in the Santa Anita Derby.

"Strategically, Scorpion seems to be better placed than Gold Trader this weekend," Lukas told Bill Christine of the *Los Angeles Times*. But Scorpion finished last. "He made a bit of a run," Lukas said in the barn afterward, "but [the other horses were] a little further down the base paths than we were." It was discovered after the race that Scorpion had a major quarter crack. The colt's campaign for the Blanket of Roses was over. Lukas had nothing to say about what had to be particularly galling to a man as competitive as he is: that his nemesis, Bob Baffert, had tied Lukas's record for most wins at the Santa Anita Derby.

Turnberry Isle

Turnberry Isle was a European horse. He was bred in Ireland by Orpendale, a financial holding company created by the influential Coolmore Stables of Ireland, which are run by legendary retired trainer Vincent O'Brien and his son-in-law, horseman John Magnier. Coolmore has three major stud farms: County Tipperary, Ireland; Hunter Valley, in New South Wales, Australia; and Versailles, Kentucky.

Turnberry Isle was owned by Michael Tabor and Susan Magnier, the wife of John Magnier and daughter of Vincent O'Brien. Susan was long involved in jumping circles, but moved to flat racing in recent years. Tabor, a resident of Monte Carlo, is a wealthy horseman who made his fortune as owner of a successful chain of English betting shops. He sold his business in 1998 for an estimated $50 million. As a horseman, Tabor has already won both the Kentucky Derby and the Preakness.

Foaled in 1998, Turnberry Isle was bred by Deputy Minister out of Blush With Pride (by Blushing Groom [Fr.]). As a two-year-old, Turnberry Isle was raced in the UK by Aiden O'Brien, a famous Irish trainer. In 2000, Aiden O'Brien started Turnberry Isle in four races. The horse responded by winning three times and finishing second once. O'Brien failed to get Turnberry Isle on the board at the Breeders' Cup, finishing sixth.

It did not go unnoticed that Lukas's two-year-olds did not show well at the Breeders' Cup either. RealRacing.com reported that "Team Lukas did not appear to have a single legitimate candidate for next season's Triple Crown. Never fear! Just when the cupboard that had once been amply stocked with the richest and the rarest two-year-olds seemed bare, it was announced that the Coolmore Team . . . was sending their talented colt Turnberry Isle to the barn of America's most flamboyant horseman."

After the race, Magnier and Tabor decided that the horse would go to Lukas, to see if he could ready Turnberry Isle for a Triple Crown campaign. It was an interesting move. "Lukas is renowned for being hard on his horses," RealRacing.com noted, "but Turnberry Isle may have matured sufficiently, in the tender care of Aiden O'Brien at Ballydoyle, to a point where he is now ready to handle rough and tough dirt racing, American style." Lukas shipped him to California and started working with the Irish chestnut colt.

By January, under Lukas, the horse was pointed toward the Santa Catalina Stakes (Grade 1). Now running with blinkers, Turnberry Isle went off at 5–2 odds, and finished a disappointing fifth. Worse, the colt never challenged throughout the mile and a sixteenth race.

Turnberry Isle suffered an injury while running in Florida. It was apparent the horse needed to rest. It was also apparent that time was running out on Lukas to produce a Derby prospect. With Yonaguska a bust, High Cascade not a possibility, and with an unproven, newly acquired prospect—Buckle Down Ben—Turnberry Isle was now Lukas's best last shot.

By mid-April all anyone in racing was talking and writing about was Lukas and his streak. D. Wayne Lukas had entered a horse in the Kentucky Derby every year for the last twenty years, and now it seemed that his almost unrepeatable streak was about to be broken. To be sure, Lukas had entered some dogs in the premiere race for the world's finest three-year-old horses. (He also had one of the worst winning percentages in the history of the race among those whose horses had won.) Lukas had won the race four times, and was now considered the grand old—if not cantankerous—man of Churchill Downs during Derby week. A Derby without D. Wayne was almost unthinkable, especially to him.

While Lukas kept a cool composure outside, insiders knew that the most flashy and successful of thoroughbred trainers was desperate. In a last-ditch effort, Lukas pointed Turnberry Isle to the Coolmore Lexington Stakes (Grade 2) at Keeneland.

When asked about the horse's injuries, Lukas replied, "We've been able to correct that. We haven't given up on him yet."

Lukas told racing writer John Asher: "The race is not a perfect situation for him in that Keeneland is showing a lot of speed bias and it's a little bit short for him anyhow. So I don't think it's a real fair test—and yet I think he has to do well in it for the Tabor-Magnier group to go on."

When asked where he thought the real talent was, Lukas said, "I think it's all in Baffert's barn," referring to Point Given and Congaree. "It would be hard-pressed for him not to win the Derby. I think he's holding all the cards."

Given the talent that was gathering for the pending Derby, Lukas said: "In order for me to even make a sales pitch for Turnberry Isle, I want to see that he's really doing well and that I'm at least a factor. Streak or no streak . . . I don't want to go over there just to be in it, I really don't. If I'm competitive even just below those two that I like, that's a different thing. It's no disgrace to finish third or fourth in the Kentucky Derby."

By race day in Keeneland the racing world was focused on Lukas's fate. Dozens of stories featured him talking about Turnberry Isle and his chances. "I think he has plenty of ability. I just don't know where I'm at with him," he said. "I'm hedging there because I really don't have a great feel for him. . . . Frankly, I'm tempering it a little bit because I don't want to put myself in the position I did a couple of years ago where somebody would say, 'He said he wasn't going to go, and he did go.' I don't want to go through that again. Believe me, of all the people in the world who would step up and say, 'Wayne, if you want to keep a string alive you can run our horse' . . . [the Tabor-Magnier group] couldn't care less. And I don't need to be barbecued over something I have no control over," he added, referring to his famous Deeds Not Words incident, where he roasted his own horse after a prep race, only to enter the horse in the Derby later. The storm over Deeds Not Words was a bitter pill for Lukas to swallow. It was apparent he had learned his lesson.

Surprisingly, there were skeptics out there in the media who were more sympathetic than they had been in years past. "Rest assured," Steve Davidowitz wrote, "if the long riding European import makes any run at all, Lukas will find a reason to put him in the . . . classic. And frankly, this time around he would have a perfect right and quite a bit of logic on his side, even if he would have no realistic chance to land in the Derby winner's circle."

"To be sure, Turnberry Isle must fish or cut bait this afternoon," Maryjean Wall wrote in the *Lexington Herald-Leader* on April 21, 2001. The morning line on Turnberry Isle was 8–1, and the horse finished sixth in a ten-horse field. The race was won by a horse named Keats, who took the lead not long after the horses left the starting gate and led the rest of the way.

After the race Lukas said: "He was trained well enough to run well but didn't. It's still the owners' decision, but I would say it would be very, very, very doubtful if he runs. . . . They've been in every big race in the world. They're not interested in the romance. It didn't fall into place this year, and that's the way it is. We can live with that."

The streak was dead. But the media frenzy was just beginning.

Churchill Downs

Regarding Lukas's streak, Bill Christine, *Los Angeles Times* horse racing writer, commented, "Lukas's Derby strategy revolves around the philosophy that you can't win if you're not there, and he's always been there. He's had 38 starters in 20 years, which is 14 more than Dick Thompson, the next trainer on the list." And Thompson was known as "Derby Dick."

Lukas had become a competitive fixture on the backstretch during Derby week, almost as much as the Blanket of Roses themselves. Since 1981, when he entered his first horse, he'd been a participant. He had six or seven horses that finished second or third, and he won the Derby four times. Only legendary trainer Ben Jones had mounted more winners, putting six horses in the winner's circle. So Lukas's nonentry was news.

The day after Turnberry Isle failed, the race results for the Coolmore Lexington were not the lead. In fact, the large headline over a column written by Rick Bailey in the *Lexington Herald-Leader* read: "LUKAS' LAST HOPE FOR DERBY RUNS OUT." The story was picked up immediately. Bailey lamented, "Lukas won't be putting his famed white bridle over a Derby entrant this year at Churchill Downs." It had been a long, exhausting campaign for the Triple Crown races thus far for Lukas, but now the media would make it both bittersweet and unavoidable.

A press that had both celebrated him and vilified him, praised Lukas and decried him, most of it deserved, now said only nice things. "The throng will sing 'My Old Kentucky Home,' and the winner will wear a blanket of roses," Ed Schuyler wrote. "But a Kentucky Derby tradition of a more recent vintage will end on the first Saturday in May."

Eric Crawford, in the *Louisville Courier-Journal*, wrote: "D. Wayne Lukas's training barn, meticulously maintained as ever, sits squarely in the middle of the Kentucky Derby backside bustle at Churchill Downs. But this week Lukas finds himself on the periphery of the race he has dominated for two decades."

A reporter, John Eisenberg, called Lukas in the early morning hours at his barn at Churchill Downs in the last days of April. He wanted to talk about the very thing he knew Lukas wanted to avoid, and asked the obvious question: How does it feel?

"You know what? I'm kind of enjoying the peace and quiet," Lukas told him.

"He was kidding of course," Eisenberg wrote. "He'd gladly take on the ritual onslaught of media demands in exchange for a Derby contender, especially with rival Bob Baffert training the favorite. But the fact that Lukas is joking instead of snarling tells you all you need to know: He is fine with the Derby shutout, which some in the racing world are toasting as an overdue humbling."

Eisenberg also pointed out what everyone in the racing world already knew: the streak should have ended four years earlier, when Lukas entered a mediocre horse named Deeds Not Words, whom he'd dismissed weeks before the race, only to enter the animal just to keep his streak alive.

Even Lukas remarked upon the fallacy of the streak: "The media likes to make a big deal of the streak, but there were times that we could have let it fall earlier than this. And yet, if you're a horse trainer, you're working for a clientele that's strong and wealthy. And if they ask you to run a horse in the Kentucky Derby, you need to step up and give them your 100 percent support."

He told Gary Long of the *Miami Herald*: "It's like an NBA franchise, or an NFL franchise, or even a college program. You get that talent pool every year, and you just assume you're going to get the players. I think our class of horses was a little bit weaker. That showed up in last year's earnings too."

In 2001, while Lukas was bothered by the lack of a Derby entrant privately, he handled it well in front of the press. As John Scheinman of the *Washington Post* pointed out: "Despite a sometimes prickly relationship with the media, Lukas is the master of the impromptu news conference, sauntering out of his No. 44 barn, leaning over a sawhorse and regaling gathering scribes with tales from his illustrious career or hard-earned insights gleaned from the battle front."

"If his detractors relish this glitch in the high-profile career of the man who reshaped a profession," Gary Long wrote, "they'd be disappointed at his equanimity in the face of failure."

"Sooner or later it was bound to happen," Lukas said. "I got realistic about it throughout the spring season. It's not like I woke up today and said, 'Holy cow, we're not in it.' Gold Trader was the one that was going to carry our colors—we thought he was going to be really good. And Scorpion was making a big move on Point Given [in the Santa Anita] before he popped that quarter crack. We had the same quality horses that we always have, but it just didn't work out."

Rival trainer Bob Baffert commented, "The Derby streak, you know, shows the caliber of horses that he's had. It's hard to come up with a Derby horse."

"It's such a tough game," Lukas said. "The longer you're in it, you realize you've still got a long way to go. Just because you've got numbers doesn't mean you've got a Derby horse. In a crop of 50,000 foals, only twelve or so of them are going to go, and eight of them shouldn't be there."

In a conversation with a reporter, Lukas said, "It's not about me running a horse—it's about not being competitive. It's not about the experience of being in the Derby. I've run in the Derby."

He continued on that same theme with another reporter, John Eisenberg: "With the emphasis I put on it and our owners put on it, we should be there." And Eisenberg wrote: "He is extremely disappointed about failing to develop a Derby horse, and he is the first to admit that it is, indeed, a failure, given the advantage he starts with as a trainer for a handful of high-rolling owners who fill his barn with well-bred contenders. Twenty-one Lukas trained horses were nominated for the Triple Crown series this year, and one-third of those were purchased for at least $375,000 as yearlings." In fact, Lukas had saddled a combined $6.2 million worth of horses in his 2001 campaign, homebred and bought combined.

There was so much hype about the streak that television executives at NBC, which was broadcasting the Kentucky Derby, decided it would be interesting to get Lukas into the broadcast booth. This rankled him. Certainly, he was still a vibrant competitor, and the television spot would likely have seemed to be something retired coaches and players do. "I couldn't see me sitting over there all day just to make a couple of comments," he said. "I've got no interest in that."

"I put that to bed in about three seconds," he told another reporter. "I never want to carry that notebook. I don't want to be the resident guru. I've got some [former assistants] in the race, and I couldn't be objective. I work with all these guys, and I don't want to make anybody mad by picking one guy's horse or another." Although, he couldn't help but take a little shot at Baffert during one of the many down moments on the backstretch, saying, "Baffert likes to act like he's not paying attention. Believe me, he's paying attention."

In fact, two former assistants of Lukas's were competing in the race. Todd Pletcher was the trainer of Balto Star (winner of the Spiral and the Arkansas Derby) and Invisible Ink (who had finished in the money at the Florida Derby and the Blue Grass), and Dallas Stewart had entered Dollar Bill (winner of the Kentucky Jockey Club and third in the Blue Grass). Both were coming out of successful spring campaigns. Stewart spoke of his former boss with the highest regard. "Twenty in a row," he said. "I don't know what to compare it to. I think that shows how special it is, when you can't think of anything to compare it to. When it comes to bringing a horse here and having him ready, Wayne is the best there is. The best."

Despite not having horses run in the premiere race, Lukas raced six horses that weekend. He watched it like any other racing fan for the first time in twenty years, except that he was in the box of his longtime owner and friend William T. Young. While Baffert's two horses, Point Given and Congaree, were considered the odds-on favorites to challenge each other for the winner's circle, it was John A. Ward's Monarchos who stole the show. But Lukas had something to cheer about. Todd Pletcher's Invisible Ink, his lesser horse in the race, finished second. Congaree finished third. And Point Given, with a horrible ride, finished a shocking fifth. Pletcher's Balto Star and Stewart's Dollar Bill took the fourteenth and fifteenth spots respectively, in a field of seventeen.

Derby week was over, but the Triple Crown series wasn't.

The Belmont

Lukas did not have a horse running in the Preakness either, making it only the second time in twenty years that he'd missed that race as well. In fact, he said he almost forgot to watch: "I was at home in Glenora [California] cleaning up the yard and putting a tarp on the pool. I glanced at my watch and saw they were getting ready to run. Half of them were in the gate when I got to the TV. I watched the race, they hit the wire, and I went back to work on the pool."

It was the right thing to say, but few in horse racing could muster up enough imagination to believe that story, especially from a man so devotedly competitive as D. Wayne Lukas.

While the Preakness is the middle child of the Triple Crown series, the Belmont stands like a mountain to be overcome. At a mile and a half, the longest premiere event in the three-year-old horse racing calendar, the Belmont Stakes is often referred to as the "Test of Champions." Twenty-three Triple Crown stories have crashed and burned before the finish line of this titanic race.

During the Derby and Preakness, Lukas had played the humble, gentlemanly winner who was momentarily out of the money. But not having a prospect for the entire Triple Crown series was too much for him to handle. As early as the Derby, he had intimated that he would have an entry for the Belmont, his last Triple Crown series prospect, Buckle Down Ben.

In 2000, when Lukas had not fared well in the first two legs of the Triple Crown, many criticized him for entering a lackluster horse named Commendable in the Belmont. It was a race Lukas and his favorite jockey, Pat Day, won, and many said they practically stole. So in 2001, mindful of Lukas's victory the previous year, few dared criticize him for entering what appeared to be an unqualified horse. After all, who could know if the old master had another trick up his sleeve?

Buckle Down Ben

Before the start of the Fountain of Youth, it was also announced that Michael Tabor had bought Buckle Down Ben for an undisclosed amount of money. Trainer Steve Klesaris would enter the horse this one last time, and after the race he would be moved to Lukas's barn. In the time Buckle Down Ben had been owned by Marcia and Philip Cohen, he'd won $111,000, plus whatever they sold the horse for. Not a bad return on their investment of $21,000.

This was not an unusual step for Lukas and Tabor, who had combined forces in just such a manner in 1995, when Tabor bought a horse named Thunder Gulch, who would become a Triple Crown series race winner. Buckle Down Ben, at the time of the sale, had a record of two wins, one place, and two shows in five starts, a solid record in the class in which the horse was racing. He looked like a good prospect.

Many people were intrigued by the news of Lukas's acquisition of the horse. The comparisons to Thunder Gulch were obvious, and it was mentioned often in columns throughout the country. One of them said: "Buckle Down Ben . . . has been purchased by Michael Tabor; and, after Saturday's Grade 1 Fountain of Youth Stakes, will toil in future chez Lukas. So, together with Turnberry Isle, this means that *Mr. Triple Crown* will now be represented this year by two horses that he did not train (ruin) as two-year-olds. Could this be the new secret formula for success?"

While there was interest in Buckle Down Ben before Tabor had purchased him, after the sale interest turned into a fascination regarding the colt's abilities. Handicappers agreed that the horse had shown promise, but now there were expectations. Those expectations were demolished when Buckle Down Ben finished fifth in the Fountain of Youth Stakes at Gulfstream. At least he finished ahead of the Lukas-trained High Cascade, who ended up last.

After the race, Lukas flew to California to saddle two horses in Santa Anita. On Sunday morning he spoke with the press, saying, "I just got Buckle Down Ben in the barn this morning and I don't know anything about him."

Buckle Down Ben was being aimed next at the Turfway Spiral Stakes. Lukas kept Velazquez as the jockey. Now, in mid-March, the press was starting to see Lukas's Derby hopes faltering, and the media was pressing him for answers.

"We haven't had a perfect spring," he told Marty McGee of the *Daily Racing Form*. "We were still feeling our way a little bit with him." He called Buckle Down "not a real fast horse, but he has very little limitations getting the distance. . . . I felt the acclimation of him to me and me to him, it'd be better if I spent more time with him out here. By going in the Spiral, that's a good five weeks between races. It's a good spot to test the waters."

As he is at many tracks, Lukas was the Turfway Park all-time stakes winner. With the withdrawal of Holiday Thunder—a colt of tremendous promise trained by John T. Ward—due to a leg bruise, Buckle Down Ben had a good chance to win the race and make a claim for a Derby bid. Bonnie Scot was also scratched from the list. It was the weekend after Gold Trader's death, and Lukas's sense of desperation was just starting to build. Two papers previewing the race ran headlines and stories touting the big colt as the favorite, and in fact his morning line odds were 5–2.

Todd Pletcher's Balto Star broke second, then sprinted to the lead. Mongoose, Meetyouatthebrig, and Buckle Down Ben followed three wide in hot pursuit down the backstretch. Turning for home, Balto Star sprinted away from a bid by Halo's Stride. Balto Star finished ahead by more than eight lengths, and was just shy of a track record. Mongoose finished third. Buckle Down Ben, beaten by 23¾ lengths, finished sixth.

"We broke okay, but he never seemed too interested in running today," John Velazquez said afterward. "He just didn't seem to respond at any point in the race."

Lukas still had Turnberry Isle's defeat ahead of him, but he now knew that his chances of gaining the Derby were slim and none.

Buckle Down Ben would be aimed at the Belmont Stakes and the Haskell. In late May, Lukas said, "We're going to try to upset some of them. We'll just take a shot. There's no pressure for us over there. We'll go into it really loose." Lukas had decided not to run a prep race, instead choosing to exercise the horse at Churchill Downs. "He puts a lot of work into his gallops. In fact, we've spent the last five or six weeks taking a little off his fastball. That horse really trains."

A day later, however, Lukas changed his mind, and he entered Buckle Down Ben in an allowance race a few days later. Lukas said: "The race is a means to an end, obviously. We just want to get a good effort from him. He doesn't have to win it. I just want to get a good mile in him before I go a mile and a half." It was a one-turn race, which is what Lukas wanted. He did not want the horse to prep at two turns. "We're not going to shake the trees—we're just going to run. Obviously we'd like a good effort. I hope it's not a gut-wrencher."

At this point Lukas took a chance and decided to switch jockeys. He went with Pat Day, who was slated in numerous races that day and was two wins shy of eight thousand. The race was fast, and Buckle Down Ben held the lead, gave it up on the stretch, then recaptured it at the end to give Day win number 7,999.

Lukas was in a good mood afterward. He joked about telling Pat Day, "If you weren't such a bad gate rider, you'd have won the last one." He added, "Whenever you ride Pat, at some place in the stretch there's always an 'Oh shit!' "

To which Day had laughingly responded, "Well, they don't pay off in mid-stretch."

And now Buckle Down Ben would go to the Belmont Stakes. He would be the eighty-first starter for Lukas in his fifty-third Triple Crown race. The press was aware that in just such a fashion, Lukas had won with Commendable the year before. In an article entitled, "Can't Count Lukas Out of Belmont" in the *Daily Racing Form*, Lukas happily found himself back in the fray. He told Jay Privman: "This should set us up good. In light of what I see this morning, I feel better about it. He's fresh and he's doing good right now."

Monarchos, the Kentucky Derby winner, would also be in New York. And Baffert had brought Point Given, winner of the Preakness.

Also in the field were Balto Star, AP Valentine, and three others. It was a strong field. Baffert had never won the Belmont Stakes, while Lukas had four Belmont trophies.

"It will be a serious test of class for him," Lukas said of Buckle Down Ben days before the race. "It's not going to be easy and we don't have any grandiose ideas that we're going to go over there and pull another Commendable either. Whatever it is, I think we've got him in a position where he's not going to embarrass anybody, and that's the main thing."

Bill Finley, of ESPN.com, noted that "the linemaker has made Buckle Down Ben 30–1, which could lead to cries that Lukas is running another bum just for the sake of running in a Triple Crown race. But no one dare accuse him of that after what he pulled off last year with Commendable."

Lukas said: "He's a horse that is going to be overlooked by a lot of people. He's an unknown. Nobody knows where I've got this horse. I'm not going to stand here and say he'll win the Belmont, and if he wins it I'm not going to stand here and say I told you so. He deserves a shot."

While Lukas would have preferred to focus on his horse and the race in the days leading up to the Belmont, he was distracted by a memorial service for Chris Antley, the troubled jockey who had mysteriously died during the winter. Antley had piloted Charismatic the year before through two victories in the Triple Crown series, and had been sixty yards shy of winning the Belmont.

Antley's death elicited public tributes in newspapers and on television. The accolades bothered Lukas, who made the mistake of criticizing the dead jockey. It left Lukas open to criticism from the media, and from horse racing fans at Belmont, who booed and hissed Lukas when he appeared in the paddock. "When you die I'm going to spit on your grave for what you did to Antley," one spectator yelled, which was a typical response.

On Belmont Day, it was sunny and warm. The racetrack was filled with people of all stripes and kinds. From the disheveled handicappers to the well-dressed visitors, the racetrack shimmered with excitement. Adults and children alike were alternately carrying ice cream cones and the *Racing Form.*

To add to the excitement of race day, Bill Clinton and New York Senator Hillary Rodham Clinton were on hand, he in a gray suit, she in a bright yellow suit. "I wanted to be here for a long time," the former President told CNN. "I was so delighted that the senator was invited to make the trophy presentation and that I could come along." Both of them were treated to alternating choruses of boos and cheers, and their presence made the event more exciting. Other well-known attendees included Mel Brooks, Ben Kingsley, George Steinbrenner, and basketball coach Rick Pitino.

As for the race itself, with Corey Nakatani up, Buckle Down Ben burst from the gate and was among the early pacesetters. But eventually it was all Point Given, who won by 12¼ lengths. By the finish line, Buckle Down Ben had faded to seventh.

Aftermath

It was reported that a well-dressed woman at Churchill Downs shouted to Lukas the week before the Derby, "Hi, D. Wayne. We're not fence jumpers. We know you're going to have something good here next year."

Lukas laughed. But he was already pitching his youngsters. Looking forward, he said, "We love our two-year-olds. We're going to be fine, more than fine."

Speaking to a reporter, Lukas again touted his youngsters, saying, "Our two-year-old crop is both deep and talented."

And ending an interview with another reporter, he pointed to a horse in his barn and remarked, "That's next year's model. The name is Jump Start. Mark that down."

COACH!

Antigo, Wisconsin

Antigo is a small town, even by Wisconsin standards. Nestled in the heart of Langlade County, it's in the northeastern part of the state, about eighty miles northwest of Green Bay. Antigo sits in a region where fishing, hunting, skiing, and snowmobiling are the activities and careers of many.

Antigo is considered "the gateway to Wisconsin's north woods recreation area." Langlade County lakes, rivers, streams, and spring holes offer a broad range of fishing. The Chamber of Commerce boasts that a visitor will find routes, in the county "that will take you through hardwood forests, through miles of pine and fir. You will speed along frozen lakes, and past hidden spring ponds." Hockey and volleyball are not just sports or hobbies in Antigo, they're a preoccupation. The Langlade County Fair is always in July. The Antigo Town Meeting takes place at seven P.M. at Town Hall. They have an Apple Festival and a Halloween Parade.

The town of Antigo is charming. The Community Profile Network notes: "A grand array of homes line the streets of Antigo and extend into the countryside surrounding the city. Clermont and Edison Streets, close to downtown, are lined with ancient maples and homes that were built in the late nineteenth and early twentieth centuries. Many splendid examples of Victorian Era architecture are represented, intermixed with Cape Cod and American Foursquare designs from the early decades of the twentieth century."

"It was the kind of place you act on your dreams," Clyde Rice, a well-known trainer of horses, and a Lukas childhood friend and neighbor, says. It was in this kind of unassuming small town—a Grant Wood "American Gothic," Norman Rockwellesque setting— that Darrell Wayne Lukas was born to Beatrice and Theodore Lukas on September 2, 1935.

D. Wayne's father, Theodore, was born of Czechoslovakian parents. Beatrice Lukas, known as Bea, was of Irish or English descent. She was originally from Lexington, Kentucky. As Bea Lukas told Ross Staaden, "My husband's mother and father met over here but they were both from the province of Bohemia. I guess you could say Wayne's father was a purebred Bohemian." Ted was in the construction business and drove heavy machinery. When his family was still young, he also took a turn delivering milk to make ends meet.

The Lukas children were all born in Antigo. Wayne was the middle child in a family of three children. His sister Dauna was eighteen months older, and his little brother Lowell came two and a half years later. "I treated them as my equal. I never talked baby talk to them," Bea Lukas says.

When Wayne and his siblings were children—Dauna about four years old, Wayne two, and Lowell a baby—the family moved around a lot. Wayne's father worked heavy construction at sites across the eastern seaboard, building roads, army bases, and airports during the Second World War.

"We lived in Maryland, New Jersey, Delaware, Pennsylvania—all over," Dauna recalls. "My first two grades, I went to four different schools because we were moving around so much." The family lived in a small trailer, "sixteen by eight feet," as they moved around. "You had to be organized and everything had a place. For instance, the dining table was like a booth and the table folded down. The cushions from the seats covered the table and that was the bed for Wayne and Lowell. My bed was a chair that folded out into a bed and fit in the aisle of the trailer. You had to get up and make your bed before you ate breakfast. Lowell slept in one spot that was one of the chairs when we ate at the table. Later on we got a bigger trailer—twenty-two by eight. That six feet made a big difference. Especially with five people."

Wayne remembers being "in a situation where every couple of months I was in a new school and meeting new kids. And to this day, even though I think I have average intelligence [and got a master's degree plus] I think I'm a terrible speller because . . . every time I looked up I had a new teacher. First, second, third, fourth, all the way into the fourth or fifth grade, we were moving all the time. And I laugh about that and think that it affected my early education.

"But the plus side of that is I think it made me very social. It taught me how to get along with everybody and not be able to walk into a schoolroom and cower down and get in the last row. I got bold as a burglar and have been all my life. . . . I gave twenty-three banquet speeches a year ago, and I can walk into the Variety Club International in Des Moines, Iowa, with three thousand people and not feel intimidated. I don't care who the hell shows up. I don't have any problems moving. None at all."

His sister, with a smile, describes young Wayne as "mischievous, like most young boys. Playful, curious. My aunt would have said he was ornery. He had a mind of his own." The Lukas family returned to Antigo when Dauna was in seventh grade, Wayne in fifth grade, and Lowell in third. They went to Fairview School, a classic one-room schoolhouse.

Lukas is known today for his extremely neat appearance. "I thought it was important," he explains. "Even as a young kid I was very conscious of my dress. I had my own money, my own checkbook. . . . In the small community of about eight thousand people, there were only about two stores. I always bought my own clothes. I was four or five years old shining my shoes. Now I don't know many kids who did that."

"My parents were particular," Dauna says. "We always had to be clean and neat, clothes pressed. . . . We weren't poor; we weren't rich.

We had the necessities. I think the neatness and orderliness came partly from living in the trailer, partly from values from my parents."

But it was on a ten-acre farm not far from Antigo that Wayne spent most of his childhood. The neighbors, mainly farming families, tended to be of the same socioeconomic background. As a result, extremes of wealth or poverty were not apparent.

"Lukas grew up as a kind of Tom Sawyer in Antigo, but without the mischief," William Nack wrote in *Sports Illustrated*. "In bed by seven, he was up and gone at four A.M., tending to his calves, delivering papers on his white pony, a mare named Queenie, and exploring the dells and hollows of the nearby Menominee reservation."

The Wolf River, a federally designated wild river, flows through the Menominee Reservation. It is one of the last pristine rivers in the state. The tribe opens the lands for camping, fishing, and white-water rafting. The countryside is as beautiful as the days when the famous nation once roamed free, and it was a haven for the young Lukas.

"My father always wanted a pony when he was a child," Wayne told Ross Staaden. "He grew up on a farm and only had the work-horses to ride. He thought every child should have a pony, so we got Queenie. I think he was living his boyhood dream through us. When we moved back to Antigo we lived on a ten-acre 'farm.' We had a few cows, some pigs, and our ponies. One pony was not enough, so we got others. There was 4-H and county fairs." Wayne raced horses and hung out around the stable area. He did trick riding and barreling riding.

Wayne had Queenie and Lowell had Daisy. And they often rode together.

"We always knew where our kids were. They were out with their horses," Bea recalled. "Nothing was too good for Queenie. Wayne would borrow my shampoo and my household bleach and bleach that horse's mane and tail so white."

Wayne's father added: "Those were back in the days when we were still feeling the Great Depression, and money and jobs were real tight. Folks criticized us for spending money on horses, but it was the best money I ever spent."

With horse in hand, Lukas rode everywhere he could. It was not unusual to go to the local county fairs and ask the trainers a million questions until they got tired of answering him.

Though his parents were not involved in racing, it was soon apparent that Lukas had a penchant for dealing with animals, any kind of livestock, and especially horses. "Wayne has a natural God-given talent with horses. From the time he was an infant he had a way with horses, an understanding with horses," Bea said. "I like to say he spoke their language. But he could do things with horses that more accomplished horsemen couldn't. He could relate to them in such a way that they responded. My mother was a horsewoman from Kentucky, and I believe that talent was passed down through the genes. Neither of the other children had that talent. They have their own talents but neither had Wayne's talent with horses."

"I remember going off by myself on that pony," Lukas says. "I'd take Spam and eggs and build a fire and pitch a tent, dam up a creek and chase the trout in it. I'd flip them out with a forked stick and come back with the smell of smoke from the fire in my clothes."

When he was seven or eight years old, Lukas met Clyde Rice. Rice's family had a farm about a mile down the road from the Lukas home. They were fast friends. Clyde's father raced quarter horses at fairs in the surrounding areas. Even as a child, Rice says, "Wayne was very outgoing, always. He was very positive. He was a natural leader. We rode our ponies around with each other."

One of the more extreme examples of Lukas's entrepreneurial zeal in those early years involved the Easter holiday. Calculating how far out he had to mate his pet rabbits, he was able to produce a den of rabbits that he sold at Easter for a profit. While Lukas claims not to remember this story, it has certainly been repeated in enough interviews with his mother that it remains part of the Lukas myth.

"He had lots of ideas. He was very ingenuous. He was a go-getter, very aggressive," Rice recalled for a *New Yorker* magazine profile on Lukas. When Wayne was nine, for instance, he leased a small field from his own uncle and grew beans during the course of the summer. He got his friends and family to help him harvest the crop, then sold it to a local cannery and made a tidy profit. He also had a far-flung paper route, delivering both the morning and evening editions on the back of his trusty friend Queenie. And, while at local parades, he sold souvenirs to onlookers.

"He was always an entrepreneur," says his amused sister. "One time he was going to raise chinchilla rabbits to make my mother a fur coat. We had pigs on our farm and they got into the rabbit hutch and destroyed the baby rabbits. That was the end of the fur coat—but years later he bought her a custom-made mink coat!"

There is also the story of the goat. A young boy, a neighbor, was allergic to cow's milk, and Wayne heard that he had to drink goat's milk. Wayne figured there must be others who also required goat's milk, and so got himself a goat. The goat loved chewing on the grass, and one day, figuring he could get it to do his mowing chores for him, Wayne let the goat munch in a pasture while tied up by a harness, and left. When he returned, not only was the pasture trimmed, but the vegetable garden was eaten as well.

By now Lukas and Rice were becoming excellent riders, learning tricks and displaying them at local and county fairs. Antigo was one of the main stops on the "leaky roof" circuit, as the quarter horse racing that takes place at small county fairs is sometimes called. They also raced on their ponies. Wayne could "trick ride off that mare," Rice recalled. "He had a pretty good routine, swinging around under the neck and vaulting—things like that." Newspaper accounts confirm these stunts, advertising Lukas the trick rider as an attraction at local fairs. Lukas raced his pony often. When asked if Queenie won many races, he replied, "I don't know if we won many, but we ran her to death."

In 1951, Wayne entered her in the saddle horse races at Northwoods Park at Eagle River, but he didn't ride Queenie himself. He had John Kaiser, who had ridden the most winners at the Thursday night meet, ride her in a boys, fourteen-hands-and-under race. They won the first race. Then, in the third race, Wayne rode Watch Me, which was owned by Art Campbell, to a victory. The *Antigo Journal* reported: "In between races an Antigo boy that is employed by a riding academy near Eagle River, Wayne Lukas, did trick riding on his horse 'Queenie.'"

"Wayne kept her until she died at a very old age—twenty some years," his sister proudly announces. "His son Jeff learned to ride on her too!"

Clyde Rice's father trained and raced both quarter horses and thoroughbreds on the leaky roof circuit, and he advised them on how to buy a horse. While he was still in grade school, Lukas was buying all types of horses at auctions. Once, when an auctioneer would not acknowledge his attempts to bid, Lukas's father, standing behind him, yelled to the auctioneer, "Take the kid's bid." And so he did. Twice each summer the Menominee Indian Nation would hold meets open to all breeds. Lukas and Rice had horses in every race—a trait, it seems, Lukas would never let go of.

As he got a little older, D. Wayne went as far north as upper Michigan to race in various county fairs. He soaked up information, hung around with old-timers, listening to their stories, watched them work their horses, and listened when they gave advice to each other. "The guys I was looking up to, my idols, were sitting there with $300 horses," he told *Sports Illustrated.* "The horses probably had bowed tendons as big as garden hoses, and I thought they were the second coming of Seabiscuit. I was just fascinated. I'd sit there and listen to those guys tell stories by the hour, and I'd pick their brains."

As Lukas entered his teenage years, his fascination with horses only intensified. His penchant for glad-handing people and talking horse-flesh made him a natural horse trader.

One of Antigo's other industries is mink ranching. After Russia, the Great Lakes region is the second largest producing area in the world. Minks are a ferretlike, meat-eating animal. The meats, with their fats and proteins, help ensure an excellent quality fur. In the Dakotas there are thousands of mustangs, running in giant herds, roaming the vast, beautiful countryside. Majestic and romantic as wild horses, these animals were considered pests by local farmers, whose crops they would graze. However, it was a lucrative business to round up small herds of mustangs and deliver them to Antigo, where they would be made into feed for the minks.

Clyde and Wayne would sit on the fences and judge the horses. "People would buy them by the pound for slaughter. I picked out the best and paid a cent or two more per pound," Lukas said. Then he and Rice would try to tame the wild mustangs, which was not always an easy job. "The problem was what they tried to do to me and my friends. They damn near killed us. But gradually we'd gentle 'em and sell 'em as saddle horses."

This experience would prove invaluable to Wayne, who learned a great deal about the psychology of horses through these long, grueling sessions. Rice's wife told Ross Staaden that "they bought thirty or forty at a time, enough to fill a railway truck, which was how they got them home." It would take five to six months of hard, grueling work, and required infinite patience.

"We served our dues," Rice said. "We didn't make much money on each one, but on those numbers, we made some money."

In high school Wayne had his eye on horses more than he did on girls. With a life so varied and rich, he had time for little else. He was also obsessed with sports. He loved all sports. However, he excelled in basketball: "I wanted to be an athlete so bad I could taste it. I was mediocre at everything, good at nothing. I was so intense that I became a student of the game of basketball. I studied what was going on. I had to have a reason why we picked and set the blind screen."

"I think his grades were average; not outstanding," his sister Dauna recalled. "I was two grades ahead of him and he got some grief from teachers who expected him to get all A's like I did. Of course Lowell, who comes along two years later, had it easier because they didn't expect as much from him after Wayne." He participated in athletics, "but was not a star." He got his letter ("A" for Antigo) in track and field and in basketball.

The Lukas house was always buzzing with active children. Lukas, popular in high school, was elected prom king his junior year. "King Lukas is active in intramurals, football, cross-country, track, student council, and is working on the prom's decoration committee," the *Antigo Journal* reported on April 19, 1952.

But horses were Wayne's life. Their forays into horse breaking only whetted his and Rice's appetite for horse trading. They wanted a bigger challenge. As teenagers, they drove an old pickup and a two-horse trailer down into Iowa and Nebraska. They would "drive all night—

buying and selling and trading. We'd buy two at one sale, shampoo 'em, clip 'em, pull up their manes, clean 'em up and sell 'em the next day."

"He always had a knack for selling things, particularly horses," Rice says. "When he'd go to talking about a horse, I had to take another look at myself, he sounded so good. People believed in him."

"We'd go through Friday, Saturday, and Sunday, and we'd roll the money over two or three times and then try to beat the first check back to the bank," Lukas recalled. "I got streetwise in a hurry about horses. You learn to judge what a good one looks like and a bad one looks like and what somebody will pay and won't pay."

Lukas was so interested in horses—in trading, selling, and racing—that by the age of seventeen he had both a quarter horse trainer's license and a thoroughbred trainer's license. This required a lot of travel to both gain and keep the license, but he loved it.

Another focus of Lukas's early life centered around two vacation spots in the summer. He worked at the Tower Ranch, which was owned by C. H. Jackson in Eagle River. This rugged camp featured swimming, golfing, fishing, flying, theatre, a separate children's facility, and, of course, horseback riding. Wayne and his younger brother Lowell both worked here. And he also worked at the Wisconsin Northernaire.

The Northernaire was an exclusive hotel run by Carl O. Marty, a former Swiss traveling salesman. It seems that this is where Lukas picked up many things that would influence his life strongly. Nestled in the heart of Wisconsin vacationland, the hotel featured a posh setting for the wealthy to relax, exercise, or a combination of the two. It was a million dollar hotel that advertised that each room cost more than $15,000 each to create, and it featured state-of-the-art amenities. It was also capped by little touches that showed sophistication and class. The hotel's expensive matchbook covers and heavyweight, bonded stationery were emblazoned with the Northernaire's crest, and the linens were rich and lush, of the highest quality, and without any adornment.

Carl Marty charged a fortune, but everything came with it, much as a cruise ship is run. "If they want steak or lobster in their rooms three times a day, we're delighted," Marty said. "And if they enjoy five desserts, that's all right too." His operation was strictly geared toward his clientele.

Service was the motto, and Marty was tough on his hired help, frequently firing them if they didn't perform or were lax. He was demanding, and his needs were paramount. "Marty has more than once fired employees for discussing the guests with coworkers," *Pageant* magazine stated in 1951. He didn't want his customers to have to ask for anything, and he believed in molding local workers to what he wanted rather than hiring people from well-known rich hotels. Once, a maitre d'hotel from a famous European redoubt shooed guests away from the resort dining room for appearing without ties. He was fired immediately. Marty worked hard to keep good employees, even offering profit sharing as far back as the 1950s.

College

There was never any doubt that Wayne would go to college. Bea and Ted, both high school graduates, "were determined that each of the three children would have a college education. At that time it was a great sacrifice."

While Lukas had made some substantial money with his hucksterish weekend forays, it never seemed to be an option as a vocation. He looked at horses as both a personal love and a way to make side money while he was in high school and college. While he might have liked the idea of being a professional trainer, had he thought about it, the hard insistence of his parents that he continue school would no doubt have precluded that course of action.

"We realized it was an essential part of getting along in this world today," Bea said. "We saw what schooling did for them not only in education but socially in learning how to deal with people and cope with situations."

As an athlete, Lukas was good enough to be recruited by Harold "Bud" Foster, the basketball coach at Wisconsin, and he went to the University of Wisconsin at La Crosse on a full basketball scholarship.

La Crosse is 140 miles southwest of Antigo, across the state line, which is the Mississippi River, from Minnesota. La Crosse was four times larger than Antigo, which was a new experience for Wayne. He majored in physical education, with an aim toward being a teacher. Most good coaches get caught up in the game within the game, and Lukas was certainly a stellar student in that way. Since he believed he could not be a great athlete, he decided to be a coach.

"You're talking about a guy who went to the University of Wisconsin and never went home at Easter or Christmas," Lukas admits now. "For four years. Stayed right there. I loved the university. And you'd think, 'Gosh you're going to come home for Christmas to your family.' Didn't go home. Stayed at the university. Knocked around playing ball."

He applied himself during the week. But the weekends were for horses. His first truck was a used Chevy pickup, and on the weekends, he would roam the countryside in it, looking for horses to buy and sell. William Nack relates the story of Lukas and his father going to an auction to bid on a quarter horse that was for sale. Lukas topped out the bidding at $360. But the horse's owner rejected the bid, thinking it too low. Lukas immediately jumped his offer to $500.

"What are you doing, bidding against yourself?" Ted Lukas asked, alarmed.

"It's money in the bank," Wayne replied. He'd had a family in mind while bidding on the horse.

"He bought him for $500 and turned around and sold him for $980. He was just *so sure* of himself," his father marveled.

Wayne's grade school teacher said he would never graduate from eighth grade. His high school teacher said he would never graduate from high school. He had a habit of getting by with jokes, but he wasn't doing very well. It was in college that he learned to study.

He also joined a fraternity, Kappa Sigma, whose reputation on the La Crosse campus was as a party house. Lukas, however, was not impressed. "All they wanted to do was drink beer and pinch the girls. I didn't have any time for that," he told Nack. "Every weekend I'm throwing my saddle into my pickup, getting on my blue jeans, and heading down the road. I was always working, always hustling, always trying to hit the sales."

As he later told Dan Peterson, a fellow Kappa Sigma: "Even before I started coaching basketball, I worked the county fair circuit. My mother wanted me to make a contribution to society, so I became a teacher, but from day one I knew what I wanted to do was train horses."

Wayne graduated Wisconsin in 1957 with honors.

Family

D. Wayne's brother and sister have stayed in touch with him over the years, though he admits they are not tight-knit. His sister, Dauna, has been a medical research administrative coordinator for more than thirty years. She has children and grandchildren. "My daughter has five doctors in her family—three are Ph.D.'s and two are M.D.'s," she says with pride. She continues to live in Wisconsin.

While she does not receive much media mention, despite the fact that little about Lukas himself isn't recorded for posterity, Dauna was on hand for Charismatic's win at the Kentucky Derby on May 8, 1999. The entire week before the Derby, Lukas had told anyone who would listen that his entry was the dark horse but not to misjudge him. He belonged. He warned everyone. Charismatic's workouts were improving. He was a dangerous horse. Dauna Moths was one person who listened to her little brother.

"My sister, bless her heart, said she wanted to bet thirty dollars across," Lukas told the press when Charismatic held off Menifee to win the Derby. "She bet ten, ten, and ten."

While Dauna had kept a fairly low profile outside of her home in Wisconsin, brother Lowell Lukas seemed to follow in his brother's footsteps. Lowell, who recently retired, was one of the most prominent golf coaches in the country. In thirty-four years as the Central Connecticut State University golf coach, his record is 4,537 wins, 1,105 losses, and 20 ties. That's an .803 winning percentage. He has guided twenty-seven players to All-American recognition. In 1993,

Lowell was inducted into the Golf Coaches Association Hall of Fame. He was the NCAA Division II golf coach of the year for the 1984–85 and 1985–86 seasons. Fourteen times under his leadership the Blue Devils finished in the top twenty. In addition, Lowell was the national chairman for NCAA Division II golf between 1976 and 1982, and for sixteen years was chairman of the Eastern College Athletic Conference Golf Committee.

In 1997 he was asked to reconsider his short-lived retirement to start a women's golf program, a challenge that he took up. The start of the program was a success and Lowell retired in June of 2000.

"All three of us are in halls of fame," Dauna says proudly. "Wayne in the Racing Hall of Fame, Lowell in NCAA Golf Coaches and the Central Connecticut Hall of Fame, and me in the Jackson Foundation Hall of Fame," the clinical research organization for which she worked.

When asked if she thought it was odd that both boys went into teaching and coaching, Dauna replied, "They liked sports, but I don't think they were athletic superstars. Teaching seems natural for all of us. We had aunts that were teachers and librarians. Both Wayne and Lowell stressed not only the athletics that they coached but the academics and other life aspects for their students."

Basketball as a Way of Life

Graduation from college meant that Wayne had to find a job. In 1958 he became a physical education teacher at Blair High School in Blair, Wisconsin. The small town, in Trempealeau County, was about twenty-five miles from La Crosse. The population was less than a thousand, and there were approximately four hundred families. In addition to teaching, Wayne also coached baseball, football, and basketball.

"At that point," he recalled, "I absolutely thought I was someday going to be a basketball coach. I loved it. All I cared about was coaching. I eventually studied all the systems, from Adolph Rupp to John Wooden. It was a disaster, and the program, especially in basketball, was a flop."

Trying to draw talent from such a small town led to an under-manned, undersized squad. After a year of employing the methods he had read about, Lukas tried to be more practical, looking for realistic methods to achieve success. But Blair was too small for him to realize his dreams as a basketball coach, and he wanted to coach in college, so he went back to the University of Wisconsin at La Crosse and got a graduate degree in education.

At the university, while working on his master's thesis, Lukas also served as assistant coach under John Erickson, himself a new coach. Erickson coached the team from 1960 to 1968, compiling a 100–114 record, but his best teams were a combined 31–17 in 1962 and 1963. Lukas planned and ran practices during his two years at Wisconsin, La Crosse, and while there assisted Johnny Orr, who was an assistant at Wisconsin under Erickson in 1959–60 and would eventually become a well-known college coach.

As for his academic life, Lukas explained: "I did my master's degree on the overload principle. I invented a basketball shoe that was one ounce per size heavier than the normal shoe. I wrote my thesis on that." The shoe had a rag-rubber sole, loaded with BBs. The theory was that if a player practiced in these shoes, which resembled a regular basketball sneaker, then the player, being released from the weight for the game, would be faster. The idea today would translate as practicing with ankle weights. "I eventually sold the shoe to the leading basketball shoe company in the country," Lukas said.

Orr and Lukas took the sneaker to the Chicago office of the Converse Rubber Company, maker of the famed Chuck Taylor basketball shoe. They marketed the shoe as the All-Star Trainer. "I did very well on that, by the way. I designed it in my basement."

"Wayne was a very energetic guy, very intelligent, articulate and neat as hell," Orr told *Sports Illustrated*'s Nack when he was head coach at Iowa State. "He'd do anything you wanted. If you told him to have a practice, he'd have it all laid out, very organized. When I got my first head coaching job at Massachusetts, I couldn't take an assistant. If I could have, I'd have taken Wayne with me. I've read how immaculate his barns are. That's him, boy! That's the way he is."

"The day [Wayne] got his master's degree we were at the ceremony," Orr said. "He came up afterward and said, 'I have my master's degree and neither my grade school teacher nor my high school teacher have theirs.'"

Calvin Klein Coach, Kmart Kids

In 1961, with his sneakers in the stores and his master's degree on the wall, Lukas needed a job. He didn't have to look far. He became a social studies teacher at Logan High School, right there in La Crosse, and also took a spot as the head basketball coach. With an eye on being a college coach, Lukas thought he could use the position to catapult himself to a university assistant's position.

La Crosse was significantly larger and different from Antigo. The town was big enough to have a "right side" as well as an "other side" of the tracks. The children from the more affluent area went to La Crosse Central. Logan, in contrast, was filled with the children of blue-collar workers, and it reflected their habits and venues. "I'm not going to say it was underprivileged," Lukas told Carol Flake, "but the railroad tracks ran right by the front door."

Logan High School is named in honor of John Alexander Logan (1826–86), Civil War general, U.S. senator, and founder of the national Memorial Day holiday. Logan's athletic teams are called the "Rangers."

The Rangers were small and undersized, a situation Lukas had had to deal with at Blair. In fact, when he arrived, the team was the smallest and worst in the conference. "I knew we were going to have to have a good year to compete in our conference. We were undermanned, sizewise and talentwise."

Lukas caused controversy almost immediately, by being a strict disciplinarian. So methodical was he that not only did he institute curfews, but periodically called the parents at home to see if the kids were obeying his curfew. He insisted that all the boys wear matching sport coats, which he arranged for with a local clothier for whom he had worked part-time.

He called in the hostess from the local Holiday Inn to teach his players manners, and what fork or spoon to eat with. He insisted that his players no longer ride yellow school buses to games, but ride in a coach bus instead. And if your shoes weren't shined, you didn't get on the bus. These ideas were all from Vince Lombardi, who was rebuilding the Packers in Green Bay in those years, and John Wooden, the renowned basketball coach at UCLA. Wooden had become famous for teaching his students how to lace up and tie their shoes properly, as well as the importance of manicures and haircuts. Both Lombardi and Wooden taught self-respect at all costs. Theirs was a coaching of life's lessons, along with proficiency in their respective sports. Lukas bought these ideas and tried to translate them for the kids at Logan.

"When I was at the U of Wisconsin," he said, "I worked at a clothing store named Spool and Son, and it was right on the capital square in Madison, and all of the assemblymen and political people all shopped there. I always had the taste for it but that made me see what the difference was between on-the-rack and tailor-made. During my coaching career I thought it was important to look right and have everything just right." Lukas himself always wore a shirt, tie, and jacket when coaching the team during games.

"We tried to give them a personal sense of pride," he later said. "We made them optimistic about themselves. They were in a community where I don't think a lot of those kids were getting that from other places. Most of them just graduated and got jobs in rubber mills, like their dads."

"He was a real taskmaster," recalled Joe Thienes, Lukas's assistant at Logan back then. "A lot of self-assurance. He dressed like a man right out of the Big Ten. He never took his jacket off on the sidelines. The gym could have been ninety degrees, and he could have died of heat prostration, but he always looked like he stepped out of *Esquire*."

"He was a Calvin Klein coach and we were Kmart kids," a former player, Terry Erickson, told Pete Axthelm. "And he really turned a lot of us around. He wouldn't settle for mediocrity."

"Most of the other teachers in school envied him," Joe Thienes said, "because of the respect the students showed him, not only because of the athletics, but also his classroom work. The others did not feel they could get close to him. He was on a pedestal, as far as they were concerned. We felt he was on a level higher than us."

"He yelled at us a lot," Erickson said. "He was like a Bobby Knight. He demanded the same kind of dedication and intensity. He was organized, prepared. When he came to Logan, everybody was sort of aimless, with no goals. He changed everybody's attitude. He just didn't coach you on the floor either. He taught you how to run your life.

"He used to say, 'Just because you win doesn't make you a winner; and just because you lose doesn't make you a loser. It's how you prepare and dedicate yourself, how much you improve.' You went to a game, you felt like you were on Mount Everest, even if you had three tubes of Clearasil in your pocket. He made you feel like a special person."

Lukas admits now that he was tough on his student-athletes, sometimes criticizing them in the press in the heat of a loss. Later, he claims, he invoked a twenty-four-hour rule on speaking out on bad play, speaking a day later to his players in private, instead of airing his anger in the press. It is a habit he fights to this day.

There were some high points in an otherwise unremarkable career. Many of the highlights were against hated archrival La Crosse Central. In 1961, Lukas was quoted as saying, "We worked hard for this baby. This is the highlight of my coaching career," when his team stunned Central. "LOGAN UPSETS CENTRAL IN 59–53 THRILLER" screamed the headline of the *La Crosse Tribune*.

In 1964 he was carried off the floor by his team when they won again over La Crosse Central, which that year had an average height advantage of three inches per player. "Hustling La Crosse Logan used a tight man-to-man defense Friday night to topple towering La Crosse Central 47–38 before 1,000 fans in the Logan High gym," the local *La Crosse Tribune* reported. Lukas only played six men that night, but credited five by name who stayed on the bench but ran the opposing team's offense and defense in the week's practices leading up to the game.

A coach from a neighboring school once told writer Ross Staaden about a game against one of Lukas's teams: " 'If we could have found him after the game, we would have lynched him,' he said, smiling rue- fully. 'His top players were a lot better than our top players, but we still rotated our ordinary and better players. Not Wayne—he played his best five players right through the game and beat us 100 to 25.' "

Meanwhile, Lukas continued to work with horses. He had never left them, and was still buying, selling, and racing. Throughout his years at Blair High School, during his master's years at Wisconsin, and even during his years of coaching at Logan, Lukas never gave up on horses. In fact, his stake in them increased.

During this time, Lukas married his first wife. He and Janet Pope, of St. Louis, had met at Wisconsin. She was perky and cute, small, with brownish-blond hair. Wayne might not have spent much time chasing girls, as he claimed, or partying with his fraternity brothers, but he'd had plenty of time for his favorite Alpha Chi Omega soror- ity girl. Their son, whom they named Jeffery, was born in 1958.

Between Lukas's relentless pursuit of perfection from his high school basketball team and his growing interest in racing horses, his little family was suffering. But his racing operation was thriving. As his successes continued to mount on the leaky roof circuit, and with his gift of gab, Lukas was able to put together a group of owners and string of horses that he had in barns in Rochester, Minnesota, more than eighty miles away. He was racing quarter horses primarily, because they were easier and faster to train than thoroughbreds. But he had some thoroughbreds as well.

Teaching gave him all summer to drag his family zigzagging across the country with him. He would pack up a camper, and spent most days at Park Jefferson, a small track near Sioux City, South Dakota. His fellow teachers—the few close enough to him to have nicknamed him—called him Luke (short for Lukas), but the trainers in Park Jef- ferson, called him by his initials, which was the custom of the horse world. And so Lukas became "D. Wayne." As Carol Flake noted, it was "pronounced as one word, drawled: 'Deewayne.' "

Bowman Farm Dairy, a large commercial operation, ran promotional weekends of trick riding and horseshows. "SEE WAYNE LUCAS [sic], FAMOUS WESTERN TRICK RIDER!" shouted the large ads. Newspapers also featured photos of the trick riding former college student, hosted by the Madison Saddle Club at the Dane County Junior Fair.

"What do high school basketball coaches do during the off season?" the *La Crosse Tribune* asked on August 15, 1962. "Lukas hits the rodeo circuit in the Midwest as a member of the Inter-State Rodeo Association." At the time, Lukas was competing in rodeos in Wisconsin, Minnesota, Iowa, Illinois, Indiana, Kansas, Michigan, and Ohio. And four years later the same paper ran photos of Wayne shaving in his side-view mirror with cold water and tending his horses.

"TEACHERS JUMP FROM BOOKS TO BRONCOS," ran the headline of a story about two high school teachers, Wayne Lukas and Clyde Rice, who were spending their summers competing in the Midwest rodeo circuits during their summer vacations. "Rice competes in bareback bronco riding and bulldogging. Lukas competes in steer wrestling, saddle bronco riding, and bull riding events," the *Antigo Journal* reported. In the article, Rice was quoted as saying: "Lukas and I have had our share of dislocations, bumps, and bruises, plus a few sprains thrown in to boot."

But Lukas also had to train during the school year. He would get up at four in the morning, drive to the stables, take care of and train the horses, and then get back in time to teach class. Then, at the end of the day, he would go out there again, tend to his animals, and then go home. As his horses became more of a demand, he started sleeping in his pickup overnight instead of going back home.

"I had some horses in Rochester, Minnesota," horseman Jack Brainard told Pete Axthelm, "and I couldn't believe that some high school coach wanted to drive sixty miles every morning to get involved with 'em. But Wayne did it. I got him five head at $125 a month, including feed and training. And he never missed a morning or night with them."

Brainard, who is known as a wizard when it comes to training all kinds of horses, recalled that "Wayne had a horse, a cutting horse, and he was having some problems with it, so I invited him up to my ranch. We'd organized a Minnesota Quarter Horse Racing Association and we built a track. . . . We had a starting gate and we had the first Minnesota Racing Futurity right there at our house. The prize money was three thousand dollars."

"I never slept in a hotel," Lukas said, looking back. "When you bed down in the back of a pickup and shave in the rearview mirror, you get to know horses, you learn a lot of other things. Maybe that's why I pay my help so well today." Even then, Lukas wore blue jeans and a pressed shirt, fresh from the cleaners.

"Racing is a captivating business, I don't know anyone who's ever left it for good after they've been involved to any degree. I know people who have tried, but once you're involved, you never really leave fully. There is a certain lure there. It's the challenge, the competition, the excitement. And if you're successful, it's a very lucrative business."

"Just like training athletes," Lukas told the *La Crosse Tribune* in 1966, in an article about his quarter horse training. The article said: "Lukas is probably better known to most people as the basketball coach at Logan High School. But people in the racing business know Lukas as one of the top quarter horse trainers in the Midwest." While he had been a public trainer up to that year, he was now under the employ of HJA Stables, which was owned by Herbert J. Alves of Prior Lake, Michigan. Alves was in the construction business, and he and Lukas were headed for a record year, and HJA was a stable to be feared at the track.

In one summer season, Lukas traveled to six different tracks around the Midwest. "You can see why the start is the most important. The race is real short, and a slow start means your horse is out of it," he said of quarter horse racing. Lukas went to Park Jefferson that season, the Illinois State Fair at Springfield, the Triple R. Track at Frankfurt, and Hawthorne in Chicago.

In 1966, Lukas won thirty-one races with his quarter horses and made $4,000, which was 60 percent of his yearly salary. He won three games with his basketball team. He considered packing it in then, but when two players found out, they convinced him to stay another year. The next season, the team lost sixteen games and won only two. "And I started looking at [the money] a little bit and I started thinking I'm just as happy training horses as I am coaching. The only reason I was coaching was for the security, because if you went out on your own in the horseracing business you were taking a helluva shot, but I, being a risk taker, it didn't affect me as much as it did my wife. Essentially it did my wife in. The season of '66–'67 was my last year. But in '65–'66 I decided I wasn't going to coach. And two kids talked me into it. Two damn kids sat down and talked me into it. And I went back and had the worst year I ever had in my life. But the most enjoyable because the whole team knew I didn't want to be there. They were great kids, they just didn't play. We were in eleven overtime games or something. Lost them all. Maybe won one. Having said that, I enjoyed it, but I knew that I was gone after that. Take my chances with the horses."

Terry Mueller, a former student, once described Wayne toward the end of his run at Logan. He gave his class an assignment and then went to work himself at the head of the room, reading up on horse care and training. Lukas's teams played a tough, man-to-man defense, and his record was 44–95.

After a big futurity win, Lukas turned to Brainard for advice. "I figured I had just killed a fat hog," he reflected. "I love racing, but Janet hates it. You think I can make it in racing?"

"I said yes," Brainaird recalled. "It cost him his marriage, but the rest is history."

"Wayne ran off and joined the circus," is how Lowell recounted their father's reaction to the move.

Lukas and Janet would stay married for another four years, but irreparable damage had already been done. At the end of the school year Lukas wrote a letter of resignation, and closed that chapter on his life in more ways than one.

THREE

QUARTER HORSES: THE FIRST YEARS

The quarter horse derives its name from the fact that it is the fastest horse up to a quarter of a mile. According to quarter horse expert Nelson C. Nye, such horses are the result of breeding a thoroughbred and a Chickasaw mare in Virginia or the Carolinas.

"Quarter horses are typically a western type horse, which means they are stockier than a thoroughbred," horse expert Audrey Pavia explains. "They have more muscular hindquarters than a thoroughbred, and are often smaller—although this is a generalization. Individuals within the breed can vary."

Colors are different too. You'll see thoroughbreds in mostly bay, chestnut, and gray, but quarter horses can be registered in thirteen different colors, including palomino, buckskin, and dun, none of which are seen in thoroughbreds.

From the starting gate to the finish line, straightaway American quarter horse racing is an explosion of speed, as every horse tries to pull away. In contrast to thoroughbred racing, there is little maneuvering. Quarter horses do not lay in wait and then attempt to pounce when the time is right. The time to gun it is straight from the starting gate. There is no turn onto the final stretch, no jockeying for position in the turns. There are few come-from-behind wins. The horses tend to finish close together. A fifth-place finish may not be more than a length out. This kind of racing makes speed, class, jockeys, trainers, and track conditions the key elements for a handicapper to consider, with little need to worry about each horse's pace and strategy. As in thoroughbred racing, quarter horses are sometimes weighted to even the field when better horses are pitted against lesser horses.

In 1967 quarter horse racing was a rough-hewn affair. The purses were small, and the grandstands were rickety. Usually, the tracks were built for both quarter horses and thoroughbreds, with the straightaways long enough for the quarter horse events. And as far as the trainers were concerned, it was pretty much a wagon caravan affair, with many trainers having a two-horse stable attached to their pickups and driving from meet to meet. However, there were those who had large strings of horses. Thus was the setting when D. Wayne Lukas was thirty-two years old and leaving behind a career as teacher and coach to pursue quarter horse training.

The burgeoning popularity of quarter horse racing in those days can be seen in the discrepancy in purse money between quarter horse and thoroughbred events. In 1967 the Kentucky Derby winner's take was $162,200, while the winner's share of quarter horses' All American Futurity was $486,600. And more and more futurities were popping up, with comparable prize money.

Futurities in the quarter horse world are a type of stakes race, usually the most lucrative. The All American Futurity, the biggest of such races, was established in 1959 as the most elite quarter horse race in the nation. At the time, it offered a purse of $129,000. By 1978 it would be the first horse race of any kind to offer a purse of $1 million or more.

At Park Jefferson, South Dakota, Lukas began some of the practices he would carry forward to this day. One of his passions was running a showplace barn. The barn was your office, your place of business. To Lukas, it said as much about you as what you wore—even more. The dirt was raked around his barn, which was landscaped with cut grass, trimmed shrubs, and neat bunches of flowers. "Janet, she liked flowers and helped him out with that," according to

José Dominguez, former Lukas employee and now a famous quarter horse trainer in his own right. "He always liked his barn nice and neat and he was good at that. They used to call him 'Mr. Clean.'"

"He ran as classy a barn then, with the budget he had, as he does now," Dick Valles, a former racing secretary, told William Nack. "He bedded his horses down first-class. I have old pictures of Park Jefferson, old winner's circles pictures, and . . . and he has on his jeans, and it's totally amazing to me what he has done. I think, 'How could you come from here and go to the top of the roof like that?'"

Those were rough-and-tumble days. Racing writer Loren Vantries had heard that Lukas had to borrow someone else's saddle because he didn't have enough money to afford his own at one point. He said that Lukas, at Arlington Park, had later confirmed the story. Ron Resch, another pioneer of racing in Minnesota, told it somewhat differently. Resch said that Lukas was looking for a competitive advantage. All the races were fought using western saddles that weighed a ton, heavily tooled with many layers of leather. Resch taught English riding, and when Wayne saw the much lighter saddle, he asked Resch if he might try it, to see if it might make a difference.

In the early days of quarter horse racing, the rules weren't as strict as in thoroughbred racing. It was still a summer sport, not a year-round business. Lukas told Pete Axthelm a story that illustrates the camaraderie and the braggadocio of those old county fair circuits. He was entering a scrawny little filly, he said, in some long forgotten fair. The trainer of the favored horse took one look at his nag and howled, "Hey, Wayne, the Shetland pony race is tomorrow."

"I'll let you into the winner's circle with her if you get a clean shirt," Wayne retorted. To make matters worse, Lukas's jockey was a skinny and tall farm boy, whose legs were so long his boots almost scraped the track. Lukas's little filly went off at odds of 52–1. The little filly won. He hadn't bet on his own horse, and learned his lesson. In the future, any time Lukas thought he had a horse that would shock everyone, he always had a ticket in his pocket.

One of the things that frustrated Lukas was that for several years he'd built up a nice stable of horses only to break it up by end of summer because he had to go back to school. Now he could create a string of winning horses, and then build up a winning stable. At a small track outside Claremore, Oklahoma, he decided to set up and put out his shingle. "I knew those Okies trained there all year 'round," he said. However, when the track didn't thaw out after two and a half months, he packed up and moved on. He finally settled in Uvalde, Texas, just outside of Laredo, for two years. While he trained both breeds of horses, he found greater success training quarter horses, and so eventually thoroughbreds were dropped from his stables.

The year 1968 was both good and bad for Lukas. While the futurities were rich purses, the average win was much less desirable. He was second in overall wins, a great accomplishment for a first-year trainer; however, there were few full-time quarter horse trainers at that time. And while he had won $14,060 by winning the Northeast Kansas Futurity, the rest of his impressive number of wins hardly made eating and staying solvent possible. "He had three or four years of pretty rough going," quarter horse trainer Jack Brainard recalled. "It was extremely hard to get going in the quarter horse racing game at that time."

In 1969, Lukas moved his operation to El Paso, which made for shorter trips to Sunland Park and Ruidoso Downs, both of which were in New Mexico. He would later end up at Ruidoso Downs. These tracks averaged more money per race, and he could make a decent living. In that part of the country all people talked about were quarter horses. However, because he had yet to build up a solid stable, his second year was difficult, and the competition was stronger. Lukas didn't even finish in the top ten for wins, but he made about the same amount of money as he had in 1968. Bob Moore, a quarter horse owner and breed enthusiast, told one writer that he remembered Lukas having only a few horses at Ruidoso Downs when he first met him.

"Wayne arrived here in a little red Volkswagen. When he started racing, he did good right off the bat, but then all of a sudden it was kind of hard. His horse could only run 120 yards. But he had good owners, he bought good horses, and he had a very good year," José Dominguez recalls.

From 1967 to 1969, Lukas led a gypsy kind of life, sometimes not seeing his wife and child for long stretches. When he finally settled down in El Paso, Janet and Jeff could live with him full-time.

Lukas met his first wealthy owner, Jacob Bunn, who made and sold coffee machines to restaurants. Bunn owned a number of horses and found success with Wayne. Unfortunately, while they would have a great run, Bunn would die at a relatively young age, giving Lukas only four or five years with the aggressive horseman.

Bunn was willing to spend money. An *El Paso Times* article in 1971 stated: "[Lukas's] group of 21 two-year-olds represents an investment of $608,000. He's especially high on First and Finest, who was purchased by Jacob Bunn of Sherman, Illinois, for a sum, which according to the stable grapevine, was one of the year's major turf transactions." This was one of the richest strings in quarter horse racing. The article went on to state that Bunn had also purchased a horse named Darling Bid at the All-American Yearling Sale for $58,000, the biggest price paid for a quarter horse at the time. Darling Bid became part of Lukas's racing stock as well.

During these years, Lukas was skipping the early season of racing. This enabled him to enter fresh horses in the later part of the season, when the purses were bigger. And because his quarter horses hadn't raced, they weren't exempt from certain races because of prior accomplishments. His clever approach meant that he could steal some lucrative races.

The *El Paso Times* marveled at his success, and concluded: "Whoever dreamed up the idea of a big-money futurity didn't really have Wayne Lukas in mind. It just seems that way."

Bobby Adair, a former quarter horse jockey, said of Lukas: "He wasn't that knowledgeable when he first came in, but he became a better horseman." Once, he recalled, Lukas was talking to a group of owners in his barn, holding forth on all kinds of subjects and guiding the conversation wherever he wanted. Meanwhile, a blacksmith was shoeing one of the horses. After Lukas had finished his musings, the crowd dispersed. At that point the blacksmith turned to Adair and said, "I hope I die the same day he does."

"Why is that?" Adair asked.

"Between now and when I die, no matter how bad I may screw up, when we reach them pearly gates, I know that Wayne can talk the both of us in."

The year 1970 was a big one for Lukas. He was the number one quarter horse trainer in the nation, with seventy-three wins. It was also the year he met Mel Hatley, who had made money in banking, oil, construction, and land development. It would grow into one of the most important relationships of Lukas's career.

Hatley had already been in quarter horse racing for some time when he met Lukas. "He approached me," Lukas said. "I trained some horses for him, we became friends and eventually partners."

"I bought a stakes-winning mare that Wayne was training and I left her with him to train," Hatley told writer Ross Staaden. "I knew he was one of the top trainers in the country. He's a very impressive young man, highly educated, very articulate and enthusiastic. I guess the outstanding thing about him is his enthusiasm for what he does. He's a very interesting person to be around. We just hit it off. I have a lot of respect for people who work hard, have enthusiasm and pride in what they are doing."

Lukas returned the compliment to Hatley, telling Staaden, "He's not only a business associate, but probably as close a friend as I have in the world."

During this period, Lukas built the core of owners who would be his mainstay and form the base of his operations for the next fifteen to twenty years. Along with Hatley, he also met Lloyd R. French, another horse enthusiast. And French in turn introduced him to Bob Beal. These men were heavily into oil, at a time when cities like Houston exploded due to oil money. There were tons of money floating in the horse world as well, where newly wealthy Texans wanted their pictures taken in the winner's circle. And Lukas spoke their language: the language of winning.

"He was a good promoter," José Dominguez said, trying to explain why Lukas was and is so good with owners. "He could sell a refrigerator to an Eskimo in a New York minute." He added, "It's his charisma, his way of speaking to people. He's just got so much class, style. He makes people feel important."

Wayne was already an expert at handling owners. Sharon Ray said at this time, "The other night I was visiting Wayne and his wife. An owner called and wanted to know why his horse wasn't entered in a futurity in which the owner had made a series of entry payments. Wayne explained why he thought the owner would be better off in the long run to miss this race." Wayne was on the phone, discussing this issue with the owner for a long time. This was not usually the case with quarter horse trainers in those days. "A lot of other trainers would have said, 'Look, if you don't like what I'm doing take your horses elsewhere. I can use the stall space.'"

Lukas said at the time: "Getting along with owners is as important as training the horses. Owners bring you stock. I believe my college background helps me get along well with these men. Their businesses interest me, and we talk about their businesses as much as about horses. College is not to train people as much as to broaden their scope, inspire them to search for more knowledge about different things." In fact, there were few horse trainers, in quarter horses or thoroughbreds, who had master's degrees.

In 1970, Lukas won $185,206 in purse money. His biggest win of the year was his first stakes win, with a horse named Reller who won the Kansas Derby. And he won the Sundland Spring Futurity with Carlotta 2. These wins combined brought in $38,437 of his year-end earnings. A trainer's cut of purse money is approximately 10 percent. Plus there are other fees. But Lukas could always make a buck in the buying and selling of horses. Dominguez said: "I'll tell you what Wayne did one time—he's awesome, just awesome—he can go out there and claim a horse for three or four thousand and by the time he's got him back in the barn he's done gone and sold him for ten. And it stays right there in his barn."

The Growing Legend of D. Wayne Lukas

Though 1970 had been good to Wayne Lukas, in 1971 he still felt that there were greener pastures to find, and his own version of California dreaming began. Concurrently, his marriage was breaking up.

"You're going to make some sacrifices if you're going to be that intense, and with me it was marriages—and any chance of a leisure or social life," he told Carol Flake.

Janet headed back to La Crosse, Wisconsin, with their son, Jeff, when Wayne made his California move. "When Wayne started moving around more, following the race meets, that really wasn't for Janet," Dauna Moths recalls. "They just grew apart."

"Jeff's mother was Midwest conservative. Wonderful person," Lukas says today. "But she married a basketball coach and got a horse trainer. So that was doomed from the get-go. Two young people. Had no shot." While he had seen the inevitable coming, it was still an emotionally charged event for the young horseman. "The marriage was not real good anyhow, way before that, but there was no other reason to separate," Lukas says. "I wasn't interested in anyone else and I guess she wasn't either, so when we did get a divorce she did one real good thing. She went back to where I was coaching in La Crosse, and so it brought Jeff back into an atmosphere where (a) everyone knew the name, and (b) all the assistant coaches and teachers were all still there. He played there. He was an all-state football player. All-star basketball player. He had a great athletic career and everything. So that was a good deal. But he worked summers with me."

So fond and proud of Jeff's abilities was Lukas that he told *New Yorker* writer Carol Flake, "I should have kept his mother pregnant five or six years in a row. I'd have an assistant trainer at every track in America, and they'd be superstars. I should have kept her in foal constantly. Little did I know she was going to be such a stakes producer."

With a divorce behind him, and what has been quoted as a "generous" settlement, Wayne was flat broke when he drove his beat-up Mustang to Los Alamitos, in southern California. "When Wayne came from New Mexico to here, he couldn't buy a Coca-Cola," former quarter horse training rival and close friend Blane Schvaneveldt says. "He owed everybody in Ruidoso, and he had to bum money to get out here, and that ain't no lie." He also arrived with a string of seven horses and Tom McKenzie, a former starting-gate attendant and cowboy as his right hand.

There were many rumors, some which persist to this day, that Lukas left numerous bad debts, including sticking El Paso, Texas, tackman Johnny Bean with a whopping bill of $20,000. "Oh, that's ridiculous," Johnny said. "Nobody had twenty thousand dollars in those days. People just say those things."

Wayne had no money, but his owners did. He needed to build a new stable—of winners. He turned to McKenzie and said, "You know what we need? One superstar horse to draw attention to the stable." This would be a growing theme in Lukas's career. He calls them "box office" horses, "superstars." And he's found them a number of times. But the horse was already there. It was a claimer he'd bought for $3,500, and it would be the first horse to help him make a name in California. Her name was Native Empress, and she would go on to be one of Wayne's first famous fillies.

"I first began to notice Native Empress way back in 1971; in the early days of that season it seemed to me she was running out of her class. The Saint Nicholas Express, on December twenty-fifth, convinced me that here was a filly that should have been right in the thick of things and where it was happening." At a distance of 350 yards, Native Express beat the highly regarded Howdy Jones and Barlimits in a time of 17.74, and won $7,500.

Owned by Chuck Nichols, one of Lukas's new owners, Native Empress's next race was one for the ages. It was the Los Alamitos Torre Pines. The purse was $12,000, a sizable amount in those days. Also entered were such legendary quarter horse names as Rocket Wrangler, Come Six, and Kaweah Bar.

"She's come off the rail in her last three races and she doesn't like it. Just wait until she gets on the outside," Lukas told Nye. She took the lead right out of the gate, on the outside, and never looked back, winning by a smashing 2¼ lengths in a sport where the photo finish is very common.

"That was a sure-enough great moment by anybody's yardstick!" Nye said. It was a huge success, and it was clear that this was the horse Lukas could showcase. It would win him money, praise, and attention. It was the kind of horse that would bring new owners into the barn or old owners back to the barn.

Al Carr of the *Los Angeles Times* wrote a story on the burgeon-ing quarter horse trainer. He said of Lukas and Native Empress, "She was overtrained, and Lukas discovered she didn't like to work hard but ran like lightning in races. Lukas spoke of matching the person-alities of grooms to the horses they handle."

"Fillies are shy and timid, sometimes high-strung," Lukas told Carr. "They don't like rough handling. I had a very good groom. But he was a big, loud, boisterous guy. I never let him handle fillies. . . . I would turn them over to an older man who would sweet-talk them."

But Lukas was considered far-out in the quarter horse world of that era. His schooling and gift for high flung gab certainly put some backstretch people off. And his discussion of psychology, when it came to horses, set some people to scratching their heads.

"Studying speech, logic, and psychology, I learned to use deduc-tive reasoning. I chart the daily works for each horse. If a horse runs well or poorly in a race, I review my charts for the previous twenty days to see what I did right or wrong."

He told another reporter: "The one difference between teaching a high school student and a horse is that the horse will usually do what you teach him to do."

Carr was impressed, and concluded: "His methods worked in the bush tracks where he owned and raced thoroughbreds and quarter horses worth as little as four hundred dollars. He's discovered it works just as well in the big time at Los Alamitos."

Lukas was named Quarter Horse Trainer of the Year in 1970 and 1971. He won $185,206 and $148,200 respectively in those years. And he would continue to win with Native Empress. She would be like a cash machine in more ways than one. First, she just kept winning. She won the 400-yard Las Damas, with a prize of $16,550; and the Los Alamitos Inaugural on June 6, 1973, for another $10,000. Then the horse was sold for $125,000 to one of Lukas's owners, Mel Hatley, so it stayed in his barn. This was the second time he'd sold her to another owner in his own barn. Over the course of her career, she would win many more races, for three more owners. But each time, Lukas got a seller's fee, and he kept the horse in his barn, except when she went to a breeding ranch.

Native Empress would be winning stakes races as late as 1974 and 1975. It was all Lukas needed. Jacob Bunn was still with him then, and he continued to buy horses. And then Lukas met Robert H. Spreen.

When they met, Lukas had a few claimers at Los Alamitos. But what Eugene Klein would become to Lukas later in his life, Robert Spreen was to Lukas in the last act of his quarter horse career. An Oklahoman who became a passionate horse owner, with a pocket to match his horse zest, Spreen teamed with Lukas to spend hundreds of thousands of dollars each year on two-year-olds, hoping to create a legendary stable. At the same time, Jacob Bunn was also increasing his holdings, and increasing Lukas's barn full of horses.

The 1972 campaign was an awful one for Lukas. He saw his earnings drop by half. The only bright note was a Grade 1 stakes win at the HQHRA Inaugural Handicap, where he won the $6,720 purse. But he rebounded in 1973 and 1974, taking home $157,186 and $497,205 in purses in those two years. He had become the sport's undisputed top trainer.

In 1973 alone, Native Empress won three Grade 1 stakes, and Lukas won a fourth with a horse called Lincoln's Sure Bet in the 400-yard Jet Deck Handicap at Los Alamitos. In 1974, Peccadillo won the Inaugural Handicap over 350 yards, and Native Empress took the Miss Princess Invitational Handicap. When Bunn unexpectedly died, Lukas bought his horses from the estate, then turned around and sold them to Spreen for more money. When Blane Schvaneveldt said, "Wayne is a sharp dealer," he knew what he was talking about.

Lukas's bust-out year was 1975. He had a staggering 863 starts, with 152 wins, 120 seconds, and 111 thirds. He brought home $926,340 in winnings that year to his owners. And some of his biggest wins were in numerous races with different horses. Sold Short won the 400-yard Golden State Futurity for $68,827. Pass Over won the Los Alamitos Invitational Championship for $55,000, which Lukas would win again the next two years. Maskeo Lad won the Los Alamitos Derby, and She's Precious won the Vessels Maturity—another race he would dominate for another two years—and the Miss Princess Invitational Handicap. And Flight 109 would capture the Inaugural

Handicap at Los Alamitos. By the end of the year, Lukas had broken all records in the quarter horse business.

Pulitzer Prize–winning sports columnist Jim Murray of the *Los Angeles Times* joked about Lukas's long work hours and dedication: "He occasionally gets to see his family. (His wife plays a game when he comes home with friends. She lines them up and defies her daughter to pick her father out of the lineup.)"

Lukas had married Pat Kaufman, daughter of Rod Kaufman, a fellow horse trainer, and at the time, Lukas thought it would be ideal. He says: "I married a trainer's daughter, who was working her tail off in the shed row from four to eight at night. She was working for her father, a *very* good horseman. A man I love to this day. I had a great relationship with him. Better with him than with her," he adds. At the least, it was a huge change from Janet, who couldn't live with his horse life and did not love it. Lukas now found himself as a father of three, with Jeff at eighteen, and Pat's daughters from a previous marriage, Terry, twelve, and Tracy, fourteen.

This marriage, however, didn't last either. Lukas says: "What happened to her was that when she saw the good life, I don't think she ever came down through the barn from the day we got married on. She found Beverly Hills and Rodeo Drive and . . . I think she understood the high side—the country club. She liked that side because she had never been introduced to that." What Pat found out, like Janet, points out brother Lowell, was that Wayne was married to his career, not her. The marriage eventually dissolved six years later. Though he says they remained on cordial grounds, to Lukas it was another personal defeat.

In racing, though, they even had to change the rules to stop him. Lukas started so many horses in each race that he was monopolizing the track. The racing secretary at Los Alamitos, Curly Smith, ruled that only a limited number of horses could be kept at the track. So Lukas shipped his horses in and out on a regular basis.

Making more money than he ever had, Lukas bought a big new house and big new cars. He owned a big new Cadillac, which was unusual for a trainer at the time. Owners had Cadillacs, not trainers. So Smith nicknamed Lukas "Cadillac."

"He owns big cars, but he never rides in them, a big house, but he never lives in it. His home is a stall, a barn, an office at shed row," Murray wrote at that time.

However, Lukas was always known as "Mr. Clean," due to his sharp dressing and personal grooming, and because of the beautiful barns he always kept. It seemed obvious to Blane Schvaneveldt that if he was going to compete, he'd have to change his methods. One of Schvaneveldt's jockeys said to him: "You've got to get more horses."

Jockey Bobby Adair told William Nack a story about Lukas begging him to come to Emporia, Kansas, to race a quarter horse named Trouble Straw for him. "He's a fast horse. Believe me, trust me," Lukas pleaded. The two-year-old colt was entered in a qualifying race, but was scared and bucked while walking by the loud crowd before being forced into the gate. The horse, however, won the race with Adair up. But Adair was not keen to ride him again. "I'll take care of this," Lukas told Adair. "Be back here next week to get your picture taken."

Using children from a nearby grade school, each of whom he paid fifty cents apiece, D. Wayne walked the horse back and forth among the jeering children now filling the grandstand. They hollered, ran back and forth and up and down the stairs of the grandstand. Some even threw paper cups. Lukas went through rolls of fifty-cent pieces that week, repeating the scene. In the weekend's race, Adair came back, climbed aboard, and Trouble Straw bolted to a lightning fast finish. "I told you I'd take care of it," Lukas said to him as they were getting their picture taken.

So strong was Lukas's hold on quarter horse racing that year that a competing owner, a woman dripping in jewelry, whose favorite palomino mare was always losing to Lukas's horses, snidely told a friend of his, "Someday, it'll be like this: he'll just come out on the track and clap his hands and the lights will go on. He'll run all the races. Then he'll clap his hands, and the lights will go off. And it will be over."

During this period, Jeff and his father saw each other over the summers. Jeff spent them with Wayne, mucking out stalls and hanging out on the backstretch. "Jeff was a two-time all-state football player," Lukas says, "and I knew some coaches at Stanford, and he was a very good student. So we went up and he interviewed for a scholarship at Stanford, and he weighed about 215 pounds and he was a linebacker, and they wanted him to beef up a little bit, which was common practice in those times." It was decided that Jeff would sit out a year. "I said . . . if he's going to do that, bring him down to L.A. and we'll put him in Cypress and he can help me with the horses. . . . So he moved in with me and he beefed up and everything, *but* when he was getting ready to go back to Stanford to play, he missed his buddies in Wisconsin and he said, 'Dad, if it's all the same to you, I don't want to go to Stanford. I want to go back to Wisconsin. . . .' So he picked up and went back to the university there." Whether Jeff liked it or not, he was being drawn into the world of horse racing.

The next two years, 1976 and 1977, were also good for Lukas, but saw a fall-off in the number of starts and number of wins, but no lessening in his major stakes victories. Little Blue Sheep won the Vessels Maturity in 1976, and She's Precious won the Go Man Go Handicap that same year. Wayne won the Los Alamitos Invitational Championship in 1976 with She's Precious and then saddled trainer C. W. "Bubba" Cascio's legendary horse Dash For Cash for a third consecutive win in 1977. Dash For Cash also won the Los Alamitos Derby, for $49,610, in 1976 for Wayne, and won the 1977 Vessels Maturity.

Over the three-year period spanning 1975–77, Dash For Cash, who ran in the name of his breeders, King Ranch and Phillips Ranch, won twenty-one of his twenty-five races, and finished second three of the four races he didn't win. "He beat good horses bad," Bubba Cascio recalled.

"I never thought I'd ever get him beat," Lukas said years later, when a race was named in the horse's honor. "I can't say that about any thoroughbred I've trained, so I would rank him as my number-one horse." Some who are envious have claimed that Dash For Cash was Bubba's horse, which was true. However, Lukas ran the horse in some premiere events. This was no mere piece of horseflesh. Dash For Cash was a highly regarded horse. And Bubba, a Quarter Horse Hall of Fame trainer who oversaw a large operation, was no fool. That the horse was entrusted to the sport's top trainer speaks volumes about his confidence in Lukas. Clearly, that confidence was warranted: Dash For Cash was undefeated in the time Lukas had him.

In 1976, Lukas had already been the national trainer-of-the-year five times. He was at Bay Meadows now, near San Francisco, and decided he wanted to set a new track record of forty-two wins. When he had forty-one wins, tying the record, "he nailed a check to the bulletin board at Bay Meadows," Wells Twombly wrote in the *San Francisco Examiner*. "It was made out for $1,800, and it could only be cashed by the nine D. Wayne Lukas grooms when the 42nd winner was in the barn. . . . It worked perfectly."

Not only did the stable exceed forty-two, it set a new mark of sixty-two wins. Lukas splurged on champagne for the stable and the corks hit the ceiling. "They had chalk talks every morning. They all had a game plan. They plotted the opposition carefully. They had slogans plastered all over the walls."

One of the wall hangings read: "The victory isn't always to the strong, nor the race to the swift . . . however, that isn't a bad way to be."

By now Lukas was considered someone with an excellent eye for horseflesh. Twombly wrote: "When he goes to the yearling sale he considers it the same as an annual draft of college football or basketball players. He knows which beast he wants on the first round, which on the second, and so forth."

But Lukas was somewhat humble, saying, "I'm a whole lot like Al McGuire of Marquette, who is a fine friend of mine. He gets a team ready to play basketball. Then he does more harm by hanging around the game. Sometimes I do the same thing." But Lukas also pointed out that horse racing was somewhat different, because, especially in quarter horse racing, there's no strategy. He got them in the starting gate and then let them go.

Twombly pointed out: "It is no jolt to learn that other horse trainers do not really understand Wayne Lukas. His methods come down from a distant planet. His dearest friends are still basketball coaches." While coaching possibilities were sometimes still dangled in front of him, Lukas was making too much money to go back to it. He was now a horse trainer.

In 1977, Lukas had an excellent year, winning seventy races and bringing in $526,296 in winnings. But he also had a run-in with the racing establishment. Moving Moon, a horse Lukas was racing at Bay Meadows, tested positive for a prohibited substance. The claim was that he had used Numorphan, a synthetic morphine substitute. Carol Flake, in her article for *The New Yorker*, discovered that it was not uncommon for quarter horse trainers to use the drug, which emboldened timid horses. Lukas did not contest the fine, and he sat out sixty days of racing. Curly Smith told Flake that Lukas did not want to contest it because he would have dragged the whole sport down. Regardless, the incident, according to Flake, was quickly forgotten.

Today, Lukas notes that the veterinarian who was responsible for suspending him was suspended from Bay Meadows himself six months later. "He was trying too hard for everybody. He was trying to build his reputation as a vet that could get 'em to run, and we probably were negligent, and I took the suspension but we were negligent in not monitoring him as much as we should."

In 1978, Lukas would take the Kindergarten Futurity with Easy Treasure, for a winning purse of $148,200. It was the biggest of his quarter horse career. Little Blue Sheep won two more stakes races that year, and a horse of Lukas's named Tex Oh won the Bull Rastus Handicap. Entering seventy-two fewer races in 1978, he won only six fewer than the previous year, and won an astonishing $827,140. It would be the second highest total of his career.

Lukas would continue to race quarter horses until 1981, though the numbers would dwindle dramatically. In the period 1970 through 1981, when he raced his last six quarter horses, he had 4,223 starts, 739 wins, 505 seconds, and 519 thirds. That gave him a win percentage of 17.5 percent. But even more remarkable was that in that same time period he had won a total of $4,215,011 in prize money (the record at the time), and finished in the money 41.74 percent of the time he raced.

However, there was one thing missing in Wayne's quarter horse career. Try as he might, he had never won the All American Futurity, the quarter horse equivalent of the Kentucky Derby. Like plums from a tree, he had picked all of sport's other ripest fruits, winning $100,000 futurities in great numbers. But in training twenty-three champions, he'd been unable to reach for that last and highest branch.

Making the Shift

In 1978, Lukas and Blane Schvaneveldt were the two undisputed kings of quarter horse racing. In 1976, Lukas's friend and rival had saddled more horses and more winners, but Lukas won more money. However, in 1977 and 1978 Schvaneveldt won everything and Lukas had fallen to third. Some people in the horse business whispered that Lukas's real reason for wanting to leave quarter horses was because he would never beat Blane Schvaneveldt. But that's probably not the reason he moved on.

In 1977, Eugene Cashman, owner of 1976 Preakness winner Elocutionist, asked Lukas to run a few thoroughbreds at Hollywood Park. One of them was Hill House, who would win eight straight races under Lukas. "I trained thoroughbreds for Gene that one summer, trying to do it all . . . and I ran myself just about ragged, up and down the highway," Lukas said. "So I gave up the thoroughbreds. I didn't think the timing was right. I backed off, reorganized, regrouped, and then took a run at it again."

Lukas credits his son for pushing him into thoroughbreds: "When Jeff got out of college we were in the thoroughbred game and we were doing real well. But although Jeff worked in the barn and it was a mom and pop deal and all that, he was never too enthused about the quarter horses. He wanted to push for the thoroughbreds. So in 1974 we decided that maybe we would slip off and try a little bit, test the water. Being of a competitive nature myself, I did not want to go in there and have four or five claimers. I wanted to test the water and all that, so we ended up buying some horses privately. And we set up a little barn over at Hollywood Park. Then, to jump ahead, we ran afternoons and nights and I hired a guy named Ed Beam and he helped me over there while I did a full set of races at Los Alamitos."

A little more than a year after making the move, Lukas said: "I think it's much more difficult to train a thoroughbred. For example: you can take good care of a quarter horse, get the right bloodlines, good confirmation, give him the ultimate in care, and he probably will run four hundred yards effectively. . . . But you take a good confirmation thoroughbred with bloodlines, and if you don't have him dead fit he's not going to run a mile and a quarter. Training thoroughbreds is a much more difficult task. . . ."

Lukas had decided he would run a public stable: "Any time you take a private job, the day you sign the contract you know two things. You know what your salary is going to be, and that you're eventually going to be fired, like a baseball manager. You're definitely going to be fired someday, so get ready for it."

In an interview years later, he noted that "the quarter horse industry was very limited. There are just not that many tracks. The purse money, other than the big, big races, wasn't there on a daily basis; the thoroughbreds at Santa Anita at that time had strong purses and the best horses."

By the end of 1977, Lukas was ready to take a shot at the big time. "Wayne and I both knew, always knew, that thoroughbreds, at the top of the game, was where the real money and the real challenge was," Clyde Rice, now an accomplished trainer himself, said. What was more important was that Lukas's owners were also ready to make the move. Bob Beal, Lloyd French, and Mel Hatley were coming along for the ride. It was going to be exciting.

The *Daily Racing Form* covered Lukas's move with interest, running a large feature article entitled "D. Wayne Lukas Is Stretching Out," by Leon Rasmussen. The article began: "Can a leading quarter horse trainer become a leading thoroughbred horse trainer?" It went on: "Several internationally known owners, such as Nelson Bunker Hunt, Robert Sangster, and Al Yank are betting top-class horses that the quarter horseman . . . will make the transition successfully." Among the other owners were the ambassador to Switzerland, Marvin L. Warner, and John Gaines, head of Gainesway Farm, the breeder of Affirmed.

Lukas was thought of as an odd duck. He bedded his horses deeper in straw and massaged each with rubber gloves on for forty-five minutes a day.

"You'd expect Raquel Welch to cook," quipped an unnamed backstretcher.

"Everyone on the backstretch is watching to see what I'll do," Lukas said at the time. "Maybe I'll fall flat on my face, but I don't intend to. This transition to thoroughbreds has me more enthused than ever before. . . . I like a challenge."

The *Racing Form* article concluded: "This linemaker makes him an odds-on choice to make it . . . and big."

When he entered his first horse, Current Concept, at Oak Tree, a steward asked Lukas if he thought the horse was fit to run. A flustered Lukas answered yes. Then he turned to Laffit Pincay Jr. and said, "I know he can run a quarter of a mile. After that you are on your own." Pincay nodded without a smile. "I don't think Laffit caught my attempt at humor," Lukas said, laughing. The horse won. Lukas's plan was to use older horses to establish the stable, and hoped that the owners would feed yearlings to him to make the thing go.

Lukas took a flier then, went to the Keeneland Auctions and purchased a filly named Terlingua, after a small Texas town. Not knowing it at the time, he had picked himself another "box office" horse. His career was about to take off, again.

FOUR

THE BIG HORSES

The Barn

D. Wayne Lukas's typical day begins in the predawn hours. Depending on the time of his life, and the location, Lukas arrives at the barn somewhere between three-thirty and five A.M. Freshly shaven, wearing a newly pressed shirt, jeans with a pair of chaps, and a white cowboy hat, he walks in with authority. There is only one man in charge of a D. Wayne Lukas barn.

As with most barns, Lukas's grooms are there early, waking their charges, mucking out stalls, and lining their horses up in a walking ring. This is a carefully arranged and choreographed display of efficiency of motion, and movement of purpose. It is designed like a pick-and-roll in basketball or an intricately designed sweep in football. And Lukas's barn is the Green Bay Packers of this kind of sweep. The movements are practiced to perfection. There are no mistakes, because every person knows his or her job, and the job comes first.

Unlike most barns, there is no coffee machine. "This ain't a coffee shop," is the practiced reply. Not anymore. Not since Jacob Bunn died. No alcohol is allowed. And there are no radios. No radio playing is allowed at all. And there's not a lot of chitchat. There is especially no cursing. It's all timed out, like the way Lukas organized basketball practices for Johnny Orr at Wisconsin.

Bunches of pink, red, yellow, and blue flowers, neatly trimmed bushes and grass, wrought ironwork, and lawn jockeys make Lukas's immaculately landscaped barns unmistakable. Many trainers have knocked this as showy. Many have snickered that maybe what he really wanted to be was a landscaper or florist. But his barns are memorable—clean and neat, with deeper straw than in other barns. They have the best oats and the cleanest tack on the backstretch. Lukas told writer Joe Palmer when he first moved into Santa Anita: "I just hope they don't think I'm too far out, the way I like to pretty up my barn."

Another thing people notice are the herringbone-raked dirt floors. As soon as someone walks over them, there's an attendant ready to rerake the floor, returning it to its perfect and dazzling pattern. "When you pay Wayne Lukas a call," Pete Axthelm wrote in *Gentleman's Quarterly*, "you're always followed by someone with a rake." Tack boxes are shined. There are no cobwebs. Everything is pin neat. Axthelm recounted that "the late racing writer Dick Joyce once suggested that Lukas was less interested in making the cover of *Sports Illustrated* than he was *Better Barns and Gardens*."

Lukas's retort? "A good appearance translates into pride."

"The stalls can be perfect, but if a saddle pony don't look right or the pony tack isn't gleaming, he'll get all over you," says Randy Bradshaw, former Lukas assistant who now oversees the California operations. "He's always looking for a way to motivate you."

The other thing Lukas is noted for are his racing silks and his bridles. Some have taken cheap shots at the green racing silks, saying they're the color of money. And Lukas's white bridles are considered flashy. They stand out. All of it is calculated and for effect.

So unique is a Wayne Lukas barn that *Sports Illustrated* sent William Nack to spend a few days trying to keep up with him, and the result was the well-received article, "While the World Sleeps," which fascinated the horse world and those interested in it. Nack captured the early morning hours and the single-minded devotion that Lukas brought to his work. The passion of Lombardi, the purposefulness of John Wooden, and the willfulness of Norman Vincent Peale were all rolled into one in Lukas. "No one ever rode into thoroughbred racing in the manner of Darrell Wayne Lukas, by himself or otherwise," Nack wrote in 1985. "There has never been anyone quite like him, no one even remotely close, in the long and colorful history of the sport—coming where he came from and doing what he has done, and all in so short a time."

Lukas would try anything to give his horses, and his owners, an edge. As with most trainers, anything legal is worth trying a couple times. Mel Hatley once told Nack about a time on an exceptionally hot day at Bay Meadows in San Francisco when an ice truck pulled in front of Lukas's stable.

"All the horses picked up their heads and went to nickerin'," Hatley said, "and I noticed that all the grooms were getting buckets and dumping ice and running water in them." This is not a particularly unusual sight in a horse barn, as it is common practice to ice down horses' legs to reduce swelling in them. Hatley asked Lukas if he was going to water down the horses' legs.

"You like to drink ice water when you're hot, don't you?" Lukas responded. "Well, so do the horses." Hatley had never seen this done before, and so he questioned Lukas further. "Some of the races are won by a photo finish," Lukas said. "If they enjoy fresh ice water on hot days, it might make 'em stick their noses out a little farther. I do every little thing I can to make these horses happy."

Another trainer who could be found on the backstretch earlier than most was Charlie Whittingham. For years, in California, Lukas and Whittingham arrived earlier than anyone else. He was less experimental than Lukas. "People are always looking for the secrets to success in this or that," Whittingham said. "There's no secret to training horses. You've just got to be there and work hard, and you'd better know what you're doing, or else they'll make a fool out of you fast."

No matter which of his many barns he's in, Lukas makes several morning phone calls with regularity. The trainer of each barn—whether it's Churchill Downs, Santa Anita, New York, or somewhere else—readies himself for the half hour barrage. Lukas discusses each horse with his assistants, a low-level-sounding title for people who have been left in charge of some of the most expensive horses in the industry. The title "Assistant Trainer" in the Lukas operation is something to be achieved.

His barns are run like other people run businesses. They are the only barns on the backstretch with time clocks, which each employee must punch; highly unusual on the sleepy backstretches across America. And Lukas is extremely picky when it comes to hiring assistants and other employees. He gets rid of nonbelievers and does what he can to hang on to people he considers good employees. Where he has a stable, he pays some of the highest salaries on the backstretch, in an effort to keep good people and keep continuity with good people. He expects his assistants to run their barns exactly as they are run elsewhere, with no variation. And his barn was the first to offer a profit sharing program for employees.

He is tough, a disciplinarian. There is one way to do anything, and that's his way. Yet few assistants who have left have negative things to say about Lukas—at least on the record. And many of his assistants have gone on to be great successes.

The assistants know what's expected of them when Lukas calls in the morning. The round robin of conversations takes hours, and for the most part Lukas seems to remember almost every horse at all the tracks where Team Lukas operates. The conversations all sound the same: a list of instructions regarding each horse, deliberate and unquestioned, like Jimmy Cagney in the movie *One, Two, Three*: "Jog that one, yeah. . . . Gallop him two miles. . . . With [him] I want to hose that ankle." The rap is the same for the next caller and the next. Lukas has given his instructions to his assistant trainers. The day can now begin.

In the years when he and his son Jeff were at Santa Anita, the two would meet at a doughnut shop earlier in the morning to plan the first part of the day, and then meet again to discuss the latter part. Lukas doesn't sleep much, and never has. He has been the same bundle of energy his whole life. He's told people that he only sleeps three or four hours a night. But Lukas is known for taking catnaps, from which he awakes seemingly refreshed and aware.

Somewhere in every Lukas barn there's a large board. It lists all the horses in the barn, with racing dates and routines to be followed. It is the equivalent of a television programmer's slotting board. This training chart will cover an entire month, and will dictate three basic instructions for each horse, one on any given day. The instructions are G for gallop, R for race, and W for walk. Horses that race on a given day will generally have light work the week before a race.

Also, Lukas scribbles constantly on yellow legal pads, making lists of things to do. Whether it's the instructions for each horse or the day's plan, it is all meticulously written down and followed. When Lukas first came over to thoroughbreds, it was said he left a half hour for himself for lunch and dinner on his things-to-do list.

Holding onto a clipboard, he'll typically begin with an "Okay, listen up!" He'll direct a cadre of riders, assigning one to a horse, giving instructions on who is to do what, directions that might sound something like this: "Bedo, you and Fernando take two and a half [laps] together. Chris, we're going to work a half mile. You gotta drop him on the rail and kinda hold him together. Just breeze him. He's not up to much more than that. If he gets a little rubber legged, don't ask him for too much. Jesse, go two solid. Martin? You're gonna jog three. Be careful. Don't let him get to playin' or he'll get rid of ya. Torey, backtrack to the middle of the backside, then gallop two and jog one. Got it?"

Then he'll turn around his expensive quarter horse, and off they go. Lukas usually heads to a far corner to watch it all take place and then to dish out criticism or advice. "We're constantly telling people why when we ask you to do something," he told Carol Flake. "We teach more than most trainers. After a period of time, if you don't improve we eliminate you. Either they're dumb, or their intensity factor isn't strong enough. The learning process involves intensity."

As Kiaran McLaughlin, independent trainer and former Team Lukas member, told Ross Staaden: "They call Wayne a teacher and a basketball coach, instead of a trainer, but that is part of what makes him what he is. He *is* a great teacher, a great coach, and a great horseman. He teaches you."

The Trainer's Daily Dozen

In every D. Wayne Lukas barn there is a plaque. It's like the Ten Commandments of Team Lukas, except it's a dozen commandments. They are the little parts of everything he's adopted and made his own. As he will loudly tell anyone, they are the rules everyone should follow, whether he or she is a horse trainer or a CEO.

The value of time
The success of perseverance
The pleasure of working
The dignity of simplicity
The worth of character
The power of kindness
The influence of example
The obligation of duty
The wisdom of economy
The virtue of patience
The improvement of talent
The joy of originating

These are the things Lukas stresses most to his assistant trainers and then to his grooms and hot walkers. Despite their obviousness, Lukas could spend hours explaining his thoughts on the Trainer's Daily Dozen, or write a book about them. They're posted in every Lukas barn. They ensure a uniformity of thinking. As mentioned before, the D. Wayne Lukas operation works on the McDonald's principle that every stable you go to will operate in exactly the same way. Employees who don't buy into his philosophy and ethic don't last long.

"Doom and gloom mumbling makes for doom and gloom mumbling horses," he has said. Attitude is everything with Lukas. Employees must exhibit enthusiasm and a desire for accomplishment, and they must have faith in his system. "They can't revert to what they think is best." But in the end, it's hard, long hours. Lukas puts in eighteen-hour days and wants his assistants to put in those same hours. "I tell my help, 'Don't buy a new set of clothes because you'll be a size smaller in thirty days.' " Anyone who is going to run one of his far-flung stables will work for a minimum of one year directly under his steely gaze. And once an assistant is ensconced in his or her position out somewhere in the Lukas empire, control is still tight, and diverging from the instructions is simply not allowed.

"I want them to tell me what they would do. Then I tell them what they are going to do. They get five minutes of democracy. The rest is dictatorship."

It even extends to language, especially in California and New York, where there are more Hispanics who work on the backstretch. As far as Lukas is concerned, it doesn't matter if someone doesn't speak English, they either follow the examples set for them or they don't last long. Lukas doesn't bother to learn Spanish, or any language other than English.

All this makes for a well-organized, no nonsense barn. It also creates a luxurious and consistently high level of living for the horses. All the horses know that no matter what barn they go to, there will be what is known on the backstretch as a "puff" outside of each horse stall, filled with hay and grass for the horses to nibble on. Psychologically, this reduces the stress on the horses brought on by traveling. Some horses don't travel as well as others, but the sameness of accommodation and routine make the moves easier on them. "We don't ship people, we ship horses," he's said. "It doesn't matter where they get off the plane. They're going to walk into the same stall, eat the same feed, get bathed and soaped at the same time, and keep the same training routine."

And for the assistants and other employees, not to mention Lukas himself, the tack is always on the same place, no matter what stable you are in—just outside the stall door. Everything is standardized and the same in every barn. If something gets changed in one barn, it gets changed in every barn.

As far as barn fees, Lukas is about mid-range in what he charges his owners. But his barns are run lavishly and his fees do not cover the costs. Other trainers charge more than he does for similar services. But that's not the way Lukas is looking to make money. He has estimated that in the beginning he was losing $1.06 per horse per day. He needed to race horses to make money. But he also realized he was beating his own brains out, as were many of his competitors. He was running his best horses against his own best horses against the other trainers' best horses. This was not the way to keep a number of owners happy, nor the way to win the most money. The thing to do was find some soft spots somewhere else where he could send his horses so they could win without taking wins away from his own barn.

So he set up barns in another part of the country. This was revolutionary, and another step away from traditional horse racing. The bluebloods demanded that you stay in your region and dominate at all costs. Because of the advances in air travel, including its lessened costs, Lukas realized he could do things differently, that he wasn't tied to one locale. He could read the *Daily Racing Form* and see the big upcoming money races that his horses could win if he could just get them there.

"I got to looking at it. You're dealing with high-class personnel. Maybe we can develop good assistants. But more importantly, I looked at the clientele. The one thing I saw in racing that was . . . that people had a tendency to stay at a location. You came to Saratoga. Whittingham had great horses, but he stayed at Santa Anita or he stayed at Hollywood. Well, not all the good horses were going to compete at that level, so what happens to the other half? Not everyone can play in the NBA or the NFL, so what happens to the other players? And I felt that in order to keep the clientele happy, we should try to make the best of every horse regardless of its ability, and the only way to do that was to set up divisions. The other thing was, I felt that if you had a top-flight horse, you were remiss if you didn't take advantage of the best possible races no matter where they were in the U.S.

"So we decided to do two things. We were going to develop a lesser string to take care of the horses that couldn't compete at Belmont, Saratoga, or Santa Anita, and we would develop the ability to move horses instead of people. See, the knock is that when you're sitting at Santa Anita and you want to take a horse to Saratoga, it's very expensive. You almost gotta win the damn thing. So people would say, 'Well, I don't know, we fly him there we gotta get an exercise rider back there, rent a car, an apartment, all these expenses.' Well, that doesn't have to be. We'll set up in Saratoga, we'll set up in California, and we can just move horses from state to state. And we do that to this day. We just put a halter on the horse and ship the horse. Exact same situation.

"I think we were in Omaha and used that for the secondary horses. We were into Churchill, and we might even have been into Monmouth Park real early . . . we started in all of those places. Then when we got the depth that we could compete on the East Coast and the West Coast, we established a base at Belmont."

It was Jeff who went out to Belmont to run that stable for his father. "He was ready and was more than happy to do it. We bought a house in Garden City and he lived the first year at the Garden City Hotel, which damn near broke us, then bought him a home and everything."

Eventually he established stables in Kentucky, at Churchill Downs, and in New York, at Belmont. These were two competitive, fertile racing grounds. But Lukas used them as hubs. He could fly horses in and out of smaller tracks, coming into town, as he had when he was a quarter horse trainer. He'd come in for the meet, and then leave when it was over. Over the years, some new stables were opened and some were closed. But all looked exactly alike.

It was through this technique that Lukas would develop a string of highly successful horses and people. Some of today's most competitive trainers got their start running one of Lukas's far-flung stables. Over the years, he has given opportunities to Bobby Barnett, Todd Pletcher, Dallas Stewart, Mark Henning, and many others who are now independent trainers. He refers to them as "his guys." These assistant trainers would eventually help him run an empire.

And it was his son, Jeff, who would run Belmont and help train some of his father's most famous horses.

Effervescing and Terlingua

Lukas rented his first stalls at Hollywood Park in the fall of 1977.

To many in the thoroughbred world, Lukas was a bit of an oddity. He was cocksure and he had an odd pedigree. He had not worked under the guiding hand of another weathered and grizzled thoroughbred veteran before setting up his own shop. And especially in those days, when the old families and the big breeding farms were still in charge, though their influence was waning, this flashy horse trader with a sheepskin on the wall was at best viewed with suspicion. And plenty of derisive snickering.

This was not Lukas's first foray into the big horses. In 1974 he'd won several races, entering horses he'd bought on the cheap. He had run them at Hollywood Park and at Pomona. While Hollywood Park was an established track, the Pomona track was what is known as a "bullring" and it was at a local fairground. It was at Pomona that Harbor Hauler won the Foothill Stakes and gave Lukas his first stakes win.

In his barn, Lukas had a string of unknowns. There were a few horses he'd bought at Keeneland, which was less of a sucker's game than it had been years before, but nobody who was anybody was going to give this apparent huckster a chance. But he had a horse he'd been working on for Albert Yank, named Effervescing.

Albert Yank was no stranger to hard work, and spent many long hours plowing dirt fields. He'd gotten involved in horses in the 1930s and slowly worked his way up to owning broodmares and stallions. He also had done a little training himself. By 1983 he was an owner/breeder. Despite several overtures by Lukas to Yank, who thought Lukas seemed like a fast talking hustler, the two were not involved until Mel Hatley offered Yank a large sum of money for a percentage of Effervescing. The only proviso was that Yank had to leave the horse with Lukas to train. This eventually started a very profitable and successful relationship between the two.

Lukas's first few months did not go well. Thoroughbred races cover longer distances than quarter horse races, and his horses proved to be fast pace setters and bad finishers. Lukas's thoroughbreds raced like quarter horses—all speed and no strategy. They didn't run, they exploded. His first winner at Santa Anita was a horse named Current Concept. He'd bought it for next to nothing, and the garden-hose-size bowed tendon came with the horse for free.

"He had to learn to slow them down," Rod Kaufman told Carol Flake. Kaufman was an experienced horse trainer who was excellent with young, inexperienced horses. Thoroughbred races are to quarter horse races what long distance running is to sprinting. Lukas had to change his approach. Thoroughbreds have to run freely but conserve energy, and then explode when they can to make their mark.

Many horse trainers, jockeys, and other training riders will tell you that personality has a lot to do with which horses will succeed. Some horses need another horse to race. Other horses only respond when far behind. Other horses want to run out front and stay there. And there are those horses that will even get bored with a big lead and squander it just so it stays more interesting. But it is the horse that fears being caught or surpassed by another that is the dream of every trainer. They want that fierce competitor that will stare down and intimidate another horse. That's the ideal. Since horses are not all the same nor ideal, each trainer tries to conceive of the right strategy for each one.

However, there was a problem with Effervescing, the horse that Hatley and Yank now co-owned. It was five years old. And it had a bum, swollen ankle. Wayne worked on it.

Lukas would make his mark faster than expected. He was able to celebrate the Fourth of July in 1978 in a most unusual way. The basketball coach turned quarter horse trainer turned thoroughbred trainer turned a lot of heads at Hollywood Park. Effervescing ran on the grass, with Laffit Pincay Jr. up, and won the $100,000 American Handicap. Lukas, Hatley, and Yank were thrilled. Yank, the old veteran, had his eye on a stakes race in Chicago, which would give the horse time to heal. But Lukas said he wasn't sending the horse anywhere. Instead, he wanted to run the horse in the $100,000 Citation Handicap at Hollywood Park—five days after its American Handicap victory. "Are you drinking your bath water?" Yank cried, incredulous. Lukas held his ground. Effervescing went out and won the race. And he would also win the Eddie Read Handicap at Del Mar, a turf race for three-year-olds and up. Pincay Jr. was in the stirrups again that day for Team Lukas.

Another of Lukas's early thoroughbred successes was Terlingua, a horse that had been bred by Tom Gentry, a high-profile and controversial figure on the thoroughbred scene. She was from Secretariat's second crop of foals. At the time, Secretariat's first crop had come up bust. Even the young man who had syndicated Secretariat, Seth Hancock, the scion of the Hancock family, had admitted as much, much to his fellow owners' chagrin. However, Beal and French were convinced by Lukas that she was worth the risk of $275,000. After the sale, Lukas had sent Terlingua to Rod Kaufman to work with her. Kaufman was good with young, fiery horses. And according to some, this horse, more than any, resembled dear old dad.

"When she came out of Tom Gentry's barn and I saw her for the first time," Lukas recalls, "she not only looked like Secretariat—she walks like her dad and looks like her mother—she was the spitting image of her mother. Tommy never knew, I think, that I was interested in the filly till the sale was over."

During her first workouts, Lukas told Pincay that this horse was special. He told the jockey to just breeze her. Pincay promised to keep her slow, but the horse was magnificent. She topped both their speed expectations.

"Oh boss, ooooh!" Pincay said after the work. "She was flying!"

On June 14, 1978, Lukas sent Terlingua out to beat the boys in the Nursery Stakes at Hollywood Park. And in doing so, he began a pattern of training two-year-old fillies that would cement his reputation as a skilled trainer. Lukas, as a quarter horse trainer, had never been afraid to run fillies against colts, which ran counter to the conventional wisdom in thoroughbred racing.

"I know it's not done. All my friends . . . came and pulled me aside and said, 'Why put your head on the chopping block?'" he said afterward. But Lukas had studied the times of the competing horses, and knew that Terlingua's speed times were better than all the horses that had ever raced there save one—Affirmed, who held the track record.

Asked much later in his career what he most looked for in a filly, Lukas replied: "She should have a head like a princess, a butt like a washerwoman, and walk like a hooker." Terlingua may not have fit that description exactly, but she could run with the best of them. She had big hind quarters, and some thought she had a bit of the quarter horse build to her. Lukas later told *New York Times* reporter Steven Crist, "The mistake everyone was making was breeding those classic distance mares to a classic horse like that." Lukas was still looking for that burst of speed.

"I have never doubted my conviction, from the first, that she was an exceptional superstar," he told a reporter. "I treated her like one, and I went right down the line with her."

She went on to to win the Del Mar Debutante and the Hollywood Juvenile. In the Juvenile, a premiere early Derby prep race, she had beaten the track record set a year earlier by Alydar.

All during her two-year-old racing season, Tom Gentry had been showing videotapes of the horse's races from that year at Keeneland. "She's trained by a quarter horse guy named Wayne Lukas," he would exclaim, like some kind of ancient mariner gone horse crazy. "You better remember his name. He's going to be the best this business has ever seen."

There was, however, a series of setbacks, and the horse could not live up to its early spectacular wins. While she had been high on the list of Derby tongues in the fall before the Derby, by the spring she was way out of it. Despite two stakes wins after the Triple Crown season had passed, Terlingua was finished.

Regardless of Terlingua's inability to gain further success beyond her immediate wins, Lukas was firmly establishing himself in the horse world. While he was winning notice from owners, however, the people on the backstretch were grumbling. It was partly Lukas's fault. He was loud and brash. He was going to do it his way. And if he was winning, he'd let you know it. While this kind of braggadocio was part of the give-and-take of the old leaky-roof circuit, it rubbed a number of thoroughbred people the wrong way. Along with his college degree and his quarter horse background, Lukas was an easy target for jibes. His assistant trainer at the time, Tom McKenzie, told Carol Flake, "People didn't like Wayne when he first changed over. He made some statements about trainers being stuck in ruts and the world passing 'em by."

This was true enough. Lukas was plastered on the cover of *Horseman's Journal* by October 1978 along with Terlingua. "I think a lot of times we're caught up in tradition," he told a writer. "Now there is something called common sense and sound judgment. . . . Until somebody shows me that we're doing it all wrong, we'll continue." Another quote from the same article was practically a declaration of war. Lukas said there were a number of trainers who were successful but didn't know anything about horses; that there were few in the thoroughbred circuit who could break a raw unraced colt and make him into a winner all by themselves. He concluded: "I know there are a number of thoroughbred trainers, very, very successful, including several in the Hall of Fame, that I wouldn't trust with my pony."

Tweaking the establishment's nose would come to be seen as vintage Lukas. And at the time, it was enough to get him noticed and raise his profile. Part feeling his oats, part fantastic showman, he was ready to raise the ante in his game of poker with the game's top players.

John Nerud, Tartan Farms, and Codex

John Nerud is a Hall of Fame horse trainer. He is one of the old-timers who remembers the old days, long before the Keeneland sales made it possible for someone with a few million bucks to buy a talented thoroughbred and call themselves a horseman. A noted curmudgeon, Nerud was once quoted as saying about the horse racing game: "It's a quick way for a rich man to get his name in all the papers. It's like buying a baseball team. There's always going to be someone with too much money who we can get interested in horse racing." Nerud is president of Tartan Farms, a premiere breeding farm based in Ocala, Florida. He was the trainer of Gallant Man and Dr. Fager for Tartan Farms before moving to an executive position overseeing breeding.

A rare mistake by Hall of Fame jockey Bill Shoemaker, who stood up in the stirrups announcing victory at the sixteenth pole instead of at the finish line, cost Gallant Man the Derby. Gallant Man and Shoemaker came back to win the 1957 Belmont Stakes, where he beat Bold Ruler, who finished third. He was voted Horse of the Year in 1958,

Champion Sprinter, Champion Grass Horse, and Champion Handi-capper all in one year—his last—1968. For Nerud, it was the perfect cap to a long and illustrious career in which he'd won more than a thousand races, in an era when plane travel and owning far-flung stables was not yet even dreamt of.

Albert Yank told Ross Staaden that he had put his longtime friend John Nerud in touch with Lukas and got him his break. "We were playing gin rummy and drinking scotch whiskey. I told him Tartan Farms should be represented on the West Coast. I told him I had a cowboy, a star-spangled cowboy, that didn't know much about thoroughbreds but would work his way through; that I was his mentor."

Nerud was retiring as a trainer to become the president of Tartan Farms, and was in fact looking for someone to train a California stable of horses. He sent eighteen horses to Lukas. "That's a large contingent of horses," he said later. "It takes trainers years to build that up. It put him in with the top group of people in the world. It gave him respectability." Nerud once described the perception of trainers by others as "men in plaid coats who steal chickens." Of course, Lukas's operation played a part in convincing Nerud to place the horses with him. He said as much in 1999: "He was a worker, he was smart, and he ran a first-class stable."

Joe Drape retold a wonderful story of Nerud and Lukas. Nerud had heard about Lukas and wanted to introduce himself to the young trainer. He saw Lukas on the track, working his horses. When Nerud approached, Lukas turned to him and said, "What can I do for you, old man?" Nerud, a sarcastic type himself, was amused.

"He works like a goddammed dog," Nerud once told William Nack. "I'm a hyper bastard too. I'm worse than 90 percent of the people. But he flies right by me."

Many years later, Nerud would describe the successful Lukas as "an arrogant man. He's got his opinions and they come out quick. He wants you to hear them and listen to them. But I believe he has earned that right for all he has done for the game."

This was a time of great personal growth for Lukas, along with some bumps in the road. During this period, Lukas would begin to expand his business. By the end of 1978 he had a record of seventy-three wins in 194 starts and had won $942,786 in purse monies. Things were looking good and were going to get better. In 1979 he had 440 starts, sixty-three wins, and earned $1,360,772.

Also in this period, in 1978, Jeff came to join his father as a trainer. Jeff had been a senior at the University of Wisconsin, when Lukas pulled him out of the university with one semester to go. Lukas told Carol Flake he simply said to his son: "You've been there long enough."

From then on Jeff would be the number two man in the operation. Neither father nor son was to be disobeyed. Where Wayne could be bristling or cool, Jeff was easier to work with. He was less like a head coach, but bad to cross. And if provoked, his temper could flare. He was twenty-two, and in the coming years, Lukas would hand over some of his best horses to his son's care. As Lukas began to build an empire, it would be his son and his assistants who spent more quality time with the horses, and Lukas would spend more time with the owners.

Kiaran McLaughlin also came to work for Lukas that year. McLaughlin was a fiery, red-headed Irishman with a wicked temper. Born a Kentuckian, he was eager to prove himself to Lukas, who was starting to develop his corporate culture, and doing it with young, hungry assistants who badly wanted to be trainers. This triumvirate would help Team Lukas get to the next plateau. Lukas's son and McLaughlin were part of his operation when Nerud handed over a difficult young colt named Codex, among the contingent of horses he sent to Lukas.

A beautiful chestnut colt by Arts and Letters out of Roundup Rose (by Minnesota Mac), Codex was foaled in 1977. When he won the Hollywood Stakes at Hollywood Park in November 1979, the inevitable question was asked: Was he Derby material? Hindsight would say yes, but at the time there was disagreement. Lukas needed a box office horse, an animal that would draw attention to the barn. But John Nerud wasn't impressed by getting attention. He wanted wins. Nerud had gone on record claiming he thought the Triple Crown races could ruin a horse, and he thwarted any move to nominate the horse for the Kentucky Derby. During Preakness week,

Lukas would diplomatically tell the press that the failure to nominate Codex to the Derby had been an "oversight." We know today that Lukas would now have nominated him in a second. Instead, Codex missed the Run for the Roses. And yet, the horse would still have a brush with greatness.

Pat Valenzuela was seventeen years old when Lukas gave him the start in the 1980 Santa Anita Derby on the first weekend in April. Fighting off Rumbo and Bic's Gold, Codex won the Santa Anita Stakes on April 5, with a time of 1:47.3 over a mile and an eighth. It was a huge win. Certainly the biggest win of Lukas's career. Afterward, Nerud assented to enter Codex in the 1980 Preakness Stakes.

It was what Lukas had been working for—his first shot at the big time. National television would be covering the event. It had taken eleven years of professional horse training to get to this point alone. Yet he'd only been training thoroughbreds for two and a half years. At the time, the newspapers referred to him as a little known California horse trainer.

The 1980 Kentucky Derby was won, surprisingly, by the first filly to win the Derby in sixty-five years, Genuine Risk. It had not been done since 1915, when Regret won the roses. With Jacinto Vasquez aboard, Genuine Risk was the clear class of the field, and beat Rumbo and Jacklin Klugman to win the race and America's heart. With the recent spate of Triple Crown winners, including Secretariat, Seattle Slew, and Affirmed, a relatively weak field, and the rising tide of feminism, Genuine Risk raised the question: Can she be the first filly ever to win a Triple Crown? The media loved the story, and in the two weeks between the Derby and the Preakness, she came to embody the equine aspirations of a whole generation of horsewomen. The battle of the sexes had taken a horsey turn.

On May 17 the horses loaded into the gate at Pimlico in Maryland. And along with them the hopes and dreams of a brash middle-age trainer named D. Wayne Lukas. With jockey Angel Cordero Jr. up, Lukas's Codex was solid out of the gate, and the trainer held his breath for the first time in a Triple Crown event. The 83,455 spectators in the stands, a record at the time, held their collective breath with him. Cordero stalked the leaders through decent fractions and made his move coming out of the final turn. The horse had the extra gas and power. Cordero could see the finish line.

What happened next is still conjecture. Few who back either camp will change their perspective on it. Joe Durso, writing for the *New York Times*, gives the right flavor of the period: "Racing's Battle of the Sexes turned into combat at the top of the stretch today when Genuine Risk, the filly from Kentucky, finally caught Codex, the colt from California, and tried to pass him. And for a few seconds, they fought one of the most memorable clashes in the 105th running of the Preakness."

From Cordero's point of view: "When he saw the gate and with all the noise in the crowd, he spooked and came out a little, but he was out there before the filly got to him. When she got to me, I already was there. I already was where I was. In this race everybody takes their chances. I hit my horse with the whip, not his."

But the opposing jockey, Jacinto Vasquez, had a different version of the incident.

"I thought this was a racetrack, not a rodeo," he railed after the race. "I think they should take his number down. They took the heart out of my filly when he brushed me. He sure brushed me hard."

He also claimed: "He hit my horse over the head with the whip. He came out and bumped me and took me outside the fence. And after that, she stopped running."

Regardless of what the truth was, Codex went wide and Genuine Risk was slightly impeded, but not cut off. A charge could still have been made. As it was, Codex won by 4¾ lengths over Genuine Risk. James Tuite, who was also covering the event for the *New York Times*, wrote: "Codex . . . gave an overpowering performance despite the controversial incident." With the protest lodged, the posted winning had to wait.

Lukas turned to Cordero as they waited for the final answer. "Take us down or not, he ran a mile and three-sixteenths." And he asked the jockey: "Did he handle nice?"

"Whatever I want, he do," Cordero replied.

J. Fred Cowill, the head of the steward's review board, denied Vasquez's complaint, and said after the winner was posted: "Vasquez said that Cordero hit his horse, but we could not see that at all. Cordero did come off the rail as Vasquez approached him with the filly. Cordero went slightly wide, but in our opinion it did not hinder the filly enough to warrant disqualification."

Asked what he thought after reviewing the replay, Nerud admitted he didn't bother to watch it. "We've already got the money," he said, smiling.

Still, Vasquez complained bitterly after the race to Durso, claiming that his horse had been struck and that he had been bumped. He charged the stewards with not wanting to cause a problem and letting Cordero get away with it. "We're friends outside, Cordero and me. But when we get in a race, we're different persons. But we're still not trying to kill each other."

Trying to leave in a hurry, Vasquez and Cordero literally bumped into each other on the back stairs of the jockey's lounge. Cordero raised his hands, as if arrested, and then laughed and hugged Vasquez. But Vasquez still fumed. Cordero told him he didn't blame him for lodging the protest, that he would have done it too if the roles were reversed.

In the meantime, Lukas's parents were very proud, and were interviewed in the local paper. "The sad thing about all of this is that I waited more than forty years for something like this. Then it happens, and I can't be there in person to see it," said Ted Lukas, at seventy-one years of age and in failing health, unable to attend the event.

Lukas's proud mother, Bea, told the local papers: "He could spend five minutes with a horse and get it to do anything he wanted to." She added: "I've got nothing against the filly. I wanted her to win the Kentucky Derby. Firestone owns Genuine Risk, and everyone knows Firestone is known for its recalls."

The day after the race, Red Smith chimed in with an article entitled, "That Was No Way to Treat a Lady," playing to the Battle of the Sexes theme embraced by the media. It began: "A tough customer who forsook Florida for Southern California came East and waylaid America's sweetheart."

Another newspaper story said: "The Equal Rights Amendment took a giant step backward at Pimlico. . . ."

And what did Lukas say to the press after his first Triple Crown victory and the controversial win? "Three qualified people watching horse races on film for years just ruled that there was no interference, and that's fine with me. I just know that I prayed a lot on the track."

After the race, Nerud called Codex "as good as any horse in the country right now." He was then reminded he had some other promising horses, and replied, "I don't want no gonna be-er. I don't want no was-er. I want an is-er, and this colt is an is-er." Then he told Lukas: "Make arrangements to ship to Belmont."

It was clear, from the press's view, that Nerud was still a very experienced man in the ways of Triple Crown events and a man very much in charge. And Lukas was looked upon as a former basketball coach and protégé. But it was fine by Lukas. He had his first win. The next day, when he arrived at the barn, he wore a huge smile, welcoming the more than forty telegrams he had received. That smile was quickly wiped off his face by the horrific offerings of their writers, accusing him of all manner of things.

Clearly, this Triple Crown series was not turning out to be a smooth ride. Now, on the way to the Belmont Stakes, absolute bedlam was about to strike. Genuine Risk's owners, Bert and Diana Firestone, filed another complaint, this time with the Maryland Racing Commission, asking them to overturn the Preakness decision. If this were done, Genuine Risk would be called the winner, and her charge for the Triple Crown at Belmont could be continued. Millions of dollars were at stake, for it was a situation in which endorsements and media hype could drive Genuine Risk's fees as brood mare up to astronomical numbers.

The Firestones insisted on reviewing the tapes with a member of the board of stewards, and stood by their position afterward. In a prepared statement, they said, "We feel that the interest of the racing public and Genuine Risk would be well served by having the matter reviewed. . . . Should the appeal be allowed, the entire purse [$180,600] will be donated to the National Museum of Racing and to furthering the interest of equine research."

On June 2, just a few days before the Belmont Stakes, the commission convened. The film was rerun seventy-eight times during the course of one day's testimony. In an article entitled "Perry Mason at the Races," Red Smith mused, "If the term 'media event' weren't already in the language, we should have to get a Latin to invent it to describe what went on yesterday in the third floor dining room of the Pimlico clubhouse. It was a circus, a television spectacular, gussied up for show biz. It was a public trial in a makeshift courtroom, and the screen credits should have read, 'By Perry Mason out of Hollywood.'"

The biggest contention, outside of the brush and other claims, was that no winner in the 105-year history of the Preakness had ever been taken down due to foul. Now, here, the media was whipping up the frenzy that the old boys' club would fix what its equine counterparts could not—it would keep the filly out of the winner's circle by any means. The commission was a zoo. Everyone possible testified, and each time, the film was run and rerun. While the television films contributed by ABC-TV showed that the horses appeared closer, Arnold Weiner, part of the group that owned Codex under Tartan Farms, showed photographs that actually showed the horses were almost three feet apart. Weiner claimed the television footage distorted the truth of the matter and was created for entertainment value, not for judging races.

There were television cameras everywhere, and the glare of hot lights was brutal. At one point Cordero was asked if he had indeed taken his horse wide. He responded, "Well, there's wide, wider, and widest," meaning his horse went wide, but not the widest it might have gone.

Red Smith quipped, "Witnesses included just about everybody involved except the horses, and they were present on film. Never before had the trackside restaurant drawn such a crowd without benefit of crab cakes."

After countless testimony and review of photographs, racing film, and television coverage, the commission denied the Firestones' bid on June 4. The board ruled three to one that while a slight brush may have occurred, the race results would not be changed. In three days the horses would challenge each other again. The money that had been withheld until then was now disbursed to the declared finishers.

All this was only part of the hype that was now building around the Belmont Stakes. The bitter rivalry that started on the track at Baltimore would now continue in the dirt of New York. Writers talked about Genuine Risk being robbed, that she would win her version of the Triple Crown, and the like. Before the race, both jockeys were addressed by the Belmont track stewards, who were aware of the rancor now growing between Cordero and Vasquez. Interest grew even keener when the post positions were drawn, and Genuine Risk and Codex were one and two in the gate. The battle lines had now been drawn.

Before the race, Cordero and Vasquez squared off in the press again. "I been riding like that for twenty years," Cordero said. "If I was afraid of controversy, I should have retired five years ago."

Vasquez rejoined, "I won't leave it up to the stewards to decide." Despite all this, Codex was installed as the favorite off his Preakness upset, with Genuine Risk and Rumbo close behind. The duel was compared to legendary rivalries like Ruffian and Foolish Pleasure, and Affirmed and Alydar.

Neither Lukas nor LeRoy Jolley, Genuine Risk's trainer, said anything inflammatory. Indeed, Lukas was deferential, saying, "I don't consider the Belmont a grudge match between our horses or between LeRoy and myself. LeRoy is a very close friend of mine." In fact, Lukas said, he was most afraid of Rumbo, another West Coast invader.

The race was anticlimatic, given its billing. It was Temperance Hill, a 50–1 shot, ridden by Eddie Maple and trained by Joseph Cantey, who took the race in a slow 2:29.4. Genuine Risk challenged hard and finished second again, by two lengths. Codex finished a disappointing seventh.

Lukas finished 1980 with sixty-four wins in 466 starts and total earnings of $2,010,841. This placed him fifth on the yearly money-winning list, which was headed by Laz Barrera with $2,969,151. Barrera, in fact, had been the money-earning leader between 1977 and 1980. Lukas was raising his image, and his career was rising.

Partez, Muttering, and Bobby Knight

The following year, 1981, would also be a successful one for Lukas, but it included few memorable moments. Except for one. For the first

bypass the race. He has won it four times, and his next victory will make him the Oaks record holder.

It is no secret that many of Lukas's friends, especially in the early years, were quarter horse people and basketball coaches. One with whom Lukas would become very friendly was Bobby Knight.

As a basketball coach at the U.S. Military Academy at West Point between 1965 and 1971, Knight had a .671 winning percentage, a remarkable achievement. He then moved on to Indiana University, which he coached to the NCAA national championship in 1976. He won another in 1981, and a third in 1987. But despite his success on the hardwood, Knight had one of the highest transfer rates out of his system than any other basketball coach. He was known for his incredible memory for detail, his passion for the sport, and his powerful and violent temper, which once culminated with him throwing a folding chair onto the court during a basketball game.

Television correspondent and *Newsweek* columnist Pete Axthelm, who more than once had run-ins with Knight, and with Lukas too, quoted Lukas talking about Knight, who had by then become a regular visitor to the Churchill Downs backstretch:

"Bob was playing at Ohio State when I was a freshman assistant at Wisconsin. I didn't know him then. But then our paths crossed a couple of times in some coaching clinics. Bobby became very prominent very quickly and he carried an aura about him. He was a bright rising star on the coaching scene and of course he claims that he even came through and watched one of our practices in La Crosse one time. I don't remember that.

"Where we actually bonded was when I became very good friends with [college and Olympic basketball coach] Pete Newell. Pete and I became friends through the racetrack. And Bobby and Pete are very close. Almost father/son relationship. Pete would say from time to time, "You and Bobby should get together, you're cut out of the same cloth and have a lot in common," even though we had no common bond at the time. We finally got together and . . . we had a lot of things to talk about. We could sit for hours and say, "What would be the best way to approach this or that," and I had enough of a basketball background that I think Bobby respected me from a coaching standpoint and we would talk hours about that. Pete Newell and I would go up to practice. I would drive over to Louisville and Bloomington. Pete and I would go up in the stands with a legal pad. We'd sit about six rows apart and we would critique the whole practice. And one night Bobby would say "What do you think," and we would, you know, really tear him down."

At the Kentucky Derby, Knight and a host of other college basketball coaches could be found hanging out at the Lukas barn. Knight and Lukas would spend more time together as the years went on, touring the country, Wayne attending basketball games, or the two of them talking on the phone.

Lukas has said that at times, when something was troubling Knight, the university athletic director would call and ask, "What are you doing in the next twenty-four hours?" And if he was free or could make the time, he'd be asked, "Why don't you run over to Bloomington and spend two days with Bob?"

"That type of thing," Lukas recalls. "Bill Parcells, Wayne Lukas, Pete Newell, and Tony La Russa, we were all in that group together. And we would be the guys that if we had to have a heart-to-heart, we'd get in a round table."

As Bobby Knight's fame would grow, so would his volatile temper. And eventually it exploded. The university put Knight on warning, and when that happened, the press flocked to Wayne, asking his opinion of the situation.

It happened while Lukas was preparing for the 2000 Preakness Stakes. Lukas had spoken to Knight the day before, and he defended his friend, saying, "I think he will probably prepare himself mentally to go into a press conference and take the high road and stick to it. I don't think he'll like it a lot, but he'll get through it." The story ran nationally.

"I have a little of that in me too," he admitted. "I know some days during the Triple Crown and Breeders' Cup some guys rub me the wrong way. Bobby is a highly intelligent guy and he's capable of making that adjustment." Lukas said this of his friend in May. By September, Knight was out of a job.

Landaluce

"The name of the most exciting racehorse in the world today sounds like one of those expressions Minnie Pearl belts out from the stage of the Grand Ole Opry in Nashville: Laaand-a-Looosse!" wrote William Leggett in a feature article for *Sports Illustrated* in 1982. A two-year-old filly from Seattle Slew (in his first year at stud) by Strip Poker (by Bold Bidder), she was an immediate sensation.

Lukas had bought Marfa and Landaluce in a buying spree of twenty-four horses for $6 million. Both would be stars in his stable. But Landaluce was the instant star. She had been named after a guide, Francisco Landaluce, at a Spanish ranch visited by the horse's owners, Beal and French. She took the stage on July 3, 1982, at Hollywood Park, and ripped off a seven-length win. A few weeks later the second place horse in that race, Some Kinda Flirt, won by a huge margin just at the Lady Sponsors' Stakes at Ak-Sar-Ben, in Nebraska, which put Landaluce's winning performance in sharper perspective. The other thing that raised eyebrows was her next win.

The six-furlong Hollywood Lassie was worth $77,500 to the winner. But Landaluce used it as a springboard—to sports pages across the country. She would battle Barzell, who was undefeated in two starts. Coming into the stretch, Landaluce was 1½ lengths ahead of the pack when Laffit Pincay Jr. tapped her on the shoulder with his whip. In response, she exploded to a twenty-one length win. Tapes were instantly reviewed to see what had happened. The evidence was clear. She had simply turned it up a notch and blown away the pack. The horse world was instantly abuzz.

No two-year-old horse had ever won by twenty-one lengths in a stakes race, or any regular race, for that matter, at Hollywood Park. Seattle Slew had won by 9¾ there as a two-year-old, and Secretariat had won one race by eight lengths. But this was something else!

Laz Barrera, the trainer who had won a Triple Crown with Affirmed in 1978, was stupefied: "Landaluce cost $650,000 as a yearling in 1981, and after looking at the film over and over again, I went to the Keeneland yearling sales and bought her full sister for $1.5 million. . . . That's how much Landaluce has impressed me."

Replays on television showed that it was a full three seconds before the next horse crossed the finish line. Said Loren Rettele, an opposing trainer: "It looks like two different races, one with Landaluce in it and another race."

"The day after she won the Lassie, the phone kept jangling off the hook," Lukas said. "*Good Morning America* had called, among others, and I didn't think I'd live to see the day when *Good Morning America* would call a two-year-old filly. We're having pictures of her made up so that if any little girl or boy in Des Moines falls in love with Landaluce, they can write to us and get a picture."

He told Carol Flake: "You search and you look, and then, all of a sudden, it comes, that star, and you know that you have been blessed with something special."

Laffitt Pincay Jr., her jockey in her first two races, said he'd never been on a horse like Landaluce: "Normally, I am not a superstitious man, but I walk around these days hoping nothing happens to her. When I see Wayne Lukas walking toward me, my instinct is to turn away. I am afraid he is going to tell me that something has gone wrong. I never want to hear that she even turned a hair." Considering the events at the end of the year, his words appeared to foreshadow the tragedy that was soon to strike.

Questioned by Leggett as to whether the horse might suffer any damage running on the hard California surfaces, Lukas said: "John Nerud called me the day we shipped her from Hollywood Park down to Del Mar. 'How did she ship?' he asked. I said, 'John, we got a special way to ship her. We wrap her gorgeous ass all up in Styrofoam so that only her head sticks out and she just moves right on down the highway.' "

In all, she raced five times and won all five races by a combined 46½ lengths. In the voting for the end of the year awards, there was speculation she might even warrant being Horse of the Year. Two more races at Hollywood Park and Lukas was convinced she was

Horse of the Year. Then, around Thanksgiving weekend or thereafter, she suddenly became ill. A virus.

"I thought we'd still be able to run her in the Starlet," Lukas told Andrew Beyer of the *Washington Post*. "After two days, I thought we'd have to miss that race and aim for the Futurity. After three days went by, I was saying, 'My God, let's just save her life.'"

With lots of effort, they relieved her stress and reduced her fever. But Lukas later realized they had taken care of dealing with the symptoms but not the cause of the problems. She was getting worse. "The third day, I knew in my heart it was a life-threatening situation. When you're that close to a horse, you're closer than a man to his wife and children. You can see the gleam in her eye change." One minute the horse would be alert, with her head sticking out the stall door, ears up and twitching, and the next she would be in her large, double stall, with her head drooping. There were more than a few times when Lukas stood outside the stall door and begged in vain for the horse to lift its head: "Come on, pick your head up!"

After five days, on a Saturday night, the horse took a turn for the worse. Sunday morning, around four o'clock, Lukas arrived and ordered the attendants to call the vet immediately.

"She started to weave and brace herself. She fell, but she was still trying to get air because of the fluid in her lungs," he told Beyer. Lukas scrambled to the barn floor, cradling the horse's head, pleading for its life. She could not breathe. "I had her head in my lap, trying to get her head up," he said. "She died in my arms."

Carol Flake remarked in her interview with Lukas that he choked up and his eyes welled with tears as he recalled the story for her years later. "He tells the story with a sad, inexorable rhythm, as though he were reciting an ancient ballad," she wrote. She related her wonder at his feel for the horses, which seemed to go beyond the numbers of winning, as Team Lukas is often caricatured. "In the Ballad of Landaluce, the horseman is destined to lose the perfect horse. All the positive thinking, the Lombardi discipline, the drill of hard work, fall away, and behind the scenes is not justice but luck."

Landaluce died on December 11, 1982, of a viral infection. It was later learned that she had died of colitis, which also struck another Seattle Slew colt, Swale, who dropped dead three weeks after capturing the Belmont Stakes. Seattle Slew himself had suffered a bout of the infection in 1978 but survived. Landaluce was buried in the infield at Hollywood Park along with the dreams of the horse world.

She was posthumously voted champion two-year-old filly, defeating another undefeated filly named Princess Rooney. A stakes race at Hollywood Park, a Breeders' Cup prep, is named in her honor and run on the first week in July every year, to commemorate her maiden win.

"Taught me never to get that close again," Lukas says today. "It was like a bad love affair. Just taught me not to open up like that anymore, and I don't. I love every horse in this barn but I don't let them get inside of me like that. That one taught me that. That was hard on me. The groom had a nervous breakdown. We all took that too hard. We didn't get over that very quickly. Our stables suffered. Took us almost three months before we got rolling again. . . .

"We were doomed from the beginning, in looking back. At the time, we didn't understand the chemistry and the medical aspect of that. We now know through research and everything that when that blood disorder hits a horse, it's over. Had we known that going in, it's like . . . I've never been involved in a close association with a cancer, but when they say it's over, it's over. We were done and we had no shot, and yet we felt like we might turn it around, but we really had no shot."

FIVE

THE BIG MONEY

Gene Klein

Landaluce had given Lukas higher visibility. But what he still lacked was money. He needed the big money to buy the big horse to win the big race. The way he was going, he usually had a star in his stable, but that star would not carry him to the winner's circle at the Derby, the Preakness, or the Belmont, and he wouldn't be able to buy the type of horse that could without really big cash reserves. To buy the right horses at Keeneland and the other big auctions, to bring Team Lukas to the next level, D. Wayne knew he needed a backer with clout.

Enter Gene Klein.

While the stereotype of a fast-talking, cowboy, used-car salesman is today considered about as hackneyed a caricature as exists in the American landscape, the prototype had not yet been forged when Gene Klein moved to California.

Eugene V. Klein grew up in New York City—in the Bronx, the son of a Russian immigrant. Always a hustler, pushy and fast-talking, Klein told *Sports Illustrated*'s William Nack that he supported himself growing up by selling cheap sets of encyclopedias door-to-door. He would mumble something very fast about taking a census for the "survey department" and then work his way to the sale of the encyclopedias. When he wasn't selling or studying his subjects, he was studying football and baseball.

Klein had always been a big devotee of New York sports. He was a baseball fan in the 1930s, following the exploits of New York's three major teams. And in the fall he could always be found on a Sunday afternoon cheering on his beloved New York Giants football team and such stars as Ed Danowski, an all-pro back who led the team, halfback Tuffy Leemans, center Mel Hein, end Jim Poole, and guard Johnny Dell Isola. And then there was the titanic coaching talent of Steve Owens, who steered the football Giants over three decades.

Klein enjoyed watching the Giants compete against George Preston Marshall's awesome Washington Redskins, who marched his team through the streets of New York in 1938 with an entire band of men dressed up in Native American costume, complete with headdresses. The Giants had been NFL champions as late as 1938, beating the hated Redskins for the division title, and then beat the vaunted Green Bay Packers of Curly Lambeau for the NFL championship. In fact, Klein was at the Polo Grounds in New York City on a cold afternoon in December 1941 when an announcement came across the loudspeaker that the Japanese had attacked the Hawaiian Islands in the Pacific.

He enlisted right away, and was assigned to the U.S. Army Air Corps. He became a navigator. But despite his day job guiding large planes on long and short distance runs, Klein never gave up his desire to sell and make a quick buck. While stationed in Wilmington, Delaware, he would take a train up to New York, buy a used car for approximately $700, then drive back to the base. Then he'd place an ad to sell the car in a Wilmington newspaper: "ARMY OFFICER TRANSFERRED; MUST SELL '39 BUICK; $900."

This perfectly exemplifies why Lukas and Klein instantly hit it off. They were kindred spirits. It was the kind of thing Lukas did in his youth (which was really twenty years later), buying horses from the glue factory and other low rent auctions, washing them down, groom-

ing them, then taking them to auctions to resell them all in one weekend, just to make a fast buck. It was this similarity, and the common
bond it forged between the two men, that would make their partnership one of the most important in Wayne Lukas's career, in Klein's
life, and in horse racing history. But that future was still a long ways
off in the waning days of World War II.

With the war career over, Klein was a twenty-six-year-old New
York street hustler with a yen for adventure and big dreams. "I
thought that California was kind of the land of opportunity," he told
William Nack, and so 1946 found Klein bound for California in a
1940 Chrysler. In the passenger seat were his wife Fran and their
infant daughter Randee. He headed for Los Angeles and started his
own small business in the San Fernando Valley. What kind of business? Used cars, of course.

He started his lot with four cars. "Prices were escalating: cars were
scarce." He sold three the first day. In the 1940s, California's car market was a booming business. And it was just the kind of opportunity
he was looking for. But Klein is more sanguine about his experience
now, telling Nack, "I didn't know what I was doing."

But that didn't stop him either. Klein was a hustler, and he saw his
opportunities and his business expand. One day he got an idea. It was
something off the wall, and it would soon change the face of car buying forever and make him rich beyond his wildest imagination. "Hamburger meat went to a dollar a pound," Klein explained. "Everybody
was screaming, 'Hamburger's a dollar a pound!'" So he decided to
sell his cars by the pound too. It was just the kind of gimmick he
needed to escalate his business. Signs on his cars read, "55 CENTS A
POUND!" OR "66 CENTS A POUND!" The obvious implication was that
his cars were cheaper than hamburger meat. And the gimmick
worked.

It was difficult to live in California in the 1950s and not know how
important a medium television was becoming. The movie industry
was waging war against the small screen, and meanwhile everyone
was trying to get one. Owning a television was a status symbol in
those days, and Klein saw it as the next big vehicle to expand his business once again. It gave him the opportunity to get his foot in the

door of every American living room, or at least into every living room in southern California. And he would not be denied. But a New York sharpie selling cars on television in southern California wasn't the way to win the locals' hearts. Klein knew, once again, that he needed a gimmick.

He transformed himself into Cowboy Gene, the fast-talking cowboy, used-car salesman. He became a slick, smiling, glad-handing good ol' boy. Yelling, "Howdy, pardner," Klein would go on the lot and slam his hand on the hood and trunks of automobiles, screaming about great prices and cheap cars. It worked like a charm. Sales skyrocketed. Klein had hit a new plateau in his business. But believe it or not, things were about to get better.

At the age of thirty-eight, another opportunity came his way. It was not as obvious, and took a bit of courage on his part. A small group of Swedish automakers came to Klein and tried to persuade him to sell a new car they were trying to establish in the American marketplace. Leo Hirsch, a hardware wholesaler, had gone to Sweden to buy nails in bulk, and discovered the Volvo automobile. He helped the Swedes find Klein, who was one of the largest forces in the car market in the mid-1950s. But this was a new adventure. Launching an entirely new car into the American auto market, then at the zenith of its power, prestige, and influence, was no small feat. It took a little extra cash and a whole lot of nerve.

Klein, ever the salesman, insisted on some changes, making the car a little sexier for the American market. In 1957, when the automakers had given him the look he was after, he and his new partner, Hirsch, launched the Volvo in southern California. It was an immediate hit. They would eventually own the western third of the United States for dealerships and distribution. Two years later, Klein and his partner decided to sell the distribution rights. The sale netted the two men $2.6 million. He was thirty-nine years old and had orchestrated one of the greatest car salesman careers in history. As he later told Nack, "My first taste of big money."

Klein then became the head of the National Theaters and Television Corporation chain, which owned 230 theaters. By 1972, after significant changes, smart moves, and a new name, National General, now a conglomerate, was valued at more than a billion dollars. But it wasn't enough for Klein: "I figured I had won the conglomerate game. I'd built a billion-dollar company, and the question I asked myself was, Do you want to go for $2 billion? And then $4 billion? Is that what you want to do? Or do you want to have some fun and buy a football team?"

In 1966, Klein had in fact bought a football team, as the general partner, for $10 million. He put up 20 percent. From then on, he was involved with the San Diego Chargers for eighteen years. "Football was fun," he said. However, he found aspects of the behind-the-scenes action to be not so much fun. He especially hated the NFL owners' meetings. He was infamous for, and later admitted to, turning off his hearing aid when some owner was being too long-winded or an owner he didn't like was speaking. He also had a long running feud with Al Davis, controversial owner of the ever-mobile Oakland/Los Angeles/Oakland Raiders.

Meanwhile, in 1976, Klein's wife of thirty years died. He remarried hastily, which proved disastrous. When the dust settled from his second marriage, and after some time had passed, he met and married the woman he would remain married to for the rest of his life—Joyce.

While the competitive nature of sports suited Klein's appetite for challenges, something turned Klein off about football: the players. He loved them but found they were unreliable. "Agents, drug problems, phone calls in the middle of the night telling me that one of my players is hanging out in drug-dealing bars. When I had the heart attack, I said, 'Bullshit!' I was burnt out." Klein sold his interest in the Chargers in 1984, cashing in for a whopping $50 million.

The end of the line in football was not far off for Klein after the 1982 season. The Chargers had beaten the Miami Dolphins in one of the most memorable playoff games ever played. Memories of Kellen Winslow, Dan Fouts, and Chuck Muncie still haunt Dolphin fans, as the Chargers won 41–38 in Miami, earning the right to play in the American Football Conference championship game. Klein was later told by federal investigators that one of his players had picked up a kilo of cocaine, and that the players were sharing it on the plane on the ride back. "On the bleeping airplane!" Klein would later comment. The Chargers were crushed in their next game by the Cincinnati Bengals, who beat them at Riverfront Stadium in Cincinnati, 27–7. Certainly the cold was a factor, the wind chill making the temperature fifty-nine degrees below zero. But Klein was already disenchanted with football.

In that same year the Chargers made it to the AFC championship game, Klein was at the Del Mar racetrack to see two brood mares his new wife Joyce had acquired an interest in. "I didn't know what a brood mare was," Klein said. He had never been a huge horse racing fan. "There wasn't enough action for me," he explained, claiming he didn't know what to do between races. In the grandstand, he ran into Dick Butkus, the Hall of Fame linebacker from the Chicago Bears. "What are you doing here?" he asked. It turned out that Butkus was part owner in two racehorses, and he told Klein he was there to watch them work out. He also wanted to spend a little time with his trainer, none other than D. Wayne Lukas.

Klein knew something about Lukas already. "Doesn't he own Landaluce?" he asked Butkus.

"Would you like to see her?" Butkus asked happily.

He took Klein down to the barn, and Klein was introduced to Landaluce and Lukas that morning. Klein and Lukas liked each other right off. One can only assume that both had found in each other what they most needed. Lukas needed someone with deep pockets who could bankroll his next big expansion, and Klein found a horse trainer who looked at the sport both like a businessman and a football coach.

They made arrangements to have lunch two weeks later. Lukas agreed to fly to the Klein home in Rancho Santa Fe. True to form, Lukas drove up to Klein's mansion in a brand new Rolls-Royce.

Lukas was at his most charming. Perfectly coiffed and impeccably dressed, he smiled and was as dapper and debonair as could be. During lunch, Lukas told Klein, "You'll get a fair shake from me if you want to do some business. I'm not going to cheat you. I don't need to fill the stalls." Klein and his wife were impressed with him. As Klein walked Lukas back to his flashy Rolls, he commented on it, saying he didn't know horse trainers drove such ritzy cars.

"I said I wasn't going to cheat you," Lukas replied. "I didn't say I was going to work for nothing." The deal was sealed.

"I had no idea of getting into racing as anything except a dabble," Klein recalled. "I had thought it would be a nice kind of hobby—ten, twelve horses. I forgot I never do anything halfway. It just kept getting bigger and bigger." The Kleins agreed to work with Lukas, and he began working immediately. Lukas immediately found three fillies, and spent $600,000 of Klein's money.

The first bump in the road might have seemed a bad omen, as one of the fillies died before she even got to the starting gate. But another, Gene's Lady, went on to win almost $1 million in prize money. They later sold the horse for $600,000.

"Horse racing helped me sell the Chargers because I knew I could get interested in something else," Klein told *Sports Illustrated*. After the sale of the Chargers in 1984, he said, "I was just happy as I could be to get out. When I signed the papers, I went to bed and woke up in the middle of the night laughing."

The third and final horse Lukas purchased was Lady's Secret, who finished her career with $3,021,425. At the time, she was the highest-earning filly in history.

Lukas told *Sports Illustrated*: "Gene is dead game. All my life I've put my head on the chopping block and it has worked. Gene has done the same thing. That's why we get along so well. He'll question me on the pros and cons of something, but if I say to him, 'Gene, this is a good deal,' he'll say 'Go!' and he never backs up."

Klein commented: "I buy so many because I believe strongly the law of averages is going to work. I don't know if it will be the million-dollar colt or the $150,000 colt. Some of them will make it, some will not. But if I have enough of them going, and they're all selected by Wayne, I feel we'll win our fair share."

The Program

One thing that particularly sold Klein on Lukas was his unconventional approach to horses and racing. Lukas didn't want to be a breeder, like so many others who are active in the sport a long time. He just wanted to race horses. He wanted to buy yearlings, race them, and when their careers as racers were over, he would sell them. Always taking the quick money and lessening the costs of keeping horses that no longer had the prospect of racing earnings, Klein and Lukas hoped to build a new model in the racing world. And they came along at the right time. Together, they would refer to this as "the program."

What Klein and Lukas were accomplishing in the 1980s would have been unthinkable only a few decades earlier. Up through the 1960s, yearling sales were considered heave-and-hope outlets for suckers. Buying a horse with potential at a yearling sale was like trying to buy a ticket to win the lottery. The class horses were kept by the big breeders with names like Whitney, Widner, Guggenheim, Kleberg, Woodward, and Phipps. They were bought by and kept at large farms like Calumet and Claiborne in Kentucky. This old money and the old establishments were a close knit and competitive bunch.

Trainer John Veitch told Carol Flake that these horses "were an extension of the family." Successful mares were kept for breeding, and the same with stallions. They mated their best horses to produce other winners. The people who were successful in this were not necessarily successful in the wallet, but had many successes to show for their hard work. These were not money-making propositions, but extremely expensive and obsessive hobbies for the dedicated rich and the few horse professionals who could make a go of it.

The only horses they sent to the yearling sales were those they felt would not be good enough to win the big races. Weaklings and losers were sold at Keeneland. Hot prospects were never sold at auction. To be sure, every once in a while a few lucky or smart trainers picked some decent winners from these sales, but for the most part they were more like tag sales than auctions.

Then, in the 1960s, horse racing began to change. Old dynasties were dying off, and the prices that could be obtained for highly rated horses could no longer be ignored. Young men entered the business. But as stallions became so expensive, and the fiscal responsibilities and risks associated with them continued to increase, it became necessary to share some of that risk. As a result, stallions that were hot prospects attracted groups of investors, called syndicates, made up of a dozen to three dozen or more parties, all of whom wanted a piece of the action. As more commercial breeders also entered the market-place, they decided to sell the yearlings off, rather than sink money into training and racing. They figured it was smarter to let someone else take the risk. And there were plenty who wanted to take those risks. Soon, horses with impeccable bloodlines were being offered for sale at auction that would never have left the farm a decade earlier. And these bloodlines were worth a fortune.

Fasig-Tipton is the premier horse auction house. An examination of its records by William Nack from 1930 to 1970 shows that only one Kentucky Derby winner was ever sold at auction in any of the decades that made up this forty-year period. Then, in the 1970s, that number shot up dramatically to four. Not so coincidently, the Keeneland auction also had two winners that decade as well.

The 1970s also saw the rise of the Europeans, the Arabs, and the Japanese as potential buyers for highly prized American thorough-breds. This influx of new money—for these groups spent extravagant sums—encouraged the breeders to put their best yearlings into the ring, drawing astronomical sums. And it was this new environment that provided the ideal setting for "the program."

Between 1970 and 1980, six out of the ten Kentucky Derby win-ners were bought at auction, whether from Keeneland or Fasig-Tipton.

Klein and Lukas attended the biggest sales. Each horse they were interested in was graded by Lukas and his team, as, for example, foot-ball players are judged in tryouts or at the big yearly combine. The horses were rated on bloodlines, physical traits, spirit, and other defin-able qualities. Each received a rating. Well before the bidding started, Team Lukas prepared its final analysis, just as owners do for pro foot-ball teams. When the bidding began, Klein, and Lukas's other own-ers, were at the trainer's side. Lukas hated to lose, especially on the horses his team had rated most highly.

Once the horses were bought at auction, they were shipped back west to Rancho Santa Fe, a huge training facility in southern California with multiple barns and hundreds of horses in training. Klein built it and owned it, but he leased it to Lukas. When the horses were two years old, after a year of carefully attended growth and development, they were shipped to Lukas's various stables across the country. From there they had to earn their keep. A successful colt could become a syndicated stallion. A successful filly could be sold at auction for big bucks. Money gained from these successes was plowed into buying more yearlings.

"I can't afford to hold on to all the great mares and keep buying at the yearling sales," Klein told Nack. "It would become an endless thing. I'd end up with two hundred mares." However, even in the 1980s the idea of selling a successful mare, even for top dollar, was unthinkable. Many were shocked by Team Lukas flaunting conventional wisdom.

"Gene Klein doesn't know this yet, but he is going to have to become deeply involved in the breeding end of the game," a Kentucky breeder said at the time. "I don't think you can only attend the yearling sales. That wheel of fortune can stop anywhere. It's just too risky, too much to ask that you repeat this thing year after year."

But Klein disagreed. "We can continue to buy the yearlings and be successful. We've done it three straight years, so I don't think it's been a fluke," he said. "It's all Wayne Lukas. He gets better every year. Oh, I'll breed some to race and hope I can get lucky. But in my book, the odds are much more against you when you breed your own because you never know when you'll breed a crooked leg foal. At the yearling sales, you can see what you get."

Eddie Gregson, a popular California trader, said of their scheme: "When a horse has been that good to you, you don't sell her like some piece of meat." However, even Gregson admitted that selling the mares was "revolutionary. It's a new notion of attacking the game. There is no loyalty to any of your retired champions. Let them go; let someone else breed them. This approach is so different."

This new team wasn't winning a lot of fans on the backstretches either. José Martin, another well-regarded trainer in California, weighed in: "If you go into a race with a horse worth $40,000 and Klein has one worth $2 million, you have to get ready to get beat eight out of ten times. And then you go to the sales and try and buy a horse, and they outbid you. You have to be jealous and you have to have anger in you."

In fact, this was how a typical trip to the Keeneland sales ended up for Billy Turner, a competing trainer. Turner got a new owner, a millionaire looking to spend some big money. Like Lukas, he graded the horses and had his eye on eight possible choices. The outcome, a disgusted Turner said, was that "the Arabs bought two of them, and Lukas bought the rest. It was a blowout. I couldn't compete."

Charlie Whittingham weighed in by saying: "I've been a horse trainer for some fifty years, and owners come and go. Anyone who puts up the kind of money that Klein has, damnit, he's in the game! Most of the people who do the squawkin' don't want to put up nothing. They want to milk the old cow, but they don't want to feed her too much."

Even the jealous Martin relented: "There's a lot of owners with as much money as Gene Klein, with more money, and no one is stopping them from doing what he's doing. You've got to have guts to do what he and Lukas are doing."

Lady's Secret

Lady's Secret was a prime example of Lukas's keen eye for horseflesh. Her dam was Great Lady M and her sire was none other than Secretariat. Now, anyone who knows anything about horse racing will tell you that while Secretariat's record as a racer was impeccable, his record as a stud was a huge disappointment. And when Wayne Lukas and Gene Klein bought Lady's Secret, everyone already knew that Secretariat's progeny had come nowhere close to the sire's personal achievements.

Lady's Secret was foaled in 1982. Robert H. Spreen was the breeder. The gray filly was bought by Lukas and Stein as a weanling. When she was two, Klein and Lukas entered her in eight races. She finished first three times, third once, and earned more than $92,000 in her first year of racing.

When she turned three, in 1985, Lukas and Klein began to push her. She had seventeen entries in her third year. She won ten races that year, and finished in the money another five. In that campaign, she won the Beldame Stakes, Ruffian Handicap, Test, Maskette, and the Ballerina Stakes. She also earned a whopping $994,349. Her star was rising.

At four years of age, 1986 was to be Lady Secret's year. She had fifteen starts. She won ten races again, and finished in the money another five. She defeated the top males in the Whitney Stakes and the Santa Margarita Handicap, and she won the Breeders' Cup Distaff. She was named Handicap Horse of the Year and Champion Older Mare that season. But the crowning success came when she was voted Horse of the Year as well. Lukas proved himself once again, and proved himself especially where it counted, with one of his biggest owners.

Lady's Secret had only five starts in 1987. She won two races and finished second once. They retired her that year. She was known for pinning her ears and digging in when rivals tangled with her in the stretch. In the three-year history of the Breeders' Cup series, no horse has compiled more Breeders' Cup points than "the Lady."

In 1992, Lady's Secret was inducted into the Hall of Fame. With career earnings of $3,021,325 when she retired, she was one of the biggest winners to come from Secretariat's line.

Klein was thrilled when Lady's Secret was voted Horse of the Year: "Her agent didn't call me to renegotiate her contract. Or tell me she wanted a bigger stall or a different grade of oats and wouldn't run on Saturday. Horses don't complain. They don't stay out all night and drink. And they don't have agents."

After the first five years as a thoroughbred owner, Klein's holdings had increased substantially. At sixty-seven, he admitted that he could have withdrawn and made more than $31 million in profits. But it wasn't all roses either. The Klein/Lukas partnership had experienced its share of disappointments. Probably their most devastating setback was Devils River. Lukas and Klein competed and won him for $1 million as a yearling at Keeneland. A son of Seattle Slew, he was one of the most expensive horses of the show, and certainly one of that year's prizes. He won less than $22,000 in prizes before he ended up with a bowed tendon. Klein told Nack, "He's gorgeous," but acknowledged that the horse was a bust. "You've just got to roll with it," he said.

In November 1989, Klein and Lukas, true to their plan, sold Lady's Secret. This was national news. Eddie Gregson commented: "Everybody was shocked. . . . You can't sell a horse like that. It destroys your karma."

Embarrassingly, Klein had to buy the gray filly back from Fasig-Tipton because she failed to reach her guaranteed price of $5.7 million. However, he eventually sold her to Fares Farm, which paid $3.8 million to purchase the 1986 Horse of the Year.

Since then Lady's Secret has been a good producer for Fares Farm. Her foal of 1992, a Mr. Prospector filly, was sold for $700,000, and her offspring of 1996, a Seattle Slew filly, brought $750,000. She produced a Mr. Prospector colt in 1994 that was bought back on a bid of $600,000.

Did Klein make a mistake by selling Lady's Secret? "There is no reason not to sell champion mares," Klein stated at the time. "You syndicate the stallions, so why not sell the mares?"

Marfa

In his first two years with entries in a Triple Crown race, Lukas had finished in the money both times. It was an excellent beginning. While the next few years would be successful ones for him in the world of racing, not a ray of hope would shine on Lukas and his owners in the main events.

On the first weekend in May 1982, Lukas boldly placed a triple entry in the Kentucky Derby, quite a turn from the trainer he was the year before. The first triple entry in the Kentucky Derby since 1946, it consisted of Marfa, Lukas's three-year-old star horse of that year; Balboa Native; and Total Departure.

Balboa Native was owned by Robert H. Spreen and had been bred by Robert E. Owens. Sandy Owens was the jockey. Total Departure was a Rebalot Stable entry that had been bred by John H. Hartagan, and Patrick Valenzuela was up. Marfa was owned by Beal, French, and Lukas himself, and had been bred by Tom Gentry. She won the Turfway Spiral Stakes (then titled the Jim Beam Stakes) and $200,000 in prize money by a then record eight-length margin. It was an impressive win. She followed up that win with a win at Santa Anita Derby, then lost the Blue Grass Stakes by a nose. Her regular jockey, Jorge Velasquez, would ride her in the Derby.

On Derby Day, she and the other two horses went off at 5–2, in a combined entry, due to racing rules and regulations. Marfa was the hot horse. She was easily seen as the favorite, and the betting on that entry reflected her stature.

As soon as the race started, Total Departure was brushed by Sunny's Halo and seemed to give up three-fourths of the way around the oval. Balboa Native found himself caught in traffic, and while he made a push late in the race, his was a lost race.

That left Marfa, who kept with the pack, but held just off the pace. At about the three-quarter-mile point, Velasquez made his move. Using his whip left-handed, he drove Marfa straight down the backstretch. But she just did not have enough gas. Sunny's Halo and Dessert Wine were ahead of her, and she was bested by Caveat and then Slew O'Gold, with whom she dueled for fourth place.

Of his triple entry, Total Departure finished last, and became an answer to the dubious trivia question: Name one of the four favorite horses to finish last in a Kentucky Derby. Balboa Native ended up ninth, and Marfa fifth.

There was much speculation before and after the race that Lukas had pushed Marfa too hard, placing the horse in too many races, and that the demanding schedule had caught up with the now exhausted horse. Others disagreed, stating simply that Marfa had been beaten by a superior horse.

The only good news during Derby week for Team Lukas was that the filly Lucky Lucky Lucky, who finished fifth in the Jim Beam Stakes behind Marfa, went on to win the Kentucky Oaks.

Keeneland

Keeneland was incorporated on April 17, 1935. Three years later the first auction of thoroughbred horses was held in the paddock. Thirty-one lots brought in $24,885, an average of $802.74. The highest price, $3,500, was paid for Marmitina, "a nine-year-old mare with a suckling colt at her side."

Just over fifty years later, Keeneland's auctions have become the Mecca of the horse world. Every July, among other months, the most powerful financial groups from across the globe come to do battle over the rights to a selection of the finest bred American horses. In 1962 the Breeders' Sales Company was dissolved, and the Keeneland Association stepped in to fill the void. By 1969 a new $700,000, 650-seat pavilion was installed on the Keeneland grounds to accommodate the growing number of bidders in the sales ring. The pavilion had a dirt floor, where the horses would be brought in, while the auctioneers stood on an elevated podium. The facility resembled an amphitheater with a roof.

It was in this arena that Lukas and his crew of owners would make 1983 a year like no other. It would signify that the monopolistic hold the old families and the old farms once had could no longer survive against buyers who were willing to pay the costs the new economy insisted on. Keeneland '83 marked the fall of old world horse racing as it was known and the beginning of how it works today.

Joining Lukas in the bidding would be two of the most highly profiled, high-spending financial powerhouses in the horse world. The first and most famous group was led by Sheik Mohammed bin Rashid al Maktoum, the defense minister of Dubai, a country then profiting greatly from newly revised oil deals with U.S. oil distributors. The sheiks from Dubai were also sometimes called the Doobie Brothers by local Kentuckians. The sheik and his brothers were advised by John Leat and Colonel Richard Warden. The other group was a powerful European contingent led by brash power broker and horseman Robert Sangster. Joining him was Greek shipping magnate Stavros Niachros. Sangster had been cock-of-the-walk at Keeneland until

1981, when the sheiks and Lukas began to challenge his hegemony over the auctions there.

As the 1983 auction progressed, the buzz honed in on horse Hip No. 308. This was no surprise, and everyone looked forward to the bidding war he would bring. No. 308 was a two-year-old colt from Northern Dancer out of My Bumpers. Northern Dancer's progeny was incredibly valuable to any syndicate, racing in Europe or elsewhere in the world. Native Dancer himself had won both the 1964 Kentucky Derby and the Preakness Stakes, and his foals had gone on to win numerous big races across Europe.

Donald Johnson, a coal mine operator, had bought a share in Native Dancer's breeding rights, and had shrewdly sold it to the Arab contingent in 1983 for $600,000, which was almost half a million more than he had paid for it. However, by 1983, Johnson still had three more colts to bring to sale, and Hip No. 308 would be the first at auction. The two others had not fared well, one having a throat problem and the other dying of a virus before the sales.

In 1981 and 1982 the sheiks and Sangster locked horns, and checkbooks were thrown out the window as the bidding for Northern Dancer bloodlines went into high gear. Each group had garnered an even share, though the acrimony in the sales ring was unusual. Everyone knew that 1983 would be wild and woolly.

Steven Crist, in his book *The Horse Traders*, captured the blasé attitude toward spending by both groups in a story of the sheik passing a television monitor featuring a horse sold for $675,000 leaving the sales ring:

" 'Who bought that?' he asked one of his advisers.

" 'Why, you did, your highness,' the acolyte answered.

" 'Ah, very good,' " the sheik said, now smiling."

Lukas opened up the bidding at $1 million on Hip No. 308. At the time, it was the largest opening bid ever in the history of the sales. It was a safe bet he wouldn't have to foot that bill. In "eight giddy minutes" the sheiks had outspent Lukas as well as Sangster and his contingent, buying the horse for an astounding $10.2 million—the previous had been just over $4 million. At one point in the sale, Johnson said, "My God, are these people spending real money?" Later the auctioneer and the bidders had to come to some kind of understanding, since the tote board did not extend above $9,999,999.

While Lukas was not a factor in this one dramatic duel, the average and mean prices of horses had risen dramatically in this one week session. In selling 301 yearlings, not including the Northern Dancer colt, Keeneland had averaged $501,495 per horse. The previous year's average had been $337,734, which amounted to a 48 percent increase in prices.

To understand the difference it made in costs, consider that Lukas bought twenty-seven horses in 1982 for a combined total of $3,649,000, giving him an average buy of somewhere around $135,000 per horse. In 1983 he bought twenty-three horses for a total of $9,470,000, for an average of $411,000, a 200 percent increase over the previous year.

Why? There are two reasons. First, the price of horseflesh had undeniably gone up. However, Lukas was also buying better quality horses. While he'd spent days at Keeneland before looking to find bargains, the escalating costs had soared over the last three years, culminating in the price explosion of 1983.

As in many years, for any trainer, the numbers probably wouldn't work out. But in 1983 he had picked three future stakes champions. And yes, one of them would be a star box office horse, just as he expected.

And what became of the $10.2 million horse? He was named Snaafi Dancer. He never raced and turned out to be infertile.

Althea and Life's Magic

In 1984, Lukas was known for three major fillies: Althea, Life's Magic, and Lucky Lucky Lucky. Lukas's barn was already thought of as a powerhouse, and his three fillies made him an even-bet threat in any fillies' stakes he dared enter. Lucky Lucky Lucky had won the Kentucky Oaks and the Black-Eyed Susan. While Althea and Lucky Lucky Lucky had won early in their careers, Life's Magic had not.

Althea was the winner of the Del Mar Futurity and the Hollywood Starlet Stakes. And she had won the Arkansas Derby just two weeks prior to her entry into the Kentucky Derby. She was nominated and voted Champion Two-Year-Old Filly in 1983. Clearly, she had done extremely well for Lukas. Althea was bred and owned by Alexander-Aykroyd-Groves, a group formed and led by Helen Alexander of King Ranch.

Life's Magic was owned by Mel Hatley and was bred by Mr. and Mrs. Douglas Parrish III. The filly had been a Lukas find at the Keeneland sales, where she was bought for $310,000.

Althea and Life's Magic were entered in another multiple entry by Lukas in the 1984 Kentucky Derby. It was the first time anyone had entered two fillies in the Derby. For the second year in a row, a Lukas horse was favored in the odds: With her wins, class, and Chris McCarron aboard, she was a bettor's choice even though she was a filly.

When the gates clanged open, Althea shot off, and set the pace for the first six furlongs. She then lost ground to the field. Life's Magic, with Don Brumfield up, sat back and waited for an opportunity to break. Coming into the stretch, she gained huge amounts of ground, but was still way too far back to catch Swale, the eventual winner, who also went on to win the Belmont Stakes that year.

Life's Magic finished eighth. Althea finished nineteenth and last. It was the second year in a row that a Lukas horse had earned the distinction of being the odds-on favorite and finished last.

"Althea didn't come to the race as well as I'd hoped," Lukas said years later. "Life's Magic fooled me. I thought she was a true mile-and-a-quarter filly. But at that point in my career I wasn't so sure I knew much about this race either."

Life's Magic would go on to win the Mother Goose Stakes, handily beating Woody Stephens's Oceana, to whom she'd finished second three times, and she was voted Champion Three-Year-Old Filly for 1984. The following year, she won win the Breeders' Cup Distaff. In her career, Life's Magic earned more than $2 million.

While Lukas oversaw her from afar, Life's Magic's distinctive career was in large part due to his son, Jeff, who was twenty-six years old at the time. She was stabled, at least part of the time, at Belmont, and Jeff Lukas worked her every day. After she won the Mother Goose Stakes, Jeff told William Leggett, "Nothing is done on whim. We try to plan things out pretty thoroughly. We don't want to leave too many things to chance."

It was apparent by now that Jeff bore the D. Wayne stamp. He wore creased jeans and freshly pressed shirts. He was polite but firm. He spoke Team Lukasspeak. It was also apparent to everyone that Lukas's concept of running satellite stables in different parts of the country was a successful and viable venture. From the few horses Lukas had in 1979, he and Jeff were now up to 115 horses in training. After the big Mother Goose Stakes win, and a chance to tweak Stephens's nose, Jeff went right back to work filling the feed tubs.

"Does your father know Life's Magic won?" Leggett asked Jeff.

"Well, he couldn't be here today because he was saddling five horses at Hollywood Park," Jeff replied. "But he has a New York phone number he can call and get the stretch calls of the races right after they're over. He probably heard Life's Magic win the race, hollered 'Whoopee!' and then threw the phone against the wall."

Success

Despite disappointments in the Triple Crown events, Lukas had breakthrough years in 1983 and 1984. In 1983, he finally emerged from Charlie Whittingham's and Laz Barrera's shadows, mounting 595 horses for seventy-eight wins and totaling $4,267,261. Still, he was $320,000 under the previous year's record earnings.

No matter. In 1984, Lukas would take the earnings title again, this time smashing the record. He saddled 805 horses, posted 131 wins, and counted $5,835,921 in winnings. Now well-known in racing circles, he was not yet a major player in the public eye. But all that was about to change.

THE BIG TIME

Keep 'Em Coming

Lady's Secret was neither the first nor the last of a long line of successful horses bought and trained by Team Lukas from the mid-1980s to 1990. This was the era of junk bonds and greed is good, and it was never so good for any trainer as it was for D. Wayne Lukas. The Rolls-Royce was replaced by a limo and a jet. Lukas was going on spending sprees on Rodeo Drive, buying $2,000 suits like he bought pansies for his barns—in bunches. Now, in the winner's circle, he was no longer sporting the look of the western cowboy, but of the well-dressed banker. In most cases, he dressed far better than many owners, whether they were his own or someone else's.

If he spent lavishly on his clothes, he spent astronomically on his horses. Joe Bagan, in his intense study of Lukas's spending habits, detailed Lukas's purchases in *Lukas at Auction*. From 1985 through 1988, between Keeneland and other sales, Lukas spent $48 million on 226 horses—a combined average of $212,389 per horse. It is important to note that prices did continue to escalate, jauntily, into the late 1980s.

In this period his successes would be as well-publicized as his failures. And in some cases, his successes became his failures. Regardless, between 1985 and 1990 few other trainers would post as many stakes winners as D. Wayne Lukas.

Lukas's 1983 class graduated three top winners, including Saratoga Six, Tank's Prospect, and Pancho Villa. In 1984 he would choose, among his twenty-eight horses, Twilight Ridge and Life At the Top. In 1985, out of fifty-three horses, his biggest stars were Sacahuista and Capote. In 1986 it was Winning Colors and Success Express, among a crop that numbered forty-six. And in 1987, Lukas found Open Mind and Houston among the sixty-three new horses in his barns.

Lukas is known for what he calls his ten point system. He judges certain aspects, and grades the horses on a scale of one through ten, ten being the highest rating. He claims never to have found a ten. He also claims that while he has spent time with many ex-assistants, teaching them what to look for, he has never told them exactly how he rates a horse at a sale.

"Every year we have the equivalent of the pro-football draft, or recruiting a new freshman class. If I give one a six, we pay attention and look for a bargain," he told Pete Axthelm. "If I come up with an eight . . . well, we must own all the eights. And for a nine, I'd give up my wife and firstborn."

But, with insight from Bagan's study of Lukas's buying habits, it's clear that Lukas's tastes are actually somewhat predictable. In the period Bagan analyzed, Lukas bought fourteen horses by Seattle Slew, thirteen from Cox's Ridge and Raja Baja, eleven from Alydar and Icecapade, and ten each from Secretariat and Saratoga Six.

Lukas bought horses from 143 different sires between 1984 and 1988. Based on the average number of winners produced by those sires, Lukas should have averaged 9 percent stakes winners; in fact, he averaged 19 percent. In his study, Bagan proved that Lukas, regardless of the money spent, could beat the averages that each stud naturally produced and increase his number of winners by 10 percent. The man can flat out pick horses.

Did the horses make money? In many cases no. While Lukas could pick out winners in a crowd, the law of averages still catches up to you.

Horse racing is a losing proposition. Lady's Secret was an exception rather than the rule. In 1985, for example, of the fifty-three horses Lukas bought at auction, fourteen went for a total of $7,245,000 and won only $318,285. And that doesn't include the barn fees and entry fees for the owners. In 1985, Lukas saddled 1,140 horses for 218 wins and $11,155,188 in prize money. And Lukas was not the biggest spender at the sales that year. However, he was able to fight off many of the big boys, and relegated many other owners and trainers to lesser animals, because he could now run the middle to upper end of the table.

In 1985 he spent a total of $17 million. His horses eventually won $6 million. Of course, that doesn't include their resale value, as well as any breeding fees that might come his way for years to come.

Bagan also evaluated Lukas's fillies versus his colts. It was clear from the results that Lukas was what Bagan referred to as a "Ladies' Man." Of the 289 horses Lukas bought between 1979 and 1987, he chose 159 fillies and 130 colts; he bought 20 percent more fillies. The fillies contributed 286 wins, of which 31 were stakes wins, and earned $16,284,222. The colts racked up 278 wins (with more than two hundred extra starts), of which twenty-three were stakes wins, and earnings of $12,294,587. Thus, the fillies racked up 25 percent more money and 10 percent more wins on two hundred less starts. Lukas knows a good filly when he sees one.

After examining the numbers, Bagan felt that in the end Lukas's program, including the selling of champion mares, was a financial success. Bagan also concluded that Lukas's selections were in the main also successful. However, Bagan realized that while Lukas made the horses pay off as much and as early as possible, he lacked success in creating strong, "classic" thoroughbreds that could win Triple Crown events with consistency.

Highlights of the Go-Go '80s

In 1985 two of Lukas's horses were voted champions at year's end: Family Style and Life's Magic. In 1986, Capote and Lady's Secret would also be named top horses, as would Sacahuista and North Sider in 1987. In 1988, Winning Colors and Gulch would take home champion trophies. And in 1989, Open Mind and Steinlen also took top honors. In the thoroughbred horse racing world, racking up these kinds of awards in these numbers was astonishing.

An interesting anecdote, related by Demi L. O'Byrne, conveys Lukas's growing prestige: "About fifteen years ago, the late Warner Jones said to me, 'Demi, there is a trainer around now that is different; this guy could be chief executive at the Ford Motor Corporation or President of the United States of America.' I said, 'Warner, who is this guy?' and he answered, 'Wayne Lukas.'"

In 1985, Tank's Prospect would be a celebrated horse. But while he got lots of press, Twilight Ridge and Family Style were burning up the track. In the Breeders' Cup Juvenile Fillies that year, Twilight Ridge and Family Style finished one-two. Earlier that year, Family Style had won the Spinaway at Saratoga with Don MacBeth aboard. Her reward was that she was named Champion Juvenile Filly for 1985. In 1986, though, she could not live up to her promise. She lost in the Bonnie Miss, though she was heavily favored. In 1987 she came back to win the Santa Anita La Brea Stakes.

In 1987, Sacahuista took the three-year-old championship trophy and North Sider was named the champion mare. North Sider had taken the Apple Blossom Handicap that year with Cordero aboard, followed by Family Style in second. Sacahuista capped a successful year with a win in the Breeders' Cup Distaff, a race for three-year-old fillies and up. And Success Express took the Breeders' Cup race for two-year-old colts and geldings.

In 1988, Winning Colors would be named the three-year-old champion and Gulch would be picked as the top champion sprinter. At the Breeders' Cup, Lukas's horses would flourish, as he took three out of ten races. Open Mind took the Juvenile Fillies; Gulch took the Sprint; and It Is True! took the Juvenile Colts.

Steinlen would help cap a wonderful 1989 for Lukas. He was named the champion turf horse and won the Breeders' Cup Mile.

Tank's Prospect

Tank's Prospect was from Mr. Prospector out of Midnight Pumpkin (by Pretense). His grandfather was Raise a Native, and his great-grandfathers were Native Dancer and Nashua. He was born to greatness, as it were. He was bought for $625,000 in 1983 by Klein and Lukas at the Keeneland sales. The horse was named by Klein in honor of Tank Younger, a former star football player with the Los Angeles Rams. This was not unusual, as Klein had once named another colt Nickel Back, which is what a defense backfield player in football in obvious passing situations is called.

The field during Tank's Prospect's two-year-old campaign in 1984 was considered the weakest in some time. One of the favorites was Chief's Crown, and another was Spend a Buck. Chief's Crown was favored in most races he entered, which was the case when Tank's Prospect came in second behind him in the Breeders' Cup Juvenile that year. Afterward, Chief's Crown was named the two-year-old champion.

Tank's Prospect followed up this disappointing yet promising finish in the Breeders' Cup with a win at the El Camino Real Derby at Bay Meadows as the Derby preps began in 1985, his first real test as a three-year-old. However, after he finished last in the Santa Anita Derby on April 6 it was discovered he had a medical condition. In nonmedical terms, the horse couldn't breathe properly because he had a paralyzed flap in his throat due to tissue swelling. Under a local anesthetic, Tank's Prospect was operated on, and began working out at a canter two days later. Lukas took a huge risk and gambled that the horse had recovered enough to run in the Arkansas Derby on April 20, 1985.

"In my mind," he said later, "the only problem was Tank's mental condition. Sometimes if a horse runs a race without getting air, he is hesitant to put out the next time." Tank's Prospect won, and in the process knocked Clever Allemont, a horse that had won six races in six starts, out of the picture for the upcoming Derby. It was a big win. Still, he was not favored in a small field for the 1985 Kentucky Derby, in which Chief's Crown was also entered. Many thought the two-year-old champion, a dominating horse the year before, was a serious Triple Crown candidate.

In the Derby, Spend a Buck went straight to the lead. He was chased by Tank's Prospect and Fast Account. Stephen's Odyssey, making a move from the back of the pack, bumped both Tank's Prospect and Fast Account, though that early in the race, it was not enough to throw the horses significantly off their pace. Spend a Buck surprised everyone by holding off late charges by Chief's Crown, who faded, and Stephen's Odyssey, who took second. It was the third fastest Kentucky Derby ever, and Spend a Buck cruised to a 5¼ length victory. Tank's Prospect finished seventh.

Lukas was disappointed, but he was ready to send his colt to the Preakness. However, while other Derby-running horses would also show up, Spend a Buck would not. Having a shot at the New Jersey Triple Crown, which offered more money than did the national Triple Crown, the horse's owners forsook the sharp turns of Pimlico for Garden State Park, a small New Jersey track.

"The eleven three-year-olds comprise the weakest Preakness field in recent years," Steven Crist wrote. The early favorites were the much-heralded Chief's Crown and Eternal Prince. Tank's Prospect only arrived at the track the day before the race. This was not the only change. Pat Day, whose Derby mount, Irish Fighter, had finished eleventh, found himself without a ride. Lukas dumped Gary Stevens in favor of Day, who was one of his favorite jockeys. By post time, Tank's Prospect was the weak favorite, at 9–2. After days of rain and gray skies, the track was fast, dry, and neat.

In front of a crowd of 81,235, Tank's Prospect was bumped coming out of the gate. Day had to place his foot back in the stirrup, which took almost a quarter of a mile. "It took me five or six jumps to get my foot back in the iron," he said after the race. "I couldn't help the horse and couldn't get him running like I'd have liked to."

Eternal Prince shot to the lead, and Chief's Crown followed in hot pursuit. Coming into the backstretch, Eternal Prince was still ahead, with Chief's Crown making his move. It was now or never for Tank's Prospect. At Day's urging, he shot through the pack around the turn near the rail and came out to the middle of the stretch for the final drive. By the time they hit the mile marker, Chief's Crown was clearly in the lead. At this point Don MacBeth was giving Chief's Crown a hand ride, while Day was pounding Tank's Prospect with his whip, as Lukas had instructed. Exploding down the stretch, Tank's Prospect beat Chief's Crown by a head in an exciting finish that had the crowd roaring.

Asked if Lukas blamed Stevens for a sour finish in the Derby, and whether Day was the reason for the Preakness win, he replied, "I couldn't blame Gary for the way he rode him, and he'll ride him again. But when a rider like Pat Day becomes available, you make a move. Pat was outstanding, perfect."

Lukas, in an understandably good mood, then told the press: "I'm just realizing what makes Laz and Woody so great: You don't know anything until you're eighty." He was referring to the well-known trainers, who were in fact not yet near eighty.

"It's so thrilling," Eugene Klein told *Sports Illustrated*. "The horse looks like a fullback and he runs like a fullback—only faster."

An interesting aside about that Preakness was that Lukas had forgotten to assign a hot walker to take Tank's Prospect back to the barn should he win. Fortunately, one was found and offered fifty dollars, bringing about the oddity of a million-dollar horse watched over by a complete stranger, a twenty-one-year-old named Mark Pratt. "You'll be the best paid hot walker in history," Lukas told Pratt about his one-time 100-yard walk.

"Mr. Lukas treated me like an equal. Some of them treat you like you're lower, " Pratt told the press.

Tank's Prospect wasn't the only good news that day. Up at Belmont, Jeff Lukas had entered Life's Magic, now four years old, in the $172,000 Shuvee Handicap for fillies and mares. She won. The Lukases were succeeding when so many people had told them they couldn't.

Lukas was quoted as saying that he rated Tank's Prospect "as good as any horse in America right now." He couldn't stop himself from a little extra selling: "These horses will beat each other all season. This is a great year, but no one wants to go out on a limb and guess who's got the best horse. It will take a lot more than the spring classics to sort this bunch out."

If the press was nice to Tank's Prospect, they were not kind to Triple Crown racing. The Preakness story in *Sports Illustrated* was titled, "Coming on Strong at the Weakness," and in it the race was lampooned as "the Peakless," and the "Black-Eyed Preakness." A headline in the *Washington Post* struck a similar note: "PREAKNESS GALLOPS TOWARD MINOR STAKES STATUS."

So, Tank's Prospect went up to New York to face down the competition in the Belmont Stakes and prove Lukas's boast. But there was a problem. Somehow, his hoof had been infected and the horse was hobbled. Lukas and his team did what they could, treating the young colt, hoping to get him ready. But even the newspapers knew something was wrong with the Preakness winner. Several writers had seen the protective bar shoe that had been placed on the animal's hoof.

In the Belmont paddock, it was obvious to many that the nervously sweating horse did not want to run that day. According to Carol Flake, writing about that wild 1985 racing season: "Tank's Prospect, covered in nervous sweat, suddenly neighed shrilly and reared, almost getting away from his groom. He was exhibiting all the most obvious signs, in horse language, for fear and anxiety. And when his groom led him into his saddling stall, he reared again."

Despite this, the odds had Tank's Prospect at 5–1.

The race was hard fought. Two sprinters took the lead, with Chief's Crown just behind as they took the first turn on the big mile-and-a-half track. Stephen's Odyssey and Crème Fraiche trailed the field. After the second turn, Chief's Crown made his move, and eventually took the lead. But Crème Fraiche and Stephen's Odyssey were moving as well. The two horses caught up with Chief's Crown and passed him. Crème Fraiche crossed the finish line with the fourth fastest Belmont to that time. Stephen's Odyssey finished second and Chief's Crown third.

Tank's Prospect was not a factor, and in fact did not finish. The horse had pulled up lame. After the race, Klein announced, after conferring with Lukas and a vet, that Tank's Prospect had injured his suspensory ligament and would be retired.

Klein eventually sold nine shares of Tank's Prospect at stud for $400,000 each. Klein himself was stuck with thirty-one shares, which was more than he wanted. But Tank's Prospect had earned a whopping $1,355,645 in his two years, with a record of five wins, two seconds, and one third in fourteen tries. He'd been a financial success. And in retrospect, while the Preakness might have suffered a tremendous image problem in a campaign in which it suffered the ignominy of being skipped for a race in New Jersey, it happened that the horses that year matured later in the season and proved themselves a solid lot, thereby raising each of them in stature.

Spend a Buck

Despite the fact that Chief's Crown was the preseason favorite, the eventual darling of the 1985 meets was Spend a Buck. Not an impressive horse to behold, Spend a Buck was a Buckaroo/Belle de Jour colt foaled on May 15, 1982, late for a racehorse. He was bred by Rowe Harper and Irish Hill Farm, and purchased by Dennis and Linda Diaz of Hunger Farm for just $12,500. Cam Gambolati was his trainer—not Lukas; Angel Cordero Jr. was his jock.

Spend a Buck showed his talent early. He was the only Kentucky Derby starter to have never finished worse than third before his Derby debut. To add to that, he was also the youngest horse in the '85 Derby out of a field of twelve starters. He had won the Cradle Stakes by fifteen lengths the previous summer at River Downs, finished second to Chief's Crown in the Young America, and was third in the Breeders' Cup, trailing a close second-place finisher, Tank's Prospect. In the spring leading up to the Derby, Spend a Buck had won both the Garden State Stakes and the Cherry Hill Mile.

On that fateful May 4, 1985, Angel Cordero Jr. rode him to a 5¼ length win under the Twin Spires of Churchill Downs, topping Stephen's Odyssey and Chief's Crown. Many considered the win a major upset.

Spend a Buck's owners and trainer had watched Cordero take their colt through the fastest mile in Kentucky Derby history, and then hold off the race's biggest names. It was a huge day for Cordero who, at age forty-two, became the oldest jockey to win the spring classic. It was his second Derby win, coming eleven years after his rousing win aboard Cannonade.

Usually, a Derby winner almost automatically advances to the Preakness to attempt to capture the elusive Triple Crown and claim a stake in the title of Greatest Horse of the Century. But Robert Brennan, promoter of New Jersey racing interests, made the owners' decision more difficult. He offered a $2 million bonus, on top of a $600,000 purse for the Jersey Derby alone, to any horse that could win the Cherry Hill Stakes, the Garden State Stakes, and the New Jersey Derby—a Garden State Triple Crown. This bold move not only said a lot about Brennan and his backers, but about the state of the Triple Crown itself and the fact that it was losing its luster.

Racing's traditionalists followed the tried-and-true path of their fathers, which almost dictated that the top thoroughbreds would go to the Derby, the Preakness, and the Belmont. Possibly more significant than the money was the prestige and honor of winning any—or all—of these premier races. But the new money in the game changed the perspective of racing, and Brennan's Garden State Triple Crown was the trump card.

The bonus money Brennan had offered was quite a carrot for the Diazes. The media spared no ink in debating what their final decision would be. They couldn't run their horse in the Preakness and the Jersey Derby, since the Preakness was scheduled to go off just a week earlier. To sway their decision, the New Jersey racetracks got together and upped the ante even more. If Spend a Buck could win the Jersey Derby, he would be eligible for an extra $1 million bonus—plus winnings from the race purses—if he won both the Haskell at Monmouth Park and the Invitational at the Meadowlands. Both were scheduled for later in the year. It worked. Spend a Buck would go to the Jersey Derby.

Spend a Buck was not Lukas's horse, but he figured into Lukas's calculations. Lukas, and Klein, figured that if Spend a Buck went to New Jersey instead of Maryland, Tank's Prospect, who finished third in the Derby, would have a good chance in the Preakness. Beyond that, they were thinking of the Champion Three-Year-Old award for Tank's Prospect. But if that was to be a possibility, Spend a Buck would have to be challenged.

If the colt was heading to the Jersey Derby, why not send a speedball horse to challenge him? Spend a Buck liked the lead, and loved fending off challengers. If another horse could challenge his pace, it would not only give Spend a Buck a run for the money, but might take some gas out of his tank for future races. So Lukas entered Huddle Up in the Jersey Derby. While the experts didn't give the horse a chance to win the race, they knew he could take a good shot at wearing Spend a Buck down.

Carol Flake remembers watching Lukas assess Spend a Buck as he was walked into the adjacent barn before the Jersey Derby. "The intense look he gave Spend a Buck did not reveal admiration," she wrote. "Only a week before, Lukas had been at the center of all the commotion with Tank's Prospect, and he seemed to begrudge the displacement."

The start of the race boded well for Team Lukas, as Huddle Up burst to the lead and Spend a Buck stumbled coming out the gate. But the Diazes' superb colt soon recovered, zeroing in on Huddle Up.

As the backstretch fell away beneath them, the two fought it out and Huddle Up began to fade. From the field, two other horses made their moves. One of these was Woody Stephens's Crème Fraiche, who even got his nose out in front of the champion for a few strides. But Spend a Buck would not be defeated. It was the kind of race that convinces people that animals have a lot more feelings, personality, and heart than we might give them credit for. Spend a Buck fought off his challengers down the stretch, eyes ablaze, legs stretched out, nostrils flaring. He won by a neck in a rousing and raucous race. Huddle Up finished sixth.

"They hooked him up front, they hooked him down the lane, they hooked him inside and outside. And he beat 'em," Dennis Diaz said. He also took home $2.6 million, having won the Cherry Hill Mile and the Garden State Stakes.

Lukas's plan died. Tank's Prospect had won the Preakness, but he broke down in the Belmont, where the eventual winner was none other than Stephens's Crème Fraiche. Spend a Buck skipped the Belmont and took a two-month rest. Even though he didn't win the Haskell at Monmouth, he still finished with over $4 million in career earnings. He was also voted Horse of the Year and Champion Three-Year-Old.

The New Jersey Triple Crown died too. The next year, a $1 million bonus was offered for the winner of the Triple Crown, a nice incentive to add to the prestige. Garden State Park burned down, was rebuilt and reopened, then closed again for good. And there has been no competing series since then to challenge the Triple Crown.

"That's very common in Europe and you get no flack for it," Lukas says today, when asked if he would do it all over again. "I would do it. I think you get a media darling like Spend a Buck or like Genuine Risk, and it's very difficult for reporters, the Andy Beyers of the world, to make brash predictions, and then when they crash and burn, to come back up on them. And so the next best thing is to take a shot at someone who's trying not to make that happen. So anyhow, I would do that again in a heartbeat if I think it would help me. I haven't been too successful doing that. One time I ran a rabbit in the Santa Anita Derby and the rabbit never even got to the front. I've had no luck doing that. I would not let the pressure of the press make up my mind."

Shari Lukas

Wayne met his third wife, Shari, at the track, of all places, studying the numbers on the exacta board. It made sense, as she was an avid handicapper. Formerly a teacher of gifted children for seven years, she was able to turn a profit handicapping at Santa Anita. It was not unusual to see her studying the *Daily Racing Form* in earnest.

Both were fastidious dressers, former teachers, and loved horse racing. Both were divorced, with children from previous marriages. They were, in fact, a beautiful couple: he, with his silver hair, big glasses, and Hollywood game show host smile and tan; she, small, lithe, trim, and pretty. They had the romance of racing and the money—their own and other people's—to enjoy one of America's biggest games, and were successful at it. Things couldn't possibly get any better.

It was a whirlwind romance, and they married during the 1984 Kentucky Derby week. For them, Derby week was their honeymoon, filled with horse racing and work. "When you're young and in love it's fun and exciting," Shari says today. "It was an exciting lifestyle, and we enjoyed it tremendously. In the beginning, we went everywhere together." Shari was as much a fixture on Lukas's arm as

French, Klein, and others were in his entourage, whether at the sales or the racetrack. Flying in for big races, all dressed up, on owner's jets, was all in a day's excitement for Wayne and Shari.

They moved into a huge home in Arcadia, California, not far from Wayne's barns at Santa Anita. Of course, the landscaping of the property was magnificent, and the backyard was filled with flowers, pools, and fountains. It was a home made as much for entertaining as it was for spoiling oneself. And it was a statement of wealth and success.

Wayne had become so much of a clotheshorse that one of the bedrooms in the house was turned into a giant dressing room/closet for him. "With Wayne, everything must coordinate," Shari told Pete Axthelm in 1989. "It carries over from the barn to himself. Sometimes he will get fully dressed and if a tie or handkerchief doesn't work just right, he'll strip down and start over." Lukas estimated at this time that he had more than two hundred sport coats and two hundred pairs of trousers. His ties were too numerous to count. "The ties are still the only problem in the marriage," Shari joked. "The burgundies with the blue stripes have got to go."

At the height of Wayne's success and the height of the late 1980s, Wayne and Shari even ventured into the highly competitive world of dog showing. They bought two Dalmatians—a male and a female, whom they called Cash and Carry—who both became champions. Cash, the male, finished third in the Dalmatian group at Westminster, one of the world's most prestigious dog shows.

Record-Breaking Years for Lukas

From 1985 to 1989, Lukas racked up title after title. He took 397 stakes races—tops among trainers—and led in earnings. He saddled 7,283 starts, took home the prize 1,443 times, and earned a whopping $74,948,843. He was, simply, the most successful trainer in the history of the sport.

In 1984 the first Breeders' Cup Championship races were held, and between then and 1989, Lukas won ten championship races out of a possible forty-two. He is still the all-time leader of Breeders' Cup wins.

In 1977 the horse racing industry established the Eclipse Awards. They are voted upon, and are considered the highest honor each year for categories such as Horse of the Year, Older Male, Older Filly or Mare, Three-Year-Old Colt or Gelding, Two-Year-Old Filly, etc. There are eleven categories given to horses, one to trainers, one to owners, one to jockeys, and one to breeders. Lukas's horses would claim ten titles between 1985 and 1989.

In 1983 and 1984, Lukas had been snubbed for the top honor among trainers. While the year's winning money earner had often won—for example, Laz Barrera and Charlie Whittingham had both won the award when they were the leaders—dollar winnings weren't the only criteria. However, in 1985, Lukas was finally recognized for his achievements. With that the floodgates opened and he took the top Eclipse Award for trainer in 1986 and 1987 as well.

In October 1985, just before the Breeders' Cup, *USA Today* ran a story, "D. WAYNE LUKAS: TRAINER'S FAST BREAKS NOW TAKE HIM TO BANK," which celebrated him as America's winningest trainer. Chet Czarniak cited the ten horses Lukas had entered in the Breeders' Cup races that season and celebrated Lukas's single-season record of winning sixty-one stakes, surpassing the record of forty-six in 1947 by trainer Jimmy Jones.

"He enjoys the trappings of success, a Rolex watch on the wrist, cars with 'D. Wayne Lukas Racing Stables' emblazoned on their doors and a list of wealthy clients who seek his counsel," Czarniak wrote. "This style, coupled with his high-priced horses, has caught the eye of other trainers, some of whom privately joke about the lawn furniture around the stables and even the large amount of straw he uses for bedding in the stalls for his horses."

When asked to comment on these snide asides, Lukas remarked, "I think we put a lot of that to rest."

The 1980s had been good to D. Wayne Lukas.

Capote

Despite all the good news, the one thing that eluded Lukas was the biggest plum on the tree: winning the Kentucky Derby. The period between 1982 and 1987 represented a no man's land of agony and suffering for Lukas each time Churchill Downs hosted its premier event.

In 1982, '83, and '84, Lukas had seen some of his best horses go down to bitter defeat. In 1985, Tank's Prospect would fall short. In 1986, Badger Land would finish fifth. But for all his success and accomplishments, Lukas's 1987 Derby would be by far his worst.

He had three horses entered: On the Line, War, and Capote. The first two were considered solid if not spectacular horses. Derby horses? Probably not. And Capote? Lukas had bought Capote for $800,000. He was out of Seattle Slew. In his juvenile year, he won three out of four starts, including the 1986 Norfolk Stakes and the 1986 Breeders' Cup Juvenile. He was named Juvenile Champion of 1986. But what had once looked like a promising career ended up a disaster. His three-year-old season spiraled out of control, and the Derby would be the icing on the cake.

Lukas's failures in the Derby were so well known that in 1987, *Sports Illustrated* devoted a whole story to him, the Derby, and a favored opposing horse, Demons Begone. In the story, titled "Doing Battle with the Demon," William Nack wrote: "For D. Wayne Lukas, the search for glory at Churchill Downs continues; his sometimes star-crossed quest to fulfill his grandest dream goes on. He calls the Kentucky Derby 'the gold ring' to distinguish it from all other titles and trophies offered in the sport."

Lukas was quoted as saying: "If you're going to coach football, you like to win the Super Bowl. Basketball the Final Four. I wouldn't want to go through life, set all those earnings and stakes records, and then sit back and say, 'By golly, we couldn't win the Derby!'"

The piece pointed out that Lukas was being criticized for bringing Capote to the Derby at all. Between "disappointing showings" and a difficult to understand training schedule, Nack wrote, Capote was a question mark at best.

Lukas defended his position: "The question is, have I got him tight enough to go a mile and a quarter next Saturday? He could be a tremendous surprise."

Nack was not impressed. "It would be a *shock* to many if Capote won," he wrote. "War is the only one who can grab the gold ring for him this year. Chances are, the ring fits elsewhere. . . ."

The *Louisville Courier-Journal* had nicknamed Capote the "blunder horse." And Ira Berkow was equally unimpressed. In a feature story, "The Narrow Horse," Berkow encapsulated backstretch conversations between insiders, discussing Capote's questionable health.

One watcher was reported as saying, "Kinda narrow, ain't he?" making a sarcastic observation that the horse was ailing, due to a virus that had diminished its girth. Berkow quoted another clocker saying: "Gaspin' like he's half dead." Lukas told Berkow, when asked what instructions he had given his riders: "It's hard to give any instructions, really. You can overcoach. When you've got great riders like Cordero and Gary Stevens and Pincay, who've got a leg up, you let them go with their experience." While the lineup of jockeys was impressive, considering they were all running for one trainer, Lukas's horses weren't scaring anyone.

In the '87 Derby, won by Alysheba, On the Line finished tenth, War thirteenth, and Capote could not complete the oval. Lukas was accused by some of having entered a hurt horse. True or not, it was the lowest point in Lukas's career as far as the big three races were concerned. It cemented the impression in many people's minds that he burned his horses out early and could not train a true classics winner.

Since scoring with a third-place winner in 1981, Lukas had endured six long years of frustration and disappointment when it came to the Derby. He also suffered under the giant load of criticism that came from fellow trainers, writers, and other know-it-alls who felt he couldn't get the job done. Six years, twelve promising horses, and a black mark against his name. For all those people who said he was doing it wrong, Lukas's record in the Derby was their trump card, and they loved to play it every May.

Pete Axthelm recounted the story about a television interview he was doing with Lukas. He had met Lukas as far back as 1982, when he asked him a particularly difficult question. "He snapped at me, 'I don't have to answer to anyone. I made more money than you last year.' It may have reflected on Lukas's good friend and master of media relations, Indiana basketball coach Bob Knight. . . . Knight was standing behind him during the interview."

Capote would be the biggest strike against Lukas. And when he took home the Eclipse Award in 1987, he still had not held the Derby's silver cup in his hands—by now more mythical grail than trophy in his covetous eyes. It was the one chink in the Team Lukas armor anyone could pierce easily and quickly.

Jeff's Winning Ways

There was never a greater show of Lukas's son Jeff's abilities than the 1989 Saratoga meet in August. While Jeff's father's name appeared on everything, Jeff was happy to work hard and increase the scope, success, and value of what was now apparently and happily the family business. Jeff never questioned the wisdom of working for his father. His father intimated many times that Jeff had been approached by others throughout his career in racing.

Jeff ran the Belmont operation, and was the man in charge when Wayne's horses beat Woody Stephen's troop. He was also in charge of running Saratoga. Jeff was well-liked on the backstretch. He was all business, and worked like his father from early in the morning until late at night. There was no question Jeff admired his dad. Early pictures, even those that appeared in newspapers, showed a proud son, always looking up to his defiant and proud father. But he was more affable and easier to approach than the former basketball coach.

But Jeff liked to enjoy himself more than his father did. With Uncle Lowell living nearby in Connecticut, the two often went golfing. "We used to sneak away," Lowell says, "and play golf. I don't think Wayne ever knew." Lowell also sent Jeff new clubs.

"Send them to my father-in-law's house," the shrewd young man told Lowell. "Don't send 'em to me."

Lowell told of days the two of them spent at the Saratoga track windows instead of the paddocks. "Jeff was the best handicapper. He was a genius with horses. We'd bet eight exactas, and we'd hit half of them."

By 1989 the horse establishment was ready to give Jeff his due. Keith Marder wrote in the *Albany Times Union*: "Even though he saddles virtually every Lukas stakes winner in New York, Jeff has never gotten credit for a victory and his name doesn't even appear on the program as the horses' trainer. Jeff has held a New York trainer's license since 1979, but his name is still listed in programs at New York tracks in parentheses next to his father's. Jeff is given credit by his father for managing the careers of Lady's Secret (Horse of the Year in 1986) and Winning Colors (Champion Filly in 1988)."

Woody Stephens thought highly of Jeff. "Things happen in the barn during training hours that you gotta make decisions on yourself. No man can be two thousand miles away on the phone and tell you. I'm pretty sure his dad's looking over his shoulder—we all know that."

"This is the greatest job in the world for someone my age," the younger Lukas said. "You get to deal with the best clients. The best horses run in the best races on the best racing circuits. You don't have the pressures of the day-to-day aggravation from the outside factors involved. I spend my summers in New York and my winters in California. How you gonna beat that?"

In fact, Jeff was increasingly running the day-to-day operations. While his father was romancing clients and selling the name, Jeff was running many things. He was the only person in the entire operation who could override Wayne's decisions, the only one who could oppose Wayne and discuss alternative suggestions with him. In a national operation, Jeff knew everything about any one of the more than two hundred horses they had at any one time. He was excellent with horses, and a few of the owners even preferred to deal with him instead.

"From jockeys to trainers to owners to former employees, Jeff Lukas receives high marks in both work ethic and horsemanship," Marder wrote.

"Jeff was very responsible for all the success in that era," says Shari Lukas. "He was terrific. He could look at a condition book and always know what he was doing."

Lukas was as proud as could be of his son. It gave him the opportunity to enjoy more of his riches, and gave him the comfort of knowing that there was someone whom he could trust running things in his absence. He was proud to say there were meets where D. Wayne Lukas Racing Stables had taken the most races in a meet, and he himself might not have saddled one horse. Jeff had done it all.

As he succinctly put it: "Other than to take time off for my funeral, I don't think the operation would miss a beat."

Winning Colors and the Wayne and Woody Show

Bred by Echo Valley Farm, Winning Colors was a roan filly foaled in 1985 by Caro out of All Rainbows (by Bold Hour). She was bought by Eugene Klein and turned over to Lukas. A big filly, the word "Amazon" was an adjective constantly linked with her name.

She raced only twice as a two-year-old in 1987, which was unusual for a Lukas-trained horse. She won both. But it was as a three-year-old, in the Santa Anita Derby on April 9, 1988, that Winning Colors turned heads and raised eyebrows with her dominating 7½ length victory over a group of well-regarded males.

"You all know how hard it is to win the Derby," Lukas said to the press corps afterward. "Maybe I do most of all. But who among you would advise me not to run?"

She had won five of her career six starts, and seemed to the viewing world as another Lukas prodigy destined for disaster, as Althea and Life's Magic had been. Writer Jay Hovdey, though impressed with the filly and referring to her as "massive," was quick to point to Lukas's dismal Derby record. But Lukas played to the bleachers, saying, "What she did today even surprised me a little. It stamped her as something truly special. One thing's for sure, we'll have all the housewives and all the gals in the beauty parlors rooting for us in the Derby."

For any writer covering the Derby in 1988, there were lots of stories to follow. But certainly many eyes were on Lukas's Winning Colors and Woody Stephens's Forty Niner. Stephens had won the Belmont Stakes five times in a row between 1982 and 1986. He was one of the older trainers in the game and easily the most popular. Like Charlie Whittingham and John Nerud, Stephens was old-school—grumbling and sarcastic—as well as competitive.

His real name was Woodward Cefis Stephens. He was born in Midway, Kentucky, in 1913. His family were farming people, and

Woody was introduced early to the concept of working with his hands from dusk till dawn. He eventually left farm life, trading a plow horse for a thoroughbred and becoming a jockey in 1932. Eventually he grew to manhood and switched to training, due to a growth spurt that cut short his riding career.

Like Lukas, Stephens had grown to be a force to be reckoned with. What Wayne was to California, Woody was to New York. They were probably the two most powerful trainers of the mid- to late 1980s. Each easily trained more than two hundred horses at any one time, and had the pick of the litter when it came to horses and owners alike.

Stephens was a raconteur, telling stories of racing and horse trading. All his stories eventually ended with his signature lines, such as, "Our steaks sure tasted sweet that night," or his favorite and most famous, "We got *all* the money." Stephens was also famous, or infamous, for telling owners off, which he loved to do, and loved to tell about.

Stephens also had a big owner behind him. Henryk de Kwiatkowski was flashy and flamboyant. He dressed impeccably and seemed to lead a charmed life. He and Stephens had such great horses as Danzig, De La Rose, and, most famously, Conquistador Cielo and Swale.

For anyone covering Derby week, Stephens and Lukas were like two schoolyard bullies testing each other. "Lukas and Stephens like winning at each other's expense far more than winning itself, and they had kept up an edgy exchange of insults throughout Derby week," Steven Crist wrote in the *New York Times*. "Stephens had said that Winning Colors did not belong in the Derby and would not win the race. Lukas said he did not expect Forty Niner to handle the Derby distance." Crist went on to point out that Stephens had beaten two of Lukas's previous fillies—Life's Magic and Althea—and for Lukas, this was settling an old score.

The week before, Lukas had told reporters: "It looks like it's going to be the Wayne and Woody show again." And he was more right than he knew.

Climbing aboard Winning Colors on that first Saturday in May was Gary Stevens. It would be the filly's first race in four weeks; if she were to win the Derby, that would be the longest layoff for a winner in twenty-five years. Lukas was trying something new. Winning Colors, who was not the favorite, would be his only entry in a seventeen-horse field.

Lukas saddled her, then went to the Racing Secretary's office to watch the race. She broke well out of the gate, and ran to an early lead. She continued to build the lead, though her fractions were not impressively fast. Forty Niner, Stephen's impressive three-year-old colt, put pressure on her in the stretch.

As William Nack reported in *Sports Illustrated*, Lukas yelled at the television, "Switch your leads, baby, switch your leads." Winning Colors stumbled as Forty Niner moved on her, first just near her hindquarters, then by her withers, then behind her by a neck. Gary Stevens was striking the horse, waving his whip, and kicking his heels as he saw Forty Niner draw up on Winning Colors. "Stay with them, Gary!" Lukas shouted at the television. "Come on! Gary, Gary, Gary, Gary, Gary, Gary, Gary, Gary!"

The horses raced on, with Winning Colors in front. Forty Niner did not catch her until two strides after the finish pole. Lukas had finally won his first Kentucky Derby, and he'd done it with a filly! The media ate it up. She was only the third filly ever to win a Derby, the first being Regret in 1915, and then Genuine Risk in 1980. It was the closest Derby finish in nineteen years, when Majestic Prince held off Arts and Letters in 1969.

Klein told Crist that it was the "greatest thrill in sports." But Crist saved his most ardent remarks for the trainer: "Lukas was glowing after today's race. The Derby had become a hex for him, and no trainer had ever sent more starters without a winner." Winning Colors's six wins in seven career starts now placed her earnings at $1.6 million.

Crist wrote: "Going over, the railbirds were yelling, 'You're o for 13.' They already conceded that I wouldn't win this time. But on the way back, when I walked past the grandstand, the people stood up and applauded. Some of the same guys who had been yelling before at me."

Still, Lukas couldn't wait to strike back at all those who had doubted him. The temptation was too great. "I hope this puts to rest all those theories that we were businessmen instead of horsemen, but with $17 million there had to be some horsemanship there," he said, crowing about his record earnings from the previous year.

Lukas then mentioned that he'd been talking to Stephens. "Woody told me," he said, " 'The filly's a good one, she's for real.' But he told me I'll never win five Belmonts, and I agree."

Lukas was also quick to note that his son Jeff had really been the horse's trainer. He boasted with a father's loud pride, "I give all the credit to Jeff. He drafted her and took her to New York last year and slept with her and nursemaided her."

After the race, when pressed for a quote, Stephens cryptically said, "We'll catch her next time." But the next day, Stephens sung like a songbird, loud enough for anyone who'd listen. "I congratulated him, but you know, I've been in that winner's circle a few times myself. I've won five Belmonts and he'll never do that. I ran second in the Derby three times and won it twice. By the time he gets to that, he'll be so old he can't walk."

And of course Stephens couldn't resist another jibe, saying to another reporter, "He's a genius now that he's won the Derby."

Then Stephens turned up the intensity. "I'm going to the lead and see if she can stand the heat. If not, she better get out of the kitchen," he said, as if issuing a challenge.

Lukas tried to take the high road, not taking the bait in public, saying, "I didn't think he'd sacrifice his horse to run with her early in the Derby and I don't think he'll do it in the Preakness."

Stephens, however, did not let up, and their battle in the press grew more heated. When Lukas announced that win, place, show, or not, he would enter Winning Colors in the Belmont Stakes, Stephens snorted, "Lukas will never get those five Belmonts. He's still looking for his first, and that filly sure won't get it for him."

Lukas retorted that "they ought to bronze Woody and put him out in the Belmont paddock next to Secretariat's statue." He told another reporter, "What Woody's got to understand is when you court the girl, the hardest part is to catch her."

After the Triple Crown races were over, *New York Times* writer George Vecsey reported that before the Preakness, Stephens had been saying, "We're going to send that filly back to the farm. My horse may finish last, but the filly will finish next to last." While Lukas had been as nice as he could be in public, he knew the strategy Stephens would employ, and warned his rider that Forty Niner would try to carry him wide.

Sure enough, when Winning Colors jumped out to the lead in the Preakness, Forty Niner challenged her, taking away the inside rail. They set a furious pace, as the two horses dueled for six furlongs. As they headed into the stretch run, Forty Niner bumped Winning Colors. Not just once, not just twice, but a few times. It was an ugly replay of the Codex–Genuine Risk duel in the 1980 Preakness.

"We were eight or nine lengths off the inside fence and we were bumping continuously," Stevens bitterly complained after the race. He carried the filly very wide and the crowd was shocked. "Pat [Day, on Forty Niner] wasn't concerned about anybody getting through or maybe even winning the race."

The two bumping horses, riding wild and wide, were slowing down, and they were passed by Risen Star and then Brian's Time. Winning Colors gamely fought on and finished third. Forty Niner had failed so miserably, he finished seventh. Accusations flew. Gary Stevens was beside himself in the jockey's clubhouse. "I don't blame Pat, I blame one man," he said. "Jealousy is a powerful thing and it cost that man more than it cost us."

Day apologized to Stevens afterward. He even tried to deflect his angry friend's tirade. But Woody Stephens would not back down. "I told the world I was going after the filly, and I did. If I left her alone she would have won again. Somebody had to take a shot."

After the race, Lukas said nothing. "Usually, I'm very outspoken," he told Ross Staaden years later, "but I didn't make any statement because I thought everybody was going to do it for me, and that's just what happened. I made a decision when I went down to get the horse, I knew it was not going to be an unnoticed or uncontroversial race."

Days later, though, Lukas sounded smart when he spoke to Dave Anderson: "You can't say, 'Woody, I'd like to win the Preakness and the Triple Crown. Why don't you run the same race you did in the Derby?' "

After the race, Stephens was lambasted, even by his most ardent admirers. "The motives and the tactics of the Preakness will always be debatable," Vecsey wrote in the *Times*. Even the *Daily Racing Form* had a comment. "Not beaten, mind you, ambushed," it said of Winning Colors. "Not outrun, but victimized in deliberate fashion."

Three weeks later, the Belmont was a zoo, as it can sometimes be. So wild did the fracas get that many fans in the stands wore shirts to annoy Klein, who had been railing against Stephens in any newspaper that would take the time to record his comments. The T-shirts read: "WHINING COLORS" and "CRYING KLEIN." The railbirds in the crowd of forty thousand were chanting, "Woody! Woody!"

But Forty Niner wasn't in it. His horse was a bust in the Belmont, and Winning Colors finished a sad sixth. She was exhausted. And the wild ride was over. Wayne and Woody would butt heads again, but never as badly as they did that season.

"In hindsight, if I look back, I don't think the Derby is so bad, I think it's the second or third leg that gets them," Lukas said. "I know my filly had a real rough race in the Preakness, and she probably took all summer, probably to the Breeders' Cup in November, to get back into form after that."

And Lukas is still in awe of Stephens's record of five Belmonts. "Woody let us have the first two but he waited on you with the fresh horse, and he even surprised me on some of them. He did a masterful job. He obviously had a grasp for it. In fact . . . at one time I took eighty-some tapes to the Garden City Hotel and stayed up all night playing *all* the Belmont tapes, trying to figure out a pattern of how to win it, because I thought I was missing the boat. I wasn't right where I wanted to be. And I studied all those tapes, and about thirty of them were in the mud so I threw those out because they had no bearing, and then the only conclusion I came to on the others was that you should have Secretariat.

"I tried to get a pattern. I watched Woody's horses and everything. And yet Woody mastered that because he took horses that were different styles of running, different abilities, and everything else, but I think the thing was he waited till he got you on his home court."

Winning Colors would win a few more races and then be retired for breeding. She would finish with more than $1.5 million in earnings, in a career that saw her record run to eight wins, three seconds, and one third in nineteen starts. She went on to become a brood mare at Gainesway Farm in Lexington, Kentucky. After five fillies, she produced her first colt in 1996, and it made international news. She was inducted into the Horse Racing Hall of Fame in 2000.

Asked what his fondest memories in racing were when he was later inducted into the Racing Hall of Fame, Lukas pointed to Winning Colors first among his other accomplishments. It would be something he would always be most proud of.

William T. Young

William T. Young was born in 1918 and graduated from the University of Kentucky with a degree in mechanical engineering in 1939. After serving in the war, he settled down with his wife Lucy and raised a family in the Lexington, Kentucky, area. He has been a proud icon ever since.

He began by making peanut butter, worked hard, and by 1946 his business had become a major national brand called Big Top. Young sold that company in 1955 to Procter & Gamble, which today sells that peanut butter under the brand name Jif. The Lexington plant is still the largest Jif manufacturing facility in the United States. But Young was just beginning. Upon selling his peanut butter company, he founded a trucking company, which is still in existence today and which still delivers Jif to stores and warehouses around the country. He also owns one of the region's largest storage facilities. He later became a chief executive at Royal Crown Cola. With his fortune, Young has founded numerous programs at the University of Kentucky, as well as the new library that bears his name.

In 1972, Young began to accumulate land in the Lexington area in order to create a farm. And by the late 1970s he was ready to populate Overbrook Farm with thoroughbred horses. He has continued to expand the farm and his holdings ever since.

Young met D. Wayne Lukas in 1989. Since then, a number of Overbrook horses at auction through Keeneland and Fasig-Tipton have found their way into the Lukas Team barns across the country. In the 1990s a large number of Lukas's winners came out of Overbrook Farm. Outside of Satish Sanan, who would join Team Lukas in the mid-1990s, Young would be the last of Lukas's major players for some time.

Young was the antithesis of Klein. Where Klein was loud, charismatic, and flamboyant, Young was quiet, paternalistic, and a traditionalist. Where Klein sought the press, the adulation, and the limelight, Young would be happy to play the country gentleman, dressed in tweeds, and stay somewhat anonymous, at least as far as national press was concerned. If Klein was a showman, Young was a proper Kentucky-bred blueblood, or at least liked to play one. He would be a supportive if demanding owner. Confident, always in charge, but open to ideas, he would stand by Lukas through the many trials and tribulations that were ahead for the trainer.

But those were personality traits. Young was essentially different from Klein because he and his staff of advisers bred thoroughbreds for a living. Where Klein had blind faith in Lukas's ability to pick horseflesh, Young and his advisers chose what horses Lukas would race, and which ones they would sell at one of the three main auctions. Where Lukas had power as both buyer and trainer in his relationship with Klein, he was now just a prominent trainer with a well-heeled, knowledgeable breeder as a client.

Criminal Type

While Lukas had entered Houston and Shy Tom as disappointments in the 1989 Kentucky Derby, and a trio of stragglers in Land Rush, Power Lunch, and Real Cash in 1990, he also campaigned the phenomenal Criminal Type, who would be entered in eleven races that year and win seven times.

Owned by Calumet Farms, Criminal Type had been campaigned in France as a two- and three-year-old, where he was unspectacular, but he did win the Prix de Caen at Deauville, a respectable stakes race. In 1989 he was brought to the United States, where his first American races were under allowance conditions. He finished in the money twice in his first three starts, then began an incredible streak in which he would get on the board in his next ten races. He was first twice, second twice, and third once in five allowance races, then won his next three races, which included two Grade 2 stakes—the San Pasqual Handicap and the San Antonio Handicap. Then, in the Santa Anita and San Bernadino handicaps, he finished second to Ruhlmann. His streak was finally boken in his next race, the Oaklawn Handicap, when he finished out of the money. But that wouldn't happen again for four more races.

On May 12, 1990, Criminal Type would meet his nemesis, Ruhlmann, once again. The occasion was the Pimlico Special Handicap, at Baltimore's historic Pimlico Racecourse (known in the 1800s as "Old Hilltop"). The race was for horses four years old and up, and Criminal Type would carry 117 pounds, compared to an impost of 124 for Ruhlmann, who at that point had taken two of the three races between them. And the purse was big. With José Santos aboard, Criminal Type edged his rival out by a nose, and set a new course record by running the mile and three-sixteenths in a blistering 1:53.

The win, and the purse money, made Lukas the first $100 million man in horse racing history. It would take Charlie Whittingham another two years to also pass the $100 million mark. But it had taken Whittingham a lifetime, and Lukas did it in less than thirteen years. He was now the all-time-winningest horse trainer in the world.

Criminal Type then won the prestigious Metropolitan Mile, triumphing over 1989 Belmont Stakes winner Easy Goer; the Hollywood Gold Cup; and the Whitney Handicap at Saratoga on August 4, 1990. In the Gold Cup, he beat Sunday Silence, a former Kentucky Derby winner. His last race was the September fifteenth running of the Woodward Handicap at Belmont.

Now a five-year-old horse, Criminal Type had won $2,351,817 in his lifetime. He was scheduled to run in the Breeders' Cup Classic and meet Unbridled, the Kentucky Derby winner, trained by Carl Nafzger, in a showdown to determine Horse of the Year. Instead, Lukas retired Criminal Type, citing the horse's sore ankles. Unbridled went on to win the Breeders' Cup Classic, but Criminal Type was named Horse of the Year, as well as Champion Older Male.

It was a masterful job by Lukas. He had proven he could make a champion of an older male, one of the few categories in which he'd failed to make a champion before. For a trainer whose reputation had been with both younger and older fillies, it proved his versatility and horsemanship.

Joe Drape wrote in the *New York Times*: "Nafzger still bristles that Lukas's Criminal Type won horse of the year over Unbridled in 1990. 'Wayne outcampaigned me. Old Criminal Type got sore ankles before the Breeders' Cup and was retired so he couldn't race my horse,' he said with a disbelieving wink. 'It just shows Wayne is smarter and shrewder than me.' "

Calumet's Criminal Type was Horse of the Year, and Calumet Farm would be named Breeder of 1990. Lukas finished the year with much to celebrate. But that would not last long.

SEVEN

THE FALL

Laz Barrera, Drugs, and D. Wayne Lukas

Trainers have been accused of juicing their charges since racing was instituted in this country three centuries ago. In fact, many trainers who were successful "juicers" were sometimes highly sought after. And it is a strange truth of horse racing that as a trainer gets older, the more well known he becomes for his strange brews. Certainly this was the case with Stephens, Nerud, and Whittingham, all of whom were known for perfectly legal but strange concoctions they used on their horses. Indeed, their magical powers were celebrated. They were crafty old wizards. "The history of racing's testing methods is riddled with inaccuracies," Pete Axthelm wrote, "and more than one squeaky clean trainer has been punished, while cheaters, who are well known to even casual fans as such, get away with their mysterious 'juice.' "

But in the world of modern racing, it is not uncommon to see successful trainers stand accused of having used illegal or banned substances to gain an edge on their competition. Some were in fact guilty, but in other instances such accusations have been examples of witch hunts rather than magic potions. And as Axthelm opined, "When you overshadow a profession the way Lukas does, your enemies don't want to behold your swelled chest, they want to behold your medicine chest."

On February 13, 1989, in Arcadia, the California Horse Racing Board announced that they were investigating Hall of Fame trainer Laz Barrera, his son Albert Barrera, D. Wayne Lukas, Bryan Webb, Anthony Hemmerick, and Roger Stein.

In October 1988, Stein's horse, Emperor's Turn, had tested positive for cocaine. Stein had been suspended for six months and fined $2,000 by the Santa Anita stewards. The announcement went on to say that Lukas and Barrera were being investigated for traces that showed up in horses they had raced in Del Mar during the summer of 1988.

The racing board said that cocaine was found in the urine sample of a Laz Barrera horse, Endow, after he won a race at Del Mar on August 31, 1988. Albert Barrera was being investigated for similar reasons in connection with a different horse. A Lukas horse, Crown Collection, who had been nominated to the Kentucky Derby, was also cited. Crown Collection won at Del Mar only two days before Barrera's.

A local anesthetic and narcotic, cocaine was not looked upon at the time as something that trainers used to juice horses. In fact, no one on the backstretch even knew if cocaine might have any effect on horses, and many of the veterinarians who were contacted said they could see no reason to administer it to a horse. However, cocaine was the drug of choice in the 1980s, it was an illegal substance, and under California racing law, nothing could be administered to race horses other than the analgesic phenylbutazone, known for short as bute.

While stories of juicing have permeated racing for a long time, the charges were shocking. Newspaper sports sections carried bold headlines on Valentine's Day, a Tuesday, in 1989. Lukas was incensed, and he decried the announcement to the press. "The bottom line," he said, "is that something is drastically wrong. In my heart, Laz Barrera is as innocent as can be and so am I, and I'd stake my children's lives on that. No horse of mine has ever received cocaine and I've never even seen it." While Lukas and Laz Barrera were allowed to continue to race at Santa Anita, the other trainers were temporarily suspended.

Albert Barrera, investigated for a horse he ran at Santa Anita, vowed to fight the sanctions: "A six month suspension would end my career. I learned how to train horses from my father, and something I didn't learn from him was to give horses cocaine and other drugs."

Two days after the announcement of the investigation, Leonard Foote, executive secretary of the California Racing Board, confirmed that the board would file claims against Lukas and Laz Barrera. Foote said the board expected to find many more horses that tested positive. "We've learned to hope for the best and expect the worst," he told reporters. Foote went out of his way to point out that while Lukas or Barrera might not have administered the illegal drug to the horses themselves, or did not know of such juicing, they were in effect responsible for the horses they raced.

By March 3 formal charges were filed and an administrative judge appointed. A hearing would be held within fifteen days. And of course it dragged on. During that period, the Kentucky Derby took place, and Lukas's entries, Houston and Shy Tom, finished eighth and tenth respectively. "Bill Young's first Derby starter was Shy Tom," Lukas recalled years later. "He ran well and had a nice spring, but I don't think either Bill or I believed in our hearts that Shy Tom was going to win the Derby."

On June 2, the day before the Belmont Stakes, which would feature Sunday Silence and Easy Goer, the California Horse Racing Board dropped the charges against all the trainers except Stein. It turned out that the trainers had been accused on a presence of a billionth-of-a-gram range appearing in the horses' blood. This amount was not only infinitesimal, but the test results when examinations were conducted again turned up no cocaine whatsoever.

At Hollywood Park, Foote said, "We don't want to charge people with accusations we cannot prove." But in fact the damage had already been done. The headline of the story about the dropping of charges was smaller than the one announcing the accusations had been, and it was buried in the back of the racing section.

"It killed Laz," Lukas says today. "Laz would call me at night and sob for an hour. He couldn't believe it. I told him, 'Laz, they're going to figure this out, it's contamination.' But he couldn't handle it. Actually, the night they told me, they woke me up, and I turned around and went back to sleep. It never affected me. . . . To this day I think that commission overreacted. And now we know that [contamination's] commonplace."

Though no one had ever proven that Lukas purposely or knowingly had dosed his horses with cocaine, a vicious whispering campaign swept through backstretches across the country. That it was the second accusation against him might have helped feed the rumor mill. To this day disgruntled losers and other Lukas snipers maintain that some kind of alchemy still exists. And when new tests are developed, they say, the truth will be found out.

This sniping should be considered in perspective. Lukas has trained more stakes winners in his career than some backstretches produce altogether. It would seem impossible that someone could or would be doping hundreds of animals, incidentally implicating numerous trainers throughout the country, to achieve the consistent success Lukas has earned year after year.

Even Chuck Jenda, a competitive trainer who has vehemently criticized Lukas in print, called the charges of cocaine against him and the other trainers "absolutely ridiculous. I mean we're talking about billionths of a gram here. I read a statistic in *Playboy* that if you checked out hundred-dollar bills, over thirty percent of them would have larger traces of cocaine on them than was found in those horses."

Mid-America Racing Stables

Horses, especially the good ones, were becoming more and more expensive. Combine that with the fact that laws passed in 1985 had taken away the tax advantages horse owners had enjoyed for many years, and now you had a perfect recipe to drive away existing owners as well potential owners. As a result, financial vehicles that could reduce risk while still offering the excitement of owning a race horse were becoming popular.

In the higher circles, select individuals would be offered shares in premium thoroughbreds. Secretariat was one of the notable early syndications offered in the blueblood world. But this idea eventually filtered down to even the lowest horses.

What was missing was a corporation that would allow you to buy stock in a racing concern, as you might buy shares in Merrill Lynch, for example. This would be helpful to horsemen who were trying to raise capital to run farms, buy yearlings, and race horses. Stock offerings could drive incredible amounts of cash toward those who knew exactly how to spend it.

There were a host of breeding concerns, including Spendthrift Farms, Blue Grass Breeders, International Thoroughbred, Kentucky Horse Center, Sovereign Thoroughbred, and Standardbred Pacers. Two of these, Spendthrift and International, were traded on the American Stock Exchange.

On the other side of the track, there were racing concerns such as Churchill Downs Inc., San Juan Racing, Santa Anita Companies, and Turf Paradise. San Juan and Santa Anita were both traded on the New York Stock Exchange. Financial writer Marilyn Bender wrote, "Big price tags are attached to thoroughbreds, the darlings of the sport of kings. They have become a commodity like art, bought and sold in an international marketplace at such huge sums that even the wealthiest breeders can no longer operate without outside financing. And now such major institutions as Citibank, Merrill Lynch, and Prudential-Bache are helping them find the money."

Even William E. Simon, former Secretary of the Treasury under Reagan, and a venture capitalist, was getting into investing in horse racing through these financial instruments. "The investing public decided the horse business was a legitimate investment and that it was more fun than owning a piece of an office building," said Michael J. Nolan, director of the American Horse Council, a horse lobbying group in Washington, D.C. But Nolan also warned that "no one should invest without a decent understanding of the business." And the article ended with a quote from Lou Guida, the biggest owner and breeder of standardbred stallions at the time: "Beware of anyone who advertises horse deals."

In 1987 a brochure announced the creation of Mid-America Racing Stables. This company would offer investors the opportunity to own race horses. D. Wayne Lukas would be the titular head of this publicly traded company that would make money buying, racing, and breeding quarter horses and thoroughbreds. It was an exciting opportunity.

The truth was, Lukas was heavily in debt, and it was not all of his own doing. He had taken out a sizable loan in 1986. The loan was secured with horses that were co-owned with Jeff and financial adviser David Burrage. But the Oklahoma City bank that had loaned the Lukases $4 million went belly up. That meant *père et fils* were responsible to the FDIC for more than $1.8 million as soon as possible. In addition, Lukas owed $700,000 to the business that ostensibly owned the horses. How were they to raise that kind of money? A stock offering.

They offered thousands of shares and raised $4 million. Lukas paid off his debts and made a little money too. As he did in his dealings with his other owners, he would receive commissions on both purchases and sales, as well as collect a salary. He also deducted management and training fees and a commission on monies won. In the end he collected more than $600,000 during the life of the company.

The only people who didn't make any money were the investors, who got screwed. The company went bankrupt in three years, and Lukas settled, with those who banded together, for the paltry sum of $250,000. For the investors, this amounted to a net loss of 94 percent. Lukas, giving his version of the events, says about the venture today: "Mid-America . . . that was a fiasco. But I never had any involvement with that. That's again where investors were trying to capitalize on our success, and I think it was doomed from the get-go. The first thing was, I think that public companies aren't conducive to racing. It's hard to train for three partnerships, let alone a public company like that. The second thing was that . . . the original assets of the company, after being scrutinized and getting a blue-sky clearance, was a quarter horse foundation. Everyone in the company knew that we were going to move to a full-blown thoroughbred operation. Much more expensive, but much more productive too. So what happened was we made the decision to do that as quickly as possible."

But that didn't happen. The prospectus had sold investors on the idea of buying into a primarily thoroughbred racing operation. In a suit later brought on by investors against Mid-America, it was alleged that few if any investors other than Jeff, Mel Hatley, and Burrage knew that the company was intending to buy out the Mel Hatley Partnership. The Mel Hatley Farms, or MHF, Partnership, was a quarter horse division that had lost money for several years in a row. It was owned by Mel Hatley, a major Lukas backer and owner, and had as minor partners Jeff Lukas, David Burrage, and Lukas himself.

According to that same suit, it was also alleged that Mid-America, after the money from the offering was secured, turned around and bought out MHF Partnership well above market value. This accusation was prompted by the fact that after the buyout Mid-America then sold the same quarter horses for more than $710,000 in losses.

This loss and the cost of buying out the partnership left the company $4 million worth of investments, with only slightly more than $1.2 million to buy, house, breed, and race thoroughbreds. Added to this was the fact that Wayne, Jeff, and Burrage were required, via an agreement with the Oklahoma Department of Securities dated March 31, 1988, to repay $753,000. The agreement went on to say, "which amount represents the approximate net benefit to such parties pursuant to the acquisition of their interests in the Partnership." Also in the agreement, in order to pay off this debt, Lukas agreed to forgive a debt of $53,000 that Mid-America owed to him, and his salary would be withheld until the amount was paid off against the remaining sum. It is also important to note that he negotiated a figure of $200,000 as a yearly fee so that the debt would be paid off or repaid within three and a half years at the very least.

"I was part of that decision [to move to a full-blown thoroughbred operation], but not totally," says Lucas. "Again you have a board, more people than one making that decision. We decided to disperse the quarter horses and take the money to go into thoroughbreds. We did it at a very inopportune time—when the market for horseflesh was crashing. We sat there and evaluated what we had calculated to be x amount of dollars going for far less. . . . We dispersed them all at one sale, with every guy who was interested in buying those kind of horses sitting there, and it was my call during the sale that they knew the market better than we did, and so I said, 'We're going to sell.' Now in hindsight, we might have pulled them all out, if there were high reserves on 'em, redid it some way and maybe waited a year or two and brought it all back. But I decided that all the players were in the room. . . . So now our assets have depleted a great deal because . . . our expectations were high and they ended up low, so there was concern among the stockholders. The second thing is, we were now limited in our financial base to jump into the thoroughbred business, so we almost had to catch lightning in a bottle. We were going to have to hit on almost every horse, which necessarily didn't happen either. So consequently the stock went south just like in any other company."

Another reason the company's stock was further affected was that by 1989 it was fighting off more than one lawsuit by disgruntled shareholders. One suit banded together eighteen shareholders, whose interest represented more than $800,000 worth of investments, suing Mid-America on a number of charges. Chief among these charges was that the "defendants . . . participated in concerted action in a common scheme to accomplish the sale of Mid-America Units during the IPO by misrepresenting certain material facts and by omitting material facts about the transaction described in the Preliminary Prospectus and Prospectus," according to documents filed with the United States District Court for the Western District of Oklahoma, on August 4, 1989.

The suit also asserted that among other reasons was that the "Preliminary Prospectus and Prospectus also represented that the chief reason that the MHF Partnership had lost money was to provide tax deductions for the limited partners." In the end the suit alleged that "the net affect of the agreement between Mid-America and the Partnership was to 'bail out' the limited partners from the Partnership at a large profit at the expense of the investors in the Mid-America public offering" and that the company's actions "constituted a continuing pattern of fraud." The suit also named the accounting firm Arthur Andersen as defendant in its allegations.

In 1986 the MHF Partnership sold off a number of horses for $147,721 that had cost it $363,207, and in 1987 it sold for $40,000 horses that had cost the partnership $285,704, according to the suit that was filed, showing that the partners knew that the market value was inflated.

Indeed, the company was bleeding money. In an SEC filing made by Arthur Andersen on behalf of Mid-America (Doc. #765028), the filing cited poor racetrack performance and losses due to the sale of the quarter horses and thoroughbreds. In 1989 Roving Cowboy, who raced four times, was sold for a loss of $170,000. Up Front never raced "and was given away rather than continue to pay for his upkeep," according to the same papers, which resulted in a loss of $62,000. Another stable mate, Sports Call, was sold off at a loss of $80,000 in 1990; and worst of all was Decoy, a horse with a breathing problem, who was eventually claimed for $25,000, which resulted in a loss of $170,000!

Added to all of this, Arthur Andersen opined, "The added financial pressure of litigation make eventual success for the Company more and more unlikely unless additional capital can be infused. . . ." In 1989, Mid-America's legal fees to defend itself from its shareholders amounted to $125,000. By the end of 1989, the company had little more than $208,000 in cash with which to operate.

"There's one other caveat: this was not my primary concern. This was something sitting out there they'd call me out to and say, 'What do you want to do?' It was such a small part of the D. Wayne Lukas racing stable—three or four horses, when I'm training 150—that I still think I have a certain amount of ego and pride that if they developed a public company right now and I did not have any other clientele, I think I can make it work. But I can't make it work with one phone call a week and three horses over here. We were doomed from the beginning, and I felt bad about it. . . . Some elderly couple called me up and said, 'We invested ten thousand dollars, we loved your program, we believed in you.' I just wrote 'em a check and sent it to them. Never even told the company. Guy's not going to lose any money with me, you know. Of course, I wouldn't do that very much, but I did do that on a number of occasions. In order for me to make that public company work I'd have to be the CEO, president, calling the shots, looking after everything, and I wasn't. I was looking after 150 other horses."

Regardless, according to SEC filings by Arthur Andersen in 1988 made on behalf of Mid-America, Lukas was listed as chairman of the board and chief executive officer, Jeff was president, and David Burrage was vice-president. Mid-America's position was that since Lukas was listed as chairman of the board and CEO, he had the power and authority to do as he wished and was not held hostage by any board. The truth was that quite possibly Lukas did not run day-to-day operations, but he did indeed have power. Keeping in mind his huge operations at the time, that five or six horses got lost among hundreds over two-and-a-half years should not be a total surprise.

By the end of 1989, Mid-America had run its course. It settled with its angry shareholders, other lawsuits were dismissed, and the company was bought for $.25 per share for a total of $1.4 million. The company was then turned into an oil and natural gas exploration company; its name was changed to Basin Industries.

Ironically, in 1990 Profit Key, one of the company's few remaining horses, actually won at Santa Anita and Hollywood Park, won $190,000 for the year, and was good enough to be entered in the Haskell Cup. Profit Key and Some More Magic, the last two thoroughbreds, were sold for a profit of $17,633.

Whether one remembers the words of the famous Roman expression about buying a horse, "Let the buyer beware," or the ringing endorsement of Lou Guida, it was one time Lukas's image rightly deserved the tarnish it received.

The World's Most Expensive Garage Sale

If nothing else, 1990 had mixed messages for Team Lukas. Lukas become the first trainer to break the $100 million mark in career winnings. Charlie Whittingham, the former number one all-time trainer, would follow him shortly. But Lukas was younger, and now every extension of his winning numbers would set new trainer records that were unlikely to be broken for years to come. However, aside from his continued, winning ways, few other things would break right for the quarter horse trainer from Antigo, Wisconsin.

Certainly the biggest blow to Lukas's fortunes was the slow but steady decline of Gene Klein's involvement in racing. The first signs of Klein's lessening influence came in 1988, when he was less conspicuous at the big events. If one of his horses was running in a big race, Klein would fly to Las Vegas instead of attending the event, bet the race in the comfort of an air-conditioned casino, and watch it on wide-screen television.

Rumors persisted on the backstretch that Klein had seen the fallacy of Lukas's promises and become disenchanted. They painted Lukas as the tailor who made the emperor's new clothes, and Klein as the deceived and newly aware king. The gossipmongers had Klein realizing that he was bleeding money and was now using a tourniquet to stop the hemorrhaging.

This was simply not true. Ross Staaden, in *Winning Trainers*, calculated that Klein had spent $39 million on yearlings and other horses, $3 million a year for training and barn fees, and $1 million a year for shipping the animals from one track to another. But he made more than $27 million in prizes. After the sell-off of Klein's empire, it was estimated by David Burrage, Lukas and Klein's financial gatekeeper, that Klein would net around $31 million.

In addition, Klein must have realized a very high profit from the sale of Rancho Del Rayo parcels and the eventual sale of the Rancho Del Rayo Racing Stables. When he bought the center, he'd sold off enough land to cover the price for the entire series of packages he put together, retaining 410 acres at no cost, after counting the money earned from the subdivisions he'd sold off.

Obviously, these are estimates. Even Klein admitted to Pete Axthelm that each year he won some money and lost more but was happy to be involved in the game. And he gleamed with pride as he sat at his desk amidst the hardware that Lukas had won him in battle all across the country.

In fact, Klein was withdrawing from racing because of his worsening health. Despite the rumblings on the backstretch and in the press, the owner had health problems that would continue to spiral downward faster than most people knew. Klein had suffered two coronary bypass operations and had been taking medications, as well as undergoing a slew of tests and other procedures. A vibrant, vivacious man, his doctors had insisted that he reduce the stress in his life, which it was obvious he craved.

In 1989, Klein held the most expensive garage sale in the history of horse racing, selling 114 of his prize horses at auction. There were eleven Grade 1 stakes winners, including Winning Colors and Lady's Secret. The value of these horses was quoted as over $30 million.

The "Klein dispersal" ranks as the sixth highest grossing dispersal of the last fifteen years. It netted more money than the Claiborne dispersal in January 1998, more than the Tartan Farms dispersal of November 1987, and more than the famed dispersal at Calumet Farm in 1990 and 1991. And eight of those top twenty dispersals featured significantly more horses sold at auction.

Klein had not only been one of the most successful owners of the 1980s, but one of the most successful of all time. He had won three Eclipse awards for owner, and six of his horses had won Eclipse awards as well. He had won more money and more stakes races than any other owner of his time.

At the time of the dispersal in November 1989, Klein said that he and his wife "have enjoyed our experiences racing more than I can describe. We've met a lot of wonderful people in racing and that too has enriched our lives."

He died four months later, on March 12, 1990.

"We used to have one owner who'd buy ten horses," trainer David Cross said. "Now we have ten owners who buy one horse. When Gene Klein left, that was the end of Lukas as we knew him."

This was true. With French, Beal, Hatley, and Klein behind him, Lukas had been the most powerful American buyer at the many auctions and sales around the country. And most of them had blind faith in their man. Lukas had carte blanche. As Lukas told William Nack: "When I went to the sales, I was answerable only to my conscience and good judgment. I bought the horse that looked like an athlete, that looked like a racehorse."

Joe Drape, in the *New York Times*, wrote: "Lukas was aware that his legend, if not notoriety, had as much to do with how he bought horses and trained owners as it did with his accomplishments on the racetrack."

Lukas, recalling his friend and partner today, says: "The toughest [owner] to deal with on a daily basis was also the most successful, and that was Gene Klein. Gene Klein was New York raised, streetwise, not very well accepted by the Kentucky establishment, and obviously created that situation a little bit himself. It isn't that they weren't crazy about him going in there and buying those expensive horses, it was just that he had a tendency to ram it back at 'em. He had all the ammunition too. I think it was a little bit the combination that he delighted in the fact that in a tradition-bound sport where everybody said you had to have connections, breeding rights, that you couldn't get the stallions, Gene Klein walked in there with a checkbook and we grabbed it, to pretty much take it over in that era. And my relationship to him was he was very, very tough. Very bottom-line conscious. He used to say to me, "Cowboy, do whatever you want, buy what you want, run 'em where you want, but if you start losing money, I'll jerk the rug out from you." See, that's the way he'd talk to me.

"When he had a third or fourth person in the room, he could be very difficult to deal with. He did not lose very graciously, and when he lost he would let everybody know it . . . whereas a lot of my clientele—Bill Young, Bob and Beverly Lewis—you can't tell if they're winning or losing, they're so gracious. But when you were one-on-one with Gene in a room or on an airplane, you couldn't have a better friend.

"His health was bad. He would not let me discuss this in the press. Covered it up because he wanted to travel. It was not going to turn around with the report he got. Once we dispersed the horses, we kept a good relationship, but he called me on a Sunday night and said, 'So what are you doing?' and I said, 'I'm trying to figure out how to make a living.' So he said, '"What are you doing next Tuesday?'—which is the dark day of racing—and I said, 'Nothing too much,' and he said, 'Ride down to Del Mar and we'll go to Remington's. We'll have lunch.' That was his favorite spot. And so I said, 'Great, what have you got in mind?' He said, 'You know, I've been sitting here thinking about it. I might send you over to Keeneland and let you do it all over again just to show those bastards it isn't luck.' And that's the way he thought. That was on a Sunday night, and on a Monday morning at nine o'clock, Joyce, his wife, called me to say that he died in his sleep."

Without Klein, Lukas would have to go backward, and find the horses that he could make. He wouldn't have the checkbook he used to have. But what some of the press corps would not admit was that, more than anything, Lukas would miss Klein's blind faith and trust. Lukas needed a believer.

Calumet Goes Bust

Calumet Farm was one of the rock solid names in thoroughbred racing. No breeder or owner so dominated the racing landscape, especially in the years between 1940 and 1960. Having bred nine Kentucky Derby winners (a record) and nine Horse of the Year winners, Calumet's claim to fame was impossible to question.

Nestled in rolling hills outside of Lexington, Kentucky, in the heart of horse country, Calumet Farms was founded in 1924. It was established by William Monroe Wright, who made his fortune as owner of the Calumet Baking Powder Co. It was after he sold his company to General Foods, for $40 million, that he decided to create Calumet. He loved standardbred horses, so Calumet became popular on the trotter circuit. But upon his death in 1931, his son, Warren Wright, changed the direction of the farm's operations and began breeding thoroughbreds.

Calumet's first big star was Nellie Flag, who burst upon the American horse racing scene in 1934. She was a two-year-old prodigy. Her rise presaged several generations of superstar horses from the sheds and barns of Calumet, which has produced such stars as Whirlaway and Citation.

In addition to becoming a premier owner/breeder, Calumet also boasted a legendary trainer, Ben A. Jones. He would win a Triple Crown in 1941 with Whirlaway, and another in 1948 with Citation. The only other man to win two Triple Crowns was J. E. Fitzsimmons, with Gallant Fox and Omaha.

Long before Team Lukas decided to run its operation like a far-flung corporation, Calumet had racing divisions on the East and West coasts. Calumet would go on to produce top money winners and breed spectacular horses into the current era. However, a series of bad debts, bad decisions, and extravagant living by J. T. Lundy, a businessman who married into the Young family and was controlling the farm, had run Calumet into the ground by 1991.

"Calumet Farm, once the pride of Kentucky racing, mysteriously crumbled," wrote gossip columnist Suzy in an article entitled "Down on the Farm—Glory Takes a Powder." She gleefully and sarcastically reported, "It seems Calumet owes a staggering $118,050,732 to banks all over the country. . . . [Its collapse] has scared the riding britches off some of those Blue Grass 'hardboots.' "

As with many other well-known trainers, the connections between Lukas and Calumet ran deep. Through the sales at Saratoga, at Keeneland or from Fasig-Tipton, Lukas had bought many horses from Calumet. As a well-regarded horse trader, he was powerful enough to secure the rights to breeding seasons on some horses that he trained and stood at Calumet, or those he raced in the Calumet name.

Among Calumet's various debtors in secured and unsecured loans was First City Bank ($32.4 million), Mutual Benefit ($21.9 million), Midlantic ($2.6 million), First National Bank ($513,194), and Peter Brant and White Birch Farms ($4 million). Another small group was also owed money by Calumet: D. Wayne Lukas and company, for premier stud, Capote. Yes, the same Capote who couldn't finish the Kentucky Derby, but had been a two-year-old champion.

In 1987, a half interest in Capote's stud rights went to J. T. Lundy at Calumet for $6.4 million. The price was to be paid in stages over the course of five years. By the time Lundy had driven Calumet into oblivion, the farm still owed Lukas, Beal, French, and Klein $2,186,582. Lundy had by now been forced to sell the farm and the farm's name, and he and his remaining cohorts operated out of an office in downtown Lexington, using the name Phoenix Corporation.

Calumet filed for bankruptcy on July 11, 1991, and was sold off on March 19, 1992, at public auction. Henryk de Kwiatkowski, an avid horseman who had owned such famous horses as Belmont Stakes winners Conquistador Cielo and Danzig Connection, and the champion filly De La Rose, bought Calumet Farm, purchasing the land and name for $17 million.

Lukas had a range of business interests represented now by Phoenix Corporation. For breeding seasons to Alydar and Criminal Type, he was owed $2.6 million. He claimed they also owed both him and Jeff substantial money for Badger Land, which they had sold to Calumet. All were lost. Most hurtful was Capote. Lukas chose to sue for loss of property. Chief Judge Joe Lee, of the United States Bankruptcy Court, Eastern District of Kentucky, Lexington, ruled that Lukas et al. could have bought back their rights during the auction for the animal by matching the highest bidder. As a result, the judge dismissed the suit.

With other claims against Calumet falling by the wayside, it has been estimated that Lukas lost another $2.1 million. "Do you know many trainers who could take that big a hit and still keep going?" Lukas asked.

Downward Spiral

The Calumet situation and the failure of Mid-America added to the financial woes Lukas was facing. Combined with the loss of Klein, Lukas was rumored to be in serious debt. And the whisperers on the backstretch were wagging their tongues about his inability to make the payroll, pay his bills, and meet his financial obligations. He lost the jet, and now had to fly like anyone else. The limo was gone.

In 1991, Lukas bought the fewest yearlings since 1984. And in 1992 he bought even fewer, with an overall price tag of $3 million. He was reaching the bottom. His winnings were $15,942,223 in 1,497 starts despite his financial setbacks. But it would take him another four years to reach that plateau again.

The following year saw Lukas in the winner's circle with 230 wins but only $9,806,436. While this was a 39 percent dropoff, he was still the earnings leader. And in 1993 he wasn't even in the top five. Bobby Frankel would take the mantle of winning earnings trainer, with seventy-nine wins, and claim $8,933,252. It was the first time in eleven years that Lukas did not win the top spot. It was also the first time since 1984 that the money winner had finished a season below $9 million.

Grand Canyon was an example of the bad luck streak that Lukas had hit, to compound his sorrowful financial state. At the end of his two-year-old season, in 1989, the horse had already won $1 million. He had won the Hollywood Futurity in the fastest time ever recorded by a two-year-old. He also won the Norfolk at Santa Anita, and the Kentucky Jockey Club Stakes at Churchill Downs. It seemed that it was going to be a good year.

Grand Canyon had been bought by Lukas for $825,000 on behalf of William T. Young and his group of managers at Overbrook Farm. In light of the horse's success, it was thought that he would be the farm's next major stud. Grand Canyon was Lukas's shining star. To use a Lukaslike basketball analogy, he would be to Team Lukas what Larry Bird was to the Boston Celtics. Not only did he race for Team Lukas, but Lukas owned a 35 percent stake in the horse.

Heading into the Derby prep season, Grand Canyon was considered one of the top horses that year. However, he was nicked up after the Hollywood Futurity, on December 17, 1989. A bruise that occurred in that race subsided and then resurfaced two months later, after he had worked out seriously for the first time since that accident. In February 1990, Lukas issued a statement stating that the horse had suffered a "muscle pull or strain of the flexor muscles of the left knee." He was pulling Grand Canyon and resting him for four months. Thus, Grand Canyon would miss the Triple Crown series. It was national news.

"It was a tough decision to make," Lukas said. "A lot of horses have been ruined chasing the Triple Crown. I didn't want to be patching him together when we were told that if we give him enough time, he'll be a hundred percent." He also said that he would "look forward to a productive fall," possibly aiming the horse for the Breeders' Cup.

But it turned out that what was initally thought to be a pull was in fact laminitis, a disease involving the bone structure where the leg or ankle meets the hardened case of the hoof. The hard case becomes infected and soft, and the leg bones, because of the pressure of carrying the horse's weight, break down through the center to the bottom of the hoof.

There are many causes of laminitis, but it is not common, nor is it clear how it develops. However, there are several things trainers can do to prevent it. One is to monitor grazing of spring grasses, especially in horses that exercise a lot. Toxemia may develop as a result of any number of viruses. Excessive weight bearing—for example, when lame horses consistently put too much pressure on one foot— is another way in which horses can develop this problem. Trauma is another, an example of which is excessive exercise on hard ground. That sounds like a Lukas horse on a hard, fast California track. However, it has been noted that Lukas, while tough on his horses, is not as tough as others, and includes plenty of rest days.

The worst thing about laminitis is that the hoof disease is fatal. Grand Canyon had to be put down. Gone was Lukas's share of the winnings as both an owner and trainer. And also gone were the lifelong breeding rights to the colt. Hundred of thousands of dollars were gone in a moment's notice.

"We've taken some hits and had some bad luck," Lukas said before the end of 1993. "It isn't as if we just caved in. We're still number one."

But he must have known that the gravy train, if it hadn't died, was certainly derailed. Whether he was just saving face or in full-blown denial, Lukas was in trouble. Debts mounted, troubles persisted, and things were about to get worse—much worse.

To be sure, the rest of the horse racing industry was also suffering in the years between 1987 and 1991. In "Hard Times in the Bluegrass," a series in the *New York Times*, Joseph Durso wrote: "After a five-year economic free fall that has wiped out scores of horse farms and sent breeding fees plunging, many people in the thoroughbred industry say its best bet is to launch a national campaign to glorify and advertise the industry's ultimate product: the race horse." Durso went on to point out that other industries had moved in on the same customers who were attracted to racing—like East Coast gambling casinos, the ever growing number of lotteries, and new riverboat gambling operations. Of course, part of this was also a result of the laws that closed loopholes that favored owning horses in the first place.

"We no longer have a monopoly on the entertainment dollar or the gambling dollar," said John Gaines, a thoroughbred industry leader. There would now be a new emphasis on racing the horses. And one of the leaders of this new emphasis was D. Wayne Lukas. He told Durso: "It was like real estate. Guys didn't have the expertise for the long haul. It was an era when we went through plan A, which was racing horses, and then skipped plan B, which was racing horses, and went straight to plan C, which was breeding horses. The horse would have a couple of races and they'd say, 'Breed him.' That's why we need to get back to the racehorse in order to revive our whole system. High purses induce you to race your horse."

Lukas was still the best front man the horse world had had in many years. He kept on selling to Durso: "Actually, the horse economy is becoming strong again. In fact, now is probably the best time to get into horses. Horseflesh is cheaper than it's been in fifteen years and the purses are higher than ever. Look, the house of cards in the bloodstock market tumbled when racehorses couldn't go out on the track and win back the money they cost."

No one on the backstretch complained when Lukas sold horse racing to the public. Part carney barker, part businessman, he was hustling for the whole industry.

Union City

"Another California star and speedball," Joe Durso wrote about Union City in an article rating each of the equine hopefuls weeks before the Kentucky Derby. "He ran second to Devoted Brass in the San Rafael and second to Personal Hope in the Santa Anita Derby. In the money seven of nine times." The line had him 8–1. He was a competitive horse in a weak field.

"There is nothing mediocre about this year's Derby horses. They are a travesty," William Nack wrote. "They are so slow that the track kitchen at Churchill Downs will be offering, for its breakfast special, a six-minute egg."

Union City was owned by Overbrook Farm, which meant that he was William T. Young's horse. He was a beautiful horse that almost always finished in the money. There was the thought that he might make a good stud despite a less than stellar career.

Union City was big, strong, and feisty. And Lukas, as usual, was selling him on the backstretch at Churchill Downs. Inviting two well-known track journalists to his barn, he stopped in front of Union City's stall. "Just look at this colt!" he said, bursting with fatherly pride. "This horse is five-to-one in the pre-Derby betting. Let me tell you something: If the 135,000 people over there could be standing where you are right now, he'd be three-to-two."

With Pat Valenzuela riding, Union City came out of the gate well, and stalked the leaders through the turns, never wavering. In the final turn, the horse swung out wide and burst up the track, then suddenly faltered. "He disappeared as though the ground beneath him had opened up and swallowed him," wrote William Nack for *Sports Illustrated*. Sea Hero won, giving eighty-five-year-old owner Paul Mellon and seventy-one-year-old trainer MacKenzie Miller their first Kentucky Derby. Union City finished fifteenth. Lukas told both friends and reporters that he was puzzled. He was also disappointed. Despite Winning Colors, he had a record of twenty-one Derby starts, one win, one third, and that was it. It was one of the worst records in Kentucky Derby history.

The horse's disappearance in the race was made more mysterious in the weeks between the Derby and the Preakness. First, Union City had no workouts between the two races. That's unusual at the classic level of racing. What was also unusual was Lukas's low profile for a Triple Crown event. What was going on over at the Lukas barn? And finally, and perhaps most significant, Union City had twice been seen standing in ice water on the backstretch at Pimlico—a practice used to shrink the swelling that occurs in horses' legs, in an attempt to reduce inflammation due to injury.

None of this was mentioned in the press before the race. After all, this was D. Wayne Lukas, who was known for shutting out writers he was angry with, and Union City had proven to be a tough, competitive animal.

When the race began, Union City proved once again that he was game. He held with the pack through the first six furlongs. As the field came out of the turn and hit the stretch, Prairie Bayou was slightly behind Union City and was ready, like the horse in front of him, to make his move. Then jockey Mike Smith, aboard Prairie Bayou, noticed a falter in Union City's step and saw Valenzuela trying to pull up his colt. It was a scary moment, for not only could Smith blow the race right here, but a major and fatal accident might easily occur. He swung Prairie Bayou outside of Union City and avoided a major collision.

"I was lucky to get by him," Smith said after the race. "And Pat was great. When he knew what was happening with Union City, he yelled, 'Breakdown! Breakdown!' That helped me and the other riders a lot." Prairie Bayou went on to win the race. Sea Hero came in second. Unfortunately, that's not where the story ended.

Union City had taken a bad step. He had completely "shattered the sesamoid bones in his right front ankle, bobbled horribly and limped to a stop."

"Lukas's face turned absolutely white," Jenny Kellner of the *New York Post* later said. He and the veterinarian were quickly at the horse's side as the crowd both cheered Prairie Bayou in the winner's circle and looked on with concern while Union City was fitted with a temporary cast before being loaded into the track ambulance. When the horse was in the ambulance, veterinarian Robert Copeland realized that the fractured leg was irreparably damaged and the horse would have to be destroyed by lethal injection.

"We never took him off the ambulance," Lukas later told reporters. He was shaken, his face ashen and his eyes red and watery.

While being closely questioned on the backstretch long after the race, Lukas snapped, "Nobody is exempt from something like this. It's happened to Mack Miller, it's happened to Charlie Whittingham, it's happened to everybody." When asked if the horse might not have been in questionable condition, he replied, "That's ridiculous! I try to be honest with you people, and I am now. I do my job. I get up every morning at three. . . . That's more than I can say for the ＊＊＊＊ who are second-guessing me."

Later, William Nack asked Lukas about the icing, which now seemed suspicious in light of the horse's demise. "That's so much ＊＊＊＊. The horse was physically fine. Periodically we ice horses. What we did was cool him down in ice water bandages each day. It is a common practice." Nack admitted that while some trainers use this method as a way to cure soreness or inflammation, Lukas was indeed right, it was also a restorative measure.

The press came after Lukas, criticizing him for his ambition, saying it blinded him when it came to the horse's obvious injuries and caused him to put the health of the stables over the health of the horses. Some writers, aware of Lukas's money troubles, wondered if he'd pressed the horse in a nervous quest for more money. Writers across the country began to enumerate the horses that had in one way or another broken down on Lukas over a fifteen-year career. Preeminent Kentucky veterinarian Alex Harthill scoffed when asked if he thought Lukas ran his horses too hard or raced unsound horses. "That's a lot of jealous talk." He also pointed out that he did not visit Lukas's barns any more than he did the others.

In his defense, as Nack pointed out in his article, there was nothing new about horses racing with injuries, and in fact some of the biggest races in America had been won by ailing horses. Others said later that if Union City were as badly hurt as some had claimed, then everyone in Lukas's barn, and the jockey, were also complicit in the horse's death. It would seem hard to believe that so great a conspiracy would stay silent for so long.

"That strengthened my character, and it strengthened my relationship with Bill Young," Lukas says today. He pointed out that on the Tuesday before the race, Union City "had a complete ear-to-tail physical by a world-renowned veterinarian, Dr. Bob Copeland . . . [and] Dr. Copeland stood right next to me at the press conference [afterward] and told everyone who would listen, and at no time did it get in print. That would have killed the sensational story. So I mean, we took a lot of heat. The thing that came out of that is you never saw Bill Young waver one iota. He stood next to me and took it all with me. Because he knew too, in his heart. That was an unfortunate thing. It happened on national television. But had we not had the backup of that complete physical on a Tuesday—we got there on a Wednesday, we galloped on a Thursday, jogged on a Friday, and ran. And Copeland was there. . . . He put the horse down and took the press conference with me. It hit the papers the next day."

Pete Axthelm once commented about Lukas: "He's the guy you love to hate, the type of guy who did all his high school homework and wouldn't let you copy it. With his perfect teeth, coiffed hair and meticulous wardrobe, he would always get the beauty queen that you wished you could ask to the senior prom." Lukas could be tough on writers and other nonhorse folks, and now, with blood on the trail, the hounds were howling with delight, the hunter was wounded and encircled. Payback is a bitch.

It was so bad that William T. Young, the man in charge of Overbrook and the owner of Union City, was so moved by the depression enveloping Lukas that he told the *Daily Racing Form*: "The decision to run in the Preakness was mine, not Wayne Lukas's. This decision was made after consultation with my staff, independent veterinarians, and, of course, Wayne Lukas. I don't fully understand the controversy surrounding this tragic loss, as we would never intentionally run an unsound horse." While Lukas could antagonize people without even meaning to, Young was respected, especially in thoroughbred horse country. His words weighed heavily. Even if some grumbling still existed, the hunt had been called off.

The Intervention

Disturbed by the viciousness of the attacks, Lukas hit rock bottom in the place where it seemed he'd been least vulnerable: his confidence. Rocked by the lambasting he'd taken in the press, and thunderstruck by what he perceived as the malice of the press, Lukas had taken to avoiding reporters and looking to go unrecognized. That was a signal to his friends.

The world of D. Wayne Lukas had been turned completely upside down. Once awash in money, horses, rich owners, and success, the 1990s had been a bit of a bust for D. Wayne Lukas. A combination of his money troubles and his losing way in major stakes races, as well as losing the earnings title after so many years, devastated him.

While a few horseman had rallied around him, they were drowned out by the vast number of doomsayers. So great was the worry among his closest friends and his son Jeff that they gathered in Jeff's Glendora living room on May 24, 1993, to intevene with D. Wayne in his hour of need. Phone calls were made, and important horse people, all across the country, dropped everything they were doing and flew on a moment's notice to confront and comfort the man who had changed racing.

Assembled were R. T. Williams, a close friend; Clyde Rice; Jeff Lukas; former assistant Kiaran McLaughlin; Paul Paternostro and Lee Eaton, two independent Kentucky bloodstock agents; Bob French, his long time owner/friend; and several others. All of them had dropped what they were doing in order to attend this impromptu "crisis intervention," as William Nack later called it in his shocking *Sports Illustrated* story, "Man on a Hot Seat." The piece recounted the many Lukas misfortunes, and created a stir in the horse community. It explained the sad truth behind Mid-America Racing, Calumet, and the intervention, all of which Lukas found humiliating, and frustrating to his ongoing business.

"Most of that was very inaccurate. I'll tell you exactly what happened there," Lukas says now of Nack's article. "He went on a witch hunt. He was trying to find a guy that had had this great run and then he was going to write this article that would dispel all this. . . . I'm not positive, but [I think] they hired a private investigator to look into the financial strength behind everything. And he interviewed a lot of people. He interviewed the deed companies. He interviewed the tack shops. He got a dead end every time. So what happened was, when he wrote the article he couldn't go where I know he wanted to go. I know he went to Kiaran McLaughlin, for example, and said, 'Kiaran, they tell me he didn't meet his payroll.' And Kiaran said, 'That is not true! He has never missed a payroll.' He tried to build this predetermined notion of where he wanted to go with the article but ended up writing an entirely different kind of article."

The investigator was legendary *Sports Illustrated* investigative reporter Lester Munson, whom Nack refers to as a "reformed lawyer." Munson's legal background gives him insights on investigative techniques not usually a part of a news reporter's training. Munson was surprised by Lukas's reaction to the piece. "I have always been surprised he did not thank us for the inspirational dimension we added to his public persona." Munson thought Nack had taken the high road in the article, insisting that Nack, in deference to Lukas and his career accomplishments, refused to use "more unsavory details of the Mid-America disaster."

"He is wrong on all counts," Munson states. "We did not start out with any predetermined agenda." Munson cited court documents, SEC filings, and other litigation papers as the source for his findings. "In addition to these public documents, we conducted telephone interviews of numerous individuals whose names were discovered in the public documents. It was nothing more than the normal reporting anyone does while working on a story with financial issues." Citing the 1988 SEC 10-K filing claiming that Lukas was chairman of the board and chief executive officer, Munson says, "It provides an interesting contrast to Lukas's claim that he was a passive participant in Mid-America."

"The consummate self-promoter, no doubt the greatest carnival barker ever to saddle a racehorse in any era of the sport, Lukas always perceived the proper role of the press as that of a cheerleader for his program," responds Nack, "and he saw as an enemy all those who did not cheer him on—or who had the temerity to condemn, criticize, or even question his operation and his practices in running it. . . . Lukas loved and embraced members of the press who sucked up to him, who never printed a disparaging word, while he chilled and blew off those who questioned his methods or wrote anything that cast him in an unfavorable light. Over the last twenty-two years, since he won the Preakness with Codex in 1980, I think I have probably been in an out of his doghouse more times than any turfwriter on the planet, and whether I was in or out depended entirely on how he perceived the last thing I had written about him. When I wrote 'Man on a Hot Seat,' I was out for several years. For him to say that I was on a 'witch-hunt,' a word that suggests a witless persecution of him, is perfectly laughable when the story is viewed in retrospect. I was simply a reporter responding to numerous racetrack rumors that he was in desperate financial straits caused, in part, by his misadventures with the collapsing Calumet Farm. The fact is that Lukas, at the time, was the leading horse trainer in America—the sport's most visible and voluble spokesman—and word that he was in trouble financially made him the natural subject of a story. So I went to California to find how much of this was true. Such activity may surprise and even offend him, but going after stories is what reporters do.

"Of course, when I learned about the 'intervention' the next day, the whole story shifted in that direction. Here were all these people showing up—Lee Eaton and Paul Paternostro from Kentucky, Bob French from Texas—and expressing their affection for him and telling him that he had to reorganize his finances. Paternostro told me that Lukas was urged to file for bankruptcy. Much to Lukas's credit, he refused to go that route. This intervention was a sudden and extraordinary turn of events, and in response I felt compelled to write about it, and so the story, dealing with what had taken place in Jeff's Glendora living room, evolved into a relatively tame response to his travails at the time. Despite what he says, by the way, there was not a single inaccuracy in the *SI* story—I defy him to cite one—and his statement that the story was filled with inaccuracies is as utterly bogus as his claim that I was out to get him."

While Nack did hammer Lukas and laid out Lukas's business misfortunes, he also took pity on the wounded horseman, in displaying how human he had become. The intervention was Nack's sympathetic portrait of Lukas's underbelly. Of course, a man as proud as Lukas doesn't want anyone to see those low moments. Lukas considers showing any signs of weakness as a character flaw.

The night before the intervention, in a Holiday Inn in Monrovia, this group of friends and supporters gathered to discuss what could they do for Lukas. Many knew that he was strapped by debt, which worried and distracted him, and caused him to forget what he was good at—training horses. While Lukas had always been a good, fast-talking horseman, he was never a financial guru. It was decided to convince him to turn over his finances to someone more experienced, and to get back to handling horses.

The next morning, Lukas was strong-armed by childhood friend Clyde Rice out of his Santa Anita barns, under the pretense of Rice wanting to see Jeff's new house. They arrived at Jeff's at nine-thirty, and when Lukas entered, he was shocked to see ten people who were important to him, standing in the room. "What are you doing here?" he asked.

Nack wrote: "French came forward and put his arms around him. 'Wayne, we love you,' said French. 'We're here to support you.' Darrell Wayne Lukas broke down and wept."

What began at nine-thirty A.M. ended at four-thirty P.M. Among the topics discussed with Lukas were his finances, his relations with writers and the media in general, and his relations with friends. It began with each man standing up and telling anecdotes about why Lukas was so important in their lives and why they were there for him now. And as Nack wrote, Lukas did indeed break down. He told the story of his life and how he'd gotten to his current troubles.

"It became an open forum," Lukas said. "They pointed out things I had done wrong." They pressed him, insisting that he pay more attention to his horse training and owners and less to his finances. He resisted vehemently. But his friends prevailed upon him. Eventually Lukas relented, and agreed to turn his financial matters over to a professional, with the understanding that all his bills and debts would be paid in full. Many could see the difference in Lukas the next day. He was no longer withdrawn, and was able to laugh for the first time in a long time. He seemed amused by his friends' efforts to save him from his own free fall.

"It was a very touchy time for us, for him," says Shari Lukas. "There was a lot of private pain. That's the very Mark Twainish thing about Wayne."

"I first met Wayne Lukas at a quarter horse sale almost twenty years ago," Paul Paternostro said. "Over a long weekend, he sold me on the idea of moving my family down to Lexington in order to devote full time to the thoroughbred horse business. Wayne has always been there for me as a constant source of enthusiasm, encouragement, and guidance." Lukas, amazed at the intervention, said to Nack: "Why does someone like Lee Eaton drop everything, leave his family on vacation, and fly out here on his expense to tell me that he loves me? I don't know if a guy deserves that. . . . I wasn't prepared for that outpouring of support. It was a beautiful thing."

Jeff and Tabasco Cat

Tabasco Cat was bred by Storm Cat out of Barbicue Sauce (by Sauce Boat). Foaled April 28, 1991, he was owned by Overbrook Farm, Storm Cat being their best stud. His lineage included Northern Dancer, Secretariat, Terlingua, and Bold Ruler. He was a feisty colt.

Tabasco Cat had won the Fort Springs Stakes as a two-year-old, and he became a leading contender for the Kentucky Derby with his third place finish in the 1993 Breeders' Cup Juvenile. He was without question the one horse Team Lukas was hoping would bring back some hardware in the 1994 racing calendar.

On December 15, 1993, stable hands were taking off the horse's bridle at the barns at Santa Anita. It was not yet nine o'clock. Tabasco Cat had finished his morning gallop, and the exercise rider had dismounted. He was about to be walked and cooled off, and then hooked to the wash harness, when he swung his head away and reared up.

Lukas noticed a commotion at the far end of the barn. "I heard people yelling that a horse was loose. I was on the phone in my office, and I leaned forward to look out and I saw Jeff." Tabasco Cat had bolted and was running toward the far end of the barn. Lukas saw his son waving his arms at the runaway horse, stepping in front of him. This is not an unusual maneuver, as many horsemen will do it to slow the horse down or make him swerve, which would also slow him down. "Usually they'll swerve or put on the brakes," Bill Smith, a fellow trainer at Santa Anita, said. "But this one just kept coming and ran right through him."

Jeff was fifty to seventy yards from the animal when it bolted toward him. At the last second, when he realized that the horse would not slow down, he moved. Unfortunately, his maneuver to slow the horse had worked—in an effort to avoid him, Tabasco Cat changed course and moved to the same side Jeff had.

"It was like two people in a hallway, awkwardly trying to avoid one another," Wayne said. The 1,100-pound colt thundered straight into his son. "Jeff went straight up into the air and upside down. When he hit, he landed on his head, and the sound was like a gunshot."

"Tabasco Cat crashed into Jeff Lukas with a sickening thud that was heard several barns away," wrote West Coast turf writer Jay Privman, whose piece on the story was carried nationally. "Jeff was flipped backward and hit the ground at the point where the base of his skull meets his neck."

"Call 911!" Lukas shouted, running to the far end of the barn.

"I could hear it and ran over right away," said Jerry Fanning, a fellow trainer, whose barn was near Lukas's. "I rushed over and could see it was bad. He was out cold. There was a girl standing over him and she said she couldn't get a pulse. That was scary." It was Fanning who called 911.

"Jeff's head was bloody, his eyes were dazed, and he lay stone still," Jay Hovdey wrote in *Reader's Digest* a year later.

Firemen arrived on the scene first. They called for immediate backup of paramedics from Los Angeles County. They called for a helicopter, which landed in the north parking lot of the Santa Anita racetrack. They would fly Jeff to Huntington Memorial Hospital in Pasadena, which was considered one of the best head trauma hospitals in California. Jeff was comatose when he was examined by neurosurgeon William Canton. He had to be put on life support systems. The news was not good. The most critical time in a head injury crisis is within the first twenty-four hours. He had multiple fractures at the base of the skull. His brain was swollen, filling up with fluids and causing intercranial pressure, called ICP, which was increasing. It was the first thing that had to be dealt with.

The procedure was to drill a hole in Jeff's skull to relieve the pressure, and insert a shunt. The second day of the ordeal seemed worse. Now in attendance in the room with Wayne were his wife Shari, Jeff's wife Linda, and Jeff's mom and Wayne's first wife, now remarried, Janet Blank. Despite the shunt, his ICP increased, and Dr. Canton prepared the family for the worst. "If there is a minister you want to call, now is probably the time," a nurse told the grieving family. Jeff was thirty-six years old, with a wife and two small children—Kelly, who was ten months old, and Brady, who was three.

He then developed pneumonia, and a tracheotomy was performed as a means of helping to reduce the fluids now building up in his lungs. He was listed in critical condition. The story was being followed nationally. Updates appeared regularly in many newspapers. On December 18, 1993, the Associated Press announced that while Jeff had been downgraded to "serious" on December 16, on the following day he was graded up to "very critical."

The family gathered each day, keeping watch over Jeff. At one point a nurse said to Wayne, "Talk to him, Mr. Lukas. We really don't know if he can hear or not. But your voice might trigger some response." During Wayne's watches, he would read the sports pages to Jeff, especially following Indiana basketball, Wisconsin football, and the Rose Bowl. "I read to him, anything I thought he would be interested in. Indiana winning a game, anything about racing. . . ." When the Rose Bowl was on, Lukas watched it from Jeff's room, speaking to him from time to time and looking, searching, for some sign of movement or recognition. There was none, and Wayne grew despondent. "It was like talking to a pile of saddles."

"Wayne and Janet didn't talk much during it all," says Shari. "But I have two boys, and I would look at Jeff and feel the emotion.

Darrell Wayne Lukas,
spring 1936.

The young Wayne Lukas with friend
Lois McPhail—a snappy dresser even
at age five.

D. Wayne in first grade.

Second-grader D. Wayne standing in front of the trailer in which he and his brother, sister, mother, and father all lived as they moved around the country following construction jobs.

Going to school in a one-room schoolhouse. Dauna (eighth grade) is wearing a dark blouse and is nearest the front blackboard; Lowell (fourth grade) is just to the left of the teacher in a light striped shirt; Wayne (sixth grade) is wearing a striped sweater and white shirt and is seated in front of the teacher.

Wayne's parents' fiftieth wedding anniversary. From left to right: Bea, his mother; Wayne; Dauna; Ted, his father, whom he adored; and Lowell.

Wayne petitioning a future alumnus while running for student government at the University of Wisconsin at La Crosse.

Striped clothes were very much the fashion at the traditional "prison party" of Kappa Sigma fraternity. The Kappa Sig pledges entertained the pledges of Alpha Chi Omega sorority.

Janet Pope, St. Louis, Mo., and Wayne Lucas, Antigo, are shown above "pounding rocks" at the party.

While at college, Lukas met and wooed pretty young coed Janet Pope. A St. Louis native, Janet fell for the aspiring coach. Here Lukas, a Kappa Sig pledge, and Janet pound rocks at a Kappa Sig theme party.

Lukas in the early quarter-horse years. A trainer with a shirt and tie made an impression as a successful trainer, despite some up and down years. As Baffert pointed out, it was always a show when Wayne came to town.

Wayne accepts a gold watch, one of his many awards, at Los Alamitos in the 1970s.

TRICK RIDING STUNTS will be among the features of the horse show presented at the Dane County Junior Fair Saturday at 2 p.m. by the Madison Saddle Club. Here some fancy riding is shown by Wayne Lucas, 124 Langdon St., a former University student from Antigo.

As a college student, Lukas often made extra money doing trick riding at county fairs and other venues. This newspaper publicity shot is from 1958.

This is an ad from the late 1950s featuring Wayne as a trick rider.

One of the most famous shingles ever hung out on the backstretch, along with his customary flowers. (COURTESY OF C. DEVITO)

Lukas, the struggling high school basketball coach and proud papa, with four-month-old son, Jeff.

Like father, like son: Jeff learns to ride on the steady and sure back of family favorite Queenie, whom Wayne owned until her death at age twenty-eight.

Arguably the most successful father-son thoroughbred horse trainers since the Joneses: Wayne and Jeff in the beginning of their run, at the 1981 Belmont. Lukas says today, "He's the best horse trainer not in the Hall of Fame."

While Grandpa Lukas admits he's not quite the family man, here he spends time with newborn grandson Brady, Jeff's first child.

Jeff, at the height of his abilities, with Brady on the backstretch in the early 1990s, before the accident.

Wayne Lukas and Laura Pinelli, an unlikely couple, share a passion for training horses. Many feel she has calmed him down, but the competitive fires rage strongly in both of them. (COURTESY OF THE *LOUISVILLE COURIER-JOURNAL*)

Charismatic and Chris Antley cross the finish line to win the 125th Kentucky Derby. The media's questionable story line coupling the troubled jockey and the courageous horse stuck in the Hall-of-Famer's craw, later erupting into a flood of bad publicity for Lukas. (COPYRIGHT © KINETIC CORP./CHURCHILL DOWNS, INC.)

I think we bonded over it. We talked on the phone. I would keep Janet updated. She's terrific."

Lukas received many calls, including expressions of concern from former President Gerald Ford and college basketball coaches Bobby Knight and Denny Crum. And every day, Linda, Janet, and Wayne took their turns watching Jeff lying there motionless.

Lukas went back to the stables each morning to oversee his continuing operations. He was being aided in his hour of need by Randy Bradshaw, his former assistant who now headed up his own successful stable. "Jeff is very important to his father," Bradshaw told reporter Jay Privman. "He ran their stakes program and their New York program all at the same time. And absolutely, he was second in command." He noted: "This has always been a very optimistic stable. That's the way Wayne is. He's a real optimist, always thinks things are going to be okay. He's been able to keep his mood upbeat."

That wasn't always easy. One time, Jeff's son Brady was talking to Wayne while Wayne was on his vigil at the hospital. He'd been filling Linda in on what was going on, and when she passed the phone to Brady, Brady said to Wayne, "Grandpa, wake up Daddy. I want to speak to him."

"I know you do. I wish I could. I wish I could," Wayne responded.

Christmas 1993 was a solemn event. The family was being drained of its energy. Now, in the same living room where Jeff had comforted his father, the family sat and hoped to hear of Jeff's recovery. Linda admitted later that hoping just for Jeff's survival would be good enough.

"Jeff's accident was the lowest point in Wayne's life, I think," his sister Dauna says today. "For the first time, the horses didn't come first. . . ."

On Christmas afternoon, when Linda was visiting the hospital, she tearfully recounted Christmas morning for Jeff, and then began reminiscing about their time together. Out of the corner of her eye she noticed something. Had Jeff's eyelids moved? Was he waking? She began to hug him and cry. No. While eye movement was a good sign, he didn't wake up. The long holiday season dragged on for the Lukas family.

Each morning, Lukas still saddled up his pony and sat on a corner of the backstretch, watching his horses being put through their morning paces. He was withdrawn, however, and sat hunched in his horse. He was irritable and sad. One morning he saw Tabasco Cat racing down the track, and he had mixed feelings. In fact, the rest of the stable viewed the young, high-strung colt as a rogue animal. But Lukas knew, and admitted later, "You can't hate this animal for what happened. If you do you'll never survive it."

It did take some time, however, for Lukas to separate the bolting monster who had ruined his son's life from the animal who sat in the stall, and who had once been his most promising star. He gathered the staff in his barn and had a long talk with his people. "We're not going to penalize this horse," he said. "It's our job to get rid of the albatross around his neck and try and turn a negative into a positive."

Lukas took over the training of the animal personally. He decided the only way to save himself and this horse, and to pay tribute to his son, was to help this horse achieve the potential for greatness that he believed the horse possessed. To take the edge off the horse, he wanted to get him out of his stall. Lukas recommended more "play time" for Tabasco Cat. He was put into a corral filled with sand, and encouraged to wear himself out playing in this romper room ring for horses. Lukas let the horse hang out in the sunlight as much as possible and graze to his heart's content.

Meanwhile, Jeff's ICP leveled off to more acceptable levels and he was gradually taken off certain medications and life support systems. His status was improving inch by inch. Slowly, there were signs that Jeff might be pulling out of his comatose state. First, it was a flinch when a nurse came to shave him with an electric razor. Another time, he squeezed someone's hand. And finally, he whispered his first word: "Linda."

On January 10, 1994, the Associated Press ran a small news item that said Jeff was now officially out of his coma and was moved from the surgical intensive care unit to a private room. He was listed in serious but stable condition.

Jeff would undergo a long and painful recuperative process. He was unable to walk without help in the beginning, had short-term memory lapses, and suffered vision loss in one eye.

In January 1994, Tabasco Cat made his first appearance on the track since the incident. He was entered in the El Camino Real Derby at Bay Meadows. He was not the favorite. As the horses came out of the turn into the backstretch, Tabasco Cat was not far behind the leaders, Delineator and Fittobetied. Both Tabasco Cat and Flying Sensation began to make their moves. Flying Sensation was out in front by more than a nose, but Tabasco Cat refused to back down and won by a neck, taking home the $300,000 prize and becoming a Derby contender.

"Maybe this horse will redeem himself, if there is some redemption, in coming back and doing a good job all spring," Lukas said. "We're trying not to penalize this horse for an accident that was very unfortunate."

"This one's for you, Jeff," said Pat Day, who had ridden Tabasco Cat for Day's 5,999th win that day. "Jeff has been at the top of my prayer list since the accident. My heart goes out to him," Day told reporters.

Jeff was moved from Huntington Memorial to Casa Colina Center for Rehabilitation in Pomona in February. He worked eight hours a day in rehabilitation. It was hard, grueling, sweating work. He was now ten minutes from his home in Glendora. And then, on February 22, he went home for the first time—for his daughter's first birthday. Afterward, he spent more time at home, and by April Jeff was ready to go back to the track.

When Linda asked Dr. Canton if Jeff would face major anxiety about this decision—as she certainly was—he told her that Jeff had no memory of the Tabasco Cat incident and had little fear. It was as if he'd been asleep for a long time.

Jeff insisted on going to the Santa Anita Derby on April 9, wanting to see the horse who almost killed him win. "He really wanted to come," Linda told Privman at the track. However, Jeff was uncomfortable around large crowds. "One problem with patients with head injuries is that loud noises, being in a crowd, is difficult." The noise, she said, would be like "banging on a bruise. That's how it feels inside his head."

So Jeff was placed in a tiny cottage, which was among a small band of trees out on the infield, by the turn for the homestretch. He would be able to see the horses warming up, and watch them bolt for the finish line later. Smartly dressed in a suit, shirt, and tie, Jeff watched from the cottage and saw the finish on a closed-circuit television.

With some jostling at the start, Tabasco Cat moved into second early in the race, and kept that spot as the horses made their way around the oval. He was chasing Flyin' J. Bryan, and Brocco—the horse of film producer Albert "Cubby" Broccoli, the man who gave the world the celluloid James Bond—and Strodes Creek were behind him. In the turn for home, all the stalkers turned up the heat, and Flyin' J. Bryan started to fade. Tabasco Cat was now out in front, with Brocco and Strodes Creek in hot pursuit. It then became a two horse race, with Tabasco Cat and Brocco pulling away from the rest of the field. Brocco then began to slowly drawl away. He won by three-quarters of a length. But Tabasco Cat's performance had assured the horse a shot at the Derby.

Watching the race whetted Jeff's desire to return to work. "He's so focused, so determined, so driven," Linda said at the time. "He wants to come back to work so bad. Jeff, before the injury, was very driven, and that helps a lot," she added, referring to his recuperative powers. "He made me go buy him a *Racing Form* last night."

The Kentucky Derby that year featured a number of qualified horses, including Holy Bull and Go for Gin. With the situation over Union City the year before, and now Jeff's recent accident, this would be a year that many track followers were expecting to see the last twinges of the Lukas empire, before it collapsed completely.

Lukas wanted the Derby badly, for numerous reasons. To vindicate him from Union City's utter collapse the previous year, to make up for Jeff's injuries, to show everyone that Team Lukas was not finished. A competitive person, he wanted to show everyone that he was not done. But his Derby record had always been disappointing, at best.

And Tabasco Cat, though game, wasn't the biggest name in the field. When Lukas saddled the horse, he was thinking of Jeff.

On a muddy track, Go for Gin took the lead, and Tabasco Cat followed the leaders from a safe distance. But Tabasco Cat didn't seem to make up any ground on them, and he faded as the pack surged ahead. With Pat Day up, Tabasco Cat finished a disappointing sixth. Go for Gin won.

"I might have wanted that one too much, just to put things back together," Lukas said after the race. But Tabasco Cat was still going to Baltimore. While Lukas and thousands of others would be there, Jeff and Linda would be home in Glendora, watching the race on television. Jeff would scour the screen with his one good eye.

In the Preakness, contested by ten horses in 1994, Go for Gin jumped to an early lead on a dry, fast track. He was followed by Polar Expedition and Silver Goblin. Tabasco Cat sat behind this group as they raced round the oval. This was the same strategy they had used in the Derby, but the horse had not been able to make up the ground on the muddy surface. Here, the ground would hold. At the far turn, Tabasco Cat showed no signs of weakness.

Pat Day then let loose the reins, and felt the horse immediately burst underneath him. As Polar Expedition started to fold up, Tabasco Cat sidestepped him and used the hole the fading horse created in the sheer wall of horseflesh separating Tabasco Cat from the finish line. Day burst through. Then Tabasco Cat was at Go for Gin's hip, his shoulder, his neck, and then the two horses were even as they fought on. Jeff whispered, "C'mon, Cat!"

Indeed, Tabasco Cat caught Go for Gin and passed him to take the Preakness. Minutes after the win, a tearful Wayne Lukas could hardly speak, which says volumes about his emotions at that one moment. "No matter how you look at it," he said, "this race belongs to Jeff." The story was a national sensation.

Later, Richard E. Glover Jr. would write for *Handicapper's Daily*: "While most people would have wanted nothing to do with a horse who had nearly killed their son, Lukas decided to take the hot blooded son of Storm Cat on as a project and turn him into something special as a tribute to Jeff. The results were amazing."

The Belmont would be a repeat of the Preakness, with Tabasco Cat taking the prize again. While Jeff would never regain his former stature within the organization, he would eventually take on administrative duties with his father. "He used to talk about going out on his own," his father said wistfully, "but he doesn't now."

The fact that Jeff Lukas is even alive is testament to his will and drive. His doctors were amazed by his sheer determination and desire. "I've been involved in hundreds of head trauma cases," Dr. Canton told writer Jeff Hovdey. "Jeff's recovery to this point is a miracle. He is at the absolute top of the class."

Jeff and Linda eventually divorced, and Jeff moved into a guest cottage on Wayne's property.

"When Jeff was hurt, the doctors called us in and I think the statistic was eighty-seven percent of these cases end up in divorce," Lukas says now. "Usually the woman leaves. And they said you should think about that, prepare for that, be involved with that. So it was no surprise that a year or so afterward that started to happen. At the time it's easy to be critical, but in light of that, Linda, his wife, has been a *great* mother, and I am not critical of that decision and I look very well on it. She has done a great job with Jeff's two children."

The fact was, Team Lukas was back. And to put emphasis on it, Tabasco Cat would go on to take second in the Breeders' Cup Classic, finishing behind Kentucky Derby show horse Concern.

At the end of 1994, Team Lukas would regain some of its luster, once more finishing on top of all other trainers, with 147 wins in 693 starts and total earnings of $9,247,457. And to top off the story, D. Wayne Lukas would be voted the Eclipse Trainer of the Year.

Tabasco Cat would go on to win $2,347,671, and take eight wins, three seconds and two shows in eighteen races. He was retired to stud in 1996 and would sire four stakes winners as well as other successful horses, establishing himself as one of the leading American sires. On October 18, 2000, Tabasco Cat was sold for $7 million to the Japan Bloodstock Breeder's Association, to stand at JBBA's Shizunai Stallion Station.

EIGHT

COMEBACK

Another Suspension

As the 1995 three-year-old prep season was about to begin, bad news shocked Team Lukas once again. On February 24 the New York State Racing and Wagering Board issued a sixty-day ban on Lukas, and the news was immediately picked up by every major newspaper in America. The problem had been brewing since September of the previous year.

In 1994, Lukas had trained two juvenile champions, Timber Country (who was already a Kentucky Derby favorite) and Flanders (a filly that had won all five of her races). Foaled in 1992, Flanders, bred and raced by Overbrook Farm, was by Seeking the Gold out of Starlet Storm (by Storm Bird). In 1994 she won the Spinaway Stakes and the Frizette. She'd also won the Matron Stakes at Belmont, with a purse of $120,000. At that point it was assumed that the highly prized filly would go on to become an exceptional brood mare.

Finishing in the money guarantees that a horse will be tested for evidence of any drug in the bloodstream. Flanders was tested after the Matron Stakes, and the checkup showed the presence of isoxsuprine, a drug that improves the circulation of the blood, especially in the legs. However, it is not considered by any racing board to improve performance. New York State law, however, prohibits the use of any drug on the days that a horse actually races.

The New York State Racing and Wagering Board had disqualified Flanders from the race and withdrawn the purse money she'd won. Lukas immediately appealed the findings. He also denied that the horse was given anything. He had the same samples sent to Ohio State University for a second opinion. Ohio State could not find any traces of the drug in those samples, but another test did find traces, and, as a result, in November Lukas admitted to the presence of isoxsuprine.

Caught up in all of this was William T. Young, the gentleman breeder who owned Flanders. Young was not about to let the New York State Racing and Wagering Board hunt down Lukas and tarnish his prize filly's reputation at the same time. If Lukas were found guilty, it could mean millions of dollars of breeding rights washed down the drain. Now the racing board was not only contending with an angry Lukas, they also had the much craftier, well-liked, and powerful Young to deal with.

The board insisted it had two tests confirming the presence of the drug, and in February announced that they would suspend Lukas for sixty days.

Turf writer Joseph Durso called Lukas at home to ask for a comment on the charges. Lukas hadn't yet seen them but replied, "I've got a good attorney and all the material is going to him. I'm busy trying to get a horse ready for the Kentucky Derby."

When pressed about the use of the drug and its presence in the horse's bloodstream, Lukas said there were "gray areas in this type of case. With the therapeutic levels we're dealing with, we've got a bit of a problem with our game." The question that immediately popped into everyone's minds was whether Lukas would be allowed to compete in the Kentucky Derby.

"We're not trying to knock him out of the Kentucky Derby or anything like that," Robert Feuerstein, counsel to the New York State Racing and Wagering Board, said. "It's just that we didn't get everything we had hoped for from the laboratory at Ohio State."

When the New York board suspended him, Lukas stayed mum on the subject. There was speculation that Jeff might be pressed back into service, now that he was working with his father again. Then, on March 2, 1995, Lukas appealed.

Robert Feuerstein responded for the racing board, stating that the review hearing would take place sometime after May 6, the date of the Kentucky Derby. "There may be numerous witnesses. It's reasonable to assume we'd go past the Derby."

The story, however, would not die, as Lukas and Overbrook Farm, which joined the battle later, skirmished with the New York State board. In fact, the case would not be settled for almost five years.

Since the Matron Stakes, Flanders had won her fifth race, taking the Breeders' Cup Juvenile Fillies event on November 5, 1994. She nosed out stablemate and fellow star, Serena's Song, was sampled and tested clean. However, Flanders had injured herself during the race, fracturing her cannon and sesamoid bones. She required immediate surgery, and was subsequently forced into retirement.

On December 16, 1999, the New York State Racing and Wagering Board announced that it had reached a settlement in the case of Flanders, Lukas, and Overbrook Farm. The machinations during the case had been endless, and the results showed it.

There were clarifications and careful wordings. As the *Lexington Herald-Leader* put it, Flanders had been disqualified after "a trace of the therapeutic substance isoxsuprine was detected in the filly's urine. A subsequent test produced a negative result, and another test found that the amount of the substance discovered was below the threshold limit for virtually every other racing jurisdiction."

In accordance with the settlement, the sixty-day suspension was withdrawn. However, Lukas was fined $500. And the disqualification would stand—but with a qualification. The board had found that the concentration found in the horse's bloodstream was small enough— sixty nanograms per milliliter—"that it is improbable that it had any effect on the performance of Flanders during the Matron Stakes."

"The money was never the issue," Lukas said, regarding the legal language obviously aimed at Overbrook. "With Overbrook, it was the principle."

Lukas's treatment in the media was mixed. Many papers ran head-lines like "FLANDERS CASE SETTLED" (*Lexington Herald-Leader*) or "FLANDERS DISQUALIFICATION UPHELD AFTER FIVE YEARS" (*Thoroughbred Times*), but some were less kind, like the *New York Post*, which had a headline that screamed, "LUKAS IS FINED FINALLY." *Post* sportswriter Bill Finley fired off the following lead: "Five years and three months after the fact, the New York State Racing and Wagering Board finally got around to punishing Wayne Lukas." He also wagged, "Treating Lukas, owner William T. Young, and the filly with kid gloves, the NYSRWB was sensitive to pressure from Young, who wanted her undefeated record restored." He noted that the $500 fine, if spread out across the entire length of time since the infraction, cost Lukas twenty-six cents a day.

The decision had taken so long that Flanders's first foal, Surfside, another in a long line of Lukas filly prodigies, had "gamely rallied in the style of her dam to win the 1999 Frizette by a head," only to come in third in the Breeders' Cup Juvenile Fillies. Surfside proved a remarkable horse.

"I'm satisfied," Lukas answered, when asked his opinion on the verdict. "It had dragged on so long that we're running her baby. I'm glad it's over."

Lukas maintains to this day that a mishap may have occurred when a stable hand was hand mixing the drug for the horse in the neighboring stall, and that if the stable hand did not wash his hands, it would have been enough to contaminate Flanders's feed.

"That's not bad in a twenty-five-, twenty-six-year run," he said of his drug suspensions. "Thousands of horses. We're pretty paranoid about that. My [former] assistants, Randy or Todd, they'll tell you, you can make plenty of mistakes, but don't make that one."

An Embarrassment of Riches

The year of that second, albeit withdrawn, suspension, Lukas had one of the best three-year-old crops in the history of his organization. It would improve throughout the 1995 Derby prep season and blossom during the Triple Crown races.

The year held so much promise not because Lukas had so many great horses—he'd always had great horses—but because he'd made a subtle change in his manner of buying horses, and in their training as well. He realized that when it came to winning the biggest prizes in the sport—the Derby in particular—whatever he'd been doing hadn't worked. So he would now aim his horses, plan his strategies, and selectively choose where his horses would race, and when, with an eye toward the classics. No more breakdowns, no more pushing and fighting. He'd race the races that would best position the horse for the Derby, and not worry about amassing every dollar the prep season had to offer. That didn't mean he was going to shy away from the biggest plums on the tree, but that he wasn't going to climb as many trees as he had in previous years.

In the beginning of his thoroughbred years, Lukas bought horses that reminded him of his best quarter horses, he told Jay Privman. They had thick necks, big rumps, and short front legs. They were sprinters. While they could chew up two-year-old courses, generally a mile and under, when it came to the classic races, which are all more than a mile, the horses would peter out. He needed to be looking for more classic-style horses, and to that end restudied the confirmations of many classic winners.

"We wanted to draft choices that fit the mold of what we were trying to do." Lukas said. "Over the years, we've adjusted our eye. It's like in football. If you want a passing offense, you draft a quarterback, not a 230-pound fullback."

He was aiming to win a classic.

Lukas is a "sports guy." His idea of relaxing is to find two college basketball games and watch them in his den on his wide-screen television, and coach each game from the La-Z-Boy recliner. And in sports, it's not how many games you've won, it's how many rings you have. The great athletes and coaches separate themselves from others by winning championships. In the thoroughbred world, the Triple Crown events and the Breeders' Cup races are the championships. Winning one wasn't enough for a competitive type like Lukas. He wanted to join the company of Ben and Jimmy Jones and James "Sunny Jim" Fitzsimmons. He pined to be one of the great ones. This is the drive of a champion, this is the must-have attitude that separates a Wayne Gretzky, a Michael Jordan, a Bill Parcells, and a Bobby Knight.

Lukas had several fine young horses, including Serena's Song, Timber Country, and Thunder Gulch. Each one would develop on its own schedule and with the help of some masterful maneuvering by the maestro himself. One of the first important moves he made was bringing Thunder Gulch to the East Coast for the Fountain of Youth Stakes at Gulfstream Park in February 1995.

"D. Wayne Lukas flew into town today with a horse, and that's usually bad news for the locals," seasoned turf journalist Joe Durso wrote.

Lukas had a barn full of talent and needed to find soft races where some of his horses could earn wins and build experience. One such place, he felt, was the Fountain of Youth. In the West, a horse named Afternoon Deelites was whipping all comers, and so, in search of a win in a soft market, Lukas thought he could bring Thunder Gulch to Gulfstream and maybe steal a race. The local talent wasn't particularly strong. But Thunder Gulch wasn't the star horse in Lukas's barn, where he was referred to, by writers only, as a second stringer.

When asked how good the colt was, Lukas responded playfully, "How good are the colts he's going to meet?" But who was this masked bandit from the West?

Thunder Gulch was the property of Michael Tabor of Monte Carlo, who had owned 114 Prince Arthur betting shops in the U.K. and sold them in 1995 for approximately $35 million. He had bought the young colt and put him in Lukas's care. In November 1994, Lukas won the Remsen Stakes at Aqueduct with Thunder Gulch, then flew the colt to California, where he could keep a better eye on him and see how he stacked up against his other stars.

The horse raced again in December, in the Hollywood Futurity. He ran a strong second, but was disposed of by the West Coast star, Afternoon Deelites, who was owned by famed songwriter/composer Burt Bacharach and trained by Charlie Whittingham. Thunder Gulch hadn't raced since then due to winter rains and off tracks. Lukas was saving this prize, not wanting to risk his health in bad spots. He soft-pedaled his horse to the locals, saying, "He is a late May foal and he is not even three yet. He's also not a real big horse."

Durso, reading between the lines, and, given his own understanding of the game, wrote: "Lukas concedes that his reasons for coming East are strategic. He is holding his first-string and other horses for the main events in California. And he is shipping colts like Thunder Gulch to places where they might stand out." As many others were seeing it also, Durso pointed out that the clash between East and West coasts would predominate the Derby prep season that year.

The race was a solid one, and Lukas's horse made a bold statement. In the turn for home, Thunder Gulch, who'd been stalking, was taken seven wide by Mike Smith and exploded down the stretch. He quickly passed the pack and knocked off horses in bunches. But the leader, Suave Prospect, was still going strong. The horses were in a duel, with Thunder Gulch inching up as they approached the finish line. At the wire, Lukas's horse was ahead by a neck.

The next day in the papers, Durso called it a "transcontinental coup." The local favorite, Jambalaya Jazz, trained by John Ward and a four-time East Coast winner, finished a distant third.

"Wayne told me to make certain I got him 'in' the race, right up there," jockey Mike Smith said after the race. "He also warned me that if I got right up to the front, he might hang on a horse and wait for someone. That is exactly what he did, but once that other horse came to him, he really dug in and ran a big race."

Lukas was jubilant: "You like to start the campaign with a win." Then the college basketball coach in him came out, and referring to the NCAA basketball tournament structure, he said, "The number one seed in the West is up for grabs with Afternoon Deelites and Timber Country." Following the same metaphor, he called Thunder Gulch "the number one seed in the South."

Lukas laid out the groundwork from here. Thunder Gulch would race in the Florida Derby, the Blue Grass, and then the Kentucky Derby. He was staking his claim, selling his horse, and hopefully scaring off a few good horses.

Whether or not he scared anyone off, Thunder Gulch also won the Florida Derby. He truly was the number-one seed in the South.

Lukas's biggest battle of 1995 loomed in the West. His Timber Country had been the best two-year-old in the country, and in fact won the Eclipse Award for Best Two-Year-Old. And Lukas had done more with more young horses than any trainer before or since. But since so many of his two-year-olds never seemed to pan out in the classics, there was the worry that Timber Country, though brazenly sold and promoted, would in fact fold. Many wanted to see results.

But in fact this was a somewhat different D. Wayne Lukas. And he was happy to talk about it. He was willing to explain his strategy, whether he fell flat on his face or not.

"This is the most discipline I've ever shown with a horse," he told Jay Privman. "It's the most planned campaign I've ever mapped out to get to the ultimate prize, and maybe even beyond the Derby."

Bred by Woodman out of Fall Aspen, Timber Country was a big horse, weighing two hundred more pounds and standing inches higher than most thoroughbreds. He was tall and long, like a basketball player. Pat Day told Privman that Timber Country required reins that were four inches longer than any Lukas had previously had in his stable. Timber Country was a different kind of horse, for Lukas. And indeed others noticed too.

"He's not a typical Lukas horse," Hall of Fame jockey Bill Shoemaker said. "He used to have those stocky horses who looked like quarter horses. This horse looks like a distance horse, and he runs like a distance horse. He's got that long body and that nice stride."

Lukas bragged that the horse was too big for the starting gate and required a larger—in fact, a double—stall, as many of his star horses got, such as Landaluce. He liked to call these "master suites."

Timber Country was big, but he wasn't as accomplished as some other popular horses. He faced some of the toughest competition of the season. And Lukas made it clear that he was going to race in a certain number of races with the colt, win, lose, or draw, and not deviate from his plan.

It rained constantly that spring season, making it difficult for Lukas to train his star. At the 1994 Eclipse Awards ceremony, where he'd picked up awards for Flanders (Two-Year-Old Filly), Timber Country (Two-Year-Old Colt), and Trainer of the Year, Lukas talked about the inclement weather: "I wouldn't say it rained a lot out here, but the animals are going around two by two."

Pat Day closed out Timber Country's two-year-old campaign with two solid wins. He won the Champagne Stakes and took the Breeders' Cup Juvenile. That made him a favorite. But early 1995 showed that the colt had some growing still to do, when he finished third in the San Rafael Stakes behind Larry the Legend and Fandare Dancer. Then, on March 19, he came in second to Afternoon Deelites in the San Felipe. And on April 8 he finished out of the money, behind Larry the Legend again, at the Santa Anita Derby, his last prep race for the Derby. Afternoon Deelites and Jumron also finished ahead of him.

Serena's Song was a beautiful and tough three-year-old filly known for her competitiveness. Lukas was betwixt and between with her chances of a Derby run. She had been an exceptional two-year-old, except for the fact that she'd had to play second fiddle to Flanders. But now Serena's Song was about to step out of the shadow of her departed stablemate who, after being hurt, had been retired to become a brood mare. With Flanders out of the way, Serena's Song was now Team Lukas's next hot young thing.

Lukas pondered publicly if she was Derby material. It seemed she had the speed, strength, and endurance to run with the big boys. But Lukas knew that if he kept her on line for the Kentucky Oaks, a filly event the day before the Derby, she could easily be the favorite there. The decision on where to run her was made more difficult when she crushed a field of three-year-old colts in the Jim Beam Stakes.

Though Serena's Song was a question mark among Lukas's big three, she was also very accomplished. She'd won four races in her two-year-old season, and finished in the money three other times. But most impressive was her march to May.

Beginning with her win at the Hollywood Starlet Stakes on December 17, 1994, at Hollywood Park, she went on a five-race roll. With Corey Nakatani aboard, they rolled through the Santa Ynez, the Las

Virgenes, the Santa Anita Oaks, and the Jim Beam Stakes. She never overpowered, but she was brilliant. And while it was questionable up to the end as to which way Lukas would go, there was no question that the press loved her.

Bob and Beverly Lewis

Bob and Beverly Lewis met while they were both college students at the University of Oregon in the 1940s. Together, they would spend sunny afternoons at Portland Meadows, a regional racetrack about 100 miles away. This is where their love for each other and racing blossomed. She was the University of Oregon's Betty Coed in 1947 (something akin to a prom queen). Bob was a cheerleader for the Fighting Ducks. He was the man who brought the real live mascot, a duck, to the many athletic events.

Bob Lewis is well known in the beverage business on the West Coast. He was tough on his drivers, and played trucking companies against one another in order to drive down rates and increase profits. In America, that kind of smart information gathering and use of power make for success. And few have ever seen the kind of success that Bob and Beverly Lewis have enjoyed.

Bob learned about horse racing early in life. His parents often took him to the track as part of family outings and spent much time at Santa Anita. Once Bob and Beverly moved to California, the racetrack bug bit Beverly as well. They spent their three-day honeymoon at the Caliente and Del Mar tracks, bought their first racehorses in 1990, and have been hooked ever since.

As in his brewery distribution business, Bob Lewis refuses—as Gene Klein did—to put all his eggs (or should we say horses) into one basket. He has split his horses among his two main trainers—Wayne Lukas and Bob Baffert.

Baffert was their first trainer. And as they bought better horses, and wanted to be more competitive in the major thoroughbred world, they decided to split their best horses among two of America's premier horse trainers instead of giving them all to one. Thus did the

Lewises become the heart of the competition between the two trainers. It should be noted, however, that they have approximately fifty horses stabled somewhere in the United Sates at any given time and have also used other, comparable trainers, including Ray Bell, Mike Molica, and Gary Jones.

As in his beer business, Lewis wanted to be able to walk out in any situation, rather than have the terms dictated to him. By dividing up his horses, he could compare rights, techniques, and results. This wasn't ideal for Baffert or Lukas, or the others, but with the new horsemen the game was drawing, they knew it was necessary to remain flexible. And if you were an owner, seeing trainers becoming rich and powerful, why let your investments sit with one trainer when you can fuel a little competition and get some extra growth?

This said, few people have ever said anything bad about the Lewises, at least in print. "Bob and Beverly Lewis are truly ambassadors for our sport," National Thoroughbred Racing Association commissioner Tim Smith has said. "Their graciousness and enthusiasm are unmatched in both victory and defeat."

About owners, Lukas says: "Over the years, we've learned that when you get to a certain status in the industry, the character and the type of people you deal with way overshadows the horses they have. If an asshole has a good horse, the horse gets to be three or four and he's gone, but the asshole's still there.

"I do not train anymore for anybody who makes my stomach knot up when I see them coming. I only train for people I really look forward to going to lunch with at the races or spending time with. And when you get to that quality of people—like Bill Young, Bob and Beverly Lewis, Michael Tabor, and John Magnier—those people understand the game and they are such good people that there is no way to get into a conflict. They'll let you buy this horse and that guy buy that horse and they'll say, 'Wayne, if you want to run in the Travers with that horse, you can take mine to the Haskell.' That part of my life hasn't always been that way, but it's very smooth right now. The quality of the person. The richer they are, the more gracious they are. Bill Young, we'll get whipped in a $500,000 and he'll say, 'I feel bad for you, I know you had your heart set on it,' because it doesn't affect his lifestyle. It affects mine."

In 1995, Bob and Beverly Lewis owned Serena's Song outright and owned a share in Timber Country, and both were with Wayne Lukas. And they had some younger horses with him as well. Like Lukas, they didn't know it yet, but they were in for the ride of their lives that year.

1995 Kentucky Derby

As the Derby approached, Lukas had two surefire bets going in—Timber Country, proven but not dominant, and Thunder Gulch, still a solid if not sparkling candidate after a bad Blue Grass Stakes, where he finished fourth.

Despite constant hounding, he still had not made up his mind what to do with Serena's Song. Then, on April 29, he announced on national television that the filly would make the Run for the Roses: "She will run in the Derby and dare to be great." Later, he told the press corps: "We're going to run the filly in the Derby. We're going to run her against the big boys and give her that chance at immortality, to give her the opportunity to be great. I've been vacillating all week."

If Lukas had been vacillating, his owners, Bob and Beverly Lewis, had been insisting. Bob Lewis was saying all along that it was Lukas's decision, but when no decision had been made, he pressed his case.

"We weighed all the pros and cons," Lewis said. "I think the bottom line is you've got to feel that she has a legitimate chance to win the race. And if you feel it in your heart, I think she deserves the opportunity." Durso remarked that even with a field of twenty horses, it was "a race still believed wide open despite a herd of Lukas stars with their conflicting ownership interests. Serena's Song is owned outright by the Lewises. Timber Country, who won the Breeders' Cup Juvenile last fall, is owned by William T. Young and Graham Beck of Lexington and the Lewises. Thunder Gulch, winner of the Florida Derby, is owned by Michael Tabor of Monte Carlo, Monaco."

Indeed, it was unique; in fact, revolutionary. Never before had a trainer run three different horses owned by three different owners or owner groups. Lukas was just making up the rules as he was going along. It would be a delicate balance.

The day after they declared that Serena's Song would be in the Derby, her workouts were followed with intense scrutiny. When she ran an incredibly fast time between poles, several writers commented approvingly to Lukas, who responded by saying, "Works don't make winning races, but they don't hurt."

One of the problems created by Lukas and the Lewises' late decision on Serena's Song was that Corey Nakatani, who would have ridden the filly, was now committed to another horse. However, Lukas didn't know this. When one of the writers at a press gathering informed him, he retorted, "They can only take twenty horses in the Derby, and there must be more than twenty jockeys walking around looking for work," and gestured at the backstretch. "Besides, it doesn't matter much who the jockey is."

But the reporters hanging out at Lukas's barn knew what he was really thinking. He wore a dark baseball cap all week that bore the name "TIMBER COUNTRY." "The bottom line is winning the Derby, and I think Timber Country can win it," he said. One morning, he nodded to the big horse while it was being washed down and said, "There's the Kentucky Derby winner getting his bath over there."

Few trainers would have had the audacity to pull off a triple entry, and even fewer could pull off selling all three. In a conversation with George Vecsey, Lukas compared all three of his horses to professional basketball players. Thunder Gulch was John Stockton, he said, solid and dependable; Timber Country was a then young Shaquille O'Neal, raw, talented, unproven; and Serena's Song was . . . Michael Jordan? Vecsey editorialized that she might be a young Reggie Miller or Anfernee Hardaway instead.

During Derby week Nick Zito, the only other Derby-winning trainer entered that year, and always a hard campaigner against Lukas, joked with the press, saying, "With all due respect, Wayne's always talking about basketball, but would you want to have him on the free-throw line with his record in the Derby?" It was true. In twenty-two starts, he'd finished in the money three times, with only one win. "Wayne's three horses," Zito said, "were me, myself, and I."

Even Lukas got some funny lines in, especially when he referred to the little-mentioned Thunder Gulch. "He's in the wrong stable. He's got a ballerina on one side and a two-year-old champion on the other. But he's not in awe of them."

The press, meanwhile, was still interested in the decision-making process that had led to Serena's Song's inclusion in the Derby. Even the ever-courteous Bob Lewis got frazzled, explaining to Vecsey, "Let me make it clear that the final decision was made by Wayne Lukas. He was kind enough to include us in it. He believes she is as suited as anybody for this race. If we could not talk about plumbing for a minute, this is a great horse."

As the event neared, the pressure on Team Lukas built. There was more spin and damage control and selling going on than during a presidential election. Serena's Song got the number 13 gate, Timber Country took gate 15, and Thunder Gulch number 16 in a field of twenty. Joseph Durso let Jeff Lukas have the last word: "Timber Country can fall in behind the early leaders. He can drop in behind the front four and settle. For Thunder Gulch, post isn't as important to him as the other two. He can break, settle inside, and save ground. The draw is nothing anybody can control. The fact that we're in the gate and have a chance to draw for the Derby is the main thing."

Even saddling up became a chore, because Wayne could not be in all three places at one time. Jeff helped him, working with Thunder Gulch. "I dragged my feet," Lukas said. "Finally, Jeff legged him up."

Serena's Song broke from the gate to a quick start, moving swiftly across the dry, fast track. She took the lead and set a fast pace. As the pack followed her, different horses jostled for position. Thunder Gulch, who had slid in just behind the pack, was within perfect striking position the entire race.

"The colt broke very sharp, and after fifty yards out of the gate I got toward the inside," jockey Gary Stevens said later. "I couldn't have imagined myself being in a better place."

He was there with Talkin' Man, the Canadian champion, who battled it out with Thunder Gulch. Talkin' Man was first to pass Serena's Song, and then Thunder Gulch passed her. As Lukas said later: "She could have got loose on the lead, and did. But she ran up fractions she couldn't live with." She had burned herself out.

Now it was Talkin' Man and Thunder Gulch, with Tejano Run coming up fast, and Timber Country. Thunder Gulch poured it on, and when Talkin' Man was asked for more, he faltered, then fell behind quickly, finally finishing twelfth.

As Stevens raced to the finish line he shouted, from fifty yards out, "Come on wire, please!" Much to his surprise, he steered Thunder Gulch to a solid win, finishing 2¼ lengths ahead of Tejano Run, with Timber Country, coming on too late, in third. It was Stevens's second Kentucky Derby win in a row. He'd won the previous year on Nick Zito's Go for Gin.

The stepchild and least talked about member of the three-horse team had won the race, and the press loved the story. Even while they could not help but write about Serena's Song and Timber Country, it was Thunder Gulch that got the headlines and the prize. At one point Lukas had described Thunder Gulch as his "blue-collar worker" when compared to the other two horses. But it was now his turn to shine.

"All week we liked this horse," he told a large gathering of press. The moans of sarcasm from the crowd were loud and laced with laughter.

Michael Tabor told the press that not only had he bet money at Churchill Downs, but also in London. "I had some sterling on it and I had some dollars on it," he said with a smile.

After the win, Lukas, on television, said that he had wanted his son to hold the winning horse's reins. "Bless his heart. He didn't want to." Lukas had now won the last three Triple Crown events, and all eyes would be on him at the Preakness.

1995 Preakness

On May 16, Lukas announced to the press that he was bringing all three of his stars to Baltimore. Thunder Gulch and Timber Country were entered in the Preakness. The big news was that Serena's Song would be entered in the Black-Eyed Susan, a race for fillies.

"There's no reason not to run her in the Black-Eyed Susan," Lukas said. "She came out of the Derby in excellent shape. She worked great. It looks like a great spot for her." Lukas was in a good mood, and he had reason to be. The railbirds had been clocking his horses' works, and each one was running faster than ever. "Air Lukas," as Joe Durso had begun calling Lukas and his team, seemed too awesome for words.

Lukas flew into Pimlico on May 17 with nine horses, not all of them his, but all of which would be competing at the weekend's coming events. Stepping out of the truck and having all the horses organized, he confidently declared to the press in a Baltimore spring downpour, "All our preparation is done."

"Had it all worked out differently last week for D. Wayne Lukas, had his gamble failed and his faith gone unrewarded," William F. Reed wrote in *Sports Illustrated* about the Preakness, "you can bet Lukas-bashing would have become as popular as crab-bashing in Baltimore's seafood restaurants. That's the price of being 'the straw that stirs racing's drink,' which is how Lukas, the sport's highest-profile trainer, was introduced at a Preakness brunch last Friday."

One of the things that Lukas was dealing with now was the controversy surrounding Timber Country, whom he still considered his best colt. And many felt that, in part, the horse's failure to win the Kentucky Derby had been attributable to Pat Day's laid-back riding style, which they believed was not a good match for a colt who needed plenty of urging. In fact, Day got caught in traffic in the Derby, and neither he nor Timber Country could fight their way out until it was too late to make a run.

All week, Lukas talked about how his head was on a chopping block. The press was still poking at him about backing the wrong horse and was criticizing him for running the filly too soon after a suicidal run at Churchill Downs, and the press and his owners wanted to know what was going to happen to Timber Country on Saturday.

On Friday, May 20, Lukas proved the boo birds wrong once again, when Serena's Song took the Black-Eyed Susan handily. The Lewises were thrilled. Lukas had also been a winner on Thursday, when Lilly Capote took the Miss Preakness. It was a good omen, and got one of the three or four monkeys off his back. He strode around the backstretch as confidently as ever, talking his horses up and sounding loud.

On Saturday, in one of the early races, his horse Commanche Trail won the Maryland Budweiser Breeders' Cup. Could his luck hold out? Before the Preakness, Lukas made a point of going into the jockey's lounge and talking to both Pat Day and Gary Stevens. But he spent more time with Day.

Make sure to "be a pilot, not a passenger," he told Day, who smilingly told the press, "My contract lasts only until the end of the race," acknowledging how important a win would be with this horse. The good news was that Day had won the Preakness and the Belmont Stakes the year before with Tabasco Cat.

Day started tapping Timber Country during the post parade, to let the horse know that it was time for business. During the race, in an eleven-horse field, Timber Country and Thunder Gulch never got caught in traffic and stalked well. And when the field turned for home, there were three horses fighting it out nose-to-nose. The third horse was Oliver Twist, a local entry from the Maryland countryside who had been a popular choice all week. Since it was trained by Bill Boniface, who had won the 1983 Preakness with Disputed Testimony, it was no surprise that he was fighting Thunder Gulch and Timber Country for the lead with yards to go. Timber Country, who had the edge, was on the outside, Thunder Gulch was in the middle, and Oliver's Twist had come up on the inside, along the rail, the three abreast. It was Timber Country who won it, by less than half a length on Oliver's Twist. Thunder Gulch was third by a neck.

"More than six months without a victory, Timber Country today arrived in the $687,400 Preakness Stakes," Vinnie Perrone wrote in the *Washington Post*. "He took the long way home." And Team Lukas took *all* the money, as Woody Stephens used to like to say. Lukas insisted that the horse not be led into the winner's circle until the entire ownership team could be assembled. "All of you lead him in there," he told them.

"Timber Country validated Lukas's insistence that the colt is special," Perrone wrote, "a posture the trainer held even after the 1994 Juvenile champion went winless in four starts, including the Derby, before this race."

Thunder Gulch was once again the stepchild.

Lukas had now tied Lucien Laurin's record of four consecutive Triple Crown victories. Laurin had won the 1972 Belmont Stakes with Riva Ridge and then swept the Triple Crown in 1973 with Secretariat.

Lukas was now in uncharted territory. No trainer had ever swept the Triple Crown races with more than one horse. If Timber Country or Thunder Gulch won the Belmont, Lukas could take home a Triple Crown of sorts. If he thought his head had been a chopping block before, the pressure on him now, despite all the wins, was intense.

1995 Belmont

At four o'clock on Friday, June 9, the day before the Belmont Stakes, Serena's Song took the Mother Goose, disposing of some of the best fillies in the United States and starting the weekend off right for Team Lukas. He was elated. But something belied his good mood.

Timber Country was suffering from a raging temperature. Lukas and his owners were faced with a dilemma. Should they try to ride the fever out and hope that the horse would recover by race time? Or should they give him a shot now to ease the fever, which would take Timber Country out of the Belmont? This being New York, Lukas well knew, as any good trainer does, that an injection would run afoul of the rules stating that no drugs shall be passed through a horse on or just before race day. Since he would be injected with an anti-inflammatory, his scratch would be a must.

At five o'clock, an hour after the Mother Goose, the smiles still hurting the faces of the Lewises, Lukas called the press box and told them to scratch the Preakness winner from the starting field, due to fever. At ten-twenty that night he clicked on the light to check in on the dozing Thunder Gulch, now his lone star for the Belmont Stakes, the perennial sidekick, the forgotten one, the leftover. He spoke softly to the big horse: "You've got to carry the whole load tomorrow." A single horse carried the dreams and aspirations of the horse world's most driven trainer.

Preparation for the race was paramount. And no one wanted to win this one more than Nick Zito, who was running with Star Standard. A native New Yorker, Zito had begun his apprenticeship in the thoroughbred profession as a hot walker at age sixteen. For years he worked for trainers up and down the East Coast. He was an assistant to such winning trainers as John Campo and Lukas's friend LeRoy Jolley, then went out on his own in the early 1970s. While Zito's overall stables were not large, compared to Lukas's, and he would never earn as much money in a year, the one thing he had over Lukas was his stunning Triple Crown record. Zito had two Kentucky Derby wins—with Strike the Gold in 1991 and Go for Gin in 1994. He also had three seconds and a third at Belmont. And he'd accomplished this with half as many entries as Lukas.

Zito had been furious with his jockey, Julie Krone, after the Derby. He felt she'd been too laid back with Suave Prospect. Now she would be on Star Standard, and Zito had insisted that she follow his instructions to the letter. He told her to get the lead at all costs and slow down the pace.

Right from the start, Krone whipped her colt to a frenzy, darting straight for the rail and cutting off Thunder Gulch. Once she had a comfortable lead, Krone let the horse slow down, and the sizzling pace became a slow burn, just as Zito had instructed. The result would be one of the slowest Belmont Stakes in years.

Lukas admitted later that he was worried. As Krone was hugging the rail and slowing the pace, Thunder Gulch was slowly stalking, along with the other horses. At the far turn, when Stevens wanted to gun the colt, Krone pushed him out wide, forcing him to fight for every inch. They battled for three furlongs, then Thunder Gulch began to gain ground, and then a little more ground.

Coming into the final stretch, Krone drifted out again, fighting her colt, who was pressing against his hard-charging adversary. "He was just getting out a little bit," she would explain. "Sometimes horses do quirky things like that. He was gritty; there was one point where I really thought he might reach over and bite at [Thunder Gulch]."

"He needs to get in the race right now," Lukas recalled thinking. "This is a bad deal."

At the sixteenth pole Thunder Gulch pulled away, and eventually won by two lengths. Zito was second with Star Standard, and Citadeed came in third.

Immediately after the race, an amazed Lukas said, "I'm a little bit overwhelmed."

Nick Zito, who was gracious as a perennial second-place finisher at Belmont, complimented Lukas: "I guess I'll have to get Pegasus to beat him. What he's done is tremendous, unbelievable." He then complimented Krone, saying, "She really proved herself as a jockey today."

Lukas said, "It surprised me a little bit. I remembered Timber Country and thought, 'Holy mackerel, we pulled it off anyhow.'"

Thunder Gulch had taken home $692,400 for Lukas and Michael Tabor, who was a happy man. "It's some thrill, Tabor told the press. "The dream lives on." It wasn't a large crowd for a Belmont, but 37,171 fans had seen the unwanted child of the Lukas stable take the second of three possible brass rings.

"I'm very, very happy," Lukas said at the end of the day, "and very, very satisfied today."

A Triple Crown of Sorts

It had been a stellar year for Team Lukas. He had completed a never-before feat, topped the earnings boards once again, and he would sweep a number of major awards.

Lukas now stood alone at the top of the trainer's world, in the present as well as in history's shadow. He'd won more money than anyone in the thoroughbred racing world ever had, and he now had a solid number of classic wins, which would enable him to compare his legacy with Ben Jones and Sunny Jim Fitzsimmons. He had also taken the number of consecutive wins in Triple Crown races from four to five, surpassing Lucien Laurin for that title. And he had a Triple Crown, of sorts, under his belt. It seemed to suit Lukas's personality. He always did things differently, and with style.

Team Lukas awards in 1995 included 197 trophies in 837 starts, worth $12,834,483. This was the second year in a row he had won the earnings battle, and the twelfth time he'd taken it in thirteen years. And then there were the Eclipse Awards. Though 1995 had been the year of Cigar, the five-year-old wonder horse, Lukas's achievements shone brightly. Thunder Gulch was the Champion Three-Year-Old, and Serena's Song was Champion Three-Year-Old Filly.

And what happened to this tremendous trio? Timber Country never made it back to the races. He recovered from his fever but injured himself during works and had to be retired to stud. Serena's Song won seven more races and finished in the money another eleven times in a career that saw her race until November 1996. She had a lifetime record of eighteen wins, eleven seconds and three thirds in thirty-eight starts, which meant that she finished in the money 84 percent of the time. And with that, she took home $3,823,388.

As for the "other" horse . . . Thunder Gulch raced only four more times. He would win in the Swaps at Hollywood Park on July 23, taking home $275,000. Then on August 19 at Saratoga, he took the illustrious Travers Stakes, known as the "Midsummer Derby," and $450,000. He raced again in September, taking the Kentucky Cup Classic and $250,000, then went to the Jockey Club Gold Cup at Belmont. There, he met Cigar, who would be Horse of the Year in 1995.

The match-up between the two was something the racing world wanted to see. The two biggest and best males of 1995, on the same track, in a field of seven. The official notes of the race say that Thunder Gulch "stalked, tired." But "tired" hardly tells what really happened. During the course of the race, Thunder Gulch had fractured his cannon bone. He was immediately treated and retired to stud. His record shows that he won nine of sixteen races, and finished in the money four more times, taking home $2,915,086 in winnings.

The second stringer had hit the three-pointer to win the game. He hadn't been the "other horse" at all. He had been *the* horse all along.

Shari Redux

If things were going well at work for Lukas, they were not going well at home. Sometime during the course of his most successful run, Wayne and Shari split up. Wayne blames work for the breakup: "Shari's a devoted . . . racetracker. Loved the game and everything. And if there was ever going to be a marriage that survived that ten- to twelve-year run, then I don't know what kind of woman it would be if they're not just going to pack up.

"She was raising two twin boys and a daughter. Our relationship was real good except that in that intense run it almost got to be a phone relationship, and I was in and out of the house. And I think a woman expects more than that and deserves more than that.

"I think we weathered the obvious things very well. I think there were other issues that might have come into play. Once, after a big win, Bill Young turned to me and said, 'It's hard to be happy when I see people I care about who aren't happy.' "

"Wayne was very successful, very driven," says Shari today. "A lot of things were sacrificed—family, wives, friends. I know he went to the barn many times instead of being there for family moments. I'm sure it was painful for him, many times."

Indeed, Lowell remembered, "Shari asked Wayne where they were going on their honeymoon. And Wayne said, 'Nowhere. I got two fillies I have to work this afternoon." Lowell pointed out that it was a repeat of Wayne's previous marriages. "The women thought that they would be number one and the horses would finish second. Pat just wanted some time for herself and her two girls. She was looking for a father for her girls. He was moving up, and his priorities were the horses. I think the marriage with Shari was like that too." Lowell also pointed out that he felt his own children also suffered from the same absenteeism due to career ambitions and success. When asked where the Lukas drive came from, Lowell replied that it might come from a desire to prove to their father that they had indeed made the right life decisions.

Even with their subsequent divorce, Shari continues to be an avid handicapper, and is still often seen sharing dinner with many of the trainers, owners, and other racing professionals who work the Del Mar and Santa Anita backstretches.

"It was hard to be a private person with such a public figure. Wayne's a very positive person. At the sales, he would always say, 'No horse remorse,'" says Shari cheerily.

Let's Do It Again

Lukas would employ the shotgun approach to ensure that his streak would remain alive in 1996. He entered a breathtaking five Derby horses, a new record: Editor's Note, Grindstone, Honour and Glory, Prince of Thieves, and Victory Speech. This was a first.

Editor's Note was an Overbrook Farm entry, but had been bred at Fawn Leap Farm. Grindstone was also an Overbrook entry, but he had been bred by Overbrook Farm. Honour and Glory was owned by Michael Tabor and was bred by Overbrook Farm. Prince of Thieves was owned by Peter Mitchell and was bred by Lowquest, Ltd. And Victory Speech was owned by a group consisting of Michael Tabor, John Magnier, and others, and had been bred by Robert W. Entenmann.

The press was having a field day lampooning Lukas. Many claimed his horses had no shot, that it was just another publicity angle that Lukas had figured out to garner the spotlight. Lukas defended himself, saying, "If you could separate them and put them with five different trainers, you'd be interviewing them now. You can make a case for each one."

There was not one certified star in the bunch, but most writers had to admit that there were no slouches either. Editor's Note had not won since 1995, but finished in the money in the Florida Derby and the Blue Grass Stakes. Lukas said that Editor's Note had to get off to a good start to be effective, or else he "could get into traffic problems if he has to negotiate twelve or fourteen horses." Grindstone had won the Louisiana Derby and finished second in the Arkansas Derby, and he'd recovered nicely from the arthroscopic knee surgery performed on him at the end of his second year. Honour and Glory was similar to Grindstone in that he had won the San Rafael Stakes but then finished a tired third in the Santa Anita Derby. Prince of Thieves had been second in the Lexington Stakes, and Victory Speech was also winless but had finished in the money in the Fountain of Youth and Jim Beam.

"You've got to like Victory Speech," Lukas said, selling to the crowd. "In the Fountain of Youth his saddle slipped, and he was beat by a neck. He has the perfect style for this race."

One writer lamented, "What anyone else in the game wants hardly matters anymore. Because D. Wayne Lukas owns it. Owns it like maybe no trainer has owned horse racing before." And his barn was always packed with curiosity seekers, writers, owners, other backstretch workers.

Lukas was selling hard during Derby week, defending his strategy, his horses, his chances, and his record. "If we win this, they ought to chisel it in stone," he said. "Because in order to beat us, somebody is going to have to win two Triple Crowns and the Kentucky Derby the year after that."

Charlie Whittingham couldn't help but take a shot at Lukas, asking a reporter, "What's Wayne up to now, ten horses?" Whittingham's entry was Corker. Whittingham continued, "He's got us surrounded. He's amazing."

Another competitor, Sonny Hine, trainer of Skip Away, said, "He is shooting buckshot and he hopes to hit something."

But Lukas, as always answering any question anyone had the guts to ask, smiled and told reporters, "What fuels me is the competition. Going over there and competing against those guys, and those guys saying, 'He didn't have a good run this spring with those horses.'"

"Championships are won with depth in every sport," he told William Nack before the race. "These colts don't compromise each other's chances."

One of Lukas's main challengers was Unbridled's Song, but the horse had cracked his hoof in the Wood Memorial, and it continued to bother the strapping colt. In the ensuing weeks, his trainer and veterinarians had tried different shoes to heel the hurt hoof. William Nack opined that "he went through more shoes than Imelda Marcos." Another challenger, Cavonnier, was from another quarter horse trainer turned thoroughbred wonder boy, Bob Baffert.

As if entering five horses wasn't enough of a publicity stunt in and of itself, Lukas had hired a publicist, Larry Feldman, to get him more publicity and speaking engagements. He felt he needed more and better exposure. During Derby week, as if things weren't crazy enough, Feldman had booked Lukas to speak with executives at a nearby General Electric plant. Lukas tried to sell the press gathering on the idea: "It's a way to carry racing to a whole crowd it doesn't usually reach. People's attitudes are, 'What could a horse trainer possibly have to say to me?' but they're surprised. It's something no one else has done before in racing."

This last part was true, but the weary writers were not impressed, though some might have given him grudging respect. It was an age in which hereos in other sports charged fees to appear or speak, so why not a thoroughbred trainer? It confirmed the stature he had reached in the sporting world.

Lukas had also been asked by then Indiana basketball coach Bobby Knight to tour the country with a group of six well-known sports personalities, speaking at motivational conventions. The others were: Bill Walsh and Bill Parcells, both Super Bowl winning football coaches; Michigan coach Bo Schembechler, winner of the Rose Bowl; Tony La Russa, then manager of the Oakland A's, who were World Series contestants; and Knight. Lukas defended himself to the writers, saying, "There are guys who do the motivational things and have never won a world championship. Bobby said why not take six guys who have reached the zenith of their professions and let them tell you how they got there."

The day of the race, an article appeared in the *Louisville Courier-Journal* in which Seth Hancock, the president of Claiborne Farm, and who at twenty-three years of age had syndicated Secretariat, criticized Lukas: "I think with Lukas the style does overtake the substance, and it bothers me. I think that's all the man cares about— what's best for him—and I think he's handled his horses that way sometimes. It's not what's best for this horse, it's what's best for Wayne Lukas." Rick Bozich, in whose column the quote appeared, was even harsher, claiming that Lukas "is Jerry Jones without the salary cap, Bobby Bowden without scholarship limitations. He is hypnotized by his own hype. . . . The word for [five entries in one Derby] is obsession."

A day later, Tim Sullivan would answer for Lukas in the *Cincinnati Enquirer*: "He is the Henry Ford of horsemen, running his stable like an assembly line, mass-producing thoroughbreds and accumulating trophies." Sullivan asked: "What's wrong with that?" And, referring to the old world families that still liked to think they ruled thoroughbred racing, he concluded: "He's a little too professional for their patrician tastes."

This view of Lukas was held by many in the sport and is still held by many. Some of the critics were sore losers, and some made good points. But overall, the bitterness and vindictiveness of their attacks and barbs often took away from the validity of their remarks. For Lukas's part, the braggadocio and bombast he'd picked up and expanded upon in his quarter horse days, the attitude of fairground jostling, was often interpreted by the traditional thoroughbred crowd as bad taste. In fact, Lukas was more complex than this. He could be a bully or a choirboy, a horseman and a con man. The contradictions melded seamlessly into the man. He could be loud, brash, and uncouth one minute, and sophisticated, charming, and doting the next.

Lukas was stung by the criticism. And it added to his increasing distrust of the press. Today he says, "I want them to be accountable. I don't want them to just write something and there's no way to defend it. . . . You never get in a fistfight with a guy that's got his ink by the barrel, know what I mean? When you stand in front of those guys, like at the Derby . . . you realize that they have a job to do and they have a story to write, and you give them two- and three-hour sessions, and then you pick up where some guy's just bashing you or criticizing you for even handing out all that, you have a tendency to say, 'Well, that's fine, I don't need to say this anymore.' You get into that damned if you do, damned if you don't situation. But as you get older you just look at it and say, 'You need the last two paragraphs, here, take it,'" and he snapped his fingers.

As early as 1991, Mike Helm of the *San Francisco Chronicle* had written: "Though there's no denying Lukas's . . . success, to many he is the Elmer Gantry of thoroughbred racing: a high-priced hustler who, with his wraparound glasses and bottom-line rap, has learned how to sweet-talk owners and parlay a cynical numbers game into a lot of money soaked in the blood of broken down horses. Though his critics acknowledge Lukas is . . . a good judge of horseflesh, they don't think it's accidental that a great horse like Grand Canyon was a winner at two and dead at three. Still, with the advent of year-round racing, Lukas's approach was probably inevitable."

In traditional thoroughbred circles, Lukas's excessive approach to the 1996 Kentucky Derby had the effect of a red flag waved in front of a bull. No one had ever had the gall or bad taste to enter five horses. Seth Hancock, whose criticism was among those that bothered Lukas, personified this old world. The scion of one of the oldest and most successful breeding farms, his attacks on the new breed of horsemen belied the fact that he'd made a fortune greater than his famous father, Bull Hancock, from these same new horsemen, who bought his horses at auctions all around the country.

"The quotes seemed an accurate portrayal of Seth's feelings about Lukas," wrote Billy Reed of the *Lexington Herald-Leader* a year later, "yet Hancock always has been careful to keep those kinds of personal thoughts off the record. Lukas was deeply offended by the comments, as were Lukas's supporters."

In 1996 the Kentucky Derby would have one of its most exciting finishes. The race began with Michael Tabor's Honour and Glory, under Aaron Gryder, racing to the front of the pack in a rocketlike burst. Matty G was right there with him, and Unbridled's Song close behind, after clearing some traffic. As they ran down the backstretch, Jerry Bailey on Grindstone was fifteenth in the field of nineteen. "It looked like there were 114 horses ahead of me," Bailey said after the race. From there he slowly started to move Grindstone up, briefly hiding behind Prince of Thieves and letting that horse run interference.

Going into the far turn, after some of the fastest splits in Derby history, Honour and Glory started to tire. But Unbridled's Song was still moving well, swallowing up large chunks of land in huge strides. Then Unbridled's Song had the lead and Grindstone was moving, picking his spots, cutting first to the inside, then the outside. As they approached the final turn, Grindstone was coming on, and Unbridled's Song made a desperate bid to stay in front, but the corrective bar shoes on his feet were slipping on the dirt. And then Cavonnier was also up close to the other two.

The fate of the race was decided when Cavonnier was unintentionally whipped on the nose by Halo Sunshine jockey Craig Perret. "As I ducked inside, the horse got hit right across the face by the whip on the horse inside me," McCarron said after the race.

Bailey had now swung Grindstone to the outside, leaving Unbridled's Song and Cavonnier on the inside, and Prince of Thieves came up. As Unbridled's Song finally started to fade, it became a two horse race between Cavonnier and Grindstone. It seemed that Cavonnier would prevail, and then Grindstone went into another gear. The two horses were abreast, Grindstone in the lead, then Cavonnier, then Grindstone again, then Cavonnier. . . . As they raced past the finish line, the crowd roared.

But who had won? Even the jockeys didn't know.

"Who won it?" Bailey asked McCarron.

"I think you did," Cavonnier's jockey replied.

"I couldn't tell who had won it," Bailey said. "The longer Chris and I waited to find out who won, the more we thought it might be a dead heat." But the applause in the stands was for Bob Baffert, trainer of Cavonnier.

Lukas thought the same thing: "When we hit the wire, we erupted. Then it hit me right between the eyes: hell, maybe we didn't win it." Frowning, Lukas warned people not to get too excited, as the board had not yet put up Grindstone's or Cavonnier's number. The stewards, it was announced, were reviewing the finish.

It was clear that Prince of Thieves had finished third. The horse, ridden by Pat Day and owned by Peter Mitchell, had produced another money finish on what would be a remarkable day, regardless. Editor's Note would finish sixth, Victory Speech tenth, and Honour and Glory a weary eighteenth in a field of nineteen.

People in the stands argued about the finish and recalled other famous finishes. There was nervous laughter, shouts, and hollers. It took four and a half minutes before the final announcement was made: Grindstone's number flashed on the board. Another roar went up from the crowd, and Lukas was amazed. Grindstone had literally won by a nose. Fans and well-wishers alike descended upon the salt-and-pepper-haired trainer.

Jockey Mike Smith said of Unbridled's Song after the race: "With bar shoes, it's tough to get a good grip, and he was bobbling. It was like wearing combat boots to try and run a foot race."

It was Lukas's sixth straight Triple Crown victory, the most in history. Between May 1994 and May 1996, no one else had won a Triple Crown event in two years. It was an unprecedented feat. Out of the $1.1 million in prize money, Lukas took $954,800, or roughly 87 percent of the total booty.

Lukas first gave praise to Grindstone's owner, William Young, who had stood by him during his darkest moments. He then praised his jockey, saying, "Jerry Bailey needs to put that in his highlight film and show it to his grandkids." But Lukas saved his breath for his critics. He asked why they harassed him, a businessman in a gentleman's sport. "I'm trying to do a job. I do it with my style and flair. I think I would be less of a person if I did it any other way."

When asked recently if he had somehow planned or orchestrated the race, using the horses as blockers as in a basketball pick-and-roll, Lukas responded, "Well, yes, but . . . if you interview Bailey, he'd tell you he got shuffled back and Prince of Thieves was right in front of him with Pat Day. . . . Bailey said he had fourteen or fifteen horses in front of him so he drafted in and got right off of Pat Day and Prince of Thieves. And he said Pat made every decision perfect. He just went in, out. He said, 'I never broke stride. At the sixteenth pole I just pulled out past him and won it.' He said, 'I got all the credit for this masterful ride between horses and all I did was follow Pat Day.'"

When asked if he'd thought that's how it would play out, Lukas answered, "No, but I knew he'd be coming from way back. But to be perfectly honest, when they were going back the downside I thought Prince of Thieves would have the better shot at it. I thought Grindstone was being shuffled back too far and had too many horses to overcome. Especially when Cavonnier cut the corner and made the jump. What I call the first run."

But in the end, Lukas credited Bailey: "I think we give the rider too much credit, but that is one case where I will go to my grave saying the rider made the difference. We would have never won with Grindstone without Bailey."

1996 Preakness

On the day after the Derby, a Sunday, Lukas found a dentist who would do work on his mouth. The dentist capped three teeth for him. He needed it done because a horse who'd swung his head had knocked those teeth loose. A reporter kidded him, "I heard you had a Triple Crown put in." Lukas laughed. They then got to talking about the race, and Lukas crowed about Bailey again. "I think Jerry Bailey made a huge difference. He took advantage of every situation all race long. Chris McCarron rode some race too."

After the Derby, it was not considered odd that the winner, Grindstone, might not be the favorite in the Preakness. Even Lukas admitted that "if Unbridled's Song trains well, he could be favored again." From his Churchill Downs barn, Lukas said that Grindstone, Prince of Thieves, Victory Speech, and Editor's Note were going to Baltimore.

But a few days later bad news hit Team Lukas. A bone chip in Grindstone's knee necessitated his retirement. It was a big blow. Lukas handled it with grace. "He gave us the ultimate thrill; he won the ultimate race. We're very happy and grateful for that." He was the first Kentucky Derby winner to miss the Preakness since Spend a Buck in 1985. The injury was not life-threatening. Apparently, Grindstone had raced on a trick knee for some time. But even as he was being retired, he was dragging around stable hands two at a time.

"It's a downer, but maybe we ought to put a positive spin on it," Lukas said. "He's only raced six times. Now all he has to do is go out to a green pasture and look for that mare."

With Grindstone out of the race, Lukas was down to Editor's Note, Victory Speech, and Prince of Thieves. As Unbridled's Song was also questionable and convalescing at Monmouth, Cavonnier was now the morning line favorite, at 9–5. He drew the number 2 post position. "I've never been one to sit down and handicap races," trainer Bob Baffert said about his horse being the favorite. "My job is to get the horse ready to run." Lukas had replaced Pat Day with Jerry Bailey, and Prince of Thieves, now with Bailey aboard, drew number 9. Victory Speech, with Rene Douglas up, drew the number 3 post, and Editor's Note, with Gary Stevens, drew number 10. Prince of Thieves was at 5–2 the second favorite, Editor's Note was at 6–1, and Victory Speech was the longest shot from the Lukas barn, at 30–1.

One of the dramatic touches to the 1996 Preakness concerned Lukas replacing Day with Bailey on Prince of Thieves. With Day thus available to ride another horse, Nick Zito jumped at the chance to get him, and Day became the jockey on Louis Quatorze.

It turned out to be a magical move. Louis Quatorze jumped to the lead at the start of the race, and held off every challenger as he flew around the track, setting some record fractions. In the end, it was Louis Quatorze in first, Skip Away second, and Editor's Note third, six lengths from the winner when Louis Quatorze crossed the finish line.

Nick Zito and Pat Day had won. Wayne Lukas and Gary Stevens were third. Jerry Bailey was seventh. "I thought we had a legitimate chance to win," Lukas said. "But I also knew that I wasn't going to come back here and kick the dog if we didn't. We've had such a great run, and I knew it wasn't going to go on forever."

He was asked repeatedly about the switch in riders. "You trade a guy and the next time you look up he beats you with a touchdown pass. That happens in sports. But I'll be the first to congratulate Pat, publicly and privately."

When asked how he felt about the streak being over, he replied, "Now we've got a chance to start a new one."

1996 Belmont

Lukas was in a unique position. He had won the last two Belmonts and had the opportunity now to win it a third consecutive time. Woody Stephens still owned the record with five straight wins. ("I don't think Woody is nervous," Lukas said.) Zito was hoping to avoid his third straight second-place Belmont finish. His horses had finished second both times to Lukas's. Put another way: Lukas wanted to continue his streak, and Zito wanted to end his.

Both trainers had two horses entered. Lukas had Prince of Thieves and Editor's Note, and Zito had Louis Quatorze and Saratoga Dandy. Prince of Thieves, third in the Derby, had been a more successful horse than Editor's Note. Though he'd finished in the money several times, Editor's Note hadn't won since the Kentucky Cup Juvenile the previous year. He'd gone nine races without a victory. So it was difficult for many to see why Lukas was running him in the Belmont. But placing a mediocre horse in a big race was nothing new for Lukas, who had fed more horseflesh into the Derby than any other trainer in history. This went along with his dictum, "You can't win it if you're not in it."

As William F. Reed wrote in *Sports Illustrated* a week after the Belmont: "The field of fourteen was more notable for who was *not* running than for who was." In the article, trainer Shug McGaughey chimed in, "I haven't seen a superstar yet." Indeed, the field was mediocre at best. The Derby winner wasn't running, and the Preakness winner, Louis Quatorze, could be had at 6–1 odds. But he wasn't the favorite; that was Bob Baffert's Cavonnier.

Gary Stevens had been slated to ride Editor's Note. But Stevens had injured his shoulder and could not race in the Belmont. He was going to be a color commentator for ABC television. Instead, Lukas called on Rene Douglas, a Panamanian, then twenty-nine years old. Douglas's agent and the injured Stevens then watched hours of tape and reviewed all the things Douglas would need to know to race the horse.

There were a few speed horses in the race, and they attempted to outdo each other when the field left the starting gate. Julie Krone jumped to a fast start on South Salem, who then gave way to Appealing Skier, who in turn gave way to Natural Selection. For the mile and a half Belmont, the pace was maniacal, and all three easily burned out. That left the experienced Triple Crown veterans, among them Skip Away, followed by Cavonnier, Editor's Note, Louis Quatorze, and Prince of Thieves. Editor's Note was twelfth and Prince of Thieves last.

As they hit the final stretch, the first to bail out was Cavonnier, who was injured. The race became a duel between Editor's Note and Skip Away. Editor's Note, on the outside, caught Skip Away and passed him. Then he slowed down, and Skip Away passed him, but only for a moment. Skip Away had been second at Pimlico and was game for a fight. Long after this race was over, Skip Away would continue to build his career winnings, and become the second highest earning horse in history. However, Editor's Note was the better horse in the Belmont. He won by a length. Skip Away was second and My Flag third.

After the race, Rene Douglas told the press, "He came close to the other horse, and he wanted to hang a little bit."

"He wasn't hanging," Lukas shot back. "He wanted to go over and take a little piece out of Skip Away. I said before the race that if it's a streetfight, a brawl, he's the one to beat." Editor's Note was owned by Overbrook Farms, and had been bought by Lukas and William T. Young for $125,000 at the Keeneland sales. On that day alone he had won $437,880 in purse money.

Young also owned Grindstone. "The excitement of these Triple Crown races has had me on the verge of tears several times," the seventy-seven-year-old horseman said, standing next to Lukas. "But now I am going to have a good cry of happiness." It was Young's second Belmont; he had won in 1994 with Tabasco Cat.

"I've been blessed with great horses and wonderful owners," Lukas said. "It's what it's all about!"

Apparently, Cavonnier's injury wasn't life-threatening, though the horse had been removed from the field via ambulance. He'd taken a bad step coming into the stretch. He was retired not too long after the race. "He has been a sound horse and always tried very hard," a stunned Baffert told the press corps. "This is every trainer's nightmare because you always wonder about a career injury and saving the horse." He also said, "When I was coming back here, I was thinking I was going to see something horrible. This horse is like a brother."

Lukas was now the undisputed king of the hill. In the past three years he had dominated the Triple Crown series like no other trainer before him. He'd won seven out of the last nine classics. And he'd won three Belmont Stakes in a row, second behind only Woody Stephens himself.

As 1996 ended, he had completed a run that will stand as long and will be as hard to duplicate as Aaron's home run record or Cal Ripken's consecutive games played record. On top of that, he was the season earnings leader, with $15,966,344, reaping 192 wins out of 1,006 starts. It was the most money he had earned in one season since 1991, during his heyday. Lukas would also celebrate the crowning of Boston Harbor, who won the 1996 Breeders' Cup Juvenile, as the two-year-old champion. Despite all this, however, he was not voted Trainer of the Year.

NINE

THE BIG RIVALRY

Deeds Not Words

If 1996 had been bold and brazen, 1997 would be desperate and cheesy. Lukas's next turn was far more detrimental to his reputation. For while he had delivered on the 1996 Derby with Grindstone, his 1997 Derby entry, Deeds Not Words, would prove that Lukas was as overreaching as he was ambitious and give his critics ammunition for years to come.

Coming out of the previous year, Lukas's stable of stars for the 1997 season included Sharp Cat and Boston Harbor, who had been the 1996 two-year-old champion and was an early Derby favorite. But Boston Harbor ran poorly in the Santa Catalina at Santa Anita Park on February 2, fading after a good start and finishing fourth, fourteen lengths behind the winner.

"We took a little roll of the dice on conditioning here, going this far," Lukas said afterward. "I still feel comfortable in what we tried to do. I think we'll get more out of this than if we sprinted him." But the shine was definitely off the apple.

Still, Lukas was considered a threat for any Triple Crown race. He could win it with a star or with an unknown. He'd pulled it off with both. In 1997 he nominated twenty-three horses, and discussed the problems of two-year-old and three-year-old racing. Not all two-year-old champions make it to the next year, he explained, because the three-year-old distances are longer and require a different build than the shorter races for juveniles. "Many of our two-year-old champions, horses like Gilded Time, probably weren't suited to the Triple Crown distances," he told writer Ed Golden. "Just because you have a horse that's well-suited to two-year-old racing, his pedigree may not equate to a three-year-old season."

Among the nominations were such horses as Boston Harbor, Alamocitos, Deeds Not Words, Gold Tribute, Partner's Hero, Wrightwood, and Sharp Cat, a highly regarded filly. Lukas went on to explain that his stable tends to overnominate because the owners want their horses mentioned, and that listing their horses early costs much less than coming in late. He rationalized this by saying, "Our ownership wants to do it, and it's their money, so we go ahead and nominate." But early in 1997 things weren't going well, and his horses did poorly.

On April 20, Lukas ran Deeds Not Words in the Lexington Stakes at Keeneland. He had been hoping, with a good win, to aim the horse at the Derby. But the horse finished a disappointing third. Lukas said that Deeds Not Words was a good horse but not yet ready, and he would not run him in the Derby. "I knew we were catching up with him, but it was a tall order, and it just didn't fall into place."

So by April 24, with the Derby nine days away, Lukas was in trouble. None of his shining stars at the beginning of the season had come through. Boston Harbor, his biggest star, had broken his cannon bone in February and was no longer a contender. In an article entitled, "Where's Lukas?" Cindy Pierson wrote, "For the first time since 1980 trainer D. Wayne Lukas probably will not have a Derby entry." She recounted his exploits and triumphs, and took a few shots. "This is a major downward turn for Lukas, however, it just goes to show all the money in the world can't always buy you a Derby horse. Lukas always has the backing to buy all the top yearlings but it just wasn't enough this year." His streak of running in the Kentucky Derby for sixteen years was about to be broken.

Lukas had tried a number of things in order to avoid the ignominy of not having a Derby entrant. He'd tried to orchestrate a sale of Concerto, a colt owned by New York Yankees owner George Steinbrenner and trained by John Tammaro III, but that hadn't materialized. He also attempted to talk Sharp Cat's owner, Prince Ahmed Salman, into letting him enter the star filly in the Derby instead of the Oaks. Lukas made this pitch public, saying: "The prince himself has such a passion for the big events; nobody enjoys racing more than Prince Ahmed. I think the voice of reason will probably be Dick Mulhall"— the prince's thoroughbred adviser. "I have a tendency to roll the dice, especially when they're going good. The thing that's warping my thinking is I've never seen this filly quite as good as I've got her right now." That was a misstatement, since the filly had failed miserably in her first try against the boys, finishing a lowly fifth in the Santa Anita Derby on April 5.

On April 26, Lukas told a reporter, "I can handle it, no problem. I'd like to be in it, but I'll feel comfortable not being there, after the run we've had." He added, "It's kind of like being Dean Smith. It's not good enough to get to the Final Four anymore, you have to win it. It's like there are two sets of standards, one for me and another one for the rest."

The Associated Press ran a story on April 28 revealing the behind-the-scenes story about Sharp Cat. Lukas admitted that he was training her for the Kentucky Oaks but that he wanted to race her in the Derby: "If I owned her, I would run her in the Derby. I really think the prince would like to go in the Derby." But Mulhall and the prince didn't fall for it. Lukas would have to go elsewhere. He told the press on Tuesday, "I'm out."

Then Lukas went to Michael Tabor, owner of Deeds Not Words. The deadline for entries was May 1. On April 29, Deeds Not Words worked three furlongs in 36.2, the fourth fastest time of twenty horses that worked the same distance that day. After this work, Tabor called officials at Churchill Downs, explaining that he planned to race the colt in the upcoming Kentucky Derby.

Lukas was in. He had his Derby horse. He also had just brought more heat on himself. The next morning, he stood outside his barn and told reporters, "I have always liked this horse. We always thought he had great ability. We thought he merits a chance." The racing community was dumbfounded.

Deeds Not Words was not a Derby horse, nor was he a mediocre horse. In 1996 he raced only twice and earned $30,865. He took his maiden win in an unremarkable venue (though he did beat the eventual Derby favorite, Silver Charm), and then finished third in the Best Pal Stakes. In 1997, as a three-year-old, Deeds Not Words came in third at the Lexington Stakes, and collected $32,350. His pedigree— Rubiano out of Charming Tiara (by Alydar)—marked him as a quality horse, but his racing performance said he was a bum.

"I won a lot of races where I didn't belong," Lukas chided reporters, and then warned them, "Be careful what kind of spin you put on this because we might end up making you look silly."

Lukas wasn't alone or the first in entering a horse of dubious distinction. There had been other stinkers in previous years. And there was even a decidedly unqualified horse entered just before his: Crimson Classic had won two allowance races in New Orleans and then finished fourth in a stakes race in Turfway Park. "Then in the Lone Star Derby, he was sent off at odds of 68–1, and promptly unseated his rider," Rob Longley of the *Toronto Sun* wrote.

The morning line on Lukas's horse was 50–1. Later, oddsmaker Mike Battaglia would say, "I've never made a Wayne Lukas–trained horse 50–1 before."

When reporters asked Lukas about it, he snapped, "If I listened to the odds, Thunder Gulch would not have been on the board."

Deeds Not Words drew the number 11 post position. But few at the drawing of numbers seemed to care. When asked why he was entering a 50–1 shot, Lukas gave a new answer: "The weather was a factor," referring to the possibility of rain. "This horse is outstanding on a muddy track."

"Oh, that's it," national columnist Ray Buck wrote. "So keep him in mind if it's a sloppy track Saturday, 5–2 Captain Bodgit and 50–1 Deeds Not Words are both mudders. But only one of them can possibly win."

There were two other 50–1 shots in the race—Crimson Classic and Celtic Warrior. Danny Hutt, Celtic Warrior's trainer, was of the opinion that Deeds Not Words would not go off 50–1. "People are going to bet on Lukas if he sends a pony over there," he said. Few reporters bothered to point out that Nick Zito had also entered a couple of 30–1 long shots in Jack Flash and Shammy Davis.

Lukas tried to counter the sarcasm and suspicions of the press, saying: "Don't be saying I'm entering him just to keep the streak going. Sure, we're rolling the dice, but we know he's a talented horse. In light of our record, I don't think we have to apologize for running him."

Another response was: "Whatever you do, please, I'm not running this horse just to have a horse in the Derby. I've won a lot of important races running horses that didn't belong there." Lukas also tried to deflect some of the criticism he was getting onto his owners: "Of my thirty-one entries, for seventeen or eighteen I could have said, 'Look, let's reconsider this.' But we're just employees. We're paid to give these people what they want when they put their money up." The press latched onto this like a pit bull on a mailman's leg. Now they had their sound bite, and they wouldn't let it go, ever.

A media circus erupted, and suddenly Lukas was the hottest news story on the backstretch. He made for better copy than Pulpit, the lukewarm favorite going into the race. "If you step into this arena, you're fair game," Lukas told one reporter. "And face it, this is the center court; this is the main arena."

"I ought to do this every year," he commented at one point. "We run an 80–1 long shot, and we get this kind of treatment." It was an attempt at humor during a difficult week, when columnists were lambasting Lukas for placing an unqualified horse in the Derby, which they saw as a move just to keep his streak alive. Dick Jerardi, for example, wrote in the *Philadelphia Daily News*: "Deeds Not Words is a testament to his trainer's lust for attention, and nothing else."

Another poke at him, which Lukas didn't joke about, was in the *Courier-Journal*, where Pat Forde called him "D.(elusional) Wayne Lukas." Lukas actually wanted to resort to fisticuffs in the parking lot to settle their differences. Forde, unrepentant, would write a year later: "The colt wallowed around the track in last place, just desserts for an act of unvarnished vanity. The fact that Lukas then went into a prolonged and petulant counterattack on the media only made it worse."

Another reporter wrote: "Derby fever is easy to catch and hard to get rid of, even for Lukas."

Michael "Roxy" Roxborough, a Las Vegas oddsmaker, told *Las Vegas Review-Journal* columnist Joe Hawk, "That horse has won just one race in his life, and he shouldn't be in this race. Lukas is like a fighter who doesn't know when his skills are gone—not that his skills are gone—but he didn't have a horse to put in this race."

"The charge against D. Wayne Lukas is obsession," wrote well-traveled horse writer Tim Sullivan, who later referred to Lukas as a cowboy Captain Ahab. "Horse racing's most accomplished trainer is allegedly afflicted with a virulent form of Kentucky Derby fever." But Sullivan did give Lukas a forum in which to defend himself. "I think we have a certain obligation to the industry to represent it, and this is our main arena . . . this is our day," Lukas said, referring to the Kentucky Derby. "If my name is thrown out and they say, 'What about this goofy S.O.B. running the horse in the Derby?' So be it. Whatever, at least they're talking about it."

And Billy Reed, in his *Herald-Leader* column, came to Lukas's defense, extolling his records and accomplishments: "Lukas, like his friend Bob Knight in college basketball, is held to a different standard. . . . Since he saddled his first Derby horse in 1981, Lukas has been accessible, quotable, and cooperative. Every writer's dream. Yet because he's confident and optimistic, he rubs many members of the media the wrong way." Reed also warned the public about the savaging of Lukas by the media types who see one horse race a year: "Lukas is the reigning king of the Triple Crown. And if the king chooses to go down in combat instead of watching from the sidelines, he deserves to be applauded for at least entering the arena and striving to win."

Interviewed on CBS television after the Preakness, Lukas complained that the accusation that he entered a horse in a race where an owner would have to put up a $30,000 entry fee was ridiculous. It was an owner's horse, an owner's money, and an owner's decision. "Michael Tabor is not going to wire thirty thousand dollars to anybody just to see his trainer in the Triple Crown. It was a joint decision and I take responsibility for leading him over there. But believe me, the ultimate decision for a thirty thousand dollar entry fee in the Kentucky Derby is going to come from the owner and the manager."

Deeds Not Words finished dead last in the Derby. And Lukas had no luck in the Kentucky Oaks either, where Sharp Cat bore out in the stretch and finished third in a tough, competitive field, but was later disqualified and placed eighth. "We had some traffic problems on the first turn," Corey Nakatani said of Deeds Not Words after the race. "A little bit of seasoning is all he needs." Kind words.

After the race, Richard Skinner said it best: "The horse backed up the critics by running last in the thirteen-horse field." It had been an ugly rout, with Deeds Not Words never racing closer than eighth and finishing twenty-five lengths behind winner Silver Charm, trained by Bob Baffert and owned by Bob and Beverly Lewis. To Lukas, while he would never say so in public, the loss to Baffert had to be particularly galling.

"It was nice to see that D. Wayne Lukas's last minute entry of Deeds Not Words, just to keep his streak of consecutive Derbies with an entry alive, proved to be as futile as it appeared," Cindy Pierson wrote. "Poor Deeds Not Words faded badly to be dead last. Hopefully the horse will be fine after the drubbing he received, but Lukas's ego should be a bit bruised now."

And another writer, Buck Johnson chimed in with, "Writers here blasted him . . . and most agree that we could have used more deeds from the horse and less words from Lukas. The nag finished last, allowing Lukas to go from first to worst as a Derby trainer in one year."

Lukas was incensed. He told the writers: "Next year we'll go to the Derby, and you'll have to deal with it because we'll be there. Don't think we won't."

A year later he would be able to say: "The biggest mistake you make is running horses that don't belong. And we're all guilty of that. But there's so much behind it that won't come out. Maybe in a book when I'm eighty-five. . . ."

Now, Lukas says: "Not only would I not run Deeds Not Words, I would have probably not run fifteen of the other thirty. You see, when you get into the Derby, the thing that you can't do is call a press conference and tell everybody what is actually happening out there. Gene Klein's an example. He calls up and he wants you to run Balboa Native or Life's Magic or someone. And you work for these people, so you're in a tough spot. Those people spend millions and millions of dollars on yearlings.

"Another example is On the Line. He won the Derby Trial. The minute he crossed the line, Gene said to me, 'Well we're going to run him in the Derby.' I said, 'Gene, I don't think he can come back in a week. And I think he's a miler.' Well, it turns out he was a top sprinter; he's only a six-furlong horse. Gene said, 'No, I've seen enough. He goes.' And then you go before the press, and do you say 'Gene Klein's a buffoon, he doesn't know a thing about racing, he's stupid, but we're going to run this horse?' So they say it for you. They say Lukas stood there and said he's gonna run On the Line, and then they go back to their typewriters and they say Lukas is a buffoon.

"So you get into that all the time. But you must defend his position. You have to say, 'Look, he paid his money, he's entitled to the moment, maybe we could go a different direction, but I'm going to do my best to get him over there.' The writer, he goes and says everything you'd like to say. Of the thirty or so we've run in the Derby, I'd say there's ten or twelve or fifteen. . . . If I ever write a book I'll tell every one of the stories behind them."

Sharp Cat was taken out of Lukas's care in December 1997 and placed in the hands of trainer Wally Dollase. Dollase and Prince Ahmed reached a three-year agreement when the prince and Lukas could not come to terms. "The prince wants all the horses to go to Dollase," Mulhall said. "We talked about maybe keeping Sharp Cat with Wayne. But Prince Ahmed wants a private trainer, and he wants the private trainer to have all the horses."

As for Deeds Not Words, on June 22, 1998, he shattered the sesamoid bone in his front right leg in an allowance race at Churchill Downs. It was his first start since the embarrassing fiasco at the 1997 Derby. The poor horse was euthanized.

While Deeds Not Words had been disparaged in the name of Lukas's overreaching vanity, his name has not died. Every spring it's dragged out by the press. Whenever they write about Lukas and the Derby, whenever they talk about horses who don't belong, poor Deeds Not Words lives again.

Bob Baffert

Over the years, Lukas has had many rivals: Schvaneveldt, Whittingham, Stephens, Zito. But the one he is most compared with is Bob Baffert. There are many reasons why. Both began racing quarter horses in the Southwest. Both became thoroughbred trainers and started out in California. When they came up in their time, both were young, good-looking, and had a carefully coiffed crop of silver hair. And since Baffert came of age, their careers have been interlinked.

The other thing they have in common is that they have both dominated thoroughbred racing. Between 1995 and 1999, Lukas and Baffert would make the Triple Crown races their own stage for one-upmanship. It would be their personal checkerboard. And it would not be until the year 2000 that someone else would seriously challenge their silver-haired reign.

In his autobiography, *Dirt Road to the Derby*, written with Steve Haskins, Baffert recalls calling Lukas when he was about to leave high school and Lukas had come to Sonita, Arizona. "When he showed up, he just took over. I mean it was a show. When Wayne rolled into town it was like Barnum and Bailey. He was a showman to the max and I really liked that." It was in 1970 or 1971, and Baffert called Lukas at his hotel room and asked for a job as a rider. "He really built me up," Baffert remembered. "When I got off the phone,

I felt really great, even though I didn't get the job." Years later, Baffert realized it was probably a good thing too. "I don't think I would have lasted too long with Wayne. He just gets up too damned early. It would have been a tough grind and he would have fired my ass in an instant." It was only the beginning of a great many conversations between the silver-haired "California" trainers.

Baffert was born on January 13, 1953, and was raised on a ranch near Nogales, Arizona. He actually rode as a jockey, with sprinters, before training his first quarter horse winner in 1971. He raced horses at Rillito Park, Los Alamitos, and many other popular quarter horse venues, and won graded futurities and other stakes races. He trained horses for quarter-horse owner Rulon Goodman, for whom Lukas had also trained, when he had quarter horses. Baffert and Lukas shared many Lukas stories with each other.

In 1983, Baffert decided to make the jump to California. He continued to race quarter horses there, and raced them exclusively until 1988. His most famous quarter horse was Gold Coast Express. Between 1988 and 1991 he raced thoroughbreds as well. "A man named Mike Pegram got me into thoroughbred racing," Baffert told the press corps after the 1997 Kentucky Derby. "I told him I'd need a bankroll, at least $300,000. I thought that would blow him away. He asked me, 'How about a million?' I said, 'I'm your man.'"

In late 1991 he was racing only thoroughbreds, and in 1992 won the Breeders' Cup Sprint with Thirty Slews. His thoroughbred career was off and running. And so was his family. Baffert had gotten married in 1984, and he and his wife Sherry now have four children: Canyon, Savannah, Taylor, and Forest.

By 1995, Baffert and Lukas were not only coming into contact, but confrontation. It was subtle and by degrees. But by the 1996 Kentucky Derby, when Baffert's Cavonnier lost by a nose to Lukas's Grindstone, they were full-fledged rivals. Baffert and Sherry had waited in the stands for the '96 Derby results. After Grindstone's number was put up and they were leaving the stands, they ran into William T. Young and Young's daughter, Lucy. "We were both in the same fraternity in college, Sigma Alpha Epsilon," Baffert said of Young, "and I slipped him the secret grip. He was so excited and he thanked me. And as much as I hated to get beat, and hated to get beat by D. Wayne Lukas, at least here was a good man who had won."

It would have been difficult for Baffert and Lukas to be friends while competing for the same stakes. Perhaps even more significant were the owners they had in common.

Certainly, if anything heats up the blood in both men, it's when Bob and Beverly Lewis are involved. Bob Lewis's goal is to keep his managers jumping, both at work and at play. He believes that pitting the two best trainers in North America against each other is the best way to make his hard earned money pay off.

A sample of this competition took place when Baffert had the Lewises come out to see Silver Charm run in an allowance race in which Baffert assumed the horse would break its maiden status. He had bought Silver Charm for the Lewises for $80,000. Out of nowhere, Lukas's horse, Deeds Not Words, blew by Silver Charm and took the race. Baffert was both angered and embarrassed.

Another time, Baffert told them that Silver Charm would blow away Gold Tribute, a Lukas-trained horse. In fact, Lukas had bought Gold Tribute for the Lewises for $725,000. The race was in Saratoga, and Lukas was with the Lewises when the race began. "Wait until you see this horse run," he told them. As they hit the stretch, Lukas said, "Here he comes. He's gonna show 'em."

"Just then," Baffert recalled, "ol' Silver Charm kicks away from him and wins going away."

Before Cavonnier, Lukas could look on Baffert as an up-and-comer whom he could trade stories with. And indeed Baffert and Lucas talked often. But winning was and is important to both men, and so, as their rivalry evolved, it was impossible for the jokester from Arizona and the basketball coach from Antigo to be anything more than cordial. Baffert's onslaught of Triple Crown winners would make it even more impossible.

Baffert claimed it was at the '96 Derby, in which Grindstone beat Cavonnier, that the relationship between them was poisoned by writer Rick Bozich. Baffert said that he and Bozich were discussing owners, and Bozich took some quotes from him out of context and used them in an article against Lukas.

Lukas was upset and confronted Baffert at a champagne toast after Baffert's horse won the Churchill Downs Handicap. He asked Baffert why he was taking shots at him in the press. Baffert, ever the jokester, admitted that he'd made fun of Lukas's ten-gallon white Stetson all week. When Lukas told him about the article, Baffert denied the quotes that Bozich had ascribed to him. But an angry Lukas didn't believe him. "You want to go toe-to-toe with me in the press," he said, "I'll go toe-to-toe with you."

Baffert said he confronted Lukas later on, at the Preakness, and tried to discuss the situation with him, to no avail. Any possibility of friendship between them was destroyed. "It was too bad, because I really liked the guy at one time," Baffert said. Their competition in the main arena and their dual involvement with the Lewises would have made them rivals regardless. As newspaper reporter Frank Angst put it: "While Baffert and Lukas are proven horsemen, they also have a knack of convincing wealthy people to spend money on top horses. Baffert and Lukas dress to run in these circles. They're top salesmen and top horsemen."

Baffert had been the Lewises' trainer first and began working with them in 1990. It was he who introduced them to Lukas, during the course of social engagements and everyday work, and in 1992 the Lewises also hired Lukas. So open is the competition between the two trainers that more than one column has been devoted to the Lewises divisive but successful strategy. Richard Eng, in the *Las Vegas Review-Journal*, wrote: "Lewis has openly pitted two incredibly gifted horsemen, Baffert vs. Lukas, to take young equine talent and mold it into the best racehorses that money can buy. By Lewis's own accounts, Baffert and Lukas have won him more than twenty Grade 1 stakes this decade. There aren't many North American owners who can boast those accomplishments."

It was 1997, the year of Deeds Not Words, that would be the turning point in the relationship between the two trainers. Baffert entered Silver Charm, while Lukas entered his uncompetitive horse. Silver Charm was spirited, and days before the race threw exercise rider Larry Damore. Other than that, all the thrills were on the track. Silver Charm had been beaten by Free House in the Santa Anita Derby, but some felt that Gary Stevens had given him a bad ride. It was assumed that the jockey would not make the same mistakes this time around, and that Silver Charm had an edge.

When the horses turned for home, Captain Bodgit and Silver Charm led the field. It was a heart-stomping duel, with Silver Charm intimidating Captain Bodgit, but not enough to encourage a formal complaint.

Baffert was in the stands with the Lewises. Lukas wasn't. In the past, Lukas had trained horses like Serena's Song and Timber Country for the Lewises—high profile, highly rated stakes winners. And up till then, Baffert wasn't getting the Lewises' best horses. Now, when his horse crossed the finish line, "Baffert's arms shot into the air and he waved his program," as the Associated Press reported the next day, "then he turned and hugged seventy-two-year-old Bob Lewis. . . ."

"When they plant me six feet under, I want my tombstone to say 'Loving husband, adoring father, and winner of the 123rd Kentucky Derby,'" Lewis said. "And if I have to come back to check it, I will."

Compare that to Lukas's fate that year: it was the second time he had a horse finish last. The previous disaster was Total Departure in 1982. Lewis told the press that Lukas "was one of the first men to throw his arms around me today. He said, 'I'm sorry I'm not part of the team, but I certainly respect and love each member of *your* team.'"

Silver Charm had won the Derby. It was Baffert's ascendancy highlighted against Lukas's lowest moment. Score one for the young, funny guy. Baffert put the big silver bowl on his head, like some kind of party animal. It was an act the nation loved. But it was no laughing matter. It took the spotlight away from Lukas. Worse yet, it meant that there was yet another high-rolling trainer that the big money guys could go spend their money with.

"Suddenly, a major client of Lukas's was shifting money and attention to this glib combination of Henny Youngman and rising star trainer," Eng wrote for the *Las Vegas Review-Journal*.

Now Baffert had a shot at the Triple Crown. And Lukas didn't have a horse to stop him with. He would have no entries in either the Preakness nor the Belmont Stakes that year. While Lukas had taken a Triple Crown of sorts, Baffert, after Silver Charm took the Preakness, was only one race away from a *real* Triple Crown winner.

Interviewed for CBS Sportsline and asked about Baffert, Lukas said all the right things, such as, "I've always known Bob, like him, respect him. I say this without any reservation—he's done a super job of handling this horse." But he went on to say he did not think Silver Charm was of the same caliber as other Triple Crown winners, like Secretariat or Affirmed. Pressed about the rivalry between them, he said: "We've crossed paths, but you have to know Bob and Beverly Lewis to appreciate the relationship we have. They like Bob. We're both very, very close to the Lewises and I think we work well together, and I don't really feel any rivalry at all on a day-to-day basis." It was good old-fashioned coachspeak. Very professional.

It happened that Silver Charm was barely beaten by Touch Gold in the Belmont, before a huge crowd that was hoping to see the first Triple Crown winner in nineteen years. Affirmed had been the last to win all three races, in 1978. It did not go unnoticed that Lukas had missed out on chasing Woody Stephens's Belmont Stakes record. Lukas's three-race winning streak came to an end that weekend.

He did take take his fourth straight training title in 1997, reaping $9,993,569 from 169 wins in 824 starts. It was the fourteenth money title earned by him in fifteen years. The accolades, however, went to Baffert, who would be named Trainer of the Year, and whose Silver Charm would be Champion Three-Year-Old.

One more thing happened in 1997: Dallas Stewart, one of Lukas's top assistants over the past three years, left Team Lukas. Stewart had been the lead man in Kentucky. He had plans to go out on his own, he said, and would base his stable out of Churchill Downs.

As Lukas was getting older, the number of his former assistants starting their own successful stables would continue to grow.

Cape Town vs. Indian Charlie and Real Quiet

Baffert was the sport's new golden boy. And Lukas was the old man now, playing the grizzled old veteran Whittingham to Baffert's brand spanking new Lukas. How the worm had turned.

But the Lukas who showed up at the 1998 Kentucky Derby was more relaxed, even if he was playing hard. The 1998 Run for the Roses would be stacked with celebrities and stories. As usual, the Derby prep season would begin with a number of good horses, slowly whittled away until the few good ones were left standing.

One of Lukas's major horses for the spring, three-year-old campaign was Cape Town, a son of Seeking the Gold. On March 14, Cape Town won the Florida Derby at Gulfstream Park when Li'l Lad was disqualified for bumping Cape Town near the wire. Li'l Lad, a Derby favorite early in the spring, was relegated to second by the stewards. He would go on to the Blue Grass Stakes, where he would take second, but would miss the Derby because of a bone chip in his knee.

"The Florida Derby was very significant for Cape Town, of course for the win, but more importantly, by the style of the victory, so we're real pleased with his victory," Lukas said after the race.

As the *Thoroughbred Times* pointed out on April 13: "The annual Kentucky Derby jockey's shuffle began on Monday when D. Wayne Lukas announced that Jerry Bailey would replace Shane Sellers aboard Florida Derby winner Cape Town in the May 2 running of the 1¼ classic."

"I've won the Derby three times, with Bailey and Stevens," Lukas said. "I feel like if I'd have gotten either one of them I'd be bettering my position, and this only comes around once." Bailey had been riding Li'l Lad, and became available when the horse was pulled out of competition.

Lukas had two other possible Derby or Triple Crown candidates: Grand Slam and Yarrow Brae. Grand Slam was an awesome specimen who had injured himself during the Breeders' Cup Juvenile and then hadn't raced until March 29 of the next year. If he had stayed healthy, he might have been a Derby horse, but it seemed his injuries might need more time to heal. Lukas decided to aim him at the Lexington Stakes and take his chances.

Yarrow Brae was a more accomplished horse, if less dazzling. He'd been runner-up in the Jim Beam on March 29, and was poised to run in the Derby Trial Stakes at Churchill Downs on April 25.

When asked to evaluate the talent out there early on in the season, the one Lukas was following most closely was Indian Charlie, Baffert's big horse. "I think Indian Charlie has been very well managed," he said, "but obviously, he's taken a very soft route, and so be it. I think we have to see him at least in graded company before we can offer any definitive opinions." Indian Charlie had won three allowance races.

Cape Town developed nicely, came in third at the Blue Grass Stakes, and was a definite Derby horse. "I don't think the Blue Grass always equates what's going to happen in the Derby," Lukas told writer Jody Demling. "If I could have gone over there with no more than I did with him and got around and won the race, I would have been ecstatic. I think if I didn't have a horse I thought could win the Kentucky Derby, I might try to win the Blue Grass." Of course, Lukas didn't want his horse to have a great day at the Blue Grass, he wanted him to have a great day at the Kentucky Derby. He also knew that one horse in the past decade had won his final prep and won the Derby, so Cape Town's third-place finish would not have concerned him. Cape Town and Lukas were in.

However, the questions about Yarrow Brae and Grand Slam remained. Yarrow Brae had finished second in the Derby trial, one of the last preps before the Derby. Lukas was waiting for the horse's owners to decide if they felt the horse was ready. It seemed unlikely.

And now here they were at Derby week.

Lukas was proud of Cape Town. He had a competitive horse and he was talking him up. "After being here sixteen or seventeen years," the grizzled veteran said, "you notice a certain stereotype about the horses that win here. This is a horse that has a marvelous disposition and can handle all the hoopla. . . . This is the strongest horse we've ever started here."

It was obvious that Lukas still had passion for the game. Asked why was he still there, he said: "Winning the first one fuels you more than ever. You constantly think about it and want to get back. Winning three Kentucky Derbies is never going to be enough."

"We're going to take one of our better horses over there in the last few years," Lukas said of Cape Town. "I think this colt has an excellent chance to win, and that we're going to be fourth or fifth choice shows you the quality of the field. You've got to consider Favorite Trick, an undefeated Indian Charlie, and it's just been an excellent field with a lot of blend."

Lukas was hoping for a fun Derby week. He didn't have to answer too many questions about his horse that were negative. Everyone thought he had a solid if not spectacular entry in Cape Town. But this would be another twenty-horse field, and there was talent in every barn.

In Baffert's Barn there were three horses of interest: Indian Charlie, Real Quiet, and Silver Charm, now a four-year-old. The previous Derby winner had won the Dubai World Cup in March. Everyone wanted to go down Baffert's stalls and take a look at the three horses.

"I have the same confidence I had with Silver Charm," Baffert said of Indian Charlie, who had now won three allowance and one stakes race, the latter the prestigious Santa Anita Derby. Indian Charlie was a popular choice.

Baffert called Real Quiet, another three-year-old, his Derby insurance. The horse had gone about his business nicely, but was not as highly thought of as Indian Charlie. He'd finished second in both the San Felipe and the Santa Anita Stakes. Both were extremely close finishes. It could be said that Indian Charlie was to Timber Country as Real Quiet was to Thunder Gulch, except they were in Baffert's barn. But how would this version play out? Early on in Derby week, Baffert told a group of writers: "I have two really good horses. Let the games begin."

The two biggest trainers on the backstretch were selling their horses, and things were about to get a lot more colorful.

In 1998, Lukas was not the only basketball coach walking the grounds. Rick Pitino, who at the time was coach of the professional Boston Celtics, had a horse with trainer Nick Zito. The two New York–area fellas were walking around pitching their colt, Halory Hunter, a horse owned by Pitino's thoroughbred stable, Celtic Pride. The personable Pitino chatted easily with everyone, and was stopped every few feet by another writer or autograph seeker. And he and Zito were using every opportunity to spin for their horse. But it wasn't all salesmanship. There was some fun too.

"The worst handicapper I've ever seen is D. Wayne Lukas," Pitino told Pat Forde, who loves a good Lukas story as much as anyone else. Forde and Pitino were discussing the difference between handicapping horses and training them. Pitino told a story of how he and a friend, whom he called Jersey Red, had been at a track when they saw Lukas, who gave them "thirty horses to bet. He told us, 'Take 'em to the window.'" Apparently, each horse was a bum. Not one of the thirty finished in the top three. So Pitino and Jersey Red went backside and found Lukas. "None of these tips have worked out," Pitino told Lukas.

"Oh, I'm the worst handicapper that's ever been," Lukas said, laughing. Jersey Red wasn't laughing. He went bust and had to go home with nothing in his pocket.

In 1998 there were few people milling around Barn 44. It was quieter, yet more upbeat, than it had been in years past. The crowds of gawking reporters were moving in smaller groups to the other barns. Lukas even joked with reporters, saying he didn't think "thirty people even knew we were in the race. It's been pleasant serenity we've had around here. And that's fine." But as competitive as Lukas is and was, the ever increasing mob surrounding Baffert's Barn 33 like a city under seige must have eaten at his stomach lining.

"Get some cameras on him too," Baffert joked with the throng of television reporters that had gathered outside his stable. The commotion got more distracting each day. Asked if he thought his horses were seasoned enough, Baffert playfully responded, "Seasoning? We're not going to eat the son of a gun, so we don't need seasoning."

But Baffert's aw-schucks, good-humored persona is only a mask hiding his competitive fire. Like Lukas, he is a horseman and a horse trader. And he was selling as well as anyone. In fact, he had them all eating out of his hand. "This horse is getting better and better," he said of Real Quiet, "and I really loved the way he went on the track today," But not wanting to skip a chance to sell his other colt too, he added: "Indian Charlie is a faster horse."

Alternately, a few reporters couldn't wait to pick at Lukas in his solitude. Neil Schmidt, in his "Derby Notebook" column for the *Cincinnati Enquirer*, wrote: "His media magnetism may be waning.

About fifteen reporters attended his press conference Wednesday [April 29], a mere fraction of the crowds he drew in past years—or what Bob Baffert or Nick Zito draw now."

For 123 years the draw at Churchill Downs for the Kentucky Derby was a simple affair, covered by the print media. In 1998 it would be televised. What better way was there to get a little extra coverage for the event than to televise it? So everyone involved gathered. Chris Lincoln, an ESPN racing analyst, emceed the event. As the balls determining post position were taken out of the traditional milk bottle, it appeared there were two number fifteens. Oops! Quickly, Bernie Hettle took all the numbers back and decided to begin again. It was a fiasco. "It made for great television, all right, if you consider those bloopers shows to be great television," wrote Bill Koch, a well-known racing scribe. "And the wonderful thing about it was that a TV guy mucked up the made-for-TV event."

Churchill Downs president Thomas Meeker said: "Matching up the pill with the sheet, apparently, is a tough job." He was joking, adding: "This is not brain surgery." While it didn't make for a great television spot, it made for a wonderful media circus.

"I feel like they did the right thing," Lukas said respectfully. "I agree with their decision to redraw the race." But he was disappointed that thoroughbred racing had come off so badly on national television. He thought the whole thing was a screw-up, that the event should have been shown and then ESPN could have conducted the interviews afterward. He told another reporter, "It was unfair for Chris to have some guy in a production truck telling him to switch to Jane Doe for an interview, announcing the pill, and worrying about commercials and everything else. That's too much to ask of one person."

At the draw, or redraw, Baffert was asked about his strategy. He replied: "Our strategy was to go have a couple of beers before we came here tonight."

"Until Chris Lincoln choked on a pill Wednesday, Madeline Paulson and Jenny Craig had pulled the silliest stunt of the 124th Kentucky Derby," Pat Forde wrote. "Milli Vanilli has a better chance of making the Rock and Roll Hall of Fame than Rock and Roll has of making it to the Churchill Downs winner's circle."

Rock and Roll was a spurious entry. He was not a very accomplished horse, but his claim to fame was that he was owned by two women, one of whom, weight-loss guru Jenny Craig, was famous. No matter that the colt was trained by Bill Mott and not a female trainer, these owners were pitching girl power. It was a publicity stunt.

Lukas made the ultimate mistake in commenting about Rock and Roll. He was upset that no one was going after Bill Mott the way the press had come after him the year before. He should have taken the high road, but he couldn't resist. "When they were on Rodeo Drive and those hats matched the shoes, Bill was dead," Lukas said. "He had no shot [at talking them out of the race]." Insert foot in mouth.

Lukas precipitated a war of words. Paulson and Craig quickly enumerated the number of Lukas horses that finished tenth or worse up to that time. Then Paulson said, "I guess you've got to love Wayne for his . . ."

"Ego?" Jenny Craig asked.

"I guess you could call it that. . . . Wayne should remember," Paulson warned, "that women live longer than men. We'll be here to throw stones after he's gone."

The day of the race, Lukas had some showmanship of his own, which he unleashed. Famous people were milling around Barn 44 while the national television cameras were there. Standing next to Lukas or walking around his barn were Hollywood starlet and horsewoman Bo Derek and legendary former University of Michigan football coach Bo Schembechler. Also on hand was former Dallas Cowboys executive Gil Brandt, who told reporters: "He also called his friend, Bob Knight, to come down here. And when Wayne calls friends here, he's confident." It was the right mix, and it was on screen in people's living rooms. It seemed that Lukas hadn't lost a step.

As for the race itself, as the horses made the near turn for the final stretch, the front-runners were Indian Charlie, Real Quiet, Victory Gallop, Halory Hunter, and Cape Town. Cape Town could not sustain his drive, and finished fifth. Indian Charlie got third, Victory Gallop second, and Real Quiet won.

Baffert had pulled a Lukas. "This is the most emotional race any trainer or owner can get involved in," he said afterward. "My guts were killing me from the pain just from screaming and trying to get those two horses going."

"I thought I had a big chance to win," jockey Jerry Bailey said. "He settled in seventh or eighth down the backside and he cruised up under his own power within a length of them, turning for home."

The next day, the Associated Press ran a story entitled, "BAFFERT'S ON THE LUKAS TRAIL." The article noted the similarities between Timber Country and Thunder Gulch and Indian Charlie and Real Quiet. Talking about Indian Charlie's third place finish after the race, Baffert told reporters, "The seasoning got him. You guys were right."

In Baltimore for the Preakness, Baffert decided to withdraw Indian Charlie. The Derby had been too much for him, while Real Quiet seemed just fine.

Lori Lewis, at Pimlico covering the week's events for Turfonline.com, wrote about Real Quiet and about Baffert—the Derby winner was the obvious and curious star. Then the Lukas horses came in. They "came off the van one by one," she wrote, "Trafalger, Baquero, License Fee, and Cape Town. Everyone was searching their memory banks for the markings that would identify them." She described what it was like as the pack of reporters, hungry for a story, followed each horse as it was walked from the van to the barn. Then Lukas arrived "and gave the folks what they were looking for." Television crews quickly set up their cameras as the webbings were put across the stalls.

Lukas was upping the ante in the Preakness. He had brought Bob and Beverly Lewis's Baquero with him to provide Cape Town with a pace setter. With Pat Day aboard, Lukas hoped Baquero would help William T. Young's Cape Town accomplish what he could not do in the Derby—win the race. "It had no bearing on anyone's horses getting injured or anything," Lukas told Pimlico officials Tuesday morning. "I planned to run all along."

Cape Town was picked to win by several racing columnists, and before the race, he would be the crowd's third favorite choice.

Another piece of news concerned trainer Shug McGaughey, who asked Pimlico executives if he could saddle his horse, Coronado's Quest, in a secluded paddock, instead of where everyone else would saddle theirs. This sparked shouts of protest from both Lukas and Baffert.

"That's an enormous edge," Baffert said.

Lukas agreed. "I'm going to saddle [Cape Town] in the exact same spot," he said. "We're all going to play on a level playing field. If he saddles behind a barn, behind an alleyway, I'm going to be there too." It was all wasted breath, as Coronado's Quest was scratched a day before the race.

A little local excitement was added to the color of Preakness day when an electrical transformer fire occurred three blocks away. The blowout disrupted betting in the clubhouse and part of the grandstand; the happy folks in the infield were unaffected. Of course, no electricity meant no air-conditioning in the clubhouse, and Baltimore can get hot and humid in late May. Some spectators saw it as a reason to leave the festivities early. Some went off to local Laurel Raceway to place bets. Many stayed. ABC television wasn't affected at all. They had brought their own generators as backup.

The race went off at its scheduled time, despite the reduced amount of betting, and at the half-mile pole Victory Gallop and Real Quiet moved off together, leaving the field behind. Real Quiet pulled away in the stretch to win it. Classic Cat, winner of the Lexington Stakes, came in third. Baquero finished seventh and Cape Town ninth in the ten-horse field.

Real Quiet's win made Baffert the only trainer ever to win the Derby and the Preakness two years in a row. It also put him on the precipice of winning the Triple Crown for the second year in a row. He boasted after the race: "If I had drawn inside, I would have guaranteed you guys a victory."

Cape Town had thrown his right hind shoe during the race, but it wasn't until days later that it was discovered he'd fractured his left front leg. He had to be retired.

Many columnists became weary of Baffert after reading Billy Reed's column in which Baffert discussed Indian Charlie's problem with the Derby's mile and a quarter distance. "You have to wonder if Baffert was clueless about Indian Charlie's distance limitations before the Derby," Jay Richards wrote, "or purposely being disingenuous."

In the days after the Preakness, McGaughey announced that Coronado's Quest would not join the field at the Belmont Stakes. And on June 2, Yarrow Brae, who had not been ready for the Derby or Preakness, was entered in the Belmont. Yarrow Brae had won the Illinois Derby, after all, and his works were excellent.

"He looks good," said Mike Maker, a Lukas assistant. "We'll be ready to run on Saturday."

Lukas was still undecided about Grand Slam, who had won the Peter Pan Stakes at Belmont. His works were good, but Lukas hesitated. "I'll probably sit like that until Thursday," he told reporters. Grand Slam had not lost a race on the Belmont course.

Meanwhile, the media circus around Baffert continued to whirl. After Real Quiet's final work, Baffert returned to his barn with the horse, only to find a horde of reporters. "I came back to the barn and saw all those people waiting for us," he said. "The Triple Crown really hit me for the first time."

The press realized by June 4, though, that with twelve challengers—five of them new horses—Real Quiet was in for a tough race. It was one of the largest fields any Derby/Preakness winner had ever had to face. The speculation was that rival owners, knowing that Real Quiet's times weren't overly impressive, were ready to take a shot at him. "They're suspect. That's why you've got a lot of new shooters," said H. James Bond, British owner of Belmont competitor Raffie's Majesty. But Baffert and Mike Pegram, Real Quiet's owner, thought the real reason for the swelled field was the newly installed $1 million purse. "Where else can you run for a million dollars this time of year?" Pegram asked.

As for the race itself, the near turn into the final stretch saw almost the same scene that horse players had been seeing all spring: Victory Gallop and Real Quiet challenging each other. Except in the closely contested Belmont, the two horses bumped in the stretch. After some controversy, a photo finish gave the definitive answer: Victory Gallop had won. Elliott Walden had won his first Belmont.

Real Quiet was second. Thomas Jo, ridden by Chris McCarron, finished third. Grand Slam finished seventh. And Yarrow Brae finished next to last.

Love Finds D. Wayne Lukas (Again)

On June 15, 1998, D. Wayne Lukas was married to Laura Pinelli. She was his fourth wife. Pinelli, thirty-one years old at the time of their marriage, was a respected public trainer of quarter horses. The couple were married in Las Vegas early in the evening, and returned to California the following morning so they could both go about training their individual stables. Ironically, Laura had once worked for Baffert.

Born in Anaheim, California, Laura Pinelli tends to wear old, cheap jeans, and is very low key. After graduating high school, she knew that horses were for her, and Los Alamitos was the closest track. "I got my first job at sixteen cleaning a tack room and rolling bandages," she said. "I worked a lot of years grooming horses, but the more I did it, the more I loved it."

She has been a trainer on her own since 1993, reaching a modicum of fame in 1997 when she took a swing at a *Racing Digest* writer whose comments about her were derisive. Nevertheless, she was generally well thought of, if not successful. At the time of her marriage to Lukas, she had earned nearly a million dollars in purses.

In six years of racing, Laura Pinelli had won the Pomona Championship, the 1993 Pacific Coast Quarter Horse Racing Association Futurity, and the 1992 Southern California Derby. She had trained such quarter horse stars as IB Quick, Jetten Setten Man, and The Royal Prince, and saddled 104 winners. She had also conditioned Mr. Bold Tac, another stakes champion. It was Mr. Bold Tac's brother, Drop Your Sox, that she came to Lukas about, advising him to claim the jet-fast horse for $10,000.

After the two were married, Lukas founded a new stable with his wife: D. Wayne Lukas Racing Stables, Quarter Horse Division. Based at Los Alamitos, Laura oversaw the operation as the trainer. But her husband, she admits, is meddlesome.

"The thing is, she understands this business and she understands me," Lukas told Joe Drape. "I'm sure a marriage counselor will tell you that I'm not a very good risk. I don't do anything but train horses." And Laura, Lukas added, is "a little old cowgirl. She'll get in there and muck out the stall herself."

Recently, in a reflective mood about marriage, Lukas said: "I tried it every way there is. If you're a horse trainer, the way I do it, I would say that you are a worse risk than probably a Hollywood type. I understand marriage a little bit. I think they take nurturing, they take caring, they take time, and I don't think you can romance a wife and this too. And I romance this. And I'm so competitive that if one of them's going to suffer, it's the marriage. I'm the first one to tell you I felt like I left every one of my relationships in great order. I'm very fond of every one of them. I think financially they're set for life because I've always had that underlying feeling that I am the reason—maybe I'm being hard on myself, but I don't think so—I think that marriages takes time, and when you get as intense as I am, . . ." he shrugged. "I don't think I'm hard to live with. I think I'm a great date, but not a long-term relationship."

Between the two of them, Wayne and Laura have eight marriages in their past, so neither has stood very long in the marital winner's circle. Laura once entered a quarter horse in a stakes race and sent her then husband out with instructions to ride to win. Laura also ventured into thoroughbreds at one point. She had been an assistant to Baffert for four years, and before that she "worked for a quarter horse trainer who yelled and screamed all the time, who turned everything into a crisis. Nobody could stand working for him. But people like working for Bob. He takes the work as seriously as anyone, but he's fair."

"Laura and I started out just to have fun, because we both like quarter horses," Lukas told *Quarter Horse Racing Journal* editor-in-chief Richard Chamberlain. "But we've gotten awful serious about all of his."

Within weeks of their marriage, Lukas was at summer sales buying thoroughbreds and quarter horses like they were going out of style. Soon Laura's barns were packed with enough quarter horses to start up the Pony Express again. And they were quality animals. Some of the current stars are First Special Dash, a two-year-old, First Down Dash filly. Drop Your Sox has already proven a stakes money finisher. Private Venture is another accomplished horse.

To give an example of Lukas's commitment to his horses and to his new venture—marriage and quarter horses—one needs to look at June 27, 1998. He saddled two horses for the Bashford Manor Stakes at Churchill Downs—Padua Stable's Time Bandit and Yes It's True. They ran one-two. That same day, he caught a plane in Kentucky to southern California and arrived at Los Alamitos in time to help Laura saddle the horses for a race that night.

"When he bought the sixth-fastest qualifier, Sir Ryon, a colt by Ronas Ryon, just before the final of the 1997 Kindergarten Futurity [Grade 2], people took notice," Chamberlain wrote. "Then, in typical modus operandi, Lukas spruced up the barn at Los Alamitos and put two finalists in the June 27 Governor's Cup Futurity, pace setter Drop Your Sox and Private Venture."

"It all goes back to my beginnings," Lukas told Chamberlain. "I've always had a fondness for the horse."

On August 13, Laura Lukas bought five quarter horse yearlings at the Vessels/Schvaneveldt sale on her husband's behalf. Lukas spent $310,000. And in October 1998, Lukas convinced William T. Young to service a quarter horse mare through artificial insemination. Storm Cat is Overbrook's leading sire. Dashing Folly was a mare owned by Henry Brown, and was a granddaughter of Dash For Cash, one of the great quarter horses of all time. This was unusual, and was done as a favor by Young for Lukas. It was by no means a new idea. The well-despised J. T. Lundy, destroyer of Calumet, had attempted to do the same with Alydar. Only one in four of those foals won any races.

Lukas continues to buy his wife horses: "I'm so competitive. I want to make sure she has good livestock, and that means a deep stable."

The Lukases were so popular in the horse world that Gastroguard, a gastric ulcers medication, asked the couple to do separate but equal ads endorsing the product. But the real-life day-to-day running of an operation like this, between two strong personalities like Wayne and Laura, can't be easy, even if you are in love.

"There is no compromise to Wayne Lukas," Laura told racing writer Steve Bisheff. "We shake on an agreement. Then he gets his way. He *always* gets his way."

But Lukas's version of their relationship differed: "This is not as rosy an arrangement as you might think. I have strong opinions. So does she. There are two votes in this operation, hers and mine. And I'm damn sure not equal on this one." He added: "Laura is very attached to the horses. I may take a more bottom-line, business approach."

Laura told Bisheff: "Jenine Sahadi laughs at us all the time. She calls us 'the Odd Couple.'" This is demonstrably true when it comes to clothes. Laura spends in a year what Wayne spends on one suit. He doesn't think about saving or spending money. He buys what he wants to buy and doesn't consider cost. Perhaps her reticence is a result of working so hard for so long for so little. "Wayne is always looking to buy new horses," she says, "and I always want to wait."

"Ever been around a woman who didn't want to spend money?" Lukas responds. "You ever heard of such a thing?"

Regardless of what a strange duo they may seem, many friends, family, and others have remarked on Wayne Lukas's newfound calm since he married Laura. They're both horse people, and that should stand for a lot between them. Wayne's sister Dauna likes Laura and says that she's good for Wayne. "I'm glad they got together," she says, and thinks he's "mellower" since he's been with her. "It is partly her, I think, and partly that he has achieved just about everything, so many records, so he can relax. . . . She is a wonderful, down-to-earth, hardworking person. I think he's finally got this marriage thing right."

Laura wants to be seen as an independent trainer who can be judged on her own merits, but her marriage will undoubtedly make her a target, simply because her last name is Lukas. This is the first wife Lukas has had who's in the business. Can these two trainers live together without driving each other crazy? Only time will tell.

When asked how much time he spends at his California home, Lukas says, "April till the second week in November, very little. Twenty days maybe. Then from November till March I'm there pretty much. I'll go three to four days, go in check the division, do this, that. I went out to my wife's stable of quarter horses and spent two days." Asked if he's spent as much time with the quarter horses as he thought he would, he answers, "Less. And that's good because I've found in life that you do not build a home with your wife, decorate a home with your wife, or help her train a horse. You think your marriage is solid, just try to decorate your house. Bobby Knight said he'd build one there in Texas, in Lubbock, and I said, 'Bobby, if I *ever* gave you good solid advice, *do not build a house* with Karen.' He said, 'Well, I can step back and let her do it.' I said, 'No way.' He called me the other day and he said, 'Guess where we're going? We're going to look at some finished houses.' "

Lukas's grandchildren live in California, with their mother. When asked if he gets to see them much, he hesitates. "Not as much as I'd like. I am removed and so busy running back and forth that if I'm there for three days, that doesn't fit into the equation very well. I've tried to, but my whole life has not been very family oriented. I don't know if that's the background of moving all the time, the fact that my father had to move and wasn't around. When my dad was living, I worshiped him," he says with longing.

In subsequent conversations, Lukas has admitted that though he may use humor sometimes in speaking about his past marriages, he was also sad regarding them, taking responsibility and lamenting their failures. He is very proud of his wife now, and, it seems, values this new chance with Laura.

End of the Year

Bob Baffert stole the headlines again in 1998, and this time the money too. For the first time since 1983, someone other than Lukas or Bobby

Frankel had won the earnings title. Lukas had done well, but certainly not as well as Baffert, who won $15,000,879. Lukas won half as much: $7,248,847. Bill Mott came in third.

Real Quiet was named Champion Three-Year-Old, and Baffert's Silverbulletday was chosen as the outstanding two-year-old filly. Baffert was voted Trainer of the Year, and to add insult to injury, as far as Lukas would have been concerned, he won the Breeders' Cup Juvenile Fillies event with Silverbulletday. However, Lukas remained the all-time Breeders' Cup winner.

But, as Lukas always likes to tell anyone who will listen, wait until you see his horses for next year. If ever he had been goaded into a fight, this was it. Everyone knew that he had to be seething inside. The year 1999 would renew the trainer battle.

TEN

THE BIG YEAR

The 1999 Preps

The spring had been a difficult one. As usual, Lukas was moving his horses around the country, trying to see which would make the cut for the Derby. For two years now, while winning other, less visible races, Baffert had stolen his look and his winnings. There's no doubt that going into the 1999 Derby season, Lukas wanted the victories for himself.

Beating everyone and taking a Derby was going to be difficult. There were a lot of talented horses out there this year, and Lukas was having trouble establishing a troupe of stars to run, as he had in 1996. He had four decent horses, including Cape Canaveral, Mountain Range, Cat Thief, and Yes It's True. Of them, only Cape Canaveral had won a race, taking the $100,000 San Miguel Stakes at Santa Anita. In the first week in February, his class of '99 wasn't impressing anyone.

In the Fountain of Youth Stakes on February 20 at Gulfstream Park, Cat Thief, under Pat Day, came in second to Carl Nafzger's Vicar. In a hard fought race, it was an impressive finish. Lukas and his team were nodding their heads in approval, and a few of the track writers were impressed too. Cat Thief was looking good.

Yet, it was only the third week in February, and Lukas was still looking for talent that might be hiding in his barn. Which one of his expensive steeds would take the next crucial step forward? Lukas did have another horse, but he was a puzzle: a colt named Charismatic.

With an expensive price tag and a great family tree, the strapping Charismatic had so far turned out to be a dud. As a two-year-old it took six starts before he got his maiden win. In those six tests, Team Lukas had tried him on turf, grass, dirt . . . they might have tried asphalt if someone would have offered a purse. Frustrated, Lukas entered the $200,000 thoroughbred whose bloodstock was the stuff of royalty in a 6½ furlong, $62,500 claiming race at Hollywood Park on November 21, 1998. There were no takers. Charismatic trailed the leaders, turned it on at the far turn, caught up at mid-stretch, and then won by five lengths.

He was then entered in two allowance races, and lost. He took fifth place in the Santa Carolina Stakes at Santa Anita on January 31, where Baffert's General Challenge and Brilliantly took first and third respectively. Using psychology on the animal, Lukas thought the horse could use a confidence boost and an easy win to get him going, so he entered Charismatic in another $62,500 claimer, on February 19, at Santa Anita. The horse won. At the time, it's understandable why no one claimed an expensive horse. He had to seem suspect, that his owners would allow him to be claimed for $62,500.

During that spring, Lukas spent more time with the big colt. He said, "Every time I'd go out there with him, I'd say, 'Boy, this horse just seems like he's getting fat.' I was even checking my groom. I thought maybe he was slipping him grain at night. Every time I drilled him, he seemed to get heavy. So I started experimenting with him a little bit."

One of his assistants, Randy Bradshaw, recalled that Lukas "started training him a little harder, and we had to watch how much hay and grain we gave him, because he was really bulking up on us, even though he'd been in a lot of races. Wayne just figured, 'If I'm train-ing him like this and he's putting on weight, if I trained him a little harder it might make him a little better.' The horse needed more training, and it made him a better athlete."

On March 6 he entered Charismatic in the El Camino Real Derby, a Grade 3 stakes race at Bay Meadows. The field was not strong, and Charismatic took second. It was nothing to write home about, but it was a step.

A week later Cat Thief made another appearance, in the Florida Derby at Gulfstream Park. This was a real test, against some of the best three-year-olds in the country. Cat Thief finished third, behind Carl Nafzger's Vicar, again, and Nick Zito's Wondertross. It wasn't overwhelming, but Cat Thief had finished in the money in three graded stakes races. Not bad. Cat Thief was going to the dance.

On the same day, Yes It's True was entered in the Swale Stakes, also at Gulfstream. It was a Grade 3 race and featured an unremarkable field. But Yes It's True took the $100,000-purse race. Things were starting to look up.

With the spires of Churchill Downs spinning in his head, Lukas began moving some of his horses around and setting up the final preps. On the first weekend in April, at Keeneland, Yes It's True took the Lafayette Stakes, and Cat Thief finished second behind Menifee in the Blue Grass Stakes. Charismatic was going to the Santa Anita Derby.

"Before Wayne saddled Charismatic for the Santa Anita Derby," Bradshaw told writer Ed Golden later, "he told his son, Jeff, and I, and Bob Lewis, 'I wouldn't be surprised if this horse won the Triple Crown.' Jeff and I look at each other and go, 'Are you nuts, or what?' "

But Charismatic faltered when he came in fourth in the Santa Anita Derby behind General Challenge, Prime Timber, and Desert Hero. Lukas chose the Lexington Stakes as the final prep for Charismatic. The horse took it strongly, making a case for his inclusion in the Kentucky Derby. What's more, with the win, Charismatic finally accrued the earnings necessary to qualify for the twenty-horse field.

At Lexington, Lukas had told jockey Chris Antley, an apparently washed-up rider on the comeback trail, to watch Jerry Bailey ride Charismatic. "Wayne told me that he'd show great improvement and that he'd go the Derby distance," Antley later recalled. "He won going away that day. Bailey had to ride another horse in the Derby, and Wayne said that he wanted to get the rider situation nailed down. That's how I ended up on Charismatic."

While Charismatic had won more than $390,000, the horse was a disappointing three for fourteen. Not exactly exciting Derby material. But he'd improved of late, so Lukas went to the big race with Charismatic and Cat Thief. Everyone liked Cat Thief. He was one of the most highly rated three-year-olds of the spring season. And there was no mistaking who the boss thought was going to win. Cat Thief was the star of the barn.

The Hall of Fame

Derby week is difficult enough for any trainer. He or she has to make sure the horses are getting in their works and that they aren't getting put off by the crowds combing the backstretch. Routine is very important to horses and trainers alike, and there is nothing routine about Derby week. This one would promise to be as smooth for Lukas as a roller coaster.

The kickoff to the Derby started off with the announcement that Lukas and three others had been elected to the Racing Hall of Fame. Among the nominees were Russell Baze, the legendary California jockey; Exceller and Miesque, contemporary male and female horses respectively; and Gunbow, named horse of yesteryear.

It had to be gratifying for Lukas, since columnists around the country were recounting his feats, singing his praises. He had won the Kentucky Derby three times, the Preakness four times, and the Belmont Stakes three times. He had won 518 graded stakes and 7 percent of the stakes races in the preceding twenty years. And he was the first trainer to come close to breaking the $200 million earnings mark. Only one other trainer had earned more than $100 million—the now departed Charlie Whittingham.

Speaking in the Churchill Downs press box, Lukas said, "I had some very good clientele that had extreme faith in me and backed it up with their bankroll and let me buy some of the best horses in the world. The $200 million represents a lot of income to a lot of people that backed me." Lukas also pointed out that the equine talent was as important as the backing. "What it comes down to—the bottom line—is the horses. A lot of people backed me, but you have to have the horses. . . ." And then he reminded everyone that "there are forty-nine sires standing in Kentucky that I trained."

But no Lukas milestone is without its own drama. While he had trained some horses as early as the 1960s, the nominating committee used 1974 as their starting point, saying that a trainer needed twenty-five consecutive years. In the past, Lukas had complained bitterly, both privately and publicly, that by the time they actually rewarded him with his election, he would refuse the honor. Obviously, reporters were going to drag up these remarks, and Lukas now had to deal with that.

"My only take is it's not my place or anyone else's to determine the eligibility," he said, "it's the Hall of Fame and its committee. If they use 1974 and that makes them happy and it's endorsed with votes, so be it, and I'm very happy to be here."

Lukas also took the opportunity to remind others that he had "graduated" some of the most competitive trainers in the business, and took a moment to acknowledge them: Mark Henning, Bobby Barnett, Kiaran McLaughlin, Dallas Stewart, Todd Pletcher, and Randy Bradshaw. All had been Lukas assistants, and he praised them as another reason he was in the Hall of Fame.

"I'm probably proudest that six of my guys—my alumni—are out on their own and doing very well. Two of them will lead horses in the Derby against me on Saturday." Barnett had entered Answer Lively in the '96 Derby, and Stewart had entered Kimberlite Pipe. Getting ready to end his press conference, Lukas joked, "On Saturday, about six P.M., I hope I'm back up here for another visit."

There was no question, despite his lack of recent Triple Crown successes, and losing the earnings title to Baffert, that the reporters were much nicer to him in 1999. It was a respect that year that Lukas thought he had deserved all along. It was difficult to rip a man with his credentials being elected into the Hall of Fame.

Of course, Lukas couldn't help getting in a dig at Baffert. Richard Eng wrote: "During Derby week, Lukas was interviewed on a Louisville television show. When congratulated for making the Hall of Fame, he replied, "When I started in racing, I thought hard work, attention to detail, and long hours would make me successful. Then along came Bob Baffert."

The 1999 Kentucky Derby

While this was a particularly strong field, the focus all Derby week seemed to be on the three star trainers: Zito, Lukas, and Baffert. Each had won two Kentucky Derbies in the 1990s. So for them, this Derby would be for all the bragging rights. Lukas had Cat Thief, his star, and Charismatic. This time the Lewises, who owned Charismatic, would be in his barn, not Baffert's. Though Baffert had won for the Lewises with Silver Charm and supplanted Lukas as the company spokesperson for the popular equine analgesic, Legend, he had spent $1.75 million of the Lewises' money on horses that had gone bust that year.

When asked his thoughts about the upcoming race, Lukas replied, "I think the horses that are battle-tested will be there at the end." Referring to Baffert's three horses and then to Elliott Walden's horses, Lukas added, "Baffert's horses have been spectacular, but I don't think they've faced tough fields like the Blue Grass horses did." Of course, one of the Blue Grass finishers was his own Cat Thief.

When Cat Thief and Charismatic were clocked during their works in the week before the Derby, the writers were asking a lot of questions. "They're just works. Be careful, because works are works," Lukas told them. "It's just like practice. Practice is practice. I was with Bobby [Knight] at practice once, and he said, 'The kids practiced great. I'm worried.'"

Nick Zito had two nice horses. Adonis had won the Wood Memorial at Aqueduct and would be ridden by veteran jock Chris McCarron. Zito's other horse was also a stakes winner, Stephen Got Even, which would be ridden by Jorge Chavez. Zito was telling one reporter about his first Kentucky Derby: "I can remember standing there looking at everything, talking to a reporter and lookin' back, lookin' back, lookin' back. Finally, she asked, 'What are you lookin' at?' I told her I didn't want to miss anything."

Asked what his thoughts were regarding a third Derby title, Zito said: "I am grateful to be in this position. I would love to finish it off. I would love to have that honor."

Baffert, who came with an assortment of three horses, said: "I feel good about this Derby. I've got two good horses who are contenders. I hope one of them wins." He was referring to General Challenge and Prime Timber. General Challenge, a large, awesome colt, had won the Santa Catalina Stakes and the Santa Anita Derby. Prime Timber had placed second in the San Rafael and won the San Felipe. By entry time, Baffert would also enter his filly Excellent Meeting, and his trio would be complete. His other star filly, Silverbulletday, would be entered in the Kentucky Oaks, one of the premier races for fillies, also run at Churchill Downs.

"I know there's going to be a year where I don't have anything, so I just try to stay calm and cool and enjoy the moment," Baffert said. "The Derby's become fun for me, like a mini-vacation." When asked about the rivalry aspect of this race in particular, with Zito and Lukas, Baffert replied, "I'm not a rivalry guy. I won the last two, so I don't see the rivalry."

There was some joshing between Zito and Baffert in the press, when Zito said he had picked number one in the post position draw because "I don't want to be near Baffert's horses."

When asked about the rivalry angle, Lukas replied, "I don't think of it that way. Each of these things is a separate race." He elaborated, saying, "There's been talk all week about the Derby, about who's going to do what and how it's going to unfold and riders and trainers and different guys doing different things, but the bottom line is it gets down to the horse." But "one guy's got three Derby wins," Lukas added, referring to himself, "and the other two guys have two, so it's catching up for them." He smiled.

Zito joked around with reporters. Both Duke and Kentucky had been hoping for a third NCAA men's basketball title, which would have made one of them the team of the 1990s. But Connecticut upset Duke in the final game. Comparing the NCAA Tournament with the Derby, Zito said, "I hope no one pulls a Connecticut." Of Lukas and Baffert, he said, "I'm not rooting for them, but I really like this Derby because Wayne seems to be somewhat not grumpy this week, and he has a good shot with his two horses, and Baffert's got his two horses, so the competition of it is really fun."

Another strong choice was Elliott Walden's Vicar. A tall, quiet, devout Christian, Walden seldom joined in the locker room bragging, joking, and jibing. Turf scribe Neil Schmidt once wrote of him: "Elliott Walden knows the part he plays. The thirty-six-year-old trainer has ascended nearly to the summit of his sport but brags only as often as his horses speak." While Lukas had hung the Trainer's Daily Dozen on the walls of his barn, Walden had hung up this little ditty: "The horse has been made ready for battle, but victory rests with the Lord."

Walden had two powerful horses in Menifee and Ecton Park. Menifee had won the Blue Grass Stakes and finished second in the Tampa Bay Derby. Ecton Park had come in third at the Arkansas Derby. Of the two, Menifee was the more accomplished and the more to be feared.

There were also two "alumni" in the field with Lukas. Bobby Barnett had entered Answer Lively, Dallas Stewart entered Kimberlite Pipe. Barnett's horse would go off at 37–1, the only horse with higher odds than Charismatic, which would be 20–1. Dallas Stewart's horse went off at 11–1. That his two former assistants were at the Derby as competitors was another compliment to Lukas, and perhaps he took it as a good omen. In the Visa Three-Year-Old Championship Series, three of his former assistants—Todd Pletcher, Stewart, and Randy Bradshaw—had finished among the top twenty trainers. Lukas would eventually win it in 1999.

The main question floating around all week was whether Baffert could keep his two Derby streak alive. Might he become the only trainer ever to take three Derbies in a row? "I really don't think about making history and would rather not think about it," Baffert said.

Racing writer Richard Skinner asked Lukas if there was an analogy between Thunder Gulch and Charismatic. "It wasn't that I didn't like Thunder Gulch, but no one really asked me about him," Lukas said. "I feel very comfortable," he said of his horses. "I don't know if they're good enough, but neither do the other guys."

Before the race, while the fun and sun blazed outside, and the festivities continued, Lukas and Chris Antley met in a dark room under the grandstands and discussed strategy. With such a large field, and being the sixteenth horse in the starting gates, Lukas told Antley not to try to do too much too soon.

"Wayne told me to stay in the second tier of horses," Antley said. "We got the chance to sit in that second tier. He was five or six down the backside, but Wayne assured me that fitness was not a problem, and that this horse would run the whole [last] half mile."

Lukas decided to sit in Cat Thief owner William T. Young's box for the race. The sun was shining brightly. With more than 151,000 spectators filling the stands and partying down on the wild infield, this was the kind of day one associated with the Kentucky Derby. The twin spires of Churchill Downs pierced the blue sky, and the brightly colored hats and bonnets that are invented just for this day moved around the grandstand, making it seem an impressionist painting.

The night before the draw for post positions, Eduardo Caramori, trainer of First American, had a dream that the winner of the Kentucky Derby would come out of post sixteen. At the draw, Caramori drew the sixteenth position, and he was convinced that fate had interceded and that he would win the Derby. But the day before the race, the number 5 horse, Aljabr, was scratched, and every horse had to move down a post. First American would start from gate 15, and Charismatic got the 16 hole. Could this be another omen?

The race was one of the toughest in history. The official recap shows that General Challenge, Ecton Park, Desert Hero, Stephen Got Even, Adonis, and Three Ring were all either jostled or bumped repeatedly during the course of the race. So rough was the ride that one column called the race the "Demolition Derby."

"This was the worst race to ride in that I can recall," Ecton Park jockey Robbie Davis said. "It was more like a bumper car race than a horse race. I was expecting someone to fall, but they were jammed in there so tight that there wasn't room to fall."

"This was my worst trip ever in horse racing," said experienced Triple Crown veteran Gary Stevens, who was atop General Challenge. A traffic jam on the far turn resulted in a lot of bumping and rubbing. "They picked me up and carried me about four strides. I don't know how I didn't fall. Then when I was over on the far turn, I got hit again."

Bob Baffert summed it up best: "It was all decided in the first turn. There were just too many horses. I knew we were dead at that first turn."

Out of this cavalry charge, coming out of the near turn, it was Menifee leading, with Cat Thief, Charismatic, and Excellent Meeting all giving chase.

"I was standing with my dearest friend in the world, Bill Young, and Cat Thief surged to the front," Lukas recalled. As Cat Thief, chased by Worldly Manner, pushed toward the wire, Lukas yelled, "He hit the front, here we go!" But then Charismatic charged. After the race, Lukas told the crowd of reporters, "I started hollering at my wife, and Charismatic's coming on the outside. You talk about being in a spot. At that point I didn't know if I should jump up and down, holler, throw my program, or what."

Charismatic's charge was coupled with Menifee's. The two of them eventually stormed past Worldly Manner, who was beginning to fade. Now Cat Thief was right there.

"I thought we were on our way to winning the Derby," Cat Thief jockey Mike Smith said. "But here came Charismatic." And there went Charismatic, with Menifee driving behind. But Charismatic held Menifee off and charged at the sixteenth pole. The two crossed the finish line among the longest shots ever to pay off in the Run for the Roses.

Dressed in a double-breasted navy pin-stripe suit, Lukas told the crowd afterward, "I'd be foolish to stand here and tell you that I thought he would win this race. I probably misread this horse as bad as any I've trained. And I've trained a lot of them." He also said:

"Besides winning with Grindstone, this is the best job I think I've done with a Derby horse."

"He got excited and gave the number one sign three jumps before the wire," Lukas said, smiling, referring to Antley holding up a finger before the end of the race. "If Menifee had caught us, that finger would be in glass in formaldehyde in the barn right now."

Lukas also had praise for Antley: "I thought Chris was a great fit for the horse. He's hungry and he's won the Derby. I liked the way he looked me in the eye and said, 'I'll get it done.' "

"Unbelievable!" Bob Lewis shouted. "Wayne said that this horse was unbelievable in the fact that the harder you train him, the better he gets. He's sound and just an incredible horse."

"This is the first lady and the first gentleman of racing. As classy as they come," Lukas said of the Lewises. Then, responding to questions about sustaining his program, he said, "Nick and Bob and I and some of the other people have been able to come here year in and year out, and that's the reason," referring to his two attending owners. "It's not anything we do special. We're not anything special. There are trainers all over that backside. Our clientele base gets us here."

As Richard E. Glover Jr. pointed out after the race: "He is right that the clientele is a big reason for any trainer's success. However, the trainer has to be good enough to produce results with those owners' horses, and he or she also has to be good enough at communicating with them to keep them happy. . . . Lukas is one of the best we will see in our lifetimes." Glover closed with a quote from Bobby Frankel, who meant it as a compliment when he said, "Wayne Lukas is the only trainer who could have won with that horse."

When asked about Baffert, Lukas said, "He should bounce back. I think he can handle it."

Before the race, Lukas had talked up Charismatic to all who would listen. What's more, despite the fact that his wife had begged him not to, he had bet $2,000 on the horse to win. Laura felt it would bring bad luck. In the winner's circle, not only did Lukas have a winning horse, he had a ticket that was roughly worth $60,000.

Lukas's sister, Dauna Moths, listened to her brother before the race and laid down thirty dollars on the horse, across the board—win, place, and show. After the win, at the press conference, a cheerful Lukas praised her for believing in him and backing it up with her bet.

"We beat everybody that showed up, that's all we can do," Lukas said to the reporters. "I guess I out-trained all those other guys. That sounds like Baffert, doesn't it?" he added, taking a shot at his rival. Asked if he thought he would be able to take a run at Ben Jones's record of six Kentucky Derby wins, Lukas said he didn't see why not: "I'm healthy, I like what I'm doing, and I'm ambitious. . . . I think there could be at least a couple more in me."

Eduardo Caramori had been right. As one writer put it, "He had the right dream, but the wrong horse."

Chris Antley

Newspapers all across the country exploded with the news that the newly appointed Hall of Fame trainer had pulled off yet another win, making him the trainer of the 1990s and ending Bob Baffert's streak at the Kentucky Derby. He was feted and celebrated in the grandest manner by almost every columnist in the country. A crowning achievement in a stellar career.

However, there was another story line that was developing. Something just as interesting to the public, and one that would eventually end in great sadness.

Chris Antley lived life like he was shot out of a rocket ship. Born in Fort Lauderdale, Florida, on January 6, 1966, Antley spent most of his formative years in Elloree, South Carolina. He rode horses all his life, mostly quarter horses. He was so taken with riding that he left school before he finished, at sixteen, and went off to become a jockey. He rode in his first thoroughbred race at Pimlico a year later, in 1983. Just a few weeks later he would win his first race.

Antley began a winning streak that would make him a notable in the world of thoroughbred racing. These wins eventually gave him the luxury of choosing to work anywhere he wanted; up and down the East Coast, and he raced mostly in New Jersey and New York. By the time he was eighteen he had 469 wins, which ranked him as the number-one jockey in the United States in 1985, at the age of eighteen. His career skyrocketed even further when he set a record by winning nine races in one day, on October 31, 1987.

Antley rode in his first Derby in 1988, aboard Private Terms, finishing ninth. He was now partying hard and living the wild life. His antics on the dance floor and at the bar were renowned. But his lifestyle had caught up with him. In that same year, he would be tested positive for cocaine and marijuana use. He voluntarily surrendered his jockey's license and entered himself into a substance abuse program.

Antley made a comeback in 1989 and set another record. Between February and May he won a race each day, sixty days in a row. He was also named that year's top jock again. He was back on top.

But Antley now had to struggle to adhere to a jockey's strict weight standards. In an attempt to keep his weight at 115 pounds, he was pressing his health to begin with, since his body build was naturally larger. He became a bulimic, purposely vomiting after meals, employing crash diets, and finally resorting to drugs to fight his out-of-control weight fluctuation as he grew out of his young man's body and into a body of a more solid and settled adult.

The typical jockey has to fight off weight, and they do it in numerous ways. Some have relied on techniques that help them to lose water weight, such as sweating in saunas or doing road work while wearing rubber body suits. Laxatives are another vehicle for extreme weight loss.

Laura Hillenbrand, in her book *Seabiscuit*, elaborates on the trials and tribulations of jockeys and weight. She tells of the ultimate weight reducer, the last resort, the purchase of special pills: "In it was the egg of a tapeworm. Within a short while the parasite would attach to a man's intestines and slowly suck the nutrients out of him. The pounds would peel away like magic." Antley never sank this low to deal with his weight, but keeping his weight down proved to be a harder problem to handle as he got older. And eventually it would be part of his undoing.

Antley decided to move to California, hoping a change of scenery would help. He became the top-winning West Coast jockey in 1991. He also rode Strike the Gold to the winner's circle in the Derby that year, and finished third in the Derby, on Dance Floor for Lukas, in 1992.

In 1997 he decided to take time off from racing and went home to South Carolina. His lifestyle, constant dieting, and mood swings were spinning him out of control. In Columbia, South Carolina, surrounded by the friends and family who always comforted him, he tried to reconcile his demanding job and his unhealthy lifestyle. Between Thanksgiving and Christmas of 1998 his weight had ballooned to 147 pounds. This was not abnormal for most five-foot-three-inch, thirty-two-year-old men. But it was unacceptable for a world-class, Triple Crown–event–winning jockey.

Antley began to work out, running as much as twenty-five miles a day. In town, he was affectionately referred to as "Forrest Gump." He lifted weights, ate healthfully, and dieted with control. He got his life back together, and his weight down to 114 pounds, without the aid of pills or succumbing once again to bulimia.

"This is the hardest thing I've ever been through," he said. "I didn't think I'd be back. My dad told me to do something else, that I didn't need to ride. He wanted me to take it easy. I told my father I have a goal in life and that I would die trying to get there."

Antley returned to Califorina and started working the backstretches trying to get rides. Many trainers were dismissive. Despite his experience and success, Antley's vices were well known, and few wanted to take a chance on him while he was trying to make his third comeback.

Lukas considered giving Antley a chance. "I spent the spring with Chris and saw an intensity in him I'd never seen before," he said. "He's hungry and he has a passion to get back to the higher echelon of the game. He's a very cool rider. He won the Derby. It wasn't like we were going with a guy that was going to break down in the post parade. He finishes well on a horse." In April, Lukas asked Antley to look over Charismatic.

"I just thought he was a great fit," he said.

After the Derby victory, Antley was jubilant. "This was a dream," he said. "Miracles are meant to happen and it happened for me today."

This was America's new story: the fat, $500,000 colt who no one claimed for $62,500, and the struggling jockey on his third comeback—the longest shots ever to win a Derby. They were the apple of America's eye and the darlings of the media. Newspapers were continually running stories on the horse and the jockey during the weeks that separated the Derby and the Preakness.

Even Zito had praise for the comeback kid, saying, "I'm also happy for Chris. He got his life back. That's great."

"This has a lot more sentimental value than anything I've done in my career," Antley said. "I had to find the depths of myself to be able to get back."

Now it was Lukas who had the comeback and had the storybook horse and jockey. Quick, get Hollywood on the phone.

The 1999 Preakness

The middle child of the Triple Crown, Pimlico has always had an image problem, half of which actually stems from its own bad and bungled management, much like the management of the city's baseball team. While the Preakness has the blanket of Black-Eyed Susans (which, incidentally, don't bloom until much later in the season—the blanket is made of painted daisies) and the playing of "Maryland, My Maryland," Pimlico itself isn't half as pretty or well-kept a park as Churchill Downs, or Monmouth Park in New Jersey for that matter.

But the Preakness has one advantage over the other two legs of the Triple Crown series: coming into it, there is always one horse that's won a race and is undefeated; a horse that can feed the fantasies of fans, trainers, and owners. In 1999 that horse was Charismatic.

"I feel confident I got my horses good, and they certainly could win," Lukas said during the time between the Derby and Preakness. Charismatic and Cat Thief were Lukas's twenty-fourth and twenty-fifth Preakness starters. And everyone was comparing them to Thunder Gulch and Timber Country. Would Lukas find another way to sweep the crown, again?

Yet, despite Charismatic's Derby win, many felt that the horse to beat was Cat Thief. Pimlico's shorter distance and sharper turns were made for William T. Young's colt, they said. Cat Thief had been in a position to win the Derby, and finished only three-quarters of a length behind Menifee. The Preakness, it was predicted, would be Cat Thief's turn.

Trainer Elliott Walden concurred. "I think the horse to beat is Cat Thief," he said. "He is a model of consistency."

Lukas countered, saying, "I can see where you can make Menifee the favorite." Then he said he thought Worldly Manner could also win the race. "I think he'll be tough. I think this race suits him real well."

Far removed from the fray was Baffert, who had entered and then scratched Silverbulletday because she had drawn the fourteenth post position. "I have to take care of her," he said. "With the good ones, you have to be so careful."

Baffert was roundly criticized for withdrawing the filly and possibly reserving her for the Belmont Stakes. Many argued that he would be doing it for the sole reason of stopping Lukas. Some had already taken shots at him for not racing her in the Derby, saying she actually had a chance. When Lukas ran his fillies, he was criticized. When Baffert pulled his filly, he was criticized. There was no winning with the media.

Meanwhile, the Lewises were spin doctoring for Charismatic the same way they had for Silver Charm, only now they were spinning for Lukas. Referring to Charismatic, Bob Lewis told writer Richard Eng: "He quite frankly has become a real professional, a real champion to Beverly and I. He has the right to be here, has a right to win this. We are so grateful to Wayne for all the thrills and joys he's brought to us."

"[Charismatic] had a little bit of a strut to his step when he came off of the track during the week. He was much more focused all week," Lukas noted.

Before the race, William Nack highlighted four horses in the Preakness: Worldly Manner, Cat Thief, Charismatic, and Excellent Meeting. Like Lukas, Nack felt strongly about Worldly Manner, writing, "The Derby sharpened him mentally and it brought him forward." Nack also pointed toward Cat Thief, saying "he always fires and looks terrific, as does Derby winner Charismatic."

"This is as good as human hands can make him," Lukas told Antley before the race. "Let's take advantage of every step."

Charismatic got off to an unimpressive start, racing in the middle of the pack down the backstretch. But around the turns he swung out and passed almost the entire pack. As he made his move, he passed Cat Thief and Kimberlite Pipe, coming out of the turn. Then Charismatic raced for the wire and destiny. Menifee and Pat Day were right with Antley and Charismatic, but the down-on-their-luck duo won again, just edging out Elliott Walden's entry. Walden would have to make the most of second again.

"I think I might have pulled the trigger a little too soon," said Pat Day, who was up on Menifee. "And then in the far turn I got a little tight and lost my position briefly."

And what about Cat Thief? He finished a disappointing seventh. He had tired badly. "There was no real excuse," Mike Smith said. "He made one move but I can't see any real reason for blaming it on anything."

Lukas, praising his colt, noted that he had come out of the Derby "more aggressive, more cocky, a strut in his step, like he knew he did something pretty special. He's getting to the point where he's starting to figure this game out."

It was Charismatic's fourth race in six weeks. And he did look as if he were getting stronger. In fact he was. The horse's times had been improving over its last four races. He was just peaking at the right time. "I told Bob and Beverly Lewis before the Kentucky Derby, 'I don't know how we'll do in the first two, but I like our chances in the Belmont,'" Lukas said after the race. "We got a Belmont Stakes horse." Asked what he thought his chances were, he answered, "I think we can win it."

"We had great hopes and anticipation, and they were fulfilled in every way here," Bob Lewis said. "We're going down this road for the second time. We're going for the Triple Crown twice in a lifetime.

How can a couple of country bumpkins from Newport Beach be so lucky?"

As for Worldly Manner, he finished next to last, just ahead of Baffert's horse, the straggling Excellent Meeting. "By the time I got halfway down the backside, she had just fallen out of the bridle," jockey Kent Desormeaux said of Excellent Meeting. "At the three-eighths pole I backed off and tried to save her as best I could." It turned out the horse had a breathing problem, and Desormeaux was praised for pulling it up.

Lukas had nothing but praise for Antley: "We picked him out and put him in the ball game and he came through. He hit three pointers every time." He added the Charismatic-Antley duo was "a nice little marriage, a nice combination."

"I'm trying to take it all in," an elated Antley said. "This whole thing is special." A *Sports Illustrated* article said that he was "seen by many as the most gifted rider of his generation." Troubled as he may have been, Antley stood at a better threshold now—that of a Triple Crown–winning jockey. Appreciative, he said, "The road back was long and hard, and maybe that's what I needed: to have it taken away and not be able to get it back."

It was Lukas's fifth Preakness, another record.

"Give the former basketball coach plenty of credit for development," columnist Richard Eng wrote. "Charismatic is the college walk-on player who became an NBA All-Star. Few colts in recent memory have blossomed so quickly, and at the right time."

A New York Minute

If America had become infatuated with Charismatic and Antley after the Derby, they had fallen in love with them after the Preakness. Now, going into the Belmont Stakes, this pair, with its remarkable stories, were the talk of the sports world, in a way that Silver Charm or Real Quiet had never been.

Between the Hall of Fame, the two big wins, and the storybook horse and rider, Lukas had a three-ring show going on, and he was presiding as ringmaster. Columnists and trainers alike blanketed him with compliments.

"I've had a nice spring," Lukas said to one reporter, "except for you guys."

Carl Nafzger, the trainer of Vicar, who had won the Florida Derby, was a cowboy from Wyoming who became a thoroughbred trainer. "He's a coach and he pushes his athletes—that's the nature of the game," Nafzger said. "The thing about him is that he's got energy and goals. When he is on top he builds, when he is on the bottom he builds."

Lukas admitted that his training methods were not only geared toward the horses, but to his personality, "and mine's aggressive. You can probably guess that when I was coaching, my teams pressed and ran. Even when the kids I had couldn't press or run."

Randy Bradshaw, who had left Lukas and become a successful trainer, and was now back as one of his top people, told writer Ed Golden, "Wayne deserves all the credit for this horse's success, nobody else. He just took him under his wing and trained him hard, and the horse just thrived on more racing and more training. But when they run a hard race, come back the next morning bucking and squealing and clean up all their feed, and it takes two people to grass them, you know you probably haven't hit bottom yet."

Another milestone was coming for Lukas. A win by Charismatic would easily put him over $200 million, making him the first trainer to hit that mark. Lukas has always been proud of that accomplishment, claiming it shows dedication, hard work, and success over a sustained period of time: "I do keep score. I think it motivates you. I don't think there's anything wrong with that. I think we've kept up a level of excellence a long time."

And, of course, the Antley publicity machine was running strong. When asked by a reporter about his thoughts on winning a Triple Crown, Antley answered, "It's hard to even think of the concept. I can't even think of it, because I'm telling you, it goes up your spine." There was also talk that with Gary Stevens departing for England to ride full-time, new doors had opened for Corey Nakatani, Alex Solis, and Antley.

But behind the scenes there was a certain amount of rancor growing. The jockeys of the two previous Triple Crown threats had not
received this much attention. Antley was interviewed, sought out, and
looking for more and more work. And with his Triple Crown streak
going, he was getting it. But Lukas was not happy with all the
attention focused on his jockey. Nor was he happy that Antley had
celebrated before the finish line—bringing to mind Shoemaker
standing up in the stirrups before the finish, when he mistook the sixteenth pole for the finish line. Lukas thought Antley was "losing
focus."

Lukas was known for switching jockeys on a whim, or when they'd
disappointed him. The relationship between a rider and a trainer is a
suspicious one by nature. To a trainer, it's always the jockey's fault, a
bad ride. And to the jockey, the trainer is a salesman who puts you
on a nag and blames the sorry horse's performance on you. Trainers
alternately rip jockeys and praise them. There are maxims in both
camps. Jockeys can't be trusted. Trainers are liars.

It was true that while Lukas had basked in the glow of the season's
success, Antley and Charismatic were more of a story line than the
trainer and even the horse. Whether Lukas was jealous of Antley's
media spotlight or if in fact Antley was losing focus, tensions behind
the scenes were running higher than success seemed to call for. Not
that the public would know about it; at least not for two years.

Of course, Lukas did not let it go unnoticed that other trainers
were not undergoing the same level of scrutiny that he'd experienced
in the past. He'd been criticized for running fillies who broke down
in the big races, but though it had happened to two different horses
in this season, no scathing articles were hammering their two trainers. Three Ring, trained by Edward Pleasant, had faltered in the
Derby, and Baffert's Excellent Meeting had hurt herself in the Preakness, and no one had demonstrably criticized them.

"If I had trained those horses," he said, "I would have been absolutely barbecued. Just ripped up, because, I guess, I rub people the
wrong way." This subject would come up again days later when Baffert entered his prize filly Silverbulletday in the Belmont Stakes, in
order to stop Charismatic.

"What if the positions were reversed, and you had entered a filly against Baffert going for the Triple Crown?" Richard Eng asked.

"You guys would have a field day," Lukas snapped. "The cockroaches would come right out of the woodwork." With a string of horses that had broken down behind him, Lukas had always made the point that his was the highest profile stable, that he bought the best horses and raced 160 horses at any given time. His operation was bound to have more breakdowns if only because he had bigger numbers. Some journalists bought this and others didn't.

In an article about Lukas after the Derby, Richard Glover Jr. made the point that Lukas had lots of high-powered owners who paid premium prices for horseflesh and expected their high-priced wards to compete in the biggest two- and three-year-old races. Lukas was under immense pressure to have these horses earn out their price tags with huge paydays. "Of course, another reason for the injuries may be the bloodlines represented," the columnist reasoned, "as some of today's most fashionable stallions often sire many offspring with soundness problems."

"He doesn't run unsound horses," Carl Nafzger said. "That's pure envy talking when somebody says that."

Silverbulletday's entry into the 1999 Belmont Stakes was greeted with whoops and hollers by the press for a number of reasons. Many had thought that Baffert should have entered the filly in the previous two races, but he had demurred. Baffert told the writers in Louisville, before she shipped out, "Doesn't she look beautiful?" After a work, he told the press, "I don't know what I was looking for, but it looked good when I saw it."

"I just hope she runs the way she worked," said her owner, Mike Pegram. Her presence was welcomed into the fray, as many insiders believed she might be a better horse than Charismatic.

"I just hope everybody who has one ready runs him," Lukas said, taking on all comers. "We don't want any second guessing on Sunday."

"If [Silverbulletday] wins it, it's going to be a great race," Baffert said to a crowd of reporters, selling them on his decision. "If Charismatic wins, it's going to be a great race. It will be good for racing." They were sold.

Except for Bob Lewis. And the obvious connection between Baffert and Lewis was immediately called into question by the press. Rumors were swirling, and Baffert was trying to deal with the negative spin. "I told Bob I was going to kick his butt on Saturday, and he said it was fine with him because he was going to kick *my* butt," Baffert said, trying to smile but obviously annoyed. "That's the way it works. We're friends and don't you worry about that stuff."

But the reporters smelled blood in the water, and Baffert knew it. He tried to claim it was a friendly rivalry and that he and Lukas ran the Lewises' horses against each other all the time. He also reasoned that since he still had Silver Charm, he had to maintain a good relationship with Bob Lewis, and the media was blowing it out of proportion.

But in truth, behind the scenes Lewis was furious that his other trainer was entering a horse against him, hoping to trip up a Triple Crown contender. While Lukas and Baffert were both touting their horses, Lewis was bubbling with anger. Baffert knew what he was doing. He had brought the Lewises to this same threshold twice, with Silver Charm and Real Quiet, two less expensive horses. Despite this, it was Lukas who was going to the sales with the Lewises' bigger checkbook. More than any other year, Baffert was feeling like their second-tier trainer.

Lewis finally exploded, offering Baffert, in public, a $200,000 bet—that Charismatic would beat his precious filly. "He was genuinely hurt by Baffert's impetuous behavior and wanted to take him to the woodshed for a spanking," Joe Drape wrote. "The challenge embarrassed Baffert and put Pegram in the difficult middle." Pegram eventually made peace between the two, and Baffert refused the challenge. Pegram, who knew the Lewises well, insisted he was an owner with a horse who had won almost every race she had raced in, and that she'd won $2.1 million.

While all sides retired to neutral corners, the Baffert and Lewis bond, while not completely severed, would never be the same. Less than a year later Baffert would experience a devastating divorce from his own wife of many years, saying that competing at the level at which he and Lukas competed laid waste to relationships of all kind.

The demands of the numerous barns, the owners, the sales, and the big races; the press appearances and business responsibilities; all of it took time that could have been spent with family, or even the horses.

Eventually, Pegram had to stand up in front of the media and say, "This is horse racing; this is about horses. This isn't about Mike Pegram or Bob Lewis or Bob Baffert or Wayne Lukas. This is about who has the best horse, and I wouldn't be able to look myself in the mirror if I thought I may have had the best horse and rolled over to let somebody win the Triple Crown."

After weathering a stormy trip to New York, escorting Charismatic and several other Belmont Stakes hopefuls, including Silverbulletday, Lukas arrived at the track. At a press conference held the next morning, he and Baffert had a rare moment of levity. Lukas was explaining that the bad weather had delayed the flight that he was on, overseeing the transport of the horses. "We had bad weather and were delayed leaving Louisville, high storms and crackling lightning. All the horses traveled just great except for Silverbulletday." With this, Lukas paused and looked at Baffert, off to the side, who had been in New York since the previous night. The room was quiet for a split second. Lukas laughed. "She was reluctant to get on. She protested every step of the way." The room laughed.

Asked if Lukas had any problem with Baffert's entry, Lukas said, "I've said to all of you over the last two or three weeks, bring them all on."

"We're going to find out if she fits," Baffert said in befuddled amusement. "I think she fits. A mile and a half—I don't know."

"The filly will add a great deal of spice," Lukas added, ever the salesman for thoroughbred racing. "Half the world is women. She'll have a built-in rooting section that don't ever read the [*Racing*] *Form*."

In the days leading up to the race, Lukas worked Charismatic at five-thirty at Belmont. The writers accused him of trying to hide the colt's works, thereby avoiding the clockers. "Charismatic goes off with the first set of horses, whether it's here, California, Kentucky, or wherever," Lukas said. "We always try to get them on the track when it's freshly harrowed; we think that's the best time. It's a routine we've followed with all our good horses over the years."

"[Silverbulletday] went really great," said Baffert, who had been ducking the media, letting his top assistant, Peter Hutton, run the morning works. "She's really full of herself."

Lukas later admitted he'd gone a little far when he compared his horse to Secretariat the day before the race. He'd said: "This is a terrible thing to say, but he looks just like Secretariat. He's almost a clone—a little larger than average, powerful, very correct through his limbs. He's perfect. And he has great heart-lung capacity." Then he tempered himself: "That doesn't mean I'm sticking my chest out saying, 'We're going to do it.' I don't know, the Belmont can be a humbling experience."

"This is unique," Baffert said on the Friday before the race. "It's like a heavyweight title match. This should be on pay-per-view, and I want a piece of the action."

"There is something about that last bump in the road that is a little bit harder than the other two," Lukas said.

The press stories before the race recounted Charismatic's run in two claiming races and retold the sad fall and triumphant return of Antley's comeback, and Silverbulletday's challenge. As one writer told it, "It was a two-horse story in a twelve-horse field."

As the horses broke from the gate, Silverbulletday raced off to join the leaders. Charismatic was not far behind. At the top of the backstretch Silverbulletday took the lead at a brutal pace, Charismatic chasing her. There was still a mile to go. "I can't believe Charismatic ran away with her," Jerry Bailey, Silverbulletday's jockey, said later. "It wasn't a killer pace, but you just hate to go eyeball-to-eyeball early in the race."

Charismatic had won the first two legs of the Triple Crown by stalking from the second group. And in a mile and half race, staying up with the speedball, untested at that distance, seemed a bad tactic. No one thought Silverbulletday could win the Belmont Stakes wire-to-wire. No one could figure out why Antley was so intent on chasing the filly.

At the turn for the final stretch, Charismatic finally took the lead.

"When Charismatic surged past the filly at the quarter pole," William Nack wrote, "the frantic, euphoric crowd sensed history being made and loosed a roar that shot like a current through the stands, scattering every pigeon in the rafters." Silverbulletday had faded, but Lemon Drop Kid and Vision and Verse, who had been stalking the two leaders all race, reserving their strength for this final burst, now came on. Antley changed leads and was urging his horse toward the wire. Then . . .

"He bobbled. It happened [all of a] sudden," Antley said afterward. "It was almost like letting out air. He eased off the run he started on." Though there was desire, the big, dynamic colt could not hold off the two charging latecomers. They passed him with sixty yards to go. Charismatic was desperate not to let them pass, but there was little he could do to stop them.

"Heading for the finish, he suddenly dipped beneath me and I could tell he was in pain," Antley said. Lemon Drop Kid took first, followed by Vision and Verse, with Charismatic taking third.

But there was something wrong with Charismatic. As soon as Antley had crossed the finish line, he jumped from the back of the animal, who it now appeared was injured. Antley fell on the seat of his pants onto the furrowed dirt track and bounced up as if on a trampoline. "I took hold of him and tried to keep him off that leg," Antley explained. Indeed, the alert jockey quickly yanked on the reins and tried to help the horse hold up its leg, trying to keep him from further injuring himself.

Lukas, in the stands, turned white. He hurried down toward the track, face pale, walking with purpose, but also like a man afraid to hear bad news. Neil Cleary, track veterinarian, got there first.

"What happened?" Lukas asked. There was already a splint on the horse's leg.

"He probably has a condylar fracture of the cannon bone, I think," the veterinarian replied.

"Sixty yards past the finish line on the old dirt course at Belmont Park, his eyes wide and his nostrils flaring and his sides rising and falling like a bellows, the chestnut colt named Charismatic stood nervously in the beating sun, chewing on the bit in his mouth as he shifted his weight awkwardly," Nack wrote, ". . . trying to keep his weight off his left front leg." Thousands of hushed fans watched in horror, and Lemon Drop Kid made a cheerful prance to the winner's circle, with thousands cheering him on. Some in the stands were not aware of who won; others were not aware that Charismatic had injured himself.

"Please be careful with him," someone shouted from the silent crowd.

Antley was pulled in front of the television cameras, his mud-caked face streaked with tears. The world watched as he choked back the sobs. "He gave America a lot. He gave us a lot. The game goes on."

"I'm sorry, I'm sorry," cried Shane Sellers, the jockey of Stephen Got Even, hugging the shaken Antley.

"That's okay," Antley said. "Things happen."

Antley remained on the track as they loaded the horse into the ambulance. He began to kick the ambulance doors. Celest Kunz loaded the colt with anti-inflammatories and painkillers then, by injecting his jugular with the quick-acting concoction. As she did, Lukas stood by the horse's head, trying to steady him. Eventually the horse calmed down.

Meanwhile, the television coverage was a mixture of euphoria and horror. They interviewed the winning jockey and trainer. "Naturally you hate to see a horse get hurt," said Scotty Schulhofer, trainer of Lemon Drop Kid. "I would have felt better if it hadn't happened."

"My heart goes out to him," Jeanne Vance, owner of Lemon Drop Kid, later said. "I didn't realize he was injured. It's one of the sad things about our business."

Intermittently, the coverage cut back to coverage of the wounded colt, with the ashen-faced trainer, the heart-stricken jockey, and the devastated owners.

"Our only concern right now is for Charismatic," Bob Lewis said. "We hope to God he is going to be fine." Of course, what no one wanted to say out loud was inferred by a quick look at the Belmont Park infield, at the grave and memorial of the great filly Ruffian, who had died tragically on national television due to fractures sustained in a 1975 match race against that year's Kentucky Derby winner, Foolish Pleasure. "He was simply marvelous," Lewis said, referring to Antley. "I think he might have saved the horse."

In the end, the horse had broken two bones. This meant he'd hurt himself at some other point in the race and was still struggling to win. "They may have happened in different strides because there are two fractures," Lukas said long afterward. "Usually, when there's multiple fractures, they don't happen at the same times, they happen sequentially." Charismatic had fractured his cannon bone and his sesamoid.

Larry Bramledge, a surgeon, gave the prognosis: "That means he's through as a race horse. We expect him to be fine as a stallion. That means it's the end of his career."

Surgery would take place in a day or two. There were some bone chips in one fracture. The other would have to heal with time and care. Almost all the veterinarians attending to the horse said that Charismatic had taken a bad step. He was a perfectly fine animal, in perfect health, except for the injuries.

Charismatic was operated on for two and a half hours by Dr. Stephan Selway, who afterward said the injury "was not the worst of this kind I've ever seen, but it was a nasty one. He'll be fine." He also said there was no evidence of any preexisting condition, which absolved Lukas of any responsibility.

Nevertheless, in the morning, when a small group of reporters gathered around the Lukas barn, Lukas was asked if he thought the horse's difficult schedule had anything to do with the fracture. In attendance was his wife Laura, who unleashed her fury.

"Do you people think we are butchers?" she asked.

Lukas eventually settled her down and answered everyone's questions. "All week we talked about how maintenance-free this horse was and how durable he is," he said. "These things happen and we have to deal with them. It's not an easy part of the game." Again, he explained, "As many horses as I train and at the level we compete, I am going to get criticized. The only critics I have to worry about are my owners, the Lewises. I can't worry about what people say."

Lukas was most concerned with lifting up the spirits of the employees in his barn. "Boy, aren't we lucky the way the horse is handling this," he said. "He's going to have a future. We didn't lose the horse." It was a tough spot for the sixty-three-year-old trainer.

"Even the Lukas-bashers won't hold him responsible for this misfortune," wrote Andrew Beyer, racing columnist for the *Washington Post* and handicapping guru. "Charismatic had given no signs of physical problems before the Belmont."

Then Lukas was asked what he had thought about Antley's ride. "If I had to draw it up on paper," he said, "I wouldn't have had him that close, but he was doing it so easy. You don't want to give up anything that comes up that easy in a horse race. The horse is always right." Lukas was being nice. This was spin doctoring.

In fact, Lukas was furious at Antley's ride. He would say to writer Joe Drape some months later, "I'm not here to be the Red Cross of the backstretch, giving out third and fourth chances. I am looking for one thing, and that's steadiness."

Few columnists would dare to criticize Antley's ride after his heroism and quick thinking. Beyer, however, did just that. In his column after the race, he asked, "Would Charismatic have won the Belmont Stakes if jockey Chris Antley had ridden him more patiently?" While Beyer went on to say that the fractures could have occurred anywhere in the course of the race, and that Antley's quick thinking was smart, he noted that Lukas had said all along that Charismatic would stalk the leader, who would be Silverbulletday, not race her for the lead. "But instead of merely putting Charismatic within striking range, Antley elected to race head-and-head with the filly. Horses don't often win the Belmont by dueling early with a formidable rival." Beyer also pointed out that despite his injuries, Charismatic lost by less than a length and a half. "If he had benefited from an easy trip . . . saving ground much of the way, stalking the leaders, I believe he would have won."

By the July 4 weekend, Belmont Park hosted a Charismatic Health Update press conference. In short, the surgery had been a success. By mid-July it was announced he would enter stud at Lane End Farm in 2000. He had spent the time recuperating in the Lukas barn at Belmont.

Even at the end of the year, sportswriters would easily recall Charismatic's rush to fame, and his heartbreaking setback. He was sixty yards from history, and it all died in a New York minute.

It Was a Very Good Year

In August 1999, at the Fasig-Tipton Sales Pavilion in Saratoga Springs, New York, D. Wayne Lukas was feted upon his induction into the Racing Hall of Fame. Certainly one of the most notable among his long list of accomplishments was the fact that in June 1999, despite Charismatic's failure to win the Belmont Stakes, Lukas was the first trainer ever to earn over $200 million dollars. It was a huge milestone for professional thoroughbred racing.

His voice wavering with emotion, Lukas pointed into the audience, where his assistant trainers—both former and current—were gathered, and said, "Those records would never have happened without these guys. You guys have propped me up, carried me. And I know I wasn't easy to work for." He also said that everything wasn't always "blue skies," but that he would make no apologies for his operation and how it works.

"It's my nature to push the envelope every time," the old coach said. "If you want a coach who wants to walk the ball up court, you better get another guy, because we are going to run and press all the time."

As Billy Reed had pointed out in one of his columns, it was easy to be elected into the Hall of Fame. "The formula is simple, really. All you have to do is be at the barn at 3:30 A.M., prepared to work. . . . All you have to do is have the personality to recruit owners with deep pockets and deeper faith. . . . All you have to do is be prepared to live out of a suitcase and spend much of your life on airplanes. . . . All you have to do is have thick skin enough to deal with media criticism of the most vicious sort. . . . All you have to do is . . . attract talented assistants and teach them the nuances of success. . . ."

"So many things have changed in our industry because of Wayne Lukas," Mark Henning told *Sports Illustrated*. "So many trainers never run multiple divisions, and he's shown us the reality that any race is just one flight away."

"He's always the consummate coach, no matter what," Randy Bradshaw said of Lukas. "He would have been a success at anything he did. . . . What bugs me the worst is when people say he is not a horseman, just a promoter. Wayne has always pushed the envelope, but we don't train horses nearly as hard today as they did in the days of Sunny Jim Fitzsimmons."

His son Jeff, of course, was at the ceremony, as well as the cadre of "my guys" who had come to honor their coach.

"I don't believe in luck in this game," Lukas said, answering a reporter's question. "If you have to depend on luck in this game, you're gonna get beat a lot."

1999 Breeders' Cup

The Breeders' Cup was held at Gulfstream on the weekend of November 5, 1999. Lukas would pull off a few upsets, and prove to the world all over again that he should never be counted out. One of the fun things noted about this Breeders' Cup was that some of Lukas's horses were wearing the nose strips that so many human athletes wear to help improve their breathing. It wasn't considered illegal. And of course as far as Lukas is concerned, any edge will suffice. Even if it didn't give the horses an edge, it was probably enough to nudge other trainers. That's also Lukas—always playing head games.

In the Juvenile Colts and Geldings, Lukas's High Yield, a Derby hopeful for 2000, came in third, behind Anees and Chief Seattle, respectively. But there were two bigger stories.

In the Juvenile Fillies, Lukas finished with two horses in the money. Satish Sanan's Cash Run, who had cost a staggering $1.2 million at Keeneland, won the event and paid $67 on odds of 32–1. Sanan's Surfside was third. Baffert's highly touted Chilukki finished second.

"We didn't think we could do it in our second year," Sanan said a few days after the meet. "We would have been happy if she was on the board." He then added, "You haven't seen anything yet from

Padua." He was referring to Padua Stables, which he and Lukas were building together. It sounded like Sanan was taking lessons from Lukas.

In the Classic, Lukas pulled another upset when Cat Thief, now without his star stablemate, finally shone through. He paid $42, the third longest shot of the day to pay off. It was a shining moment for Lukas.

"He's been a hard knocker all year, been consistent, just hadn't gotten the brass ring," Lukas said. When asked about the nose strips, Lukas replied, "I don't think those nose strips beat the other horses. Cat Thief beat the other horses."

Andrew Beyer wrote of Cat Thief's win, "The lightly regarded three-year-old, who had won only once all year, astonished most handicappers with his win and confused the debate about who should be 1999's horse of the year."

Cat Thief's win was such a shock that Ed Golden wrote in *Golden Glimpses*, a racing newsletter, "The Classic could be run again this minute, and I still couldn't bet on Cat Thief."

"Cat Thief, best known for flirting with victory, embraced it Saturday," Jay Privman wrote.

When the dust settled, Lukas had taken two out of eight races, and increased his all time Breeders' Cup winning total to fifteen races. "It's been a great day," he said. "You never know, but I thought we had a shot."

Collecting the Prizes

Lukas racked up numerous awards that year as well. He took two of the Visa three-year-old championship titles. And he won the trainer award based on victories in various graded stakes races. Baffert came in second. It was Baffert, however, who won the Eclipse Award as Trainer of the Year, most likely because he won the earnings title. Lukas finished second in both categories.

"Bob Baffert . . . seemed stunned he had been chosen champion trainer over Lukas," wrote Jay Privman, who covered the event in

Beverly Hills. Baffert's emotions got the best of him twice. At one point he said, "See, if Wayne would have won, he would have had a better speech." He paused again. He admitted that it was a "humbling and a tough year." Baffert had gone winless in the Triple Crown events and the Breeders' Cup, had a humiliating episode with one of his owners, and endured the breakup of his marriage. He went on to thank his staff for helping him get through it. "We had to gain our yardage two yards at a time," he said. "We just kept getting up."

Baffert's Chilukki won an Eclipse for Best Two-Year-Old Filly, and Silverbulletday won Best Filly.

Lukas had won the Kentucky Derby, the Preakness, and two Breeders' Cup races, and claimed Eclipse awards for Charismatic, who was named Best Three-Year-Old Horse and Horse of the Year. It was Lukas's third Horse of the Year award. He'd won previously with Lady's Secret (1986) and Criminal Type (1990).

"When Tim Smith, the commissioner of the NTRA, opened the envelope," Jay Privman wrote, "and announced that Charismatic was the winner, a roar erupted from the crowd, the loudest from the table where Charismatic's owners, Bob and Beverly Lewis, and trainer, D. Wayne Lukas, were seated."

In his acceptance speech, Bob Lewis thanked Lukas "for the great thrills you brought us."

Lukas, in his moment to speak, thanked the Lewises "for staying with me as I blundered through the spring, until I got it together."

Indeed, it was a *very* good year.

ELEVEN

THE BIG MESS

Long Shot

In the spring of 2000, Wayne Lukas was moving his horses around the country, as usual, trying to see which would make the cut for the Derby.

His colts included High Yield, True Confidence, Sun Cat, Commendable, Millencolin, and Exchange Rate. His fillies coming into the season, Surfside and Cash Run, were extremely impressive, to which Spain would soon be added.

By Derby time Lukas had three entries: High Yield, Exchange Rate, and Commendable. Of the three, High Yield undoubtedly belonged in the Derby. He had won the Fountain of Youth, and the Blue Grass, and finished second in the Santa Catalina Stakes and the Florida Derby. He was tough, maturing, and impressive. But the Derby field promised to be tough. Exchange Rate won the Risen Star Stakes in February and had been unimpressive since, coming in a tired fourth in the Louisiana Derby and finishing a forgettable ninth in the Wood Memorial. Commendable finished fourth in both the Coolmore Lexington Stakes and the San Felipe Stakes.

The Kentucky Derby in 2000 featured the high-strung colt Fusaichi Pegasus. He was owned by the flamboyant sixty-four-year-old Japanese entrepreneur Fusao Sekiguchi, who had been among the small group of top bidders at Keeneland fighting to win the highly sought colt. One of the other bidding groups was made up of D. Wayne Lukas and computer industrialist Satish Sanan.

"We competed against each other to get good horses," Sekiguchi said. "They came to the auction as well to bid on Pegasus, and I thought, whatever I have to pay, whether $4 million or $5 million, I am going to get this horse." Sekiguchi chose Neil Drysdale to train the horse.

Fusaichi Pegasus was the first favorite to win the Kentucky Derby in twenty-one years, and it was the first time in five years that the event hadn't been won by either Baffert or Lukas. And neither finished in the money. They were that dominant in the sport. Lukas had three Kentucky Derby winners in that time, and Baffert two.

Their hegemony would be tested and breached a second time when Red Bullet won the Preakness. It was the first time in six years that either a Lukas or a Baffert horse hadn't finished in the money in Pimlico's Triple Crown event. Lukas had taken the Preakness as far back as 1994 with Tabasco Cat, then followed up with Timber Country in 1995 and Charismatic in 1999. Baffert had won it twice.

Now the stage was set for the Belmont. Again, one had to go back as far as 1994 to find a year in which a Lukas or a Baffert horse hadn't finished in the money. Lukas had three Belmont Stakes wins and a third place with Charismatic in that period. His only entry in June 2000 would be Commendable.

What the public didn't know until after the race was that the Lewises were having second thoughts about entering their disappointing colt in the Belmont. They'd had horrific luck in New York in the past, and Commendable wasn't actually all that, well, commendable. He'd finished seventeenth in the Derby.

Bob Lewis called Lukas on the Wednesday morning before the race and said, "Coach, are you sure we're doing the right thing here?" Lukas convinced the Lewises to stand firm. Only a few hours before the draw, Commendable was entered.

Sports Illustrated's Mark Beech rated all the horses before the Belmont, and commenting on Commendable, wrote: "On the down swing . . . other than the fact that he's rested . . . I see no reason to recommend him here." And that pretty much summed up what all the experts were saying about the horse.

Before the race, Lukas looked at the field and, wondering if he had a shot, wrote a list of pros and cons on a legal pad, posing questions and answering them.

"I listed the horses and wrote down their strengths and weaknesses," he revealed after the race, "and then made observations like, 'Can Hugh Hefner set all the fractions on the pace?' Yes. 'Can he finish a mile and a half? No.'" So, in his prerace discussion with Pat Day, Lukas told the jockey to stalk Hugh Hefner. "He'll clear you, then go to the outside of him and he'll fall apart at the mile pole."

"Who else was a horse to beat in this race? I said, 'Can Impeachment make a half-mile run and beat you?' No," Lukas continued. Aptitude? "I thought he'd probably leave himself too much to do," he said. Basically the plan was to pick the pace setter's pocket, as Hugh Hefner's people had promised their horse would set the pace, and then to get a jump on the closers before they jumped.

It was ninety-five degrees and the track was baked; 67,810 people were present, and few of them were betting on Commendable. By the time the race went off, Commendable's odds were 18–1, which were lower than should have been expected, given the horse's lackluster record and the horrid predictions from virtually every prognosticator in the country.

While in the paddock that afternoon, Commendable had twisted his foot and lost a shoe. "He took it off just as clean as a whistle, all eight nails," Lukas said. "It didn't bother me too much. I think the blacksmith was a lot more nervous than I was. I was trying to calm him and kid him a little bit."

While the early fractions were tough, it turned out to be the second slowest Belmont Stakes since the mid-1970s. Commendable plodded along, behind then on the hip of Hugh Hefner. When Hugh Hefner started to fade, as Lukas said he would, Pat Day made his move. Commendable turned it on at the top of the stretch.

"He took me to the lead around the far turn," Day said after the race. "I hadn't asked him for anything, I wasn't sure how much horse I had. I shoved him a little bit and got a favorable response. I felt at that point they were going to have to come running to get past him." As the field neared the wire, it was Commendable and Aptitude. At the finish line it was Commendable by a length and a half. And he paid $39.60, a handsome reward for a little faith.

Afterward Lukas told reporters about his legal pad and list, and his thoughts about Commendable. He said he believed after reviewing the sheet that "he could run his natural race with his tactical speed."

"It was a wonderful trip," Day said. "I talked to Mr. Lukas before the race and he said, 'Have an energy saving ride.' He told me to get alongside Hugh Hefner and wait as long as I could. And that's what I did."

"Wayne Lukas not only knew his horse, but knew everyone else's horses too," Joe Hirsch wrote the next day in the *Daily Racing Form*, in a column entitled, "Lukas Knew Everyone's Horse."

"We didn't have any grandiose ideas that we could come in here and overwhelm this field," Lukas said after the race. "In fact we didn't even feel that we could do what we did, as easily as we did it."

The Lewises were elated. Lukas had delivered to them what they had been denied twice before: a Belmont Stakes win. "I've won two Derbies and two Preaknesses and now the elusive Belmont is finally ours," a beaming Lewis remarked. "He had a five-week rest and I was convinced the Kentucky Derby was not his race. He just didn't click." Lewis added. "The heartaches and trials of Silver Charm and Charismatic, a lot of that is erased by the victory today."

While the fans and railbirds were in shock, the opposing trainers and the turf writers immediately started making excuses for Commendable's improbable win. The pace was too slow. The best horses weren't entered. It was understandable why the other trainers might make excuses, but the writers seemed just as mystified and pissed off.

"We all know why Commendable won the Belmont," Michael Watchmaker wrote. "Kentucky Derby winner Fusaichi Pegasus, who beat him by twenty-six lengths at Churchill Downs, wasn't there, nor was Preakness winner Red Bullet. At the same time, his victory is inexplicable. Here was a colt who couldn't hit the board in six starts since winning his career debut."

Andrew Beyer wrote, in the *Washington Post*: "Commendable didn't exactly blossom; he won by default. His time of two minutes thirty-one seconds for 1½ miles was the second slowest Belmont since 1970." Yet Commendable had the fourth best Beyer Speed Figures of any of the entrants, making him better than seven of eleven horses in the field, which was pointed out by columnist David Litfin.

"Commendable showed up," Litfin wrote in the *Daily Racing Form*. "He won, and nobody, this handicapper included, gave him a ghost of a chance even though he was THIS CLOSE on ability with the obvious contenders. Cry and moan all you want, but let's not punish the horse for our shortcomings."

Lukas had now taken his ninth Triple Crown event victory in the last six years. Another long shot in the winner's circle. Wayne had pulled a Lukas, again.

Still a Ladies' Man

Commendable wasn't the only star in Lukas's barn in 2000. He had three fillies that were alternately incredible and disappointing: Spain, Cash Run, and Surfside. They were mercurial and intoxicating, and the media was as amazed by them as their trainer. What they lacked in consistency they made up for in pizzazz.

There was no mistaking that Surfside was destined to be another filly star in the Lukas firmament. By Seattle Slew out of Flanders, Surfside was bred and owned by Overbrook Farm. Her talent showed as a two-year-old, when she took the Frizette handily and then, on December 7, the Hollywood Starlet Stakes by seven lengths. She followed that up on January 9, 2000, as a three-year-old, with an impressive eight length win in the Santa Yasabel Stakes at Santa Anita. She then took the Las Virgenes on February 1, but this time by a mere three-quarters of a length. Still, Surfside was considered one of the top fillies in the country when she ran in the Santa Anita Oaks on March 15.

She won by less than a length over an unimpressive field. It was the third slowest Oaks in more than forty years.

"My filly was starting to labor a little in the stretch," Pat Day remarked. "I had to get after her a bit. Hopefully, this will be good for her. Her status is not diminished in my eyes. She keeps on winning. She's got those number ones by her name."

William T. Young, her owner, admitted that there were Derby hopes for Surfside, but that her next test, the Santa Anita Derby, would be the telling moment for the filly that had already won $1,040,230.

"I know you guys would like to see her waltz off by seven or eight lengths, and obviously for the next one we'll try to do a little more," Lukas said after the Santa Anita Oaks. "We're going to stay right on course. We'll find out April eighth. We'll find out if she can beat the boys." But her stock had already started to go down. Jay Privman, respected West Coast turf scribe, was already asking if she belonged in the Derby after the unimpressive win.

At the Santa Anita Derby, Surfside looked promising. She took the lead immediately and led for a good period. But then she started to fade, and finished fifth in a six-horse field. Asked several days after the disappointing loss if Surfside was going to go to the Kentucky Oaks, the filly event the day before the Derby, Lukas snapped, "The check writer has the last word."

But ten days later it was announced that the floundering filly had bone chips in her two front ankles. She would miss the big money events of the spring. A crestfallen Lukas said Surfside "never showed any sign that there was a problem. I've never trained a sounder horse. She was absolutely as good as I can make one." The backstretch whisper mill was cranking up the same accusations about Lukas. He trained her too hard, raced her too hard. If he didn't, why did she break down? Regardless, she would hopefully return to action in two or three months.

Spain, another promising filly, began the year with California trainer Jeff Bonde. The year before, as a two-year-old, she'd come in second in the Vinery Del Mar Debutante and third in the Oak Leaf Stakes at Oak Tree. In the latter, she finished behind Chilukki and

Abby Girl. She then finished fourth in the Breeders' Cup Juvenile Fillies.

Her first race in 2000 was the Las Virgenes, in February, where she placed behind Surfside. She was subsequently entered in both the Santa Anita Oaks and the Fantasy Stakes, and finished last. In May, Spain was transferred to Barn 44 at Churchill Downs, and Lukas entered her in the Dogwood Stakes. While there were high hopes for her, the newly transferred filly, subbing for Surfside, her injured star stablemate, finished a disappointing sixth.

Some changes were needed. A little rest and some new training and she was ready. The results, as John Piesen of the *Daily Racing Form* noted, were wonderful: "A change of equipment, a nip here, a tuck there, and a drop from Grade 1 competition produced a long-awaited win on July 12 at Belmont Park, where Spain buried a good allowance field with a mile in 1:35.63 seconds." Piesen rated her before her next race, the more challenging Monmouth Oaks: "She has won only twice—a maiden-special and a one-other-than allowance—during a 12-race career spanning 13 months. But don't let her record fool you. Spain clearly is the one to beat." And she lived up to his prediction, taking the race by an impressive 4¾ lengths.

In what was billed as the three-year-old filly-of-the-year stakes, Spain was entered in the Alabama, at Saratoga. It was a disappointing trip, but she managed to take second. And then on September 18, Spain pulled off her biggest win when she took the Turfway Breeders' Cup. It was a huge win. Lukas was working his magic with this lady, as she now had three wins in five races under him.

"We'll go right into the Breeders' Cup," he said. But Lukas changed his mind and sent her to the Three Chimney's Spinster Stakes first, explaining, "I'm always of the belief that if you've got something good right in front of you, go ahead and take it. This filly has been doing so well that I thought this was the best way to go." She finished second.

Cash Run, meanwhile, a third Lukas filly, had been a puzzle. She won the Breeders' Cup Juvenile Fillies in 1999, then won the Bonnie Miss and the Devona Dale. But in her next three starts she finished fourth in the Ashland Stakes at Keeneland, thirteenth in the Kentucky

Oaks at Churchill Downs, and fourth in the Black-Eyed Susan at Pimlico. And in her next two races, the Princess Stakes and the Hollywood Oaks, she came in third and fourth respectively.

Then, during the Saratoga meeting of 2000, where Lukas went through one of the worst droughts of his career, winning only two of thirty-four races, Cash Run was fouled by Dream Supreme in the Ballerina Handicap. Dream Supreme's jockey was Pat Day, certainly one of Lukas's favorites. Lukas claimed foul. The stewards disallowed it.

Cash Run went on to lose the Floral Stakes in late August and the Indiana Breeders' Cup Oaks. In the end, despite the high hopes both her trainer and the media had for her, she would not pan out.

By now it was October, and Surfside was ready to make a comeback. Lukas entered her in the Breeders' Cup Distaff. Spain was also entered, and her odds were 55–1. Surfside was 10–1. In one of the biggest upsets in Breeders' Cup history, Spain won the Distaff, with Surfside finishing second. It was a huge coup for Team Lukas. Newspapers trumpeted the feat: "SPAIN? SURFSIDE? YES, IT'S LUKAS-LUKAS!" Jay Privman's article began: "Spain, who had yet to win a Grade 1 stakes race, picked an opportune time to win her first when she led a parade of long shots across the line in the $2.36 million Breeders' Cup Distaff, the first Breeders' Cup race of the day, Saturday at Churchill Downs."

After the Breeders' Cup race, Spain would come in second against lesser competition in the Falls City Handicap, and thus fail to secure her place in the fillies grouping that year. But Surfside would win a race that would cement her reputation, despite her lengthy layoff, as the nation's best filly.

In the $445,600 Clark Handicap at Churchill Downs on November 24, Surfside would be facing colts, including Bobby Frankel's Aptitude, who had been favored in the Belmont—only to lose to Commendable. Surfside shot out of the gate, took the lead, set sizzling fractions. She stayed four lengths ahead of Guided Tour, who chased her all the way around the oval and finished second, ahead of Aptitude, who was another eight lengths. Surfside literally ran away with the race, securing her reputation as the class three-year-old filly of 2000. She had earned $1,824,987 and won eight starts in thirteen races.

The Aftermath of Chris Antley

A year after his incredible run with Charismatic, Chris Antley was back in Kentucky, back at Churchill Downs—as a spectator. He had ridden as late as March 2000, but a knee operation due to a racing injury, and his battles with weight, began to resurface. Since then, he'd spent time with his father in South Carolina and then in his Pasadena home, and also met Natalie Jowett, an ABC television producer, and gotten married.

A year after his magical Derby win, Antley's father was interviewed by reporters. "He loved that horse," Les Antley said. "He told me he probably got more publicity for [his quick action to save Charismatic] than he would have if they had won the race." A married Antley was about to begin a new phase of his life, his father told the press.

But nothing could be further from the truth. Antley was distraught by his battles with his weight, and was turning again to drugs. When Cathy Parks, a family friend and local realtor who'd sold the Pasadena house to Antley, let Antley's brother Bryan in on December 2, 2000, she knew Bryan was there on a mission. In fact, he was there to pick Chris up and bring him back to his father's home, in order to dry him out and get him back on his feet. Instead, they found Chris lying facedown in a pool of blood.

Interviewed at the scene of the crime, Parks told of a young man, Timothy Wyman Tyler Jr., who had been in the driveway earlier in the day and was a former house guest of the jockey. The police considered him a suspect.

The racing world was shocked and saddened. A murder? A top, winning jockey? "He seemed to have some fear that this type of thing was going to happen," Gary Stevens told reporter Beth Harris. "A lot of things he was saying were not making sense to me. He had a lot of demons haunting him."

"He instinctively came to the aid of this horse. It was a very heroic and admirable circumstance," Bob Lewis said. "We just thought so highly of Chris."

Lukas called Antley, "a very, very talented rider . . . a very likable guy." He expressed surprise that Antley had not continued riding. "He had some personal problems."

Lukas was taking the high road. In fact, he'd bottled up his true feelings about Chris Antley. As Joe Drape wrote in *The Race for the Triple Crown*, Lukas had gone as far as stopping the taping of a television magazine feature when he felt the reporter was forcing the story of how Chris and Charismatic had become inseparable soulmates. He snapped at the reporter, "The first time he ever saw the horse was in the paddock at the Derby." This was not true. Antley had ridden the horse once earlier in the season. "Chris never once came by the barn to take a look at that colt. Don't tell me they needed each other."

Lukas had told several people that he thought Antley gave the horse a horrible ride in the Belmont, making it a speed duel too early in the race, with Silverbulletday. It was not an uncommon point of view on the backstretch. "Lukas believed that Antley was becoming distracted again, and, in Lukas's mind, was close to blowing his second chance," Drape wrote, and he quoted Lukas: "I'm not here to be the Red Cross of the backstretch, handing out third and fourth chances. I'm looking for one thing, and that's steadiness."

Eulogy upon eulogy was written for Antley in the press. Dozens of articles and features about the brilliant but troubled jockey were in sports pages all over the country. One of the few dissenting voices was that of Jay Hovdey, who wrote a moving account of Antley's life, but also leveled it with: "Antley had a paper thin psyche, susceptible to tearing and shredding under the pressure of his work. He publicly confessed use of drugs, and alcohol became a chronic reference . . . he lumped himself in with a modern sports pathology."

It was discovered that Antley had in fact died of a drug overdose. And then on January 12, 2001, Natalie Antley gave birth to a daughter, Violet Grace Antley.

Many thought the story would pass, but Chris Antley, even in death, would not go away. As the 2001 Kentucky Derby approached, reporters asked Lukas about the departed jockey. At one point Lukas, finally fed up, said: "I thought he lost a little focus after the Preakness in that three-week span. I think when you're going for a Triple Crown—you have it in front of you and you have that much at stake—I'd have felt a lot better if he would have slept with the horse. I couldn't find him sometimes." He added: "If I had to do it again, I'd have probably changed riders." His comments did not create a furor. But that was about to change.

As the Belmont Stakes approached, tributes to Antley began to build again. NBC would be airing a feature on him during its Belmont coverage, and a memorial service was planned for the jockey.

Of course, with a horse in the Belmont Stakes—even the undistinguished Buckle Down Ben—the reporters came around to Lukas's barn, and they asked about Antley again. Lukas was not in a mood to mince words. "I don't think they bonded," he said simply. "I know I bonded with the horse, but I don't think he ever bonded."

Lukas noted that Antley had no contact with him or the horse in the days after the accident. "I'm not saying it was insincere, maybe it was an emotional response. It may have been sincere in that second, but it wasn't carried far after that."

After more questioning, Lukas recalled the day's events immediately after the incident, which included a press conference outside the barn. "If you tearfully tell the media that you saved this horse and he was your only concern, wouldn't you then walk twenty feet to his stall and see if he was dying or was going to make it?" Lukas reasoned. "But he turned, got in a limo, and left."

Lukas went on to explain that he had seen Antley three times during the Triple Crown run, and then only minutes before each race. If Antley had had the kind of bond with the horse that he claimed, Lukas said, or even an interest in a horse that had the potential, after the first two races, to win the Crown, why didn't he call and see how the horse was doing? He revealed that he and the owners had discussed making a switch and using a different rider. He hadn't spoken about these things before, he said, especially after the jockey's death, because he didn't want to ruin Antley's reputation.

"We had a great ride together. It was a chapter his family could look back on pride with. We'll leave it at that." But Lukas couldn't let it go: "I was saddened by his death. It was a tragic thing, but no one was surprised."

With the memorial service planned, and the outpouring of goodwill for the dead jockey, Lukas's comments made headlines. The story was carried by hundreds of newspapers. The horse world was shocked and horrified. It showed bad timing and bad taste.

On the day of the Belmont Stakes itself, when Lukas led Buckle Down Ben out of the paddock and out to the track, the local New York railbirds, never shy about speaking up, booed, hissed, shouted epithets, and spat at the beleaguered trainer. They yelled, "I can't wait to stand over your grave, Lukas," and the like. Everywhere he went, the crowd jeered him.

Writer Don Engle best summed up the horrified public's shock when he wrote: "Why in the world is he saying this? On NBC's Belmont Stakes telecast, an emotional, laudatory feature on Antley and his rescue of Charismatic makes Lukas's comments appear even more churlish. In seeking to diminish Antley, Lukas diminished himself far more. Why?" Indeed, many columnists were asking the same question.

Natalie Antley fired back in the press a week or so later, saying, "Lukas said that Chris couldn't be bothered to go back and see the horse in the barn, and that's not true. He was upset. He was emotionally spent, so he left."

The Lewises had called her up and said many nice things about her husband, she said, noting that they thought Chris had saved the horse's life and rewarded him with a share in the colt's breeding rights. "Mr. Lewis did it as a thank-you for saving Charismatic's life," she said in a telephone interview with West Coast writer Jay Privman. "Wayne should be on his knees thanking Chris for saving the horse, because if the horse had been put down, the blame would have come back to Wayne Lukas, not Chris Antley." Privman called Lukas, and Lukas repeated his comments. Then Privman spoke to Antley's father, who was also fraught with anguish about his son's tragic death and Lukas's harsh words.

A salient comment was added by former *New York Times* reporter and now *Daily Racing News* editor-in-chief, Steven Crist: "The Antley-Charismatic love story is the kind of 'human interest' fable that has come to dominate far too much sports reporting and broadcasting. In an effort to give niche-interest sports a more universal appeal, journalists and producers fall all over themselves to create little soap operas about ever-popular topics like death, disease, religion, sex, and drugs." Crist ended his article by noting Lukas's successes and reasoning that he "speaks his mind with increasingly less regard for nicety. In doing so, he may perturb friends and families of the deceased but should not be reviled for telling the other side of a story."

The Rise and Fall of Lukas and Padua Stables

Satish Sanan is a large man with large appetites. Born in Batala, Punjab, India, he studied computer science and electronics at the University of Liverpool and graduated in 1973. While in school, he met his wife to be, Anne, then a schoolteacher. Sanan was broke, and his wife supported him through school and through his first job. He worked first in England and then went to Canada. He founded his own company, Information Management Resources Global, in 1988 in Clearwater, Florida. IMR Global is one of the providers of technology in the manufacturing/distribution, retail, insurance, and health industries. The company grew through acquisition, and has offices in Australia, India, Japan, and the U.K.

In his first year in business, Sanan procured a $1.8 million contract. The problem was, he didn't have the capital to meet his payroll or commitments. He called an old school buddy whom he hadn't seen in three years, who was now a banker at First Boston, and secured the money necessary to keep his company afloat. This was not unusual. Over the years, IMR has survived countless problems, only to emerge stronger each time. Once, in 1993, when the company was shy $600,000 to meet the payroll, Sanan's employees donated cash, jewelry, and other valuables to the tune of $400,000, and with the help of a banker for the rest, the payroll was met, the company was saved, and it continued to grow.

Under Sanan's guidance, IMR Global became a consulting colossus. And in 1996 he took his expanding company public. At one point the company was valued at $486 million, with three thousand employees. Sanan has been credited in some quarters for starting the twenty-four-hour workday, by establishing computer support offices in different parts of the world to maintain work projects on a twenty-four-hour basis and provide constant services for his clients. This concept was termed the "virtual workday." Some of his highest profile customers were Merrill Lynch, Amtrak, and Michelin. He was honored in 1999 by the consulting firm Ernst and Young for this major IT innovation.

Sanan is affable and hearty, and has inspired loyalty in employees and friends alike. He has by all reports always put his family first, and it is known that he has two heroes in life—the famed Mahatma Gandhi, and General Electric CEO Jack Welch. But Sanan always liked horses. And with his pockets lined with cash, he wanted to establish a truly great thoroughbred program.

He started buying thoroughbreds with D. Wayne Lukas as early as 1995, but Sanan was a small-time owner then, dabbling in the sport of kings. However, he became more aggressive, and in April 1998 bought Silverleaf Farm, a 586-acre spread in Ocala, Florida, that he and his wife renamed Padua Stables. In that same month, Sanan named D. Wayne Lukas general manager of Padua Stables and made him a minority partner. Jeff, recuperating from his accident and reeling from his divorce, held administrative duties at the stables. It was clearly understood that Lukas would be the exclusive trainer of Padua's horses. Now, they just needed horses.

Lukas knew where to buy them. He, Sanan, and Sanan's wife Anne attended the Keeneland sales, to shop around. They made quite a splash. It was no coincidence that the September Keeneland sales posted record numbers that year. The news shot through the industry, since the September sales are not usually the ones that set records—presumably because the best horses are sold in July and August. And the stars of the show were Satish Sanan and D. Wayne Lukas. They went on a shopping spree that would have made Liz Taylor blush, including a Mr. Prospector colt for $2.3 million.

The first three sessions showed a 10 percent gain in net sales, according to news reports. Sanan and Lukas were intent on recreating the same kind of successful operation that Lukas and Gene Klein had been so successful with back in the 1980s.

The following July, Lukas and his new owner were at it again. This time they made an even bigger splash. In the first session on Monday, Sanan and Lukas bought $4.4 million worth of horses. They paid $2.2 million for a Pleasant Colony colt, $1.1 million for a Thunder Gulch colt; and bought two other colts for the bargain basement price of $1.1 million.

"You mark my word, this is a Triple Crown winner," Sanan boldly stated after buying the Pleasant Colony colt. "We've invested a lot of money, we are a prestige player, we're in for the long haul. This is not a flash in the pan. To play at the top level, you've got to spend some money."

As if that weren't enough, on the second day they spent more. They bought one colt for $5.35 million and then three more fillies within a twenty-minute run that brought their tab to $8.6 million.

Ironically, Lukas lost out on the prize possession, a Mr. Prospector colt, out of Angel Fever, that he cajoled Sanan and the Coolmore group to join forces for, which made them a formidable and spend-thrift coalition. However, they dropped out at $3.8 million, and the young, strapping colt went to a Japanese entrepreneur named Fusao Sekiguchi, who eventually paid $4 million.

"His ambition and goals seemed to blend with what I wanted to do," Lukas said of Satish Sanan. "We're just now in the process of trying to build a high-class, visible racing operation. . . . These are calculated decisions."

He said to another reporter: "I told everybody that we were going to be very busy in this sale. There were a lot of good horses. . . . We have a plan to build the world's best thoroughbred operation. We are just carrying out that plan." Sanan had just spent $13,350,000 for fourteen horses. They bought nine colts and five fillies.

When asked if he thought he was responsible for the increase in prices in the last two sales, Sanan replied, "There are a lot of strong people here, strong horses. That's what drives the price, not me."

The press loved the duo, since they were great poster boys for the sales, along with the flamboyant and odd Japanese tycoon. Track writer Jay Richards wrote: "Trainer D. Wayne Lukas has found a new client with an apparently unlimited cash supply named Satish Sanan, whose horses run under the name of Padua Stables. Remember that name—you'll be hearing it a lot in the next year or two." Yes, because they would continue on one of the largest buying sprees in thoroughbred history, not excluding the Sangster Group or the sheiks of Dubai.

However, in July 1999, IMR Global's stock took a huge hit. It had been trading as high as $17.42 on the NASDAQ exchange, and would sink as low as $2.37. When Lukas showed up at the sales pavilion, he was only the second most disappointed man in the small theater— the first was the auctioneer. Lukas was there to buy some horses, which he could not do much of, and to do damage control. "He wanted to be in his office," Lukas said of Sanan, "obviously to deal with the problems of the stock dipping. He wanted to be there to take care of his principal business instead of his hobby, so he could get it righted and going the right way. From the horse standpoint, we haven't had any discussions."

In the meantime, the competition was still buying fast and furious. Bob and Beverly Lewis laid out $6.65 million for twelve yearlings, and Sheik Mohammed bin Rashid al Maktoum spent a paltry $3.9 million. However, before the end of the sale, Lukas was able to form a partnership between Padua and Coolmore to buy a filly by Gone West out of Miraloma for $2.8 million. It was the second highest price ever paid for a filly at Keeneland.

"Wayne loves the pedigree, and she is one of those fillies who could make your brood mare band," Sanan said. The seller was Bob and Beverly Lewis. They had received lower than expected bids on another horse and were disappointed with their sales. "Thank goodness for Satish," Lewis told the press.

By now Padua Stables was coming into fruition. As some stables in the area were selling, J. J. Pletcher's Payton Training Center and Padua were being built up.

"Just a few cosmetic things to put in place," Bruce Hill, general manager of Padua, said in August 1999. "The turf gallops should be ready in a week or so." The farm had now expanded to seven hundred acres. And the training center facilities were finally being finished. During an interview, Hill pointed and said, "These just arrived from Keeneland. There are twenty-three of them in all. And, of course, there is Saratoga to go and the Keeneland fall sales." Padua now had twenty-two racing horses, who had won fifteen races as two-year-olds. The stables had won four stakes. Things were looking up.

Hill had been right. There were still more horses to come from more sales. Glenye Cain wrote in the *Daily Racing Form* that "Sanan, ever seated beside trainer D. Wayne Lukas, spent a total of $1,250,000 at the session, which put him in the good company . . . of the auctioneer. . . ."

In September, however, IMR's stock price fell again, when Bank of America dumped one million shares. By October, Padua Stables and all its contents, including brood mares, weanlings, yearlings, stallion shares, and real estate, had cost Sanan more than $100 million.

The year 1999 ended with a splash. Padua's filly Cash Run, bought at Keeneland for $1.2 million, upset Chilukki and stablemate Surfside in the Breeders' Cup Juvenile Fillies race. Sanan and his wife Anne joined Lukas in the winner's circle. A jubilant Sanan told the press, "We didn't think we could do it in our second year. We would have been happy if she were on the board."

"She was my number-one pick at the Keeneland sale," Lukas said. "She was spectacular in her debut, that was no big surprise."

"You haven't seen anything yet from Padua," Sanan said.

But he had already scheduled a reduction sale in Lexington, and it took place the next day. In an effort to pay off some of his debts,

Sanan was selling some of his stock through Eaton. Padua sold fourteen horses and netted $10,845,000. Sanan had been a late addition to the catalog. There were rumors that he owed the auctioneers, from previous sales, but officials denied the rumor. Earlier in the month, he had privately sold off shares in stallions A.P. Indy, Gone West, Woodman, Belong to Me, and Phone Trick in an effort to increase his cash flow.

"That was painful," Sanan would say of these sales later.

Then, on November 24, Sanan had to sell approximately 6 to 7 percent of IMR Global in order to raise the necessary cash to right his business and personal life. The sell-off helped him alleviate more debt with Bank of America.

The spring would not be good to Sanan and Lukas, and by May it seemed that the promise of the previous fall had fallen flat, prompting Jay Privman to write a scathing article entitled, "Padua's Riches May Not Buy Blanket of Roses." In it, he told the cautionary tale of how Lukas and Sanan had bought thirty-nine horses to campaign in the spring season toward the classics. Many had been bought in excess of $1 million. Only one, Exchange Rate, would make it into the Derby. Otherwise, the stable had little to show in two years' time. A top sprinter had been produced in Yes It's True, and there was Breeders' Cup winner Cash Run (who had been bought for a pricey $1.2 million). Other stakes winners included Magicalmysterycat, Millencolin, Mycatcandance, and November Slew. The rest, to be polite, had been a bust, the biggest being the $2.2 million colt who was now named Colonial Boy—and running in allowance races at Aqueduct.

Exchange Rate had won the Risen Star Stakes at the Fair Grounds in New Orleans, and come in second to Captain Steve in the Louisiana Derby. He finished horribly at the Wood Memorial, however. He was a solid, if not spectacular horse, who cost $1.4 million and won $226,000.

"We've put him into the Breeders' Cup and he's going to be in the Derby," Lukas said, referring to Sanan. "Whether he's 1–9 or 90–1, he's here. I think the report card at this standpoint is good."

But Exchange Rate finished twelfth. No matter what kind of spin Lukas was putting on it, the cards did not seem to be coming his way.

The facts and figures that Privman had highlighted in his article did little to hinder the spending spree that continued. At Keeneland in July, Lukas and Sanan spent another $4.8 million, including a $2.5 million purchase in a first-time partnership with William T. Young's Overbrook Farm. At one point on the first evening of the sales, Aaron Jones, an Oregon lumber tycoon, dueled with a team of Lukas, Sanan, and Demi O'Byrne, who were sitting a few rows away. Tensions rose as the crowd watched the bidding war escalate like a tennis match. There was a huge roar when the bidding went over $1 million. Jones won.

Lukas admitted that night that they were "paying a little more than we expected for all of them." That was an understatement. In one of the most exorbitant thoroughbred markets since the halcyon days of the early 1980s, Sanan and Lukas were buying everything in sight. By the time the July sales ended in 2000, Sanan had spent $14.4 million. They had paid the unheard of sum of $3.6 million for a yearling filly, the second highest price ever paid for a filly. Upon signing the ticket, Anne Sanan said, "This is what the game is all about. . . . We love the game, and we're committed to it."

The news again hit the wires quickly. RealRacing.com opined: "Since entering the fray, some five years ago, Mr. Sanan has spent a king's ransom at the behest of the cliché-ridden exhortations of his trainer D. Wayne Lukas. Yet, to date, successes on the track have been few and far between."

In 2001 the direction of Padua Stables was starting to change. It went from being solely a training facility to a stallion station. It started with three stallions: Yes It's True, Dance Master, and Prospect Rate. "Yes It's True generated well over two hundred applications and it was decided to book a hundred," Bruce Hill told the press. But there were whispers in the thoroughbred industry that Lukas was in a make-or-break year, and his spring campaigns had failed miserably. It would be the first year in twenty that he would not have a Kentucky Derby entry, and he would also miss the Preakness. In June he would race in the Belmont Stakes, but not with a Padua Stables horse. Things were looking tough.

Just before the Belmont, Sanan made a decision after discussing the matter with Lukas. Padua Stables took over control of the training and breaking facilities, which had previously been managed by Lukas Racing Stables. The center would now break and train horses from outside its own stables.

"Nothing really is changing," Nadia Sanan, Satish's daughter, told the press. "[Wayne Lukas] is still the exclusive trainer for all our horses. We're just going to take over the accounting at the farm." Lukas's employees had been handling billing and accounting, and now Lukas would no longer be involved in the day-to-day running of the operations.

"It wasn't confusing when we only had six horses," Nadia Sanan explained. "But now we have brood mares and stallions, and more mares for boarding, and we plan to bring on three more stallions. It got to be too much."

In July, Exchange Rate was injured and retired to stud. He had cost $1.4 million, and out of fifteen starts, had won only six races, for a grand total of $479,803. A week later a $3.6 million Mr. Prospector filly named Born Perfect was injured during training and retired. She was scheduled for breeding the following year. And there were whispers through the horse world that Sanan was talking to people. To lots of people. And that Lukas could possibly be on his way out completely.

Finally, in August 2001, Lukas and Padua Stables parted ways. It was not a real surprise. A large percentage of horses were taken from Lukas and dispersed among other competing trainers, including Steve Asmussen, Bob Baffert, Michael Dickinson, Bill Mott, and Todd Pletcher. Nadia Sanan, when pressed by the media, admitted that the reason for the move was due to disappointing performances on the racetrack.

"Anytime you make this type of investment that we have with Padua, you are hoping to do a lot of things in this business, and hopefully we can accomplish a lot of them," she said.

"I wanted him to do well," Lukas said of Sanan. "He has made a commitment to this sport." Lukas admitted he was "frustrated," that it was a personal disappointment, but that he harbored no ill will toward the Sanan family, who had been very good to him.

"There's a lot of people pulling at him because he's the new kid on the block," Lukas said. "He's getting a lot of advice. But I like him very much and I wish him well. It goes back to what I said before. I'm at a point in my career—I'm sixty-six and I don't want any disruption. I don't want Padua to be a problem for Bob Lewis or Overbrook . . . that, coupled with the fact that . . . it frustrates me to not do as well for him, more than it frustrates him to not do well for me. And I told him that. 'This is my whole life. I don't have anything else. I don't play golf, I don't go to movies, I don't go to dinner—I haven't eaten one meal at the restaurant here at Saratoga, not one meal. I go to my room, throw a sandwich in the microwave that I get at the filling station.' So I said, 'I'm living this every day so it's much more frustrating for me than for you, frankly, and I want you to try.' I said, 'Pick five or six people you really respect and give them each four or five horses, and one of them might hit.' I don't think the karma was there, the aura wasn't there, with him and I."

Jeff, to both his own and his father's satisfaction, would remain on at Padua, retaining his administrative duties. Randy Bradshaw was named the training center manager.

A week after the announcement, Lukas showed up at the Saratoga sales with owner David Shimmon. Baffert bid by cell phone, Nadia Sanan bid from a soundproof booth, and life went on.

TWELVE

LEGACY

The Lukas Record

D. Wayne Lukas's record speaks for itself. He has led or leads in almost any category a horse trainer would want to lead. He has led the nation in total earnings fourteen times. He surpassed Charlie Whittingham and the $100 million mark back in 1988. He was the first and only trainer to break the $200 million mark. But for all of those who say money isn't everything, Lukas has other milestones.

"Wayne doesn't care too much for the money," says Hall of Fame football legend, radio talk-show host, and racing afficionado Paul Hornung. "That's not what drives him. His drive comes from winning. That, and he likes nice clothes, a McDonald's cheeseburger, and a college basketball game on when he goes home at night."

"He's cocky. He's brazen. He's confident," says Hornung. "And he can back it up. And that rubs some people the wrong way."

He's won more premier thoroughbred events than any other living trainer, including four Kentucky Derbies, five Preakness Stakes, and five Belmonts. He has won fifteen Breeders' Cup races and is the all-time Breeders' Cup winner in races and money. And he's won countless stakes races throughout the county. There's hardly a track where his stables have not raced, and few tracks where he does not hold some kind of record or milestone. He has more than four thousand wins and a thousand stakes wins. His record for wins places him fourth on the all-time list, behind Dale Baird (8,490), Jack Van Berg (6,301), and King Leatherbury (5,916). However, these three trainers mainly ran claimers, and less than a thousand of Lukas's wins were in claiming races. His one thousand stakes wins is the record, and make up a quarter of all the races his horses have appeared in.

These accompishments are the result of a massive organization. Where's the horsemanship? Lukas's critics might ask. By the end of 2001, Lukas had campaigned twenty-one Eclipse champions, including: Althea, Boston Harbor, Capote, Charismatic, Criminal Type, Family Style, Flanders, Golden Attraction, Gulch, Lady's Secret, Landaluce, Life's Magic, North Sider, Open Mind, Sacahuista, Serena's Song, Steinlen, Thunder Gulch, Timber Country, Winning Colors, and, most recently, Surfside. Woody Stephens had eleven, and Charlie Whittingham had ten. Ben and Jimmy Jones together had sixteen. The closest active trainer, Shug McGaughey, has seven. Bill Mott and Baffert have five, and Bobby Frankel four.

Lukas has also been Trainer of the Year three times and is a member of the Hall of Fame. There is no denying his record. The man has accomplished everything any trainer could possibly wish to achieve. He has taken broken-down, older horses and made winners of them; he's taken cheap horses and made them famous; and he has successfully campaigned expensive horses bought at auction. Even with the failures of Padua Stables factored in, Lukas certainly has one of the best track records in the industry for picking winners from the sales.

"There are going to be guys that shoot at these marks, and that's the way it should be, and I accept that," Lukas says. "The thing I think that brings out your position in the industry is not doing it once or twice, but the consistency level, and standing the test of time. We throw around in sports the words 'great' and 'legendary' way too easy. I think greatness comes from standing the test of time. Doing it over and over and over the way Sunny Fitzsimmons and Whittingham did. I think we put guys in the Hall of Fame too frivolously. I made a comment when I went in. I said I think we ought to put one in each year and take one out each year. Look back at some of the records of the guys we put in.

"Jeff made a great point about ten or twelve years ago. He said, 'Dad, do you realize we had a better August-September-October than that guy had a career?' He told me that and it was true. We had more stakes winners in championships in a three-month run than he had in a career. So sometimes you gotta look back. Greatness stands the test of time only. I don't know where it'll all go. Let me put it this way: I don't wake up every morning thinking, 'Who do I have to beat today?'"

"He brought marketing to the game. The real successful trainers are those who market themselves and the game," says Hornung. "He brought the game two steps further and five classes higher. He dressed and talked like a businessman. He wore a suit and tie. He showed class and elevated what it meant to be a trainer."

Where does this place Lukas in the pantheon of horse trainers? Like it or not, he has to be considered one of the twentieth century's top five trainers. Sunny Jim Fitzsimmons and Ben Jones, *père et fils*, are the only trainers whose records are close to that of Lukas's. Compared to the most prominent of his contemporaries, Bob Baffert, Lukas's earnings, Triple Crown, and Breeders' Cup record are currently well beyond reach, despite Baffert's recent current success and popularity. Certainly, if anyone currently on the thoroughbred scene can catch Lukas, it will be Baffert, though it will take a long time and a high level of commitment to get there.

Then there's Charlie Whittingham and Woody Stephens. The highly regarded Whittingham was both a friend to Lukas and a critic. And Woody Stephens's run of five consecutive Belmont Stakes is seemingly unapproachable. But while the cantankerous Whittingham and the irascible Stephens were both extremely well-liked by the horse world and by the media, Lukas's record far surpasses theirs.

The Alumni

There are many trainers who have worked for Lukas in one capacity or another. While there are six well-known alumni with whom Lukas has established long-lasting relationships, there are in fact another half-dozen successful trainers who worked for Lukas earlier in their careers.

The alumni represent the crème de la crème of Lukas's invaluable assistants from over the years. Bobby Barnett, Randy Bradshaw, Kiaran McLaughlin, Mark Henning, Dallas Stewart, and Todd Pletcher are his most notable successors—his legacy in and of themselves. Many have emulated their mentor's ways, and some have put their own personal stamp on their operations, but Lukas's influence on these successful trainers is unmistakable.

"If they are made out of the right stuff, they're going to want to go out there on their own at some point, and my guys are made out of the right stuff," Lukas has said.

Here are the stories, briefly, of the men whom Lukas refers to as "my guys."

Bobby Barnett

Barnett was one of the original assistants who formed the corps of Lukas's success. He worked for Lukas between 1981 and 1984, but despite this short span, set the tone for other assistants yet to come, and in fact recruited several others. Barnett and Jeff Lukas were two key individuals who enabled Lukas to begin expanding his operation.

Robert C. Barnett was born on July 30, 1949, in Pampa, Texas, but he grew up on his parents' ranch in Oklahoma. "We had Black Angus cattle and quarter horses," he recalls. "Mom and Dad started match racing, and I started riding in those races when I was about twelve." He met Lukas when Wayne was still a quarter horse trainer and Barnett was a quarter horse jockey. The two became reacquainted years later, and Barnett began working for the man he considers "an excellent teacher."

Barnett has been a success over a sixteen-year career as an independent trainer. As recently as 1999, he ranked eleventh in earnings with $4,626,737 in prize money, and stood in the winner's circle eighty-five times. He has trained one Eclipse champion, Answer Lively.

For the most part, Barnett operates in Arkansas and Louisiana, where he is a perennial force. He has taken top honors in earnings three times at Oaklawn (1993, 1995, and 1996) and twice at Churchill Downs. He trains approximately fifty horses for ten to twelve owners, the most prominent of whom is John Franks.

"The three things I credit to my success," he's said, "are working for Wayne, from whom I learned a lot, hooking up with Mr. Franks, and when Frankie Brothers went back to Kentucky." Frankie Brothers was John Franks's trainer before leaving the circuit.

Barnett is currently a resident of Bossier City, Louisiana, where he lives with his wife Debbie and his daughters Tiffani and Traci.

Randy Bradshaw

Bradshaw originally went to work for Lukas in 1984, after having trained a few horses on his own. He served several tours of duty with Team Lukas and left several times, but has had an excellent relationship with his former employer. When Jeff Lukas was injured by Tabasco Cat, for instance, Bradshaw, who was training his own string, came back to help Lukas in his time of need. He primarily worked the Churchill Downs division of Team Lukas before leaving in 1993.

Bradshaw campaigned several successful horses, including Hedonist and Artax, whom he entered in the Kentucky Derby in 1998. Many writers made light of the fact that Artex was his first Derby horse, and he answered: "I've been in a lot of Grade 1 races. This one is a little more hype, but they're all important." He has won several graded stakes, most notably the Santa Anita Oaks, the San Felipe Stakes, and the Santa Catalina.

Among the lessons Bradshaw admits he's learned from Lukas was to enter horses in other races during a big stakes day. Asked if this was a distraction, he responded, "I think if you didn't, you'd want to mess around your horse all day. Your horse is used to a routine. You don't want to change everything the last few weeks that he has learned in the last two years."

Bradshaw returned to Lukas's fold on April 1, 1999, and was reportedly very well compensated. When he rejoined Team Lukas,

Mike Marlow, Lukas's then-California assistant, was moved to New York.

"In two years, I'll be fifty," Bradshaw told the *Thoroughbred Times*. "I want the security for my family. I think it's important I give that to them."

He currently works with Jeff Lukas managing Padua Stables for Satish Sanan, following Sanan's amicable parting with Wayne Lukas.

Kiaran McLaughlin

The fiery redheaded Irishman was one of the key players in the Lukas Racing Stables' successes during the incredible runs of the 1980s.

Born on November 15, 1960, in Lexington, Kentucky, McLaughlin dropped out of the University of Kentucky to go into horse racing. He worked for a number of trainers, including John Henning, Mark Henning's father, and worked for Lukas from 1985 to 1992. At one point he ran both the Louisville and Lexington stables for Team Lukas. He then went to New York to run the Belmont division, where he trained a number of Lukas's Eclipse champions, including Open Mind.

McLaughlin married Letty Henning, daughter of John and sister of Mark, and they have two children—a daughter, Erin, and a son, Ryan. When he left Lukas in 1992, McLaughlin became a jockey's agent for a short time, before accepting a position with the sheik of Dubai.

Currently, he runs the stables of Sheik Mohammed al Maktoum in Dubai in the United Arab Emirates, training more than 150 horses. He splits his time between Dubai—from November to March/April—and New York—from April to October/November—and keeps a string of forty to fifty horses at Belmont. He has won stakes races in the United States, Dubai, and Japan, and usually races in the Breeders' Cup before returning to Dubai in the fall.

Mark Henning

Born in 1965 in Mansfield, Ohio, Mark Henning's father, John Henning, was an accomplished trainer, so Mark grew up around horses.

Intending to become a veterinarian, he attended Ohio State University after graduating from high school in 1982. The best-laid plans of mice and men. . . .

Henning worked first for trainer Neil Howard. In May 1987 he went to work for Hall of Fame trainer Jack Van Berg for a short period, before accepting a job with Lukas. His first job was to run the New York division, which he did for two years. He was then given his own string, and competed at Churchill Downs, Keeneland, and Gulfstream Park, among other places.

Once, when Henning was running the Belmont stables, he saddled three winners in one day. He eagerly anticipated Lukas's call to tell him the good news, and when Lukas called to check in, Henning told him, "The horses ran real good."

Lukas, who had watched the races on simulcast, yelled: "You hillbilly, those horses didn't run good! Don't you know anything?"

Henning was devastated. He wondered what he'd done wrong, recounted the rest of the day's events to Lukas, then made the mistake of repeating his assessment of the day's results: "The horses ran good."

"Horses don't run good!" Lukas yelled again into the phone. "Horses run well!"

Henning left Lukas in 1992. "I don't know at that time that he anticipated any of us moving on," he said. His departure precipitated Todd Pletcher's, Dallas Stewart's, and Kiaran McLaughlin's. His first move was to California, where, in 1993, Henning's stable would rank fourth in earnings.

Today Henning has two stables, one in New York and one in Kentucky, and his two biggest backers are Team Valor and Edward P. Evans. He has won the Arlington Million, the Santa Anita Derby, and more than eighty other stakes races. And, like the other former Lukas assistants, he's gone head-to-head with his old boss.

"As each of us has been successful, Wayne's a little more receptive to the idea," Henning recently said at Belmont. "He takes great pride, as he should, with our success." Henning has great respect for his former employer: "He gave us the ability, knowledge, and exposure. He gave us the opportunity to deal with owners and the press. He gave us a lot of rope, and he tightened it once in a while. He's a great teacher, always has been."

Henning lives on Long Island with his wife and two children, and winters in Florida, with the New York horses.

Dallas Stewart

Born in McComb, Mississippi, on September 15, 1959, Stewart, one of the longest serving of Lukas's assistants, was with Lukas from 1986 to 1997.

Stewart's introduction to Lukas occurred through Randy Bradshaw. Stewart was galloping horses on a track in Louisiana when he approached Bradshaw, who was running Lukas's stables there. "I introduced myself," he recalled, "and asked him about the possibility of a job. It was perfect timing. They were looking for somebody."

Stewart was the exercise rider in 1988 for Winning Colors. He also worked with Lady's Secret, Thunder Gulch, Serena's Song, Timber Country, and Tabasco Cat. In 1992 he was promoted to Lukas's top Kentucky assistant. And by 1995 he was in charge of Kentucky, Florida, and Saratoga for Team Lukas.

"I had one of the best jobs that anybody could ask for. . . . It was a lot of hard work, for sure. But it was a whole lot of fun too." About going out on his own in 1997, Stewart said: "When you leave a stable like Lukas's, you give up a lot." He felt, however, that "doing it for yourself, that's got to be more exciting and satisfying."

When Stewart was about to leave Lukas, he wondered where he'd find a pony as nice as the expensive ones his employer provided him with. One morning he talked to Lukas, wondering aloud where he could find a nice lead pony. Before Stewart left, Lukas called him over. "I think you forgot something," he said, and offered the pony as a gift to his longtime loyal assistant.

"Actually, the one that I probably was the closest to in a day-to-day relationship was Dallas," Lukas said, when thinking about his former assistants, "because I spent so much time with him in Kentucky. He was always there. Dallas probably worked side by side with me more than the others. Randy was in the farm situation, the racetrack situation, but he wasn't right where *I was*, talking to him every day."

Stewart's barns are a picture perfect copy of Lukas's. Walls and trim are painted white. The stable's colors are green-and-white. Stewart's saddle pads carry the initials DS, however, not the DL used by Lukas.

The former assistant's first stakes win was at Turfway Park in December 1997. Rod and Staff won the Prairie Bayou Stakes. And in 1999, Stewart's Kimberlite Pipe was entered in the Louisiana Derby. Lukas did not have an entry, but he watched the simulcast at his home, rooting for Stewart. As the horse barreled down the stretch, it fought off two desperate challengers and won by a head. Lukas went nuts.

"I was up hollering and banging on the furniture. My wife said she had never seen me show that kind of emotion, even after some of my big wins. I said, 'Well, that's my guy.' "

The admiration was mutual. Stewart once said to a reporter: "That man's a legend. I am very proud to say that I was associated with him and his son Jeff. . . . He gives you the stock, but then he challenges you to develop 'em and make yourself a force. That's what we're trying to do here."

Stewart resides in Louisville, Kentucky, with his wife Yvette and son Wesley.

Todd Pletcher

Born on June 26, 1967, in Dallas, Texas, Todd Pletcher grew up around horses. His father is famed horseman J. J. Pletcher, whose farm is not far from Padua Stables in Florida. Todd graduated with a degree in animal science from the University of Arizona, and began working for Lukas in 1990. He was an instrumental figure in the big run Team Lukas made between 1994 and 1996, after which he went out on his own.

In 2000, Todd Pletcher had four entries in the Kentucky Derby. Unlike his former employer, no one criticized him for it.

"There's bigger purses, but there's no bigger event, no bigger prize," Pletcher said. His entry of Impeachment took third, and More

Than Ready took fourth. His horses Trippi and Graeme Hall finished eleventh and last respectively. Impeachment also finished third in the Preakness Stakes that same year.

"I am proud of all these horses," Pletcher said. "Of course, we came to win . . . I've said all along we came here with four horses we thought would run well, and that we had a chance." Sound like anyone you've heard before?

"He is an attention-to-detail guy," Pletcher said of Lukas. "He runs a great organization. He is very meticulous, and hopefully I've carried some of those things with me."

Pletcher had one of the top fillies of 1998 in Jersey Girl. In 1999 his stables finished in the top ten for earnings, and finished fifth in 2000. He lives in Garden City, Long Island, not far from Belmont, with his wife and his sons Payton and Kyle.

Lucas on His Assistants

"The assistants all had a certain common thread that ran through every one of them, and that would be a good work ethic," Lukas says today. "They were good people. There were a number of assistants that didn't make it. We went through a bunch of people who couldn't take the work ethic or the schedule and *me*. You know, they just couldn't handle it. And yet the ones that did survive, they all brought a little something to the table. Their own individual mannerisms and so forth.

"See, we had like a head coaching–assistant relationship. You may be appalled to hear this, but in all of those assistants, those six or seven, I probably haven't had dinner with them one on one. In all those years with all those assistants, I don't think there'd probably be five sit-down dinners. I always keep an arm's length. And yet they know that I was there for them, and I think we have a great bond with every one of them. The ones that are left know that I'm a hundred percent behind them. I did not get very close to them, nor did I get close to their families.

"Dallas Stewart—which would be thirteen, fourteen years, whatever it was—I have never seen his home, in Louisville. And I'm there months on end. I have never seen Todd's home in New York. You'd think surely you'd go to dinner or the house to drop off something, but it's a little bit different relationship. Very much on a professional basis. But underlying that, there was an affection that worked both ways."

Asked if they come to him for advice, Lukas chuckles, saying, "They will if they really get in the grease, and I think they pride themselves on being able to handle any situation. Every once in a while something will come up, but they'll sort of circle around. I don't think Dallas or Todd or any of them will just come right up. Kiaran will probably be the most open about saying, 'Hey boss, how do I handle this?' But they are so conditioned in our program, so conditioned in my way of thinking, that they might feel that's a moment of weakness. They might ask their dad before they ask me."

While many of these men are now considered top trainers, more often than not their names in newspaper and magazine articles are followed by the phrase "former Lukas assistant." Asked if he thought that was a compliment to him, he responded, "I wish they would not do that. Because I think those guys need to step up and have their own legacy. I even told the press when Todd was at the Derby. Every day I said, 'Todd's his own man, he's bringing his own ideas to the table. If we've helped him get this far, well, so be it, but you need to quit referring to him as my assistant and refer to him as a guy with a horse in the Derby.' I tried to water that one down, and it happens every interview."

But he says that he is proud. "Oh, yeah. I'm proud of all of them. All of those guys I'm extremely proud of. But I want them to have their own legacy. I don't want them to always have that footnote."

Overview

In varying degrees, Lukas's former assistants all keep nice, neat, pretty barns. You will most certainly see most of them chasing the Triple Crown events or, as Lukas likes to call them, the classics. And they relentlessly chase stakes races and many races on the national stage.

"Another important measure of the man is the top trainers who apprenticed under him," Richard Eng wrote of Lukas in 1999, during the trainer's Hall of Fame induction. "The list is impressive. Here's where they finished last year in earnings: Todd Pletcher (ninth), Bobby Barnett (eleventh), Mark Henning (fifteenth), Randy Bradshaw (twenty-eighth), Dallas Stewart (fifty-fourth), and Kiaran McLaughlin, the leading trainer in Dubai last season."

"Six former Lukas assistants have gone on to compete successfully at the sport's highest level," horse racing columnist Gary West wrote. "And they're living proof, much more convincing than any numbers, of Lukas's influence on the sport and of his dazzling success."

In the 1999 Visa Three-Year-Old Championship Series, where trainers are awarded points on winning graded stakes, only Lukas finished in the top ten. But his alumni filled the ranks of the next fifteen, with Pletcher twelfth, Dallas Stewart sixteenth, Randy Bradshaw seventeenth, and Bobby Barnett twenty-fourth.

In August 2000, Todd Pletcher took the Visa Three-Year-Old Championship. Lukas finished second to his former protégé. Baffert finished fourth. In the twenty-four months of the Visa championships between 1999 and 2000, Lukas's former assistants finished in the money twenty-six times in ninety-four races. Lukas himself finished in the money thirty-one times in that same span. Combining the records of Lukas and the "alumni," they were in the money fifty-seven times in ninety-four races. That's dominance.

The 2000 Breeders' Cup proved a turning point, with four of Lukas's former assistants entering horses in the events: Mark Henning, Kiaran McLaughlin, Dallas Stewart, and Todd Pletcher. Bobby Barnett had three entries in the 1998 Breeders' Cup.

In 2001, Todd Pletcher finished in the top ten in the Visa championships and Mark Henning in the top fifteen. Lukas was also in the top ten, just behind Pletcher, who also had two Kentucky Derby entries, Invisible Ink and Balto Star, the latter among the prerace favorites. Pletcher then skipped the Preakness and entered his two horses in the Belmont. Stewart had Dollar Bill, who raced in all three Triple Crown events.

Jeff

One can see the emotion in Lukas's eyes when he talks about his son. He will proudly tell you of his son's ability to personally get beyond his accident. He can even lace a little humor into it: "He's doing very well. He can't drive and it's a hardship. He lost complete eyesight in his right eye and has very limited vision in the left and he can't see peripherally, so when he drives he sideswipes everybody. And he's a bad driver anyway. It's in the gene pool. He inherited that. But he's very energetic yet. He may want a pizza at nine o'clock at night, and somebody's gotta drive him. He'll wake up at three o'clock in the morning and wonder why someone's not there to take him to the barn. So that's a problem. So we try not to move him very much.

"He's got a golf cart, he's got a thousand acres down there, and he runs into everybody in the golf cart. The surprising thing is, before the injury he could not have handled any of this, mentally. You'd have had to put him in a straitjacket. He had so much energy. But the injury would let him accept this, and it's made him reasonably happy, I think. That's the only thing you can say about it."

Asked if his son still follows his operation closely, Lukas says: "He's more like the interested spectator now. He'll call up and say, 'Boy, Dad, that horse ran well.' But he might call me five days later, where he used to call me after five minutes."

Still, Lukas can't help but wistfully remonstrate on what might have been. "One of the most successful trainers in the world is not in the Hall of Fame," he says. "Jeff. Unbelievable, his influence. And I think one thing that is a complete tribute to the organization is that we've been able to sustain a certain level of excellence without him. Because he brought *huge* to the table.

"I never even came [to Saratoga]. We won thirteen stakes at a twenty-eight-day meet, if you look it up. Thirteen stakes in twenty-eight days. I only saddled one of 'em. Jeff handled them all. He's got the best credentials of anyone in the world and he's not in the Hall of Fame. Every top stable in the country running at him on a private job, including the big ones. He turned 'em all down. He wanted to stay with it, you know. He had everything going for him. To extinguish that star is one of the real tragedies of this industry because . . . I think he would have surpassed everything I ever did."

The Legacy

Anyone who has come to the stage in their career that Lukas has asks one burning question: Have I changed the game? And Lukas certainly has. It has to be considered ironic that on the backstretch these days, many barns are decorated with large bunches of flowers, are cleanly kept and handsomely appointed. From the days when local trainers poked fun at how he "prettied up" his barns, Lukas must laugh inside when walking past the barns of his current competitors.

It's also ironic that Lukas's impressive records are assailable because a younger generation of horsemen and horsewomen have adopted his approach of racing on a national level. While Baffert may seem to Lukas as a relentless pursuer and incalculable usurper, he is in fact a Frankenstein of Lukas's own making. Lukas befriended the young trainer, who at one time looked up to him, and inspired him to give chase. If you love competition, Baffert's chasing after Lukas's milestones is thrilling sport. And of course there are the men he calls "my guys," several of whom may take a shot at chasing the master himself. They know how he did it.

"The bottom line for me would be, did I make the game better?" Lukas says. "I never hurt it, I don't think. And there was a run of time there when, with some of the adversity, people would say, 'Was he good for the game?' I think I've been good for the game. I think I've changed it a little bit for the better. And I'd like to be thought of as having made changes that were positive.

"The second thing would be, we were labeled as a corporate, unfeeling, hell-bent, win-at-all-costs operation, with little horsemanship, and now that my assistants are all doing so well, and are so well sought after, somebody's going to have to step back and say, 'Wait a minute, they're doing the same things, and now it's okay.' There had to be some horsemanship. Not all these guys could come through the program and not develop something. And yet they all have their own individual thing. But you go over there, and there's a mirror of what you see here."

For many years Lukas had an excellent relationship with the press. He was the silver-haired, good-looking, fast-talking horse trader with a Hollywood smile. And he whipped everybody who tried to beat him. There was rarely a bad article written about him. Always a control freak when it came to his image, he was able to mold his public persona in a way that no other trainer ever had. He could be loud and boastful, but he could back it up. As in any business, getting to the top is easier than staying on top, and Lukas's record has been delivered with consistency over the years.

But since the early 1990s, Lukas has found himself in a battle with the press. Once the wheels came off with Mid-America, Calumet, and Union City, Lukas found himself in a state of constant confrontation, instead of adulation. This soured him on the press and made him somewhat combative and defensive during what has to be considered one of the best runs (1994–96) in horse racing history. Like an animal who was wounded, Lukas fought hardest when he was backed against a wall. A man as proud as he is cannot show weakness. It's not allowed. Put up a fist and he will fight you.

Like any man sixty-six years of age, Lukas is now concerned with his legacy. It seems that this is the time for him to mend his relations with the press, to be more understanding and less combative. But that may be difficult. There are those in the press who love him to excess, and those who will criticize him for breathing. It's easy to get under his skin, and that game doesn't look to end anytime soon, unless he takes the fun out of it by not rising to the bait.

The Horses

Lukas first looked for a quarter horse build in his horses—with huge haunches and short stocky chests. He changed that model before he made the big run in the mid-1990s. He says now that he looks for both, hopefully taking the best possible horses available. But his aim is still to win the classics.

Asked what he thought his best training accomplishments were, he answered, "One of the best horses I ever trained was [the quarter horse] Dash For Cash. He was very special. Tabasco Cat was a pretty good training job in light of that was a rough year. Obviously some of those fillies, Serena's Song and Lady's Secret—we won the Whitney with Lady's Secret, the Haskell with Serena's Song—those were probably achievements that as a horse trainer, if you're out there, if you ask Nick or one of these guys here, they're going to say, 'Boy, that's not easy to pull those off.' "

The record is what it is. Monumental and monolithic. And in the coming years, with none of his fire for competition doused, Lukas is hoping to add to that record. He knows people will make a run at his records. Should he respond graciously to their attempts, it would be wonderful, but sometimes those who are most competitive with him are those he has problems dealing with.

A legacy is how we are remembered. How will Lukas be remembered? Certainly there is good and bad. His high-profile wins were as controversial as his high-profile disasters. His running five horses at Churchill Downs will be remembered as an over-the-top attempt to win a Derby. Certainly there is his reputation for working horses too hard, whether it is deserved or not. Capote and Union City bring to mind other young horses who broke down while in Lukas's hands.

In explanation, Lukas says: "The first thing is, U.S. racing has a tendency to swing the pendulum toward speed, and speed kills. We have put so much emphasis on speed in the U.S., rather than distance racing. See, in Europe you can gallop on a soft turf course for a mile and then sprint the last quarter of a mile. Here there are no spots like that. You run from the get-go from the gate and someone's always following you. So speed has compromised the soundness of horses a great deal, and we're breeding for it. We're breeding them faster and quicker, and I think that's a lot of our problem. The other thing is, our purse structure's gotten so lucrative in two- and three-year-olds that nobody wants to sit back and wait on them."

Lukas in Perspective

Lukas's relationship with the press recently has been difficult at best. Can he be too boastful? At times, yes. Can he be too proud? Yes. He has admitted to rubbing some people the wrong way, and he does.

Regardless, D. Wayne Lukas has changed the game. The barns on the backside are in general much nicer than you would have found them twenty years ago. They are now a place of business, instead of barns on a backstretch. People now race their horses in white bridles with regularity. He proved to be hugely successful, proved that you didn't need a breeding operation behind you, that you could go out and, with a keen eye for horseflesh, you could stake a claim to greatness by buying it. The way trainers pursue the game has changed, as they now operate on a national level, shipping horses, not people. Trainers today try to find the weakest spots in the national schedule to get the most success out of their horses. And the big trainers, the ones who want the national reputations, chase the classics. This is all due to Wayne Lukas's influence.

Lukas is now at the same age Charlie Whittingham and Woody Stephens were when he broke into the game. Asked if he had a different view of the game from his current vantage point, he said: "I've thought about that a little bit. When you're coming up through the ranks and trying to establish your position in the industry, I think the underlying thing that causes the jealousy or the animosity is that you're not really secure in your position. Insecurity causes jealousies. When you're totally secure in what you're doing, you don't have those feelings. When you're even a little insecure, the threat comes from the new guy—the quarter horse trainer coming over and whipping up on you and venturing into your territory. . . . So I have over the years thought, 'Why would I feel any animosity for John Doe coming up through the ranks?' I don't feel threatened at all. I feel more threatened when I don't feel I have the material in the barn. I do not feel threatened by John Doe over here.

"And I'm one of the few guys who I think you'll find in racing who's quick to offer advice to new guys. I'm always going to go up and compliment them if they do something that I think is spectacular. I make it a point. Even sometimes when it just about kills me to do it. I'll go over and say, 'That was a helluva job. You whipped up on us and made us like it.' . . . Charlie and I never fought. Laz Barerra and Charlie were very different. Of course, we were right there in California, but I never thought Laz resented me, and I never thought Woody resented me. I think they both stood back a little bit in awe. Whittingham'd say, 'Man, cowboy, you got it going.'

"And another guy who always made me feel that he was never resentful or threatened was Alan Jerkens. Every time I'd run into Alan Jerkens he'd even ask me questions. Why did you do that? What about the gate? What do you do here? And Mack Miller, when we won with Tabasco Cat in the Belmont, he wrote me a letter which is framed on my office wall. He said this might be the greatest training job I've ever seen in my life. He wrote Bill Young the same letter. But there were some guys that I could feel the resentment coming off, and I feel it's the insecurity."

More than anything, Lukas will be remembered as the agent of change in an industry that was in flux. He took a game that was the hobby of old-moneyed families and transformed it into a business at a time when those old families had dissipated or no longer had the capital to make a go of it on their own, especially as the value of individual horses rose astronomically. Some of the same people who complained about Lukas (and Gene Klein) were in fact selling him horses. Regardless, Lukas made it a business, and a successful business, and was part of the movement that changed how the entire game was played. If it was not him, it might have been someone else. The game was bound to change. It was time for a change. Nothing goes on unchanged as long as horse racing in America did. The signposts were everywhere.

When Lukas entered the thoroughbred game—"full-blown," as he likes to say—he saw how the game was not played, and challenged the old rules and notions. He did what Calumet and Claiborne had done, but from a trainer's perspective. He raced horses in different parts of the country. He changed the balance of power. Becoming a superstar trainer, he changed the relationship between trainer and owner and breeder. The trainer used to be someone who worked for a rich family or farm. He was an employee. Lukas changed that. And in a sport that was controlled by a handful of people or families, he—and others like him—threw the game wide open, and in doing so changed it forever.

What if there had been no Lukas? Impossible. With Sangster and the sheiks holding personal bidding wars and buying everything in sight, Lukas was one of a handful of Americans who were attempting to keep some of the best bloodstock in America. Was he doing it out of patriotism? It seems doubtful. But the simple fact is that if there were a void there, some American, or group, modeled on Sangster's group, would have eventually found its way in.

That's changing the game. That's a legacy.

The Future

What does the future hold for D. Wayne Lukas? What hurdles does he have yet to overcome? Where is he headed?

Since Lukas is driven by competition, it would seem that he'll follow the lead of a number of great horse trainers who have gone before him, like Whittingham and Stephens: he'll train until he can't do it anymore.

Even for Lukas there are still records to chase. He is chasing the legends now. He's chasing Ben Jones's six Kentucky Derbies. But Lukas wants seven. He's chasing R. W. Walden's seven Preaknesses. But Lukas wants eight. And he's chasing James Rowe Sr.'s eight Belmont Stakes, but Lukas wants nine.

Asked if he had any interest in trying to take the English or Irish Derby, Lukas answered: "I don't want to go into any arena where I think I'm overmatched or I don't think I have at least a level playing field. In order to do that, (a) I want to make sure I have a good enough horse, but (b) you'd better prepare for it. And that would take pulling off from this and going over there. I don't think you can win the Irish Derby without being at Coolmore."

And he still has the dream, like any other horseman, that somewhere in his barn is that animal, as elusive as Pegasus, that will deliver him a Triple Crown. For Lukas and other good horse trainers, the future is and always has been the next horse.

In August, this writer met with Darrell Wayne Lukas outside his barns in Saratoga. He was tall, wearing creased blue jeans; a starched, white, freshly pressed shirt; a white cowboy hat and a pair of wraparound sunglasses. He was suspicious and wary, as he often is of the press these days. He could be defensive, both against charges and about competitors, and argumentative, but was more often funny, charming, witty, and a wonderful raconteur. He was on his best behavior.

We sat at a little table, on a sunny bright morning on a Tuesday. The sky was a bright blue and the horses were neighing in the background as we discussed his career. Lukas told stories, defended his positions, discussed his personal life. But in the end it always came back to the horses. He was having one of the best runs he'd had in Saratoga, a million miles away from the horrors of the year before.

Scorpion, a brutal disappointment earlier in the year, had won the Jim Dandy. It was an unprecedented upset. Lukas was on a roll. And he had a young colt, named Jump Start, whom he was talking up. As we departed, he told us to remember that name. The next day, a colt by the name of Jump Start won the Grade 2 Saratoga Special and $150,000.

Jump Start was suddenly Derby material, according to several press reports. And he was highly rated in the 2001 Breeders' Cup Juvenile at Belmont. But Jump Start broke his leg in two places after challenging for the lead halfway through the race. This was on the same day as Spain's attempt to win a second Distaff in a row came painfully close; she finished second.

The future is only as close as the next good horse away.

ENDNOTES

Prologue

Every horseman . . . Joe Drape. *The Race For the Triple Crown.*
  New York: Atlantic, 2001, 1

I've probably . . . John D. Ferguson, "Derby 1999: Charismatic,"
  Theturfonline.com

We're devastated . . . "No Crown for Charismatic," *Holland
  Sentinel*, June 6, 1999

There's a certain element . . . "Charismatic has surgery on broken
  leg," CNNSI.com, June 7, 1999

Chapter One: The Last Big Race

Notable for his . . . Bill Finley, "Saratoga Journal: Day 2, August 2,
  2000," ESPN.com

If we're going . . . "D. Wayne Lukas' Summer of Discontent,"
  ESPN.com, August 20, 2000

Cash run was . . . Ibid.

Every time I look . . . Richard Rosenblatt, "Race for 3-Year-Old
  Champ to Begin," AP, June 11, 2000

The Preps

But the maiden . . . "High Cascade Heads North for GG Derby,"
    Horseplayerdaily.com, January 10, 2001
Last year he . . . "Lukas Enlists Baze for High Cascade,"
    Thoroughbredtimes.com, February 15, 2001
Lukas told me . . . Ibid.
Russell Baze was . . . "Barn Notes," Gulfstream Park, February 18,
    2001
Trainer D. Wayne Lukas . . . "Golden State Mile," Thorough
    bredtimes.com, February 10, 2001
It's time to . . . Jennie Rees, "Gold Trader Can Regain Derby
    Luster in San Felipe," *Louisville Courier-Journal*, March 16,
    2001
He was running fine . . . Ibid.
These horses are . . . Ibid.
Was a great blow . . . Marty McGee, *Daily Racing Form*, March
    22, 2001
We think we've got . . . Ibid., Rees
Strategically, Scorpion . . . Bill Christine, "Lukas Is Playing Catch
    Up," *Los Angeles Times*, March 17, 2001
He made a bit . . . "Jockey and Trainer Quotes," Santa Anita, April
    7, 2001
Team Lukas did not . . . "Lukas' Main Hope for 2001 Derby Is
    Irish," Realracing.com
We've been able . . . Ibid., McGee
The race is not . . . John Asher, "Turnberry Isle to Get a Chance at
    Coolmore," Churchilldowns.com, April 16, 2001
I think he has . . . Jennie Rees, "Lukas May Be on Last Leg,"
    Louisville Courier-Journal, April 20, 2001
Rest assured . . . Steve Davidowitz, "Across the Board,"
    axcis/TrackMaster.com, April 21, 2001
To be sure . . . Maryjean Wall, *Lexington Herald-Leader*, April 21,
    2001
He was trained . . . Rick Bailey, "Lukas' last hope for Derby runs
    out," *Lexington Herald-Leader*, April 22, 2001

Churchill Downs

Lukas' derby strategy . . . Bill Christine, "Lukas Is Playing
    Catchup," *Los Angeles Times*, March 17, 2001
The throng will . . . Ed Schuyler, Jr., "Trainer D. Wayne Lukas's
    streak of 20 straight Kentucky Derbys about to end,"
    YahooCanada.com, April 27, 2001
D. Wayne Lukas' training . . . Eric Crawford, "A Derby Without
    Lukas," *Louisville Courier-Journal*, May 2, 2001
The media likes . . . Ibid., Crawford
It's like an . . . Gary Long, "Gary Long Commentary," *Miami
    Herald*, May 4, 2001
Despite a sometimes . . . John Scheinman, "Without an Entry,
    Lukas Still a Presence," *Washington Post*, May 2, 2001
If his detractors . . . Ibid., Long
Sooner or later . . . Ibid., Eisenberg
The Derby streak . . . Ibid.
It's such a tough game . . . Ibid., Scheinman
It's not about . . . Pete Coates, *Bloomberg News*, April 24, 2001
With the emphasis . . . Ibid., Eisenberg
I couldn't see me . . . John Clay, "Lukas Shrugs Off Ending of the
    Streak," *Lexington Herald-Leader*, May 3, 2001
I put that to bed . . . Ibid., Crawford
Baffert likes to act . . . Ibid., Clay
Twenty in a row . . . Ibid., Crawford

The Belmont

I was at home . . . Bill Finley, "Lukas stays cool through dry Triple
    Crown," ESPN.com
Buckle Down Ben . . . "Jinxed again!" Realracing.com, February
    14, 2001
I just got . . . "Gulfstream Park, Barn Notes," February 18, 2001
We haven't had . . . Marty McGee, *Daily Racing Form*, March 22,
    2001
We broke okay . . . "Balto Star Wins $600G Spiral Stakes,"
    CasinoMagazine.com

We're going to try . . . "Point Given Returns to Churchill,"
  MSNBC.com, May 24, 2001
The race is . . . John Asher, "Belmont Hopeful Buckle Down Ben
  Prepping at Churchill Downs," Churchilldowns.com May 25,
  2001
If you weren't . . . Jennie Rees, "Day now at 7,999 wins, rides one
  at Belmont today," *Louisville Courier-Journal*, May 28, 2001
It will be a serious test . . . "Point Given Skips Through Slop in
  Strong Churchill Work," Churchilldowns.com
The linemaker has . . . Ibid., Finley
He's a horse . . . Ibid.
I wanted to be . . . "Clintons among celebrities in attendance at
  Belmont, New York," AP, CNNSI.com, June 9, 2001

Aftermath

Hi, D. Wayne . . . Ibid., Long, May 4, 2001
Our two-year-old . . . Ibid., Clay, "Lukas Shrugs off ending of the
  streak"
That's next year's model . . . Ibid., Crawford, "A Derby Without
  Lukas"

Chapter Two: Coach!

Antigo, Wisconsin

The gateway . . . Community Profile Network, Antigo, Wisconsin
Langlade County lakes . . . Antigo Chamber of Commerce
A grand array . . . Ibid., Community Profile Network
It was the . . . Carol Flake, "Profiles, The Intensity Factor," *The
  New Yorker*, December 26, 1988, 54
My husband's mother . . . Ross Staaden. *Winning Trainers.*
  Karawara, Australia: Headway International, 1991
Lukas grew up . . . William Nack, "While the rest of the world
  sleeps," *Sports Illustrated*, May 6, 1985, 78
Wayne has a . . . Ibid., Staaden, 29
I remember going . . . Ibid., Nack, 78
Wayne was very . . . Ibid., Staaden

He had lots . . . Ibid., Flake, 54
Trick ride off . . . Ibid.
The guys I . . . Ibid., Nack, 79
People would buy . . . Pete Axthelm, "Smelling the Roses, Pricked by a Thorn," *GQ*, May 1989, 290
They bought thirty . . . Ibid., Staaden, 30
I wanted to be . . . Ibid., Nack, 79
He always had . . . Ibid., Flake, 54
We'd go through . . . Ibid., Nack, 79

College

Were determined . . . Ibid., Staaden, 29
We realized it . . . Ibid.
What are you . . . Ibid., Nack, 79
Wayne's grade school . . . Ibid., Staaden
All they wanted . . . Ibid., Nack
Even before . . . Dan Peterson, "D. Wayne Lukas, King of the Sport of Kings," Kappasigma.com

Family

My daughter . . . Ibid., Staaden, 28
My sister . . . Ed Schuyler, "Right dream, wrong horse at Derby," AP, Sunday, May 2, 1999

Basketball as a Way of Life

At that point . . . Ibid., Nack
I did my . . . Ibid., Staaden, 30
Wayne was a very . . . Ibid., Nack, 80
The day . . . Ibid., Staaden, 29

Calvin Klein Coach, Kmart Kids

La Crosse was . . . Ibid., Flake, 56
We tried to . . . Ibid.
He was a real taskmaster . . . Ibid., Nack, 81
He was a Calvin Klein . . . Ibid., Axthelm, 290
Most of the . . . Ibid., Nack, 82

He yelled at us . . . Ibid., Nack, 81
If we could . . . Ibid., Staaden, 33
Pronounced as one . . . Ibid., Flake, 56
I had some . . . Ibid., Axthelm, 291
Wayne had a . . . Ibid., Staaden, 34
I never slept . . . Ibid., Axthelm
I figured I . . . Ibid., Axthelm
At the end of the school year . . . Ibid., Flake, 56

Chapter Three: Quarter Horses: The First Years

Nelson C. Nye . . . Nelson C. Nye. *Outstanding Modern Quarter
    Horse Sires.* New York: William Morrow, 1948
From the starting gate . . . *A Guide to Wagering On America's
    Fastest Athlete, The Racing American Quarter Horse.*
    American Quarter Horse Association, 2001
Quarter horses are . . . Audrey Pavia, interview, July 6, 2001
Janet, she liked . . . Ibid., Staaden, 36
He ran as . . . Ibid., Nack, 82
Hey, Wayne . . . Ibid., Axthelm, 291
One of the things . . . Ibid., Flake, 56
He had three . . . Ibid., Staaden
Wayne arrived here . . . Ibid.
He wasn't that knowledgeable . . . Ibid., Flake, 57
I hope I . . . Ibid., Nack, 78
He approached me . . . Ibid., Staaden, 35
I bought a . . . Ibid., Staaden, 35–36
He was a . . . Ibid.
I'll tell you . . . Ibid., Staaden, 37

The Growing Legend of D. Wayne Lukas

You're going . . . Ibid., Flake
When Wayne came . . . Ibid., Staaden, 38
Oh, that's ridiculous . . . Ibid.
You know what . . . Ibid., Flake, 57
I first began . . . Ibid., Nye, 247
She's come off . . . Ibid.

Wayne is a sharp . . . Ibid., Staaden, 39
You've got to . . . Ibid., Flake, 62
So strong was . . . Ibid.
I never thought . . . release, "Dash For Cash Races Honor One of
the All-Time Greats," Lone Star Park at Grand Prairie,
October 20, 2000
Moving Moon . . . Ibid., Flake 63

Making the Shift

Wayne and I . . . Ibid., Staaden, 41

Chapter Four: The Big Horses

The Barn

This ain't a . . . Ibid., Flake, 44
I just hope . . . Ibid., 37
When you pay . . . Ibid., Axthelm, 238
A good appearance . . . Ibid.
The stalls can be . . . Joe Drape, "Lukas Makes Himself Heard
Again," *New York Times*, May 30, 1999
All the horses . . . Ibid., Nack, 82
People are always looking . . . Mike Helm. *A Breed Apart*. New
York: Henry Holt, 1991
Jog that one . . . Ibid., Nack, 73
Bedo, you and . . . Ibid., Nack, 74
No one ever . . . Ibid.
We're constantly telling people . . . Ibid., Flake, 46
They call Wayne . . . Ibid., Staaden, 135

The Trainer's Daily Dozen

Doom and gloom . . . Ibid., 133
I want them . . . Ibid., Joe Drape, *The Race for the Triple Crown*

Effervescing and Terlingua

He had to . . . Ibid., Flake, 63
Are you drinking . . . Ibid., Nack, 83

She should have . . . Ibid., 77

The mistake everyone . . . Steven Crist. *The Horse Traders*. New
    York: W. W. Norton, 1986, 82

She's trained by . . . Billy Reed, "Legendary Lukas Honored,"
    Lexington Herald-Leader, April 28, 1999

People didn't like . . . Ibid., Flake, 64

John Nerud, Tartan Farms, and Codex

It's a quick . . . Ibid., Crist, 104

We were playing . . . Ibid., Staaden, 43

That's a large . . . Ibid., Flake, 63

Men in plaid . . . Ibid., 46

He was a . . . "Breeder's Cup Profile: D. Wayne Lukas,"
    BreedersCup.com

He works like . . . Ibid., Nack, 84

An arrogant man . . . Ibid., Drape, "Lukas Makes Himself Heard
    Again"

You've been there . . . Ibid., Flake, 43

Oversight . . . James Tuite, "Codex Wins Preakness Foul Claim
    Disallowed," *New York Times*, May 18, 1980

Racing's Battle of . . . Joseph Durso, "Race Finishes as Jockey
    Battle," *New York Times*, May 18, 1980

When he saw the gate . . . Ibid., Tuite, "Codex Wins Preakness. . . ."

I thought this . . . Ibid.

He hit my . . . Ibid., Durso

Codex . . . gave an . . . Ibid., Tuite

Take us down . . . Red Smith, "That Was No Way to Treat a Lady,
    New York Times, May 18, 1980

Vasquez said that . . . Ibid., Tuite

We're friends outside . . . Ibid., Durso

A tough customer . . . Ibid., Smith

The Equal Rights . . . James Tuite, "Genuine Risk and Codex in 1,
    2 Posts," *New York Times*, June 6, 1980

Three qualified people . . . Ibid., Tuite

As good as . . . Ibid., Smith

We feel that . . . James Tuite, "Preakness Appeal Is Made," *New
    York Times*, May 20, 1980

If the term . . . Red Smith, "Perry Mason at the Races," *New York Times*, June 3, 1980

Well, there's wide . . . James Tuite, "Preakness Hearing Begins in Maryland," *New York Times*, June 3, 1980

Witnesses included just . . . Ibid., Smith

I been riding . . . Ibid., Tuite

I don't consider . . . Ibid., Tuite, "Genuine Risk and Codex . . . ."

Partez, Muttering, and Bobby Knight

I thought we were . . . James Tuite, "Pleasant Colony Wins Kentucky Derby," *New York Times*, May 3, 1981

Comparatively speaking . . . Ibid., Staaden, 48

I think . . . Steve Wilstein, "Knight Keeps His Job, but for How Long?" Topic Newspapers, Associated Press, May 26, 2000

Landaluce

The name of . . . William Leggett, "Just Like Dear Old Dad," *Sports Illustrated*, August 9, 1982

Landaluce cost . . . Ibid.

It looks like . . . Ibid.

You search and . . . Ibid., Flake, 65

Normally, I am . . . Ibid., Leggett

John Nerud called . . . Ibid.

I thought we'd . . . Andrew Beyer, "I had her head in my lap . . . She died in my arms." *The Horseman's Journal*, February 1983, reprinted from the *Washington Post*, January, 6, 1983

Chapter Five: The Big Money

Gene Klein

Army Officer . . . William Nack, "Another View From the Top," *Sports Illustrated*, May 8, 1988, 102

I thought that . . . Ibid.

Prices were . . . Ibid.

Hamburger meat . . . Ibid.

My first taste . . . Ibid.
I figured I . . . Ibid.
Football . . . Ibid.
Agents, drug problems . . . Ibid., Nack, 104
I didn't know . . . Ibid., Nack, 100
You'll get a . . . Ibid., Nack, 104
Horse racing helped . . . Ibid.
Gene is dead game . . . Ibid., Nack, 106

The Program

Horses were an . . . Ibid., Flake, 66
I can't afford . . . Ibid., Nack, 107
Gene Klein doesn't . . . Ibid., Nack, 108
When a horse . . . Ibid.
If you go . . . Ibid.
I've been a . . . Ibid.

Lady's Secret

Her agent didn't . . . Ibid.
There is no reason . . . Ibid.

Keeneland

A nine-year-old . . . "About Keeneland, History 1950–1959,"
    keeneland.com, 2001
Who bought that? . . . Ibid., Crist, *The Horse Traders*
Eight giddy minutes . . . William F. Reed, "My God, Are These
    People Spending Real Money?" *Sports Illustrated*, August 1,
    1983, 26

Althea and Life's Magic

Althea didn't come . . . John Clay, "Let's hear it for the girls,"
    Lexington Herald-Leader, May 1, 1999
Nothing is done . . . William Leggett, "Another Touch of Lukas
    Magic," *Sports Illustrated*, June 25, 1984
Does your father . . . Ibid., Leggett, 69

Chapter Six: The Big Time

Keep 'Em Coming

If he spent . . . Most of the numbers in this section are generated
from or calculated from: Joe Bagan. *Lukas at Auction*.
Denver: Sachs-Lawler, 1989
Every year we have . . . Ibid., Axthelm, 292
Ladies' Man . . . Ibid., Bagan, 309

Tank's Prospect

In my mind . . . Ibid., Staaden, 55
The eleven three-year-olds . . . Steven Crist, "Two Overshadow
Field for Preakness," *New York Times*, May 18, 1985
It took me . . . Demmie Stathopolos, "Coming on Strong at the
Weakness," *Sports Illustrated*, May 27, 1985
I couldn't blame . . . Steven Crist, "Tank's Prospect Takes the
Preakness," *New York Times*, May 19, 1985
I'm just realizing . . . Steven Crist, "Wayne Lukas: Be Prepared,"
New York Times, May 19, 1985
It's so thrilling . . . Ibid., Stathopolos
You'll be the . . . Ibid., Crist
As good as any . . . Ibid., Stathopolos
Tank's Prospect, covered . . . Carol Flake, *Tarnished Crown*.
Garden City: Doubleday, 1987, 334–35

Spend a Buck

The intense look . . . Ibid., Flake, 325
They hooked him . . . Dave Anderson, "Don't Get in His Way,"
New York Times, May 28, 1985

Capote

For D. Wayne Lukas . . . William Nack, "Doing Battle With the
Demon," *Sports Illustrated*, May 4, 1987, 42
The question is . . . Ibid., 48

Blunder horse . . . Ira Berkow, "The Narrow Horse," *New York Times*, May 2, 1987

He snapped at me . . . Ibid., Axthelm, 239

Winning Colors and the Wayne and Woody Show

You all know . . . Jay Hovdey, "Winning Colors is First on Coast," *New York Times*, April 10, 1988

What she did . . . Ibid.

Our steaks sure . . . Ibid., Crist, *The Horse Traders*, 185

Lukas and Stephens . . . Steven Crist, "Winning Colors Is the Winning Ticket," *New York Times*, May 8, 1988

It looks like . . . Steven Crist, "Filly and Forty Niner Set for Rematch," *New York Times*, May 9, 1988

Switch your leads . . . William Nack, "Kentucky Derby," *Sports Illustrated*, May 1988

Lukas was glowing . . . Ibid., Crist, "Winning Colors. . . . "

Going over . . . Steven Crist, "Had to Be Some Horsemanship," *New York Times*, May 8, 1988

Woody told me . . . Ibid.

I give all the . . . Robert McG. Thomas Jr., "Jeff Lukas Is Injured Seriously by Runaway," *New York Times*, December 16, 1993

We'll catch her . . . Ibid., Crist, "Winning Colors. . . . "

I congratulated him . . . Ibid., Crist, "Filly and Forty Niner. . . . "

He's a genius . . . Demmie Stathopolos, "One Heavenly Star," *Sports Illustrated*, May 30, 1988, 32

Lukas will never get . . . Steven Crist, "Chance of Surprise," *New York Times*, May 21, 1988

What Woody's got . . . Ibid., Stathopolos, 32

We're going to . . . George Vecsey, "No Regrets From Lukas," *New York Times*, May 22, 1998

We were eight . . . Steven Crist, "Risen Star Outruns Filly in Preakness," *New York Times*, May 22, 1988

I don't blame . . . Ibid.

I told the . . . Ibid.

Usually I'm very . . . Ibid., Staaden, 143

You can't say . . . Ibid., Anderson

The motives and . . . Ibid., Vecsey

In hindsight . . . Ibid., John Clay, "Let's Hear it for the Girls"

William T. Young

The information in this section is drawn from Dan Liebman, "Teaming With Success," Overbrookfarm.com

Criminal Type

Nafzger still bristles . . . Ibid., Joe Drape, "Lukas Makes Himself Heard Again"

Chapter Seven: The Fall

Laz Barrera, Drugs, and D. Wayne Lukas

The history of . . . Ibid., Axthelm, 238

When you overshadow . . . Ibid.

The bottom line . . . "Barrera and Lukas Cited in Drug-Use Investigation," *New York Times*, February 14, 1989

A six-month . . . Ibid.

We've learned . . . "Accusations Filed," *New York Times*, February 16, 1989

Bill Young's first . . . Tim Sullivan, "First Saturday in May is Lukas time," *Cincinnati Enquirer*, May 3, 2000

We don't want . . . "California Drops Charges Against Lukas and Four Others," *New York Times*, June 2, 1989

Absolutely ridiculous . . . Ibid., Helm, *A Breed Apart*

Mid-America Racing Stables

Big price tags . . . Marilyn Bender, "Winner's Circle Goes Public," *New York Times*, April 28, 1985

The investing public . . . Ibid.

The World's Most Expensive Garage Sale

The "Klein Dispersal" . . . David L. Heckerman, "The Claiborne-Gorman Dispersal," auctions.bloodhorse.com

When I went . . . William Nack, "Man on a Hot Seat," *Sports Illustrated*, June 7, 1993, 48

Lukas was aware . . . Ibid., Drape, *The Race for the Triple Crown*, 48

Calumet Goes Bust

Calumet history courtesy of the website Calumet.com

Calumet farm, once . . . Ann Hagedorn Auerbach. *Wild Ride*. New York: Henry Holt, 1994, 303

Chief Judge Joe Lee . . . United States Bankruptcy Court, Kentucky, Lexington, case no. 91-51414

Do you know . . . Ibid., Nack, "Man on a Hot Seat," 49

Downward Spiral

It was a . . . Steven Crist, "Grand Canyon Out of Triple Crown," *New York Times*, February 16, 1990

We've taken some . . . Ibid., Nack, 48

After a five . . . Joseph Durso, "To Lessen Malaise, Industry Looks to Up the Purse for Promotion," *New York Times*, April 24, 1991

We no longer . . . Ibid.

Union City

Another California star . . . Joe Durso, "Date With the Derby," *New York Times*, April 19, 1993

There is nothing . . . William Nack, "A Discredit to Their Race," *Sports Illustrated*, May 3, 1993

This horse is . . . Ibid., Nack, "Man on a Hot Seat"

I was lucky . . . William F. Reed, "Blew By You," *Sports Illustrated*, May 24, 1993

Shattered the sesamoid . . . Ibid., Nack, "Man on a Hot Seat," 45

We never took . . . Ibid., Reed, 35

Nobody is exempt . . . Ibid.

That's ridiculous . . . Ibid., Nack, 46

That's so much . . . Ibid.

The decision to run . . . William T. Young, *Daily Racing Form*,
    May 23, 1993
For a decade . . . Jim McKay. *The Real McKay*. New York: Dutton
    Publishing, 1998

The Intervention

What are you doing here . . . Ibid., Nack, 50
It became an open . . . Ibid.
Why does someone . . . Ibid.

Jeff and Tabasco Cat

I heard people yelling . . . Stephanie Diaz, "Lukas Hopes to Cap
    Amazing Career with Triple Crown," *Detroit News*, June 4, 1999
Usually they'll swerve . . . Ibid., Thomas Jr.
It was like . . . Jay Privman, "For Lukas Family, the Highest
    Stakes," *New York Times*, January 23, 1994
Jeff went straight . . . Ibid., Diaz
Tabasco Cat crashed . . . Ibid., Privman
If there is . . . Jay Hovdey, "Journey to the Winner's Circle,"
    Reader's Digest, May 1995, 88
Talk to him . . . Ibid., Hovdey
I read to him . . . Ibid., Diaz
Jeff is very . . . Ibid., Privman
Grandpa, wake up . . . Ibid.
We're not going . . . Ibid., Hovdey
Maybe this horse . . . "A Victory for Tabasco Cat," *New York
    Times*, January 23, 1994
This one's for . . . Ibid.
He really wanted . . . Jay Privman, "Far From Crowd, Lukas Is on
    Track to Recover," *New York Times*, April 10, 1994
He's so focused . . . Ibid.
I might have . . . Ibid., Hovdey
No matter how . . . Ibid.
While most people . . . Richard E. Glover Jr., "Houdini Lukas,"
    Handicapper's Daily, June 2000

He used to talk . . . Ibid., Diaz

I've been involved . . . Ibid., Hovdey

Chapter Eight: Comeback

Another Suspension

I've got a good . . . Joseph Durso, "Lukas Gets 60-Day Ban in
   Flanders Drug Case," *New York Times*, February 25, 1995

Gray areas in . . . Ibid.

We're not trying . . . Ibid.

There may be . . . "Lukas Files Appeal of Suspension," *New York
   Times*, March 4, 1995

A trace of the . . . "Flanders Case Settled," *Lexington Herald-
   Leader*, December 18, 1999

That it is improbable . . . Bill Heller, "Flanders Disqualification
   Upheld After Five Years," *Thoroughbred Times*, December 16,
   1999

The money was never . . . Ibid.

Five years and . . . Bill Finley, "Lukas Is Fined, Finally," *New York
   Daily News*, December 17, 1999

Gamely rallied in . . . Ibid., Heller

I'm satisfied . . . Ibid.

An Embarrassment of Riches

We wanted to draft . . . Jay Privman, "In Timber Country, Great
   Expectations," *New York Times*, April 7, 1995

D. Wayne Lukas flew . . . Joseph Durso, "Lukas Will Test Thunder
   Gulch, a Second Stringer, in Fountain of Youth," *New York
   Times*, February 17, 1995

How good are . . . Ibid.

He is a late . . . Ibid.

Lukas concedes that . . . Ibid.

Wayne told me . . . Ibid., Joseph Durso, "California Second
   Stringer Captures Fountain of Youth," *New York Times*,
   February 19, 1995

The number one . . . Ibid., Privman
This is the . . . Ibid.
He's not a typical . . . Ibid.
I wouldn't say . . . Joseph Durso, "Eclipse Awards Reflect Lukas's Big Comeback," *New York Times*, January 13, 1995

1995 Kentucky Derby

We're going to . . . Joseph Durso, "Lukas Changes Tune About Serena's Song," *New York Times*, April 30, 1995
We weighed all . . . Ibid.
Works don't make . . . Joseph Durso, "Filly Has a Faster Answer for Doubters," *New York Times*, May 1, 1995
The bottom line is . . . Ibid., Durso, "Lukas Changes Tune. . . . "
With all due respect . . . George Vecsey, "Lukas Improves His Average," *New York Times*, May 7, 1995
He's in the . . . Ibid.
Let me make it . . . George Vecsey, "Lukas Filly Can Shoot the Three," *New York Times*, May 5, 1995
Timber Country can . . . Joseph Durso, "Draw Leaves Favorites on the Outside," *New York Times*, May 5, 1995
The colt broke . . . Andrew Beyer, "Thunder Gulch Is Electric in Derby Shocker," *Washington Post*, May 7, 1995
She could have got . . . Joseph Durso, "Thunder Gulch Is No.3 in Barn, but No. 1 in Derby," *New York Times*, May 7, 1995
Come on wire . . . Chuck Culpepper, "Angel on my back turns tears of sorrow to tears of joy," *Lexington Herald-Leader*, May 7, 1995
All week we . . . Ibid., Vecsey, "Lukas Improves His Average"
I had some . . . Ibid., Beyer

1995 Preakness

There's no reason . . . Joseph Durso, "Lukas's Filly to Run in Black-Eyed Susan," *New York Times*, May 17, 1995
All our preparation is done . . . Joseph Durso, "Lukas Flies Favorites to Pimlico," *New York Times*, May 18, 1995

Had it all . . . William F. Reed, "Two for One," *Sports Illustrated*, May 29, 1995

Be a pilot . . . Ibid.

More than six . . . Vinnie Perrone, "Lukas Rules, Timber Country Reigns at Preakness," *Washington Post*, May 21, 1995

All of you . . . Ibid., Reed

Timber Country validated . . . Ibid., Perrone

1995 Belmont

You've got to . . . William F. Reed, "The Triple Double," *Sports Illustrated*, June 19, 1995

He was just . . . Vinnie Perrone, "Thunder Gulch Wins Belmont, Puts Lukas on Top," *Washington Post*, June 11, 1995

I'm a little . . . Ibid.

I guess I'll have to . . . Ibid., Reed

She really proved . . . Ibid., Perrone

It surprised me . . . Ibid., Reed

It's some thrill . . . Ibid., Perrone

I'm very . . . Ibid.

Let's Do It Again

If you could . . . "Training five derby entrants isn't enough for Lukas," Bloomberg/Nando.net, May 1, 1996

Could get into . . . Ibid.

You've got to . . . Ibid.

What anyone else . . . "Giving racing what it doesn't want," Bloomberg/Nando.net, May 4, 1996

What's Wayne up . . . Ibid.

What fuels me . . . Ibid.

Championships are won . . . William Nack, "Coming Through," *Sports Illustrated*, May 13, 1996

It's a way . . . Ibid., "Training five derby entrants. . . . "

There are guys . . . Ibid.

He is the Henry . . . Tim Sullivan, "Lukas Wins, and He Wins His Way," *Cincinnati Enquirer*, May 5, 1996

Though there's no denying . . . Ibid., Mike Helm, *A Breed Apart*

The quotes seemed . . . Billy Reed, "Come on, Seth, say
  something," *Lexington Herald-Leader*, May 1997
It looked like . . . Andrew Beyer, "Grindstone Puts Nose to the
  Wire, Wins Derby," *Washington Post*, May 5, 1996
Who won it . . . Ibid., Nack
The longer Chris . . . "Wrap Up of the Kentucky Derby," UPI,
  May 4, 1996
When we hit . . . Ed Schuyler Jr., "Grindstone by a Nose,"
  Associated Press, May 5, 1996
With bar shoes . . . Ibid.
Jerry Bailey . . . Ibid., Nack

1996 Preakness

I heard you had . . . Ed Schuyler Jr., "Lukas Still Aglow in Wake of
  Thrilling Derby Victory," Associated Press, May 6, 1996
If Unbridled's Song . . . "Lukas Goes for Preakness," *Detroit
  News*, May 6, 1996
It's a downer . . . Ibid.
I've never been one . . . "Cavonnier installed as 9–5 favorite in
  Preakness," Nando.net/Scripps Howard News Service, May
  16, 1996
I thought we . . . "Lukas' streak is over; time to start a new one,"
  Nando.net/Associated Press, May 18, 1996
You trade a guy . . . Ibid.

1996 Belmont

I don't think . . . "Rivals Lukas, Zito will start two horses in
  Belmont," Nando.net/Associated Press, June 6, 1996
The field of . . . William F. Reed, "Note Worthy," *Sports
  Illustrated*, June 17, 1996
He came close . . . Ibid.
The excitement of . . . "Editor's Note wins Belmont Stakes,"
  Nando.net/Associated Press, June 8, 1996
He has been . . . Ibid.
When I was . . . Vinnie Perrone, "Note: Lucas wins at Belmont
  Again," *Washington Post*, June 9, 1996

Chapter Nine: The Big Rivalry

Deeds Not Words

We took a . . . "Santa Catalina Stakes," www.iglou.com, February 3, 1997

Many of our . . . Ed Golden, "Mr. Triple Crown Lukas Could Dominate This Year," *Golden Glimpses #58*, webcom.com

I knew we were . . . "Lukas enters a horse in Derby," *Sportsbytes*, www.kernal.com, May 1, 1997

For the first time . . . Cindy Pierson, About.com, April 24, 1997

The prince himself . . . "Lukas Out of Derby," *TRC Thoroughbred Notebook*, April 24, 1997

I can handle . . . "A Derby without Lukas? It could happen," Associated Press, April 26, 1997

I'm out . . . Detroit News wire services, May 1, 1997

I have always . . . Ibid., *Sportsbytes*, April 24, 1997

I won a lot . . . Maryjean Wall, "Wayne's World," *Lexington Herald-Leader*, May 19, 1997

Then in the . . . Rob Longley, "Lukas could have last words," *Toronto Sun*, April 30, 1997

I've never . . . "Santa Catalina Stakes," www.iglou.com, February 3, 1997

If I listened . . . Ibid., Wall

The weather was . . . Ray Buck, "Even after the post, Derby picture is cloudy," CBS Sportsline, April 30, 1997

People are going . . . Neil Schmidt, "Lukas Bucks the Odds," *Cincinnati Enquirer*, May 1, 1997

Don't be saying . . . Ibid.

Whatever you do . . . Ed Schuyler Jr., "Derby is Pulpit's Platform to Make History," *Detroit News*, May 1, 1997

If you step . . . "Derby Notes," *Lubbock Avalanche-Journal*, May 3, 1997

I ought to . . . Ibid., *Sportsbytes*

Deeds Not Words is . . . Dick Jerardi, *Philadelphia Daily News*, May 2, 1997

The colt wallowed . . . Pat Forde, "Like it or not, Rock and Roll is here to stay," *Louisville Courier-Journal*, May 1, 1998

Derby fever . . . "Pulpit battles history," *Beloit Daily News*, May 3, 1997

That horse has won . . . Joe Hawk, "Derby for Dummies," *Las Vegas Review-Journal*, May 3, 1997

The charge against . . . Tim Sullivan, "Not Derby Without Lukas," *Cincinnati Enquirer*, May 3, 1997

Lukas, like his . . . Billy Reed, "Media Be Darned: Lukas earned spot," *Lexington Herald-Leader*, May 2, 1997

Michael Tabor is not . . . "Lucas on his frustrations and criticism," CBS Sportsline, Triple Crown 1997

Lukas is the . . . Ibid., Reed

We had some traffic . . . "Deeds Not Words," iglou.com, Triple Crown 1997

The horse backed up . . . Richard Skinner, "Beam winner comes up short," *Kentucky Post*, May 5, 1997

It was nice . . . Cindy Pierson, "My First Live Derby," About.com, May 7, 1997

Writers here blasted . . . Buck Johnson, "Hot horses may wage more duels," *Chattanooga Times*, May 5, 1997

Next year we'll . . . Jody Demling, "D. Wayne home at the Downs," *Louisville Courier-Journal*, April 30, 1998

The biggest mistake . . . Tim Sullivan, "First Saturday in May is Lukas time," *Cincinnati Enquirer*, May 3, 2000

The prince wants . . . "Sharp Cat to Dollase," *Thoroughbred Times*, December 16, 1997

Bob Baffert

He really built me up . . . Bob Baffert with Steve Haskins. *Dirt Road to Glory*. Lexington, Kentucky: Bloodhorse Books, 1999

A man named . . . "Baffert repays old debt with Derby victory," Nando.net/Associated Press, May 3, 1997

We were both . . . Ibid., Baffert, 18

Wait until you . . . Ibid., 30

You want to go . . . Ibid., 31

It was too bad . . . Ibid., 32

While Baffert and . . . Frank Angst, "Mountains of Victories," *Sunday Gazette Mail*, April 1, 2001

Lewis has openly . . . Richard Eng, "Lewises benefit from Baffert-Lukas rivalry," *Las Vegas Review-Journal*, May 16, 1999

Cape Town vs. Indian Charlie and Real Quiet

The Florida Derby . . . Ed Golden, "Lukas goes on the 'town' in bid for 4th Derby," *Golden Glimpses #113*, April 1998

The annual Kentucky . . . "Bailey to Ride Cape Town in Derby," *Thoroughbred Times*, April 13, 1998

I think Indian Charlie . . . Ibid., Golden

I don't think . . . Jody Demling, "Trainers tell why their horses faltered," *Louisville Courier-Journal*, May 2, 1998

After being here . . . Steve Bailey, "Lukas Sees another Derby contender in Cape Town," Associated Press, April 27, 1998

Winning the first . . . "Lukas Makes the Derby," Associated Press, April 27, 1998

We're going to take . . . Ibid.

I have the same . . . "Baffert confident about Indian Charlie," Associated Press, April 30, 1998

I have two really . . . Ibid.

The worst handicapper . . . Pat Forde, "Pitino at the Downs," *Louisville Courier-Journal*, April 28, 1998

Thirty people . . . Jody Demling, "D. Wayne home at the Downs," *Louisville Courier-Journal*, April 30, 1998

Seasoning? . . . "Baffert charmed with two entries," Associated Press, April 29, 1998

This horse is . . . Ibid.

His media magnetism . . . Neil Schmidt, "Derby Notebook," *Cincinnati Enquirer*, April 30, 1998

It made for . . . Bill Koch, "How to muck up a Derby tradition," *Cincinnati Post*, April 30, 1998

Matching up the . . . Ibid.

I feel like . . . Ibid.

It was unfair . . . Neil Schmidt, "Lukas: TV taking over
   horseracing," *Cincinnati Enquirer*, May 1, 1998
Until Chris Lincoln . . . Ibid., Forde, "Like it or not. . . . "
When they were on . . . Richard Rosenblatt, "Items on Rock and
   Roll, McCarron, Lukas; Derby Facts," Associated Press, May
   2, 1998
I guess you've . . . Ibid.
He also called . . . "Derby Notes: Lukas gets famous visitors,"
   Associated Press, May 2, 1998
I thought I had . . . "Quotes from the Kentucky Derby,"
   Associated Press, May 2, 1998
The seasoning . . . "Baffert's on the Lukas trail," Associated Press,
   May 3, 1998
Came off the . . . Lori Lewis, "Preakness Journal," Theturf
   online.com, May 13, 1998
It had no bearing . . . John Harrell, "Indian Charlie out, Baquero
   in for Preakness," *Thoroughbred Times*, May 12, 1998
That's an enormous . . . Daniel J. McCue, "Belmont's Quest Casts
   Long Preakness Shadow," *Floral Park Dispatch*, May 22, 1998
If I had drawn . . . "Real Quiet moves to within one step of the
   Triple Crown," Associated Press, May 17, 1998
You have to wonder . . . Jay Richards, "Belmont field weaker as
   Coronado's Quest won't run," *Las Vegas Journal-Review*,
   May 22, 1998
He looks good . . . "Yarrow Brae works, Grand Slam status still
   undecided," *Thoroughbred Times*, June 2, 1998
I came back . . . Reuters, "Let the Hype Begin," CNNSI.com,
   June 2, 1998
They're suspect . . . Tom Keyser, "Belmont Stakes Notebook,"
   Baltimore Sun, June 4, 1998
Where else can . . . Bob Ehealt, "Challengers ready to disrupt
   Baffert's harmony," *Stamford Advocate*, June 4, 1998

Love Finds D. Wayne Lukas (Again)

The thing is . . . Ibid., Drape, *The Race for the Triple Crown*
A little old cowgirl . . . Ibid.

I worked for a . . . Larry Bortstein, "In Bob Baffert's barn, everyone must get along," *Orange County Register*, May 1, 1998

Laura and I . . . Richard Chamberlain, "D. Wayne Lukas," *Quarter Horse Racing Journal*, August 1998

When he bought . . . Ibid.

I'm so competitive . . . Steve Bisheff, "She's the Lukas of Quarter Horses," *Orange County Register*, July 12, 2000

There is no . . . Ibid., Bisheff

Chapter Ten: The Big Year

The 1999 Preps

Started training him . . . Ed Golden, *Golden Glimpses* #167, May 25, 1999

Before Wayne saddled . . . Ibid.

Wayne told me . . . Clift Guilliams, "A charismatic finish," Scripps Howard News Service, May 1, 1999

The Hall of Fame

I had some . . . Richard Rosenblatt, "Lukas enters Horse Racing's Hall of Fame," Associated Press, April 27, 1999

What it comes . . . Rick Cushing, "D. Wayne Lukas elected to Racing Hall of Fame," *The Tennesseean*, April 28, 1999

My only take . . . Ibid., Rosenblatt

I'm probably proudest . . . Ibid.

During Derby week . . . Ibid., Eng, "Lukas-Baffert rivalry. . . . "

The 1999 Kentucky Derby

I think the . . . "Baffert, Lukas, Zito all aiming to add to Derby windfall," Associated Press, April 27, 1999

Baffert's horses have . . . Neil Schmidt, "Kentucky Derby Notebook," *Cincinnati Enquirer*, April 30, 1999

They're just works . . . "Lukas duo works early," *Thoroughbred Times*, April 26, 1999

I can remember . . . "Baffert, Lukas, Zito aim for third Derby victory of the '90s," Associated Press, April 30, 1999

I am grateful . . . Ibid., "Baffert, Lukas, Zito all aiming. . . . "

I know there's . . . Ibid., "Baffert, Lukas, Zito aim for third Derby"

I don't think . . . Ibid., "Baffert, Lukas, Zito all aiming. . . . "

I hope no one . . . Richard Skinner, "Training Trifecta," *Cincinnati Post*, May 1, 1999

Elliott Walden knows . . . Ibid., Schmidt

I really don't think . . . Ibid., Skinner

It wasn't that . . . Ibid.

Wayne told me . . . John Scher, "A closer look," CNNSI, May 1, 1999

This was the worst . . . "Demolition Derby," CNNSI.com, May 9, 1999

This was my . . . Ibid.

It was all . . . Ibid.

I was standing . . . Ibid., Eng, "Lukas-Baffert rivalry . . . "

He hit the front . . . Richard Skinner, "Unlikely Derby Champ," *Cincinnati Post*, May 3, 1999

At that point . . . Ibid., Tim Sullivan, "Lukas laughs last and best"

I thought we . . . "D. Wayne's world," CNNSI, May 9, 1999

I'd be foolish . . . Ibid., Sullivan

He got excited . . . Ed Schuyler Jr., "Trainer had right dream, wrong horse," Associated Press, May 3, 1999

I thought Chris . . . Ibid., "D. Wayne's World"

This is the . . . Mark Story, "Luck, drag race, land Lewises a win," *Lexington Herald-Leader*, May 2, 1999

Nick and Bob and I . . . Richard E. Glover Jr., "The D Stands for Derby," *Handicapper's Daily*, May 5, 1999

We beat everybody . . . Rob Longley, "Lukas finds his swagger," *Toronto Sun*, May 3, 1999

I'm healthy . . . Ibid.

Right dream, but the wrong . . . Ibid., Schuyler Jr.

Chris Antley

In it was . . . Laura Hillenbrand. *Seabiscuit*. New York: Knopf, 2001, 68–69

This is the . . . Steve Bailey, "Bouts with drugs, weight problems sweeten Antley's Miracle," Associated Press, May 1, 1999

I spent the spring . . . Ibid.

He's hungry and . . . George Solomon, "Redemption is the Sweetest for Winning Jockey," *Washington Post*, May 2, 1999

This was a dream . . . Ibid., Bailey

I'm also happy . . . "D. Wayne's world," CNNSI, May 9, 1999

This has a lot . . . Ibid., George Solomon, "Redemption is the Sweetest. . . ."

The 1999 Preakness

I think the . . . Ed Schuyler Jr., "Past could become the present for Lukas at Preakness," Associated Press, May 15, 1999

I can see . . . Ibid.

I have to take . . . Richard Eng, "Lewises benefit from Baffert-Lukas rivalry," *Las Vegas Review-Journal*, May 16, 1999

He quite frankly . . . Ibid.

[Charismatic] had a little . . . "Two down, one to go," CNNSI.com, June 3, 1999

The Derby sharpened . . . William Nack, "The Picks," CNNSI.com, May 15, 1999

I think I . . . "What the jockeys said," Associated Press, May 15, 1999

There was no . . . Ibid.

More aggressive . . . Ibid.

I told Bob . . . Ibid., "Two down, one to go"

We had great . . . Ibid., Eng, "Lewises benefit from. . . ."

By the time . . . Ibid., "What the jockeys said"

We picked him . . . Ibid., "Two down, one to go"

I'm trying . . . "Ride of his life," CNNSI.com, June 3, 1999

Give the former . . . Ibid., Eng, "Lewises benefit from. . . ."

A New York Minute

I've had a nice . . . "A Charismatic win would toast Lukas," *Amarillo Globe News*, June 4, 1999

He's a coach . . . Ibid., Drape, "Lukas Makes Himself Heard Again"

And mine's aggressive . . . Jim Litke, "Everybody in the game wants to be there," *Slam!*, June 7, 1999

Wayne deserves all . . . Ed Golden, *Golden Glimpses #167*, May 25, 1999

I do keep . . . Ibid., "A Charismatic win. . . ."

It's hard to . . . Ibid., Golden

If I had . . . Ibid., Drape

What if the . . . Richard Eng, "Lukas gunning for Triple Crown," *Las Vegas Review-Journal*, June 4, 1999

Of course, another . . . Richard E. Glover Jr., "The D Stands for Derby: Lukas Bags His Fourth," *Handicapper's Daily*, May 5, 1999

He doesn't run unsound . . . Ibid., Joe Drape

Doesn't she look . . . "Lukas Wants Nothing but the Best for Charismatic," *The Tennesseean*, June 2, 1999

I just hope . . . Ibid.

I told Bob . . . "It's Bob against Bob," Associated Press, June 3, 1999

He was genuinely . . . Ibid., Drape, *The Race for the Triple Crown*, 118–19

This is horse racing . . . Ibid., Eng, "Lukas gunning for Triple Crown"

We had bad . . . "Charismatic weathers stormy trips to Belmont," *Jefferson City New Tribune*, June 3, 1999

Charismatic goes off . . . "Charismatic's ready to go," *Slam!*, June 4, 1999

[Silverbulletday] went really . . . Ibid.

This is a . . . Rob Longley, "Charismatic triple threat," *Toronto Sun*, June 4, 1999

This is unique . . . Ed Schuyler Jr., "From claiming races to the edge of greatness," Associated Press, June 4, 1999

There is something . . . Ibid.

When Charismatic surged . . . William Nack, "Broken Dream," *Sports Illustrated*, June 8, 1999

He bobbled . . . William Gildea, "For Charismatic, Broken Leg, Broken Hearts," *Washington Post*, June 6, 1999

It was almost . . . "Triple Frown," CNNSI, June 7, 1999

Heading for the . . . "Charismatic Injured at Wire," *Cincinnati Enquirer*, June 6, 1999

Sixty yards past . . . Ibid., Nack, "Broken Dream"

I'm sorry . . . Ibid., Gildea

Naturally you hate . . . Ibid.

My heart goes . . . "Charismatic loses, hurt stalking Silverbulletday," *Slam!*, June 5, 1996

Our only concern . . . Ibid., Gildea

He was simply . . . Ibid., "Triple Frown"

They may have . . . Ibid.

That means he's . . . Ibid., "Charismatic loses, hurt stalking Silverbulletday"

Was not the worst . . . Ed Schuyler Jr., "Charismatic has surgery," Associated Press, June 6, 1999

Do you people . . . Ibid., Drape, *The Race for the Triple Crown*, 54–55

All week we . . . Ibid., "Charismatic Injured at Wire"

As many horses . . . Ibid., Jim Litke, "Everybody in the game wants to be there," *Slam!*, June 7, 1999

Boy, aren't we . . . Ibid., Schuyler Jr., "Charismatic has surgery"

Even the Lukas-bashers . . . Andrew Beyer, "Jockey's Costly Mistake, Horse's Tragic Accident," *Washington Post*, June 7, 1999

I'm not here . . . Ibid., Drape, *The Race for the Triple Crown*, 128

Would Charismatic . . . Ibid., Beyer

If he had . . . Ibid.

It Was a Very Good Year

Those records . . . "Lukas basks in glory," *Sports Illustrated*, August 10, 1999

It's my nature . . . Ibid.

The formula is . . . Billy Reed, "Legendary Lukas Honored," *Lexington Herald-Leader*, May 1, 1999

So many things . . . Ibid., "Lukas basks in glory"

He's always the . . . Ed Golden, *Golden Glimpses* #177, August 3, 1999

I don't believe in luck . . . Ibid., "Lukas basks in glory"

1999 Breeders' Cup

We didn't think . . . David Greening, "Cash Run pays dividends for Sanan," *Daily Racing Form*, November 6, 1999
He's been a hard . . . Ibid.
The lightly regarded . . . Andrew Beyer, "Cat Thief Snatches a Classic Triumph," *Washington Post*, November 7, 1999
The Classic could . . . Ed Golden, *Golden Glimpses* #187, November 9, 1999
Cat Thief, best . . . Jay Privman, "Persistent Cat Thief steals top prize," *Daily Racing Form*, Nov. 6, 1999
It's been a . . . Ibid., Greening

Collecting the Prizes

Bob Baffert . . . Jay Privman, "Charismatic's new claim to fame," *Daily Racing Form*, Jan. 20, 2000
See, if Wayne . . . Steve Andersen, "Baffert proudest of 1999," *Daily Racing Form*, Jan. 20, 2000
When Tim Smith . . . Ibid., Privman

Chapter Eleven: The Big Mess

Long Shot

We competed against . . . Kathryn Tolbert, "Sekiguchi: Easy to single out; Sees a kindred spirit in Pegasus," *Daily Racing Form*, May 17, 2000
Coach, are you . . . Steve Myrick, "Lukas' Commendable Milestone," *Lawrence* (Mass.) *Eagle-Tribune*, June 11, 2000
On the down swing . . . Mark Beech, "Belmont Rankings," *Sports Illustrated*, June 9, 2000
I listed the . . . Richard Rosenblatt, "Race for 3-Year-Old Champ to Begin," Associated Press, June 11, 2000
He took it . . . Ibid., Myrick
He took me to the lead . . . Ibid.
He could run . . . Joe Drape, "Top 3-Year-Old to Be Decided," *New York Times*, June 12, 2000

It was a wonderful . . . "Commendable victory!" *Sports Illustrated*, June 11, 2000

Wayne Lukas not . . . Joe Hirsch, "Lukas Knew Everyone's Horse," *Daily Racing Form*, June 16, 2000

We didn't have any . . . "D. Wayne Lukas thought Commendable was a long shot," CNNSI.com, June 11, 2000 (audio wave file)

I've won two . . . Ibid., "Commendable victory!"

We all know why . . . Michael Watchmaker, "An improbable win," *Daily Racing Form*, June 16, 2000

Commendable didn't exactly . . . Andrew Beyer, "Belmont winner will soon join cast of 'Where are they now?'" *Washington Post*, June 6, 2000

Commendable showed up . . . Dave Liftin, "Commendable deserves some credit," *Daily Racing Form*, June 15, 2000

Still a Ladies' Man

My filly was . . . Brad Free, "Unspectacular win for Surfside," *Daily Racing Form*, March 15, 2000

I know you . . . Ibid.

Never showed any . . . Marty McGee, "Surgery Next for Surfside," *Daily Racing Form*, April 22, 2000

A change of . . . John Piesen, "Spain is better than she looks," *Daily Racing Form*, July 27, 2000

We'll go right . . . Marty McGee, "Easy does it for Caller One," *Daily Racing Form*, September 18, 2000

I'm always of . . . Marty McGee, "Spain to take her next step in Spinster," *Daily Racing Form*, October 13, 2000

Spain, who had . . . Jay Privman, "Spain? Surfside? Yes It's True, Lukas-Lukas," *Daily Racing Form*, November 6, 2000

The Aftermath of Chris Antley

He loved that . . . Bob Spear, "A year after magical ride," *Akron Beacon Journal*, May 3, 2000

He seemed to . . . Beth Harris, "Derby Winning Jockey Antley Found Dead," *Detroit News*, December 4, 2000

He instinctively came . . . Ibid.

A very, very . . . Ibid.

Chris never once . . . Ibid., Drape, *The Race for the Triple Crown*, 128

Lukas believed that . . . Ibid.

Antley had a . . . Jay Hovdey, "Small-town kid chased most elusive prize," *Daily Racing Form*, December 6, 2000

I thought he . . . Richard Rosenblatt, "Lukas said he should have changed riders," Nando.net/Associated Press, May 1, 2001

I don't think . . . Bob Ehalt, "Lukas disputes Antley's 'bond' with Charismatic," *Daily Racing Form*, June 8, 2001

If you tearfully . . . Ibid.

We had a . . . Ed Fountaine, "Lukas Laments Not Giving Antley Boot," *New York Post*, June 9, 2001

Why in the . . . Don Engle, "Editor's Notebook," *TIA Newsletter*, June 10, 2001

Lukas said that . . . Jay Privman, "Antley's wife rebuts Lukas comments," *Daily Racing Form*, June 20, 2001

Mr. Lewis did . . . Ibid.

The Antley-Charismatic . . . Steven Crist, "No tolerance for zero tolerance," *Daily Racing Form*, June 23, 2001

The Rise and Fall of Lukas and Padua Stables

You mark my . . . Tim Whitmire, "Sanan spends heavily for yearlings," Associated Press, July 21, 1998

His ambition and . . . Ibid.

I told everybody . . . "Keeneland Sale sizzles," *TRC Thoroughbred Notebook*, July 23, 1998

There are a . . . Ibid., Whitmire

Trainer D. Wayne . . . Jay Richards, "Purchasers often pay when they pony up millions for yearlings," *Las Vegas Journal-Review*, July 26, 1998

He wanted to . . . Deirdre D. Biles, "Extreme Prices," auctions.bloodhorse.com, July 1999

Wayne loves the . . . "Record-high purchase wraps up yearling sale," *The Tennessean*, July 21, 1999

Just a few . . . Dave Goldman, "Flurry of Farm Sales," *Daily Racing Form*, August 1, 1999

Sanan, ever seated . . . Glenye Cain, "Yearlings up, up away," *Daily Racing Form*, August 13, 1999

We didn't think . . . David Greening, "Cash Run pays dividends for Sanan," *Daily Racing Form*, November 6, 1999

That was painful . . . Janet Patton, "We're off to a tremendous start, *Lexington Herald-Leader*, July 18, 2000

We've put him . . . Jay Privman, "Padua's riches may not buy blanket of roses," *Daily Racing News*, May 6, 2000

Paying a little more . . . Ibid., Patton

This is what . . . "News Archives: What's Satish Sanan's game?" Realracing.com, July 27, 2000

Nothing really is . . . Matt Haggerty, "Padua, Lukas simplify business," *Daily Racing Form*, June 5, 2001

Anytime you make . . . Jay Privman, "Padua, Lukas go their separate ways," *Daily Racing News*, August 3, 2001

I wanted him . . . Ibid.

Chapter Twelve: Legacy

The Alumni

If they are . . . Gary West, "Nothing brings Lukas more pride than his guys," *Dallas Morning News*, November 3, 2000

An excellent teacher . . . "Bobby C. Barnett," *Training*, Thoroughbred racing biographies, Keeneland.com

The three things . . . Ibid.

I think if you . . . "Trainer of Artax likes being left alone," *Slam!*, April 29, 1998

In two years . . . "Bradshaw rejoins Lukas flock," *Thoroughbred Times*, March 2, 1999

The horses ran . . . Ibid., West

I don't know . . . Rick Bailey, "Henning giving ex-boss Lukas run for money," *Lexington Herald-Leader*, November 3, 2000

As each of . . . Ibid.

I introduced myself . . . "Dallas Stewart," *Training*, Thoroughbred racing biographies, *Keeneland.com*

I had one . . . Ibid.

Doing it for . . . "Lukas losing top assistant," *Thoroughbred Times*, August 10, 1997

I think you . . . Billy Reed, "Lukas protégé striking it big," *Lexington Herald-Leader*, April 23, 1999

I was up . . . Ibid., Reed

That man's a . . . Ibid.

There's bigger purses . . . Tim Sullivan, "First Saturday in May is Lukas time, *Cincinnati Enquirer*, May 3, 2000

I am proud . . . "Baffert-Lukas monopoly busted after five years," CNNSI, May 6, 2000

He is an . . . Nick Charles, "Four of a Kind," CNNSI, May 3, 2000

Overview

Another important measure . . . Richard Eng, "Lukas most worthy of Hall induction," *Las Vegas Review-Journal*, February 28, 1999

Six former Lukas . . . Ibid., West

INDEX